THE LIFE OF NAPOLEON BUONAPARTE

THE LIFE OF

NAPOLEON

BUONAPARTE

SIR

WALTER SCOTT

EDITED BY

RICHARD MICHAELIS

GIBSON SQUARE

This edition published in the UK for the first time by Gibson Square

UK	Tel:	+44 (0)20 7096 1100
US	Tel:	+1 646 216 9813
Eire	Tel:	+353 (0)1 657 1057

info@gibsonsquare.com
www.gibsonsquare.com

ISBN   978-1-906142-21-6

The Gibson Square Speakers Bureau provides a wide range of authors for speaking events all over the world. To find out more contact us through the above details.

The moral right of Richard Michaelis to be identified as the author of this work has been asserted in accordance with the Copyright, Designs and Patents Act 1988.

Printed and bound by CPI Group (UK) Ltd, Croydon, CR0 4YY

$\mathscr{C}$ONTENTS

Introduction

In his introduction to *The Betrothed,* Sir Walter Scott informed the public of the intention, of the author of *Waverley,* to switch genre:

> I will lay my foundations better than on quicksands – I will rear my structure of better materials than painted cards; in a word, I will write HISTORY!
>
> I intend to write the most wonderful book which the world ever read – a book in which every incident shall be incredible, yet strictly true – a work recalling recollections with which the ears of this generation once tingled, and which shall be read by our children with an admiration approaching to incredulity. Such shall be the LIFE OF NAPOLEON BUONAPARTE by the author of *Waverley.*[1]

Scott began this 'new species of work'[2] – perhaps the most ambitious history attempted, in English, since Gibbon's *Decline and Fall* – in late summer 1825. In January 1826 the over-exposed publishing businesses with which he was associated collapsed under the weight of speculative failures in London, leaving him with colossal debts. Typically, he decided to repay his creditors in full rather than suffer the disgrace of bankruptcy, combatively remarking to his 'giurnal', that 'I do not like to have it thought that there is any way in which I can be beaten',[3] 'Besides, I must re-establish my fortune for the sake of the children and my own character'.[4] On 15 May 1826 Scott suffered the additional blow of losing his wife.

Despite these desperate distractions, he 'finished Bony' on 7 June 1827. Originally planned as a four-volume contribution to the *Miscellany,* Archibald Constable's latest publishing venture, *The Life of Napoleon Buonaparte* had, by then, spiraled into nine volumes – Scott's single greatest literary endeavour – acquiring, among other things, a two-volume preliminary sketch of the Revolution, an extensive discussion of Napoleon's exile to Saint Helena and a large documentary appendix.

Astonishingly, during the same two year period, Scott also wrote *Woodstock, The Chronicles of Canongate,* numerous reviews, campaigned successfully against the abolition of small banknotes in Scotland through his *Letters of Malachi Malagrowther,* travelled to London and Paris in pursuit of material for the *Life,* and carried on with his duties as principal clerk to the court of sessions and sheriff-depute of Selkirkshire.

To the modern reader there is, of course, something faintly ironic about Scott declaring that he is about to write HISTORY since it is now widely believed that, in the broadest sense of the term at least, he had been doing just that for years. Georg Lukács famously argued that the French Revolution and Napoleonic wars transformed history into a mass experience, creating modern historical consciousness, and that, in his finest historical novels, Scott was the first author accurately to portray historical cultures and to depict the historical process.[5] He could portray historical cultures because he had devoted so much effort to familiarizing himself with a variety of periods and folklores; he could depict the historical process because he was equally familiar with the fundamental concerns of the different social groups about which he was writing. By abstracting himself, and deliberately under-characterizing his heroes and heroines – they are representatives of the societies, classes and cultures that produced them rather than fully-fledged characters – Scott permitted different historical voices to speak for themselves and, in doing so, exposed the underlying dynamics of the historical process. At his best, Scott's natural conservatism and his melancholy comprehension of the inevitability of historical change combine to excite sympathy for both helpless sides as they struggle for historical supremacy, in *Waverley,* doomed Jacobitism and its inevitable replacement, modernising Hannoverianism. The influence of Scott's lively depictions of the past on nineteenth century historians and historical thinkers cannot be overstated. George Malcolm Young argued that Scott's ability to empathize with a wide range of historical actors, and to make them come alive, taught succeeding generations to listen to the voices of the past: 'when once the canvas of fiction had been enlarged the canvas of history could be enlarged too'.[6] Many of the giants of nineteenth century history-writing, Augustin Thierry, Thomas

Carlyle, Leopold von Ranke, owed Scott a profound debt of inspiration, while among those who liked to make history as well as write it, Scott's fan club encompassed figures as diverse as Marx and Bismarck.

British readers could hardly wait to get their hands on the *Life*. *The Times* fanned their impatience, and paid unprecedented homage to Scott's towering reputation, by publishing five columns of selections from the *Life* as a sampler.[7] Europe was similarly eager; Goethe was ecstatic:

> What could be more delightful than leisurely and calmly to sit down and listen to the discourse of such a man, while clearly, truly, and with all the skill of a great artist, he recalls to me the incidents on which through life I have meditated, and the influence of which is still in daily operation.[8]

Scott's continental reputation was such, and the subject he was addressing so central to European preoccupations, that, in a pioneering literary Eurovision, the *Life* was due to be published simultaneously in German, French, Italian and Spanish.

The first edition of the *Life* was a stupendous commercial success. Scott was accustomed to receiving large sums for his writing but even he happily wondered whether 'more was ever made by a single work or by a single author's labours in the same time'. More modestly, he went on to ruminate 'whether such good fortune was deserved or not'.[9] Privately he hoped it was, that the *Life* would become an enduring classic and that, besides contributing to pay off his gigantic debts, subsequent editions would provide for his somewhat less industrious offspring. The work did not live up to his daydreams and, despite impressive sales, became peripheral to the Scott canon some time before his novels fell out of fashion. Thereafter the *Life* suffered a long spell in literary limbo from which it has only recently begun to be rehabilitated by literary scholars and historians.[10]

With the *Life*, Scott, the inventor of the romantic history novel, was branching out into new territory, he was quite literally writing a 'new species of work', a largely 'reflective'[11] and analytical book, just as Napoleon was becoming transformed into the pre-eminent romantic icon of the age. The irony was not lost on the public and may to some extent explain the work's fate. That is not to say that Scott absolutely jettisoned his literary muse. It was too deeply ingrained, and Napoleon's career too 'wonderful', for him altogether to resist nine-volumes worth of temptation. The author realized, for instance, that the epic of Napoleon's existence – his triumphs, at one stage, were greater 'than had ever before been recorded in history'[12] – required an epic language, the essentially unhistorical but very much more vivid language of metaphor. In the same unhistorical vein, Scott exalts the men he admires above all others, patriots, irrespective of their nationality. In the revolutionary section, the republican soldiers who saved France at Valmy in 1792 are praised while the aristocratic *émigrés,* who sought sanctuary abroad and attacked their homeland, are condemned. Likewise some of the finest passages of the *Life* are reserved for the loyal inhabitants of distant and backward provinces. This is logical. Scott was the poet of the Highlands and an opponent of the levelling, universalizing tendencies of the Enlightenment. The regionalisms he praises in the *Life,* were, like the Highlanders of his novels, threatened by progress, in this case in the shape of Enlightened French expansion. Thus the *Life's* fundamental historical gravitas is broken by admiring descriptions of the proud, stubborn and courageous Spanish peasants at whose hands France first tasted defeat under Napoleon; of the sharp-shooting, fanatically loyal Tyrolean rebels of 1809; and, without question the greatest heroes of the *Life,* of the dauntless Cossacks – Scott's 'children of the desert' – as well as the Russian people in general, whose fighting skills combined with supernatural heroism not for the last time to stop evil in its tracks. Besides reminding the reader of Scott's literary pedigree, these passages underline an openness to cultural variety that was significantly absent from the Enlightenment historical tradition. The historians Scott studied in his youth, notably David Hume, could be cruelly contemptuous of so-called backward or unenlightened peoples.

Stylistic surprises aside, the *Life* burdened under two major critical handicaps. The first was the technical complaint that it was poorly edited and researched; the second, the exceedingly hostile reception it received at the hands of particularly influential interest groups. That such a complex and monumental work, undertaken in haste – Lockhart estimated that, in total, Scott spent a year working on it – during an exceptionally trying period, should have contained factual errors, editorial lapses, as well as the occasional longueur, is hardly surprising. Most history books and biographies do to this day. Scott was aware of this and, even before the first edition appeared, was making plans to correct and review the text (as in the later edition of the *Life* on which this book is based). The number of errors and blemishes was and is, however, routinely exaggerated. Those that do occur are usually trivial, and rarely detract either from the extremely high quality of the prose or the sustained intelligence of the argument. The linked accusation of poor scholarship is equally unfounded. Given the time Scott had at his disposal, and the conditions under which he was working, the effort he put into his research was little short of formidable. Relying to a small extent upon material he had previously produced for the *Edinburgh Annual Register,* he went on methodically to absorb the principal published memoirs, used the bait of literary stardom to wheedle private papers out of some of the leading actors of the period, notably Wellington and Bernadotte, and even acquired a full set of the *Moniteur.* The extent of his researches, and his exceptional capacity for assimilation, become abundantly clear when, for instance, he deals with the military campaigns that, much to his personal sorrow, dominate the text. These are consistently anchored in brief but excellent surveys of international politics. The manoeuvres that precede and follow battles, as well as the bloody choreography of the battles themselves, are clearly and economically described, while the strengths and weaknesses of the combatants, their tactics and strategies, are systematically and intelligently assessed. As a result Scott provides a sophisticated account of Napoleon's tactical and strategic abilities, demythologizing one of military history's most mythologized figures in the process. While recognising that Napoleon was a brilliant and audacious strategist and tactician, he demonstrates that this was by no means the only reason he regularly won. He did so just as often because of the quality and resilience of the men and officers brought to the fore by the Revolution and the superior flexibility of mass French tactics developed since 1792 – tactics that, again according to Scott, carried within them the seeds of the terrible brutalisation of war observed between 1799 and 1815. Nor does he overlook the fact that wars are lost as well as won. The generals opposing Napoleon are subjected to his scrutiny and more often than not turn out to be lousy tacticians who regularly fail to learn from the mistakes of their predecessors.

Within Scott's broad treatment of Napoleon's military career, three campaigns stand out for the thoroughness and lucidity with which they are analysed. Napoleon's first Italian campaign in 1797 – the one that proclaimed his genius and is still considered by many experts as his finest – is reproduced in deserving detail, as is the brief Belgian campaign in 1815. Scott is at his most impressive, however, when dealing with the ill-fated Russian campaign of 1812. His intelligent emphasis on Russian fighting qualities, and his devastating indictment of Napoleon's arrogant exculpatory gloss on the campaign, the excuse that blamed *Général Hiver* – an excuse that is touted with misplaced conviction to this day – justly earned him the undying gratitude of Russian and Soviet historiography.

Scott's treatment of political developments in France is equally assured, particularly with regard to the different parties forged in the fire of Revolution and their evolving relationship with Napoleon. More interestingly, perhaps, for a modern reader, Scott used his contacts in the Cabinet to provide him with previously unpublished documents relating to Napoleon's surrender to the British after the Hundred Days and subsequent captivity, enabling him to address what were, at the time, politically fraught questions with considerably more authority than any of his predecessors had done, or indeed many of his successors. Access to these papers enabled him to rebut the claim, made at the time and since, that Captain Maitland of the *Bellorophon* had deliberately misled Napoleon in order to lure him into British custody. Significantly, Scott went on to argue that, legally at least, the dispute was in any case irrelevant. Napoleon did not throw himself upon British mercy only to be betrayed, as his entourage claimed and his apologists have argued ever since, rather he made the only possible choice between surrendering, as a prisoner of war, to the British squadron blockading La Rochelle, or sitting around and waiting to be arrested by vengeful French Royalists. Under the circumstances, and given that he had forfeited all Treaty rights by escaping from Elba – that he was quite literally an outlaw – he had no grounds upon which to expect generous terms from, or dictate terms to, the Crown. By establishing this important point, Scott can contest most of the grounds upon which Napoleon and his entourage regularly complained on Saint Helena, something he does with forensic skill. The reader even discovers what sort of wine Napoleon and his aides drank and how much it cost the British taxpayer, although Scott tactfully opines that 'there was rather too much said and thought about the quantity consumed'.

The fallen Emperor's minions were predictably enraged at Scott's sceptical treatment of their hero. General Gourgaud, who accompanied Napoleon to Saint Helena, and whose double-dealing on the island Scott exposed for the first time in the *Life*, publicly threatened to shoot him.[13] Despite by now being unwell, Scott was keen to accept the challenge, if only because he owned a set of duelling pistols that had belonged to Napoleon and thought it would be amusing to use them against one of his generals. Louis Bonaparte, the one time 'pageant king' of Holland, whom Scott treated remarkably generously in the *Life*, composed a virulent pamphlet against it, frenziedly accusing the author of turning the 'novels and libels fabricated against France and Napoleon into history'[14] while singularly failing to substantiate most of his accusations with more evidence than his own dubious word.

Unfortunately, opinion formers who had not been close to the Emperor were also outraged. This was particularly the case of British radicals who attacked the *Life* less with regard to its content than the well-known Toryism of its author.[15] Typically, their criticisms emerged well before the *Life* had been published. William Hazlitt, for one, was so perturbed by the potential Tory propaganda value of the book that he set out, in the event disappointingly, to write his own corrective biography of Napoleon before Scott's came out.[16] Other radicals had the decency to wait until the book was published before delivering themselves of their pre-determined verdicts. They duly accused Scott of not writing a biography so much as an epic Tory manifesto against the Revolution, Napoleon and, by implication, the reforming movement that was gathering momentum in Britain in the mid-1820s. In other words that, just as Edmund Burke had written a book about the superiority of British institutions and called it *Reflections on the Revolution in France,* Scott had written a book about the excellence of the British constitution and the risks attendant upon great reforming movements and called it *The Life of Napoleon Buonaparte.* Frederic Denison Maurice accused Scott of being too conservative to write history, and hoped he would never try again. He described the *Life* as 'the longest and most tedious of his novels', a 'wretchedly and despicably insufficient' portrait of 'one of the marked epochs of the world'.[17] In a far more important review, John Stuart Mill was much better disposed towards the author's story-telling ability but similarly unimpressed by his talents as an historian.[18]

Scott's *bien-pensants* critics had a point. He *was* a Tory who deplored most of the developments in France and Europe between 1789 and 1815. He deplored them because they destroyed his ideal of social harmony, wrecking what Talleyrand, remembering the ancien-régime long after its demise, famously called its *douceur de vivre,* the paternalistic feudal fantasy Scott himself attempted to create at Abbotsford, replacing it with the dismal prospect of an age of violent clashes between irreconcilable political cultures, an era that Scott memorably lamented as 'the iron age in which it has been our fate to live'.[19] In his euphoria at Napoleon's first abdication, Scott thanked

> Divine Providence, which I trusted could never permit the permanent duration of a system which was calculated to bring the world back to all the ignorance and ferocity of the darker ages without the spirit of high honour and chivalry by which their ignorance was gilded and their tempers softened.[20]

His language here echoes Burke's famous paean for Marie-Antoinette and the age of chivalry, emphasizing the extent to which he interpreted the revolutionary and Napoleonic periods in terms of the harmonious social relations they had supposedly undermined, relations that he hoped to see reconstituted after 1814. The revolutionary and Napoleonic wars also led, *inter alia,* to mass-murder, military despotism, over twenty years' ruinous conflict, and immense suffering throughout the continent, something Scott felt reasonably enough justified deploring.

By the mid-1820s, as he was contemplating writing the *Life,* and reformers and reactionaries were yet again squaring up in Britain and Europe, it became obvious that Divine Providence had played a singularly nasty trick on him in 1814. The challenge of the new had neither been annihilated by France's defeat nor cynically suffocated at the Congress of Vienna; it had merely been postponed. Worse still, Europe's fickle collective memory was rapidly succumbing to gross moral and factual amnesia. Napoleon was, partly thanks to the propaganda he had cleverly peddled from Saint Helena, in the process of becoming transmuted into the patron saint of freedom and modernity. This re-branded Napoleon, as well as the renewed political challenges of the 1820s, needed to be contested. In this respect, the fact that the *Life* was initially due to be included in the *Miscellany*, an imprint deliberately created for the rising number of less affluent readers, is surely significant. Scott saw the urgency of bringing the lower classes onside. The object of the *Miscellany* was to prevent them from getting hold of *bad* ideas:

> to place the best and soundest works of every kind within the reach of the lower classes, whose shelves will be otherwise unquestionably filled with that sort of trash which is peculiarly dangerous both to their morals as men and their loyalty as subjects.[21]

In this respect, Scott almost certainly viewed the *Life* as an opportunity to educate politically beyond the confines of his habitual readership. As a result, he is occasionally prone to making unhistorical political and social comparisons between France and Britain, comparisons from which Britain, her wonderful monarchs, loyal and intelligent gentry, and outstanding, manly constitution, invariably emerge victorious. Similarly, when he is not vigorously defending Tory policies and attacking Whig naivety, Scott is vigorously attacking the Tories for being too soft on Napoleon, while his habit of ingratiating himself with the great and the good, particularly if they happen to be monarchs, aristocrats, or the Duke of Wellington, can make the reader fast-forward through such sections in the original work.

Scott's overarching intention, therefore, was unquestionably to demonstrate that much that had occurred during the revolutionary and Napoleonic periods was disastrous. It must be emphasized, however, that, obvious propagandist passages aside, he overwhelmingly sought to convince through careful and well-substantiated argument and rebuttal. Indeed, taken as a whole, and contrary to the assertions of radical critics, the *Life* is strikingly moderate and impartial. If anything Scott feared that he was being too fair and would ultimately antagonize both sides of the reforming divide, telling Constable that

> I am pretty sure I shall offend the high fliers both of Whigs & Tories and must expect treatment accordingly for which I do not care a d—n so they let me have fair play with the public.[22]

Most of the time, Scott lets his substantial evidence do the talking, merely sitting in judgment and, honest judge that he was, giving the benefit of the doubt to the accused. Terrible accusations require damning evidence, thus, while he raises a number of well-known accusations against Napoleon – the massacre of royalist prisoners in Toulon in 1793, the poisoning of French sick at Jaffa in 1798, or the alleged maltreatment of Pius VII in exile – he does so only to dismiss them categorically for want of proof. Even Napoleon's daring escape from Elba was to some extent justified, at least to Scott, by the restored Bourbons' refusal to pay his alimentary pension. Likewise, while Scott intelligently defends the Crown's decision to intern Napoleon on Saint Helena, and argues that the small company of exiles were more to blame for their supposititious sufferings than the British, he insists that 'the very best accommodation was due to fallen greatness',[23] accommodation that Napoleon did not receive at the hands of his truculent gaoler, the inept Sir Hudson Lowe who, he argues, did not have the character to deal with a situation 'that was in every respect a painful one'.[24] From a grizzlier perspective, Scott gives Napoleon every conceivable opportunity to clear his name before coming to a considered verdict on the massacre of Turkish prisoners at Jaffa or the murder of the Duke d'Enghien.

Mill's review unintentionally reveals the extent of Scott's ideological moderation. While significantly admitting that the 'work contains juster views, and above all, breathes a less malignant spirit, than almost any other Tory publication on the Revolution', he castigates Scott for lending naive credibility to a number of reactionary canards, notably that there was a scheming republican party from the very beginning of the Revolution, that the Duke d'Orléans contributed substantially to the overthrow of the monarchy or that the Enlightenment was associated with the decline of public mores – an argument, incidentally, that recent historiography to some extent bears out. In doing so he misses the much more important and dramatic concession Scott the diehard Tory does make, namely that the Revolution was inevitable and represented a legitimate 'exertion of the public will of France to free the country from public grievances'.[25] The French had been provoked into a national reforming effort by a century of governmental failings. The system had been crumbling for ages, the victim of a corrupt Regent, lazy or hapless monarchs, the Crown's assault on traditional liberties, and France's all too evident decline as a world power.

When it comes to the French aristocracy, Scott's surprising impartiality carries him even further away from habitual Tory nostra. Indeed, his analyses of class and the Enlightenment pre-empt those famously made by Alexis de Tocqueville by thirty years. He argues that, over the eighteenth century, the aristocracy forfeited the 'respect and love' of the people but continued to enjoy abusive rights and immunities at their expense. Simultaneously they patronized philosophers who resented privilege and questioned birthright.

> [Aristocrats] assumed the tone of philosophers as they would have done that of Arcadian shepherds at a masquerade, but without any more thoughts of sacrificing their own rank and immunities in the one case, than of actually driving their flocks a-field in the other.[26]

It was precisely this irresponsible patronage of the Enlightenment that transformed an inevitable and legitimate Revolution into a catastrophe. Inexperienced philosophers who, in the absence of a genuine free press, came to believe in their own simplistic reforming rhetoric – 'the theory of government was kept studiously separated from the practice'[27] –

became the formal opposition and, once in power, liberated the destructive, levelling spirit of the age. The great Constituent Assembly was, again according to Scott, made up of talented men, the representatives of a rising middle-class justifiably fed up with aristocratic privilege, but their inexperience combined with their exposure to the Enlightenment to provoke them into wholesale experimentation.

Mill ignored the strikingly moderate substance of Scott's analysis. He also ignored the very fundamental political and historical points Scott was trying to score by including a two-volume preliminary sketch of the Revolution. Politically, Scott was demonstrating that the anti-revolutionary thinker whom he most admired, Edmund Burke – 'no political prophet ever viewed futurity with a surer ken'[28] – was right, great revolutions will throw-up military dictatorships. Historically, he was demonstrating that Napoleon was the product of the genius of Revolution rather than, as his champions alleged, a romantic superman who rose unassisted to greatness or, as Napoleon himself appeared at times to believe, was fated to it. In this respect at least, Scott the historian is admirably consistent with Scott the historical novelist. Like the fictional heroes and heroines of his finest works, his Napoleon is first and foremost the product of an age of dramatic dislocation. To emphasize the priority of period over individual, Scott does not mention Napoleon in the first volume of the *Life* and only gives him a walk-on part towards the end of the second, during the siege of Toulon in 1793. Even then Napoleon is simply one of a number of successful revolutionary generals who, for all his undeniable qualities, could have whistled for supreme power had his more favoured rival, Joubert, survived the battle of Novi, had he not landed, on his return from Egypt in 1799, exactly 'at the happy crisis'[29] in national affairs, or had either of the Jacobin generals, Bernadotte or Jourdan, had the courage, integrity, or presence of mind to oppose the coup d'état of 18-19 brumaire.

Mill ignored the point of Scott's treatment of the Revolution because, spectacularly, he saw no need for a biography of Napoleon. The man who once dominated Europe, and continues to excite historical imaginations and debates was not, for the supercilious philosopher, a subject worthy of serious analysis. With breathtaking arrogance, Mill wrote Napoleon's towering career off as the triumph of low, selfish cunning:

> [T]here have never been wanting just such men as he, when such prizes have been attainable by them: the most obvious causes suffice to account for every event in his history: to comprehend it thoroughly, there needed no extraordinary depth of philosophy; the lowest impulses of the lowest description of human beings are the moving principle of the whole...

Napoleon evidently grated; Mill's object in 1828 was to preserve reformers from their Tory critics, not to remind the educated public that great reforming movements can degenerate into oppressive despotisms.

Scott did not share Mill's moral and intellectual snobbery. In the *Life* he records that virtually all the hardened British sailors who conveyed Napoleon to Elba and, over a year later, to Saint Helena, fell under the Emperor's spell, charmed by his extraordinary capacity to charm. Scott's correspondence, coupled with the text of the *Life*, suggest that he underwent a similar transformation himself. As a vehement Tory and patriot, he had loyally despised Napoleon during the war. Then, the Emperor was the arch-enemy of mankind:

> [T]he most accursed and relentless military despotism that ever wasted the blood and curbed the faculties of a civilized people. – I should have as soon expected the blade of a sword to bear a crop of corn, on its polished and hardened side, as any good or liberal institution to flow from Bonaparte.[30]

In 1814 Scott was disappointed to learn that Napoleon had received Elba for his troubles, he would sooner the mob had torn him to pieces. By the mid-1820s, however, as memories of bloody wars gave way to Promethean visions of fallen greatness fastened to sea-girt rocks, Scott's attitude, like that of his great French counterpart, Chateaubriand, had noticeably softened. The pathos of lonely captivity had endowed Napoleon with the trappings of tragedy:

He was a strange mingled phantom of grandeur and terror and a little meanness withal as ever bestrode the destinies of the world and his own close was as extraordinary as his rise..... He might have been a great man and was only a great soldier – he might have been the benefactor of the human race and he was the cause of more blood being spilled than had flowed for an hundred years before. He lowered the standard of virtue and public feeling among the french and spoiled their soldierly character by associating it with perfidy and dishonour. Still I think the sufferings attending his double fall are a great atonement for the faults of his character.[31]

Scott does not, for all that, allow himself to be captivated, like so many of his contemporaries, into forgetfulness. He never forgets Napoleon's gigantic failings – the monstrous egoism that led him to crush liberty, suffocate the press, murder the Duke d'Enghien, brutalise warfare, bleed France and Europe dry in ultimately fruitless wars before blaming the weather and everyone but himself for his failures:

The miscarriage of his plans was seldom imputed by him to the successful wisdom or valour of an enemy, but to some accidental circumstance, or blunder, which deranged the scheme which must otherwise have been infallible.[32]

Scott notes that even during his enforced leisure on Saint Helena, Napoleon cannot bring himself to imagine that he might somehow be morally responsible for his dismal fate.

Nor is Scott dazzled, like so many historians before and since, by Napoleon's DIY-Empire. Where others are mesmerised by the apparent power and glory, Scott, at his most incisive, sees only a wonderful sham, unsteadily located somewhere in the political lexicon between 'oriental despotism' and 'splendid masquerade', acted out by greedy players united by the prospect of dividing up the spoils of endless conquests, men whose loyalty Napoleon pays for in kind, and who are the first to desert him when his star finally wanes. Within this essentially condemnatory structure, however, Scott is prepared to do justice to, and praise, what Mill could not recognize, namely Napoleon's extraordinary abilities as a soldier and statesman, the absolute identification with France that for so long mitigated his egoism, and his essential humaneness, qualities that might have enabled him to establish a successful dynasty had he not been bent on world domination. In the process Scott identifies what is perhaps the key to the Emperor's lasting historical attractiveness, namely the apparently inexorable self-confidence that made what was, by contemporary social and historical standards, an extraordinary trajectory appear momentarily predestined:

> Arrived at the possession of supreme power, a height that dazzles and confounds so many, Napoleon seemed only to occupy the station for which he was born.[33]

Under Scott's close scrutiny Napoleon is not simplified into unalloyed greatness but, at the same time, he ceases to be an enemy of the human race. Instead he becomes the protagonist of an epic of extraordinary human qualities squandered by monumental egoism and ambition – world domination was the 'Sisyphæan stone' that Napoleon 'rolled so high up the hill, that at length he was crushed under its precipitate recoil.' Anticipating some of the standards of Victorian biography, Scott's *Napoleon Buonaparte* becomes a moral tale of transgressions to some extent redeemed by ennobling punishment.

Frustratingly, perhaps, for a modern readership brought up on tell-all biographies, Scott eschews Napoleon's private life. He does not dwell on his subject's childhood, nor does he expose his dubious private mores. Depicting him as a fine and upstanding private gentleman devoted to his two wives, he makes a single, belated, and oblique reference to Maria Waleska and the child she had with Napoleon, and tactfully skirts his many other paramours. For Scott, as for so many of his nineteenth century successors, the measure of a man's life lay almost entirely in his public persona. Fortunately, the quality and variety of the writing more than makes up for the absence of prurient detail. The great tableaux of the Napoleonic saga are all evocatively reproduced. Fierce battles in which magnificently attired Mamelukes desperately wheel their horses around to kick their way into French squares they have not been able to break compete for space with sublime renderings of frozen landscapes as an entire French army struggles over Alpine passes barely wide enough to accommodate a mule, the men volunteering to pull the artillery by hand, before pouring into Italy to crush a startled Austrian host, or, later on, chilling descriptions of another, far less fortunate army, dragging itself from the ruins of Moscow through an equally frozen wilderness. Between the bloodthirsty episodes, Scott successfully retains the reader's attention by mixing up his styles. The poetic: Elba 'possesses so much both of beauty and variety, as might constitute the scene of a summer night's dream of sovereignty' alternates with the philosophical musings of wearied experience. On his baleful return from Waterloo, Napoleon, 'like most men in difficulties', 'received much more advice than offers of assistance'. His abusive exploitation of plebiscites, in which most Frenchmen did not vote, to justify his constitutional amendments, is easily dispatched:

This argument, being directly contrary to the presumption of law in all similar cases, is not more valid than the defence of the soldier, who, accused of having stolen a necklace from an image of the Virgin, replied to the charge, that he had first asked the Madonna's permission, and, receiving no answer, had taken silence for consent.

Scott's irrepressible bonhomie also pervades the text. He informs us that many men
sighed for Napoleon's sister Pauline, adding suggestively that 'it is said they did not sigh in vain'. Talleyrand's notorious political opportunism, by contrast, reminds him of 'the personal virtue of a female follower of the camp, which consisted in strict fidelity to the grenadier company.'[34]

*

The rehabilitation of the *Life* does not only represent belated recognition of Scott's talents as an historian, it restores a vital missing link from the evolution of historical writing in English. His indirect influence, through his fiction, on nineteenth century historians, has rarely been in question. His direct influence, however, has for too long been ignored. While he may never enjoy the reputation of a Gibbon, a Hume or a Robertson, or, among his successors, a Carlyle, Scott's *Life* connects the two ages of historical writing, underlining their similarities and exposing their differences. The scope and range of the *Life* mark it out as the heir to Gibbon's *Decline and Fall* or Hume's *History of England*, with the important difference that it is no longer sustained by the intellectual self-confidence of the eighteenth century. Carlyle, for his part, was largely piqued into writing his *History of the French Revolution* by reading the *Life*.

In his review, Mill suggested that the historian

> ... must be familiar with generalizations and general views; a man whose knowledge is systematic, embraces classes as well as individuals, who can discriminate between the results of narrow and partial observation, and those of enlarged experience; in short a *philosopher*.[35]

As such, besides being superlatively informed, Mill's historian has to be able to suspend his personal sentiments and opinions as he works in order to arrive at an authoritative version of the past. Scott, by contrast, believed that the historian's primary duty was to recreate another quality of truth, not the truth of the dispassionate and omniscient historian writing with the ironic benefit of hindsight, but the warts and all truth as it was experienced – a vision of history-writing that is as concerned with prejudice and emotion as it is with fact:

> That which is present possesses such power over our senses and our imagination, that it requires no common effort to recall those sensations which expired with preceding events. Yet, to do this is the peculiar province of history, which will be written and read in vain, unless it can connect with its details an accurate idea of the impression which these produced on men's minds while they were yet in transit.[36]

It is now widely acknowledged that it is impossible to write history objectively, that the historian cannot abstract himself or his opinions from the text he produces. The complex processes by which evidence is evaluated and assimilated, and the barely comprehensible mechanics of literary creation, combine to turn the pursuit of objectivity into an exercise in futility. Scott's radical contemporaries thought otherwise. In their optimistic estimation, historical objectivity seemed attainable. Almost two hundred years later, with history ever more insecure about its mixed literary and scientific pedigree and humanity ever more confused and despondent about both itself and progress, it is Scott, his passion and engagement clearly in evidence in his *Life of Napoleon,* who seems more realistic and relevant.

$\mathscr{E}$NDNOTES

1   Introduction, *The Betrothed* (1825).

2   Letter to John Gibson, Junior, 15 September 1826, *The Letters of Sir Walter Scott,* H.J.C. Grierson ed. (London, 1932) vol. x. p. 105.

3   17 June 1826, *The Journal of Sir Walter Scott* W.E.K. Anderson ed. (Oxford, 1972) p. 159.

4   Ibid, 26 May 1826, p. 150.

5   G. Lukács, *The Historical Novel* (1962).

6   G.M. Young, 'Scott and the Historians' in *Sir Walter Scott Lectures 1940-1948* (Edinburgh, 1950) pp. 81-107.

7   30 June 1827.

8   Cited in E. Johnson, *Sir Walter Scott, The Great Unknown* (1970) vol. ii. p.1019.

9   30 January 1827, *The Journal of Sir Walter Scott….,* p. 272.

10. See for instance J. Sutherland, *The Life of Walter Scott. A Critical Biography* (1995), R.S. Alexander, *Napoleon* (2001).

11   H. Ben-Israel, *English Historians on the French Revolution* (Cambridge, 1968).

12. W. Scott, *The Life of Napoleon Buonaparte, with a Preliminary Sketch of the Revolution* (Edinburgh, 1827) p. 231.

13   G. Gourgaud, *Réfutation de la vie de Napoléon par sir Walter Scott, par le general G**** (Paris, 1827).

14   L. Bonaparte, *Réponse à sir Walter Scott sur son histoire de Napoléon* (Paris, 1829).

15. Reading the *Life*, Heinrich Heine concluded that Scott had purely and simply lost it, positing him as yet another one of Napoleon's British victims: 'Strange! The dead Emperor is, even in his grave, the bane of the Britons, and through him Britannia's greatest poet has lost his laurels!', see J.O. Hayden ed., *Walter Scott: The Critical Heritage* (repr. 1995) p. 304.

16. *The Life of Napoleon Buonaparte* (1830).

17. *The Athenaeum,* vol. xiv (11 March 1828).

18. *The Westminster Review* (April 1828) pp. 251-313.

19   P. 240.

20   To Walter Henry Watts, 21 June 1814.

21   To Sir William Knighton, 30 October 1825. Lockhart eventually adapted the *Life* for John Murray in 1829.

22   To Constable, 21 August 1825, *The Letters…* vol. ix. p. 266.

23   Vol. ix. p. 118.

24   Vol. ix. p 156.

25   Vol. ii. p. 66.

26   Vol. i. p. 50.

27   Vol. i. p. 76.

28   Vol. i. p. 278.

29   P. 285.

30   To Matthew Weld Hartstrong, 12 April 1814, *Letters…,* vol. iii. p. 428.

31   To Lady Abercorn, 21 April 1824, vol. viii. pp. 284/5.

32   Vol. iv. p. 111.

33   Vol. ix. p. 312.

34   Vol. viii. p. 298.

35   The Westminster Review…., p. 252.

36   Vol. i. p. 4.

Comment on Walter Scott's Original Text

The object of abridging *The Life of Napoleon Buonaparte* has been to provide readers with a digestible version of Scott's longest historical work that retains the extraordinary range of the original while delivering a sustained narrative of Napoleon's life and career. In order to achieve this difficult balance, it has been necessary to remove passages that are not directly relevant to the narrative. The preliminary sketch of the French Revolution and the documentary appendix have consequently been cut. Together these amounted to two and a half of the original nine volumes. Internal French political developments and military campaigns during the Directory, in which Napoleon did not play a direct part, have also either been cut or abridged. Scott devoted considerable space to the evolving political situation in Britain as well as to British involvement in the revolutionary and Napoleonic wars. These sections, particularly Scott's detailed renderings of the naval contests between Britain and France, and his extensive narratives of the Peninsular War, have been pared down to a bare minimum both on the assumption that they will be reasonably well-known to interested British readers and in order to restore the episodes in question to their relative significance. In contrast, the extensive survey of the proceedings that led up to Napoleon's internment on Saint Helena has largely been retained as it reveals issues and arguments with which modern readers may be less familiar and that may therefore be of particular interest. Finally, the lengthy chapter headings have been removed both to save essential space and because, in almost every instance, they no longer accurately reflect content.

Within this remit, cutting the text has posed considerable difficulties, not least because of the richness of Scott's prose and the elegant, interlocking construction of the narrative. As a result, while every attempt has been made to retain textual continuity, the reader will have to forgive the occasional caesura and thematic jump. Where absolutely necessary, brief summaries of the missing text have been inserted in italics. These provide paraphrases of Scott's narrative and arguments and in no way reflect the views or opinions of the editor.

To facilitate what is always a difficult task, the 1834-5 Edition of the *Life,* rather than the first edition, published by Ballantyne & Co., in Edinburgh, in 1827, has been used, both because the later edition was better formatted for scanning and because it had been cleaned and revised, correcting many of the errors that had crept into the original as Scott raced to finish it. A number of errors, however, remain. It is fondly hoped that most of the egregious ones have been footnoted in this edition. Less significant errors – dates off by a day or two, exotic geographical confusions, the names of peripheral figures – have been ignored so as not to interfere with textual continuity. Curious spellings have been footnoted only when they threatened to undermine the cogency of the text. The editor's footnotes are designated by Arab numerals, Scott's by Roman ones.

THE LIFE OF

NAPOLEON

BUONAPARTE

Sed non in Caesare tantum
Nomen erat, nec fama ducis, sed nescia virtus
Stare loco, solusque pudor non vincere bello;
Acer et indomitus, quo spes quoque ira vocasset,
Ferre manum et numquam temerando parcere ferro,
Successus urguere suos, instare favori
Numinis, inpellens, quidquid sibi summa petenti
Obstaret, gaudensque viam fecisse ruina.

Lucani, *Pharsalia,* Book I

But Caesar had more
than a mere name and military reputation : his
energy could never rest, and his one disgrace was
to conquer without war. He was alert and head-
strong ; his arms answered every summons of ambition or resentment; he never shrank from using
the sword lightly ; he followed up each success and
snatched at the favour of Fortune, overthrowing
every obstacle on his path to supreme power, and
rejoicing to clear the way before him by destruction.

Translation by J.D. Duff
Loeb Classical Library (1962)

CHAPTER I

All that is known with certainty of Napoleon's family may be told in few words. The Buonapartes were a family of some distinction in the Middle Ages; their names are inscribed in the Golden Book at Treviso and their armorial bearings are to be seen on several houses in Florence. But attached, during the civil war, to the Ghibellines, they were persecuted by the Guelphs, and being exiled from Tuscany, one of the family took refuge in Corsica and there established himself and his successors, who were regularly enrolled among the noble natives of the island and enjoyed all the privileges of gentle blood.

The father of Napoleon, Charles Buonaparte, was the principal descendant of this exiled family. He was regularly educated at Pisa in the study of the law and is stated to have possessed a very handsome person, a talent for eloquence, and a vivacity of intellect, which he transmitted to his son. He was a patriot also and a soldier, and assisted at the gallant stand made by Paoli against the French. It was in the middle of civil discord, fights and skirmishes that Charles Buonaparte married Laetitia Ramolini, one of the most beautiful young women of the island, and possessed of a great deal of firmness of character. She partook of the dangers of her husband during the years of civil war and is said to have accompanied him on horseback in some military expeditions, or perhaps hasty flights, shortly before her being delivered of the future emperor. Though left a widow in the prime of life, she had already borne her husband thirteen children of whom five sons and three daughters survived him: 1. Joseph; 2. Napoleon himself; 3. Lucien; 4. Louis; 5. Jerome. The females were: 1. Maria Anne, afterwards Grand Duchess of Tuscany, by the name of Eliza; 2. Maria Annonciada, who became Maria Pauline, Princess of Borghese; 3. Carlotta, or Caroline, wife of Murat, and Queen of Naples.[1]

The family of Buonaparte, being reconciled to the French government after the emigration of Paoli, enjoyed the protection of the Count de

Marboeuf, the Governor of Corsica, by whose interest Charles was included in a deputation of the nobles of the island, sent to Louis XVI in 1779. As a consequence, he was appointed to a judicial situation – that of assessor of the Tribunal of Ajaccio[2] – the income of which aided him to maintain his increasing family, which the smallness of his patrimony, and some habits of expense, would otherwise have rendered difficult. Charles Buonaparte died at the age of about forty years of an ulcer in the stomach on the 24th February 1785.

The subject of our narrative was born upon the 15th day of August 1769 at his father's house in Ajaccio. We read with interest that his mother's good constitution and bold character of mind induced her to attend mass upon the day of his birth, it being the Festival of the Assumption, obliging her to return home immediately, and, as there was no time to prepare a bed or bedroom, she was delivered of the future victor upon a temporary couch prepared for her accommodation and covered with an ancient piece of tapestry, representing the heroes of the Iliad. The infant was christened by the name of Napoleon, an obscure saint, who had fallen out of the calendar, so that his namesake never knew which day he was to celebrate as the festival of his patron. The politeness of the Pope promoted the patron in order to compliment the god-child, and Saint Napoleon was accommodated with a festival. To render this compliment, which no one but a Pope could have paid, still more flattering, the feast was fixed for the 15th August, the birthday of the Emperor, and the day on which he signed the Concordat[3] so that Napoleon had the rare honour of promoting his patron saint.

The young Napoleon had, of course, the simple and hardy education proper to the natives of the mountainous island of his birth, and in his infancy was not remarkable for more than that animation of temper, and wilfulness and impatience of inactivity, by which children of quick parts and lively sensibility are usually distinguished. The winter of the year was generally passed by the family of his father at Ajaccio, where they still exhibit, as the ominous plaything of Napoleon's boyhood, the model of a brass cannon, weighing about thirty pounds. We leave it to philosophers to inquire whether the future love of war was suggested by the accidental possession of such a toy; or whether the tendency of the mind dictated the selection of it; or, lastly, whether the nature of the pastime, corresponding with the taste which chose it, may not have had each their action and reaction, and contributed between them to the formation of a character so warlike.

The Count de Marboeuf interested himself in the young Napoleon, so much as to obtain him an appointment (April, 1779,)[4] to the Royal Military School at Brienne, which was maintained at royal expense, in order to bring up youths for the engineer and artillery service. The malignity of contemporary historians has ascribed a motive of gallantry towards Madame Buonaparte as the foundation of this kindness, but Count Marboeuf had arrived at a period of life when such connections are not to be presumed, nor did the scandal receive any currency from the natives of Ajaccio.

Nothing could be more suitable to the nature of young Buonaparte's genius, than the line of study which thus fortunately was opened before him. His ardour for the abstract sciences amounted to a passion, and was combined with a singular aptitude for applying them to the purposes of war, while his attention to pursuits so interesting in themselves, was stimulated by his natural ambition and desire of distinction. Almost all the scientific teachers at Brienne spoke of the talents of Buonaparte and the progress of his studies with admiration. Circumstances of various kinds, exaggerated or invented, have been circulated concerning the youth of a person so remarkable. The following are given upon good authority:

The conduct of Napoleon among his companions was that of a studious and reserved youth, addicting himself deeply to the means of improvement and rather avoiding than seeking the usual temptations to dissipation. He had few friends and no intimates, yet when there was any joint plan to be carried into effect he was frequently chosen dictator of the little republic. In winter, Buonaparte upon one occasion engaged his companions in constructing a fortress out of the snow, regularly defended by ditches and bastions, according to the rules of fortification. It was considered as displaying the great powers of the juvenile engineer and was attacked and defended by the students until the battle became so keen that their superiors thought it proper to proclaim a truce.

The young Buonaparte gave another instance of address and enterprise. There was a fair held annually in the neighbourhood of Brienne where the pupils of the Military School used to find a day's amusement;

but on account of a quarrel betwixt them and the country people, the masters had directed that the students should not, on the fair day, be permitted to go beyond their own precincts, which were surrounded with a wall. Under the direction of the young Corsican, however, the scholars had already laid a plot for securing their usual day's diversion. They had undermined the wall which encompassed their exercising ground with so much skill and secrecy that their operations remained entirely unknown till the morning of the fair, when a part of the boundary unexpectedly fell and gave a free passage to the imprisoned students, of which they immediately took the advantage by hurrying to the prohibited scene of amusement.

But although on these occasions Buonaparte displayed some of the frolic temper of youth, mixed with the inventive genius and the talent for commanding by which he was distinguished in after time, his life at school was in general that of a recluse and severe student, acquiring by his judgment, and treasuring in his memory that wonderful process of almost unlimited combination, by means of which he was afterwards able to simplify the most difficult and complicated undertakings. His mathematical teacher was proud of the young islander, as the boast of his school, and his other scientific instructors had the same reason to be satisfied. In languages Buonaparte was less proficient, and never acquired the art of writing or spelling French, far less foreign languages, with accuracy or correctness; nor had the monks of Brienne any reason to pride themselves on the classical proficiency of their scholar. The full energies of his mind being devoted to the scientific pursuits of his profession left little time or inclination for other studies. Though of Italian origin, Buonaparte had not a decided taste for the fine arts, and his taste in composition seems to have leaned towards the grotesque and the bombastic. He used always the most exaggerated phrases; and it is seldom, if ever, that his bulletins present those touches of sublimity which are founded on dignity and simplicity of expression.

Notwithstanding the external calmness and reserve of his deportment, he had, while a student at Brienne, a full share of that ambition for distinction and dread of disgrace, that restless and irritating love of fame, which is the spur to extraordinary attempts. On one occasion a harsh superintendent imposed on the future Emperor, for some trifling fault, the disgrace of wearing a penitential dress and being excluded from the table of his students. His pride felt the indignity so severely that it brought on a severe nervous attack; to which, though otherwise of good constitution, he was subject upon occasions of extraordinary irritation. Father Petrault, the professor of mathematics, hastened to deliver his favourite pupil from punishment by which he was so much affected.

In October, 1784, Napoleon Buonaparte, then only fifteen years old, was, though under the usual age, selected by M. de Keralio,[i] the inspector of the military schools, to be sent to have his education completed in the general school of Paris. It was a compliment paid to the precocity of his extraordinary mathematical talent, and the steadiness of his application. While at Paris he attracted the same notice as at Brienne. His taste did not become correct, but his appetite for study in all departments was greatly enlarged; and notwithstanding the quantity which he daily read, his memory was strong enough to retain, and his judgment sufficiently ripe to arrange and digest, the knowledge which he then acquired; so that he had it at his command during all the rest of his busy life. Plutarch was his favourite author; upon the study of whom he had so modelled his opinions and habits of thought that Paoli afterwards pronounced him a young man of an antique caste.

Napoleon Buonaparte, in his 17th year, [September, 1785] received his first commission as second lieutenant in the regiment of La Fère, then quartered at Valence. He mingled with society when he joined his regiment more than he had hitherto been accustomed to do; and exhibited the powers of pleasing which he possessed in an uncommon degree, when he chose to exert them. His handsome and intelligent features, with his active and neat though slight figure, gave him additional advantages. His manners could scarcely be called elegant, but made up in vivacity and variety of expression, and often in great spirit and energy, for what they wanted in grace and polish.

In 1786, he became an adventurer for the honours of literature also, and was anonymously a competitor for the prize offered by the Academy of Lyons on Raynal's question, "What are the principles and institutions, by application of which mankind can be raised to the highest pitch of happiness?" The prize was adjudged to the young soldier.[5] In 1789, Buonaparte, then quartered at Auxonne, had composed a work, which might form two volumes, on the political, civil, and military history of Corsica. He addressed a letter to General Paoli, then residing in London, on the subject of the proposed work and the actual condition of his countrymen. He also submitted it to the Abbé Raynal, who recommended publication. With this view, Buonaparte invited M. Joly, a bookseller of Dole, to visit him at Auxonne. He found the future Emperor in a naked barrack room, the sole furniture of which consisted of a wretched bed without curtains, a table placed in the embrasure of a window, loaded with books and papers, and two chairs. His brother Louis, whom he was teaching mathematics, lay on a wretched mattress in an adjoining closet. M. Joly and the author agreed on the price of the impression, but Napoleon was at the time in uncertainty whether he was to remain at Auxonne. The work was never printed. In 1790 Buonaparte composed a political tract in the form of a letter to M. de Buttafuoco,[6] major-general, and deputy of the Corsican noblesse in the National Assembly. 100 copies were printed and sent to Corsica; where it was adopted and republished by the patriotic society of Ajaccio, who passed a resolution, attaching the epithet *infamous,* to the name of their noble deputy.

Sterner times were fast approaching, and the nation was now fully divided by those factions which produced the Revolution. The officers of Buonaparte's regiment were also divided into Royalists and Patriots; and it is easily to be imagined that the young and the friendless stranger and adventurer should adopt that side to which he had already shown some inclination, and which promised to open the most free career to those who had only their merit to rely upon. "Were I a general officer," he is alleged to have said, "I would have adhered to the King; being a subaltern, I join the Patriots." Napoleon has himself recorded that he was a warm patriot during the whole sitting of the National Assembly; but that, on the appointment of the Legislative Assembly, he became shaken in his opinions. If so, his original sentiments regained force, for we shortly afterwards find him entertaining such as went to the extreme heights of the Revolution.

Early in 1792, Buonaparte became a captain in the artillery by seniority; and in the same year, being at Paris, he witnessed the two insurrections of the 20th June and 10th August. He was accustomed to speak of the insurgents as the most despicable banditti, and to express with what ease a determined officer could have checked these apparently formidable but dastardly and unwieldy masses. Buonaparte, anxious for the safety of his mother and family, was now desirous to exchange France for Corsica, where the same things were acting on a less distinguished stage.

It was a singular feature in the French Revolution that it brought out from his retirement the celebrated Pascal Paoli, who, long banished from Corsica, the independence of which he had so valiantly defended, returned from exile with the flattering hope of still witnessing the progress of liberty in his native land. On visiting Paris, he was received there with enthusiastic veneration, and the National Assembly and Royal Family contended which should show him most distinction. He was created president of the department, and commander of the national guard of his native island, and used the powers entrusted to him with great wisdom and patriotism. But Paoli's views of liberty were different from those which unhappily began to be popular in France. He was desirous of establishing that freedom which is the protector not the destroyer of property, and which confers practical happiness instead of aiming at theoretical perfection. In a word, he endeavoured to keep Corsica free from the prevailing infection of Jacobinism; and in reward, was denounced in the Assembly. Paoli, summoned to attend for the purpose of standing in his defence, declined the journey on account of his age, but offered to withdraw from the island. A large proportion of the inhabitants took part with the aged champion of their freedom, while the Convention sent an expedition, at the head of which were La Combe Saint Michel and Salicetti, one of the Corsican deputies to the Convention, with the usual instructions for bloodshed and pillage.

Buonaparte was in Corsica, upon leave of absence, when these events were taking place; and although he himself, and Paoli, had hitherto been on friendly terms, the young artillery officer did not hesitate to choose a side. He embraced that of the Convention with heart and hand; and his first military exploit was in the civil war of his native island. In 1793, he was despatched to surprise Ajaccio, then occupied by Paoli or his adherents. Buonaparte was acting provisionally, commanding a battalion of national guards. He landed in the gulf of Ajaccio with about fifty men, to take possession of a tower called the Torre di Capitello, on the opposite side of the gulf and almost facing the city. He succeeded in taking the place; but as there arose a gale which prevented his communicating with the frigate which had put him ashore, he was besieged in his new conquest by the opposite faction, and reduced to such distress that he and his little garrison were obliged to feed on horse-flesh. After five days he was relieved by the frigate, and evacuated the tower, having first in vain attempted to blow it up. The Torre di Capitello still shows marks of the damage it then sustained, and its remains may be looked on as a curiosity, as the first scene of his combats.[7]

The strength of Paoli increasing, and the English preparing to assist him, Corsica became no longer a safe residence for the Buonaparte family. Indeed, both Napoleon and his brother Joseph, who had distinguished themselves as partisans of the French, were subjected to a decree of banishment from their native island; and Madame Buonaparte, with two of her daughters, set sail under their protection, and settled at Marseilles, where the family remained in obscurity, until the dawning prospects of Napoleon afforded him the means of assisting them.

On his return from Corsica, Buonaparte arrived at Nice, and was preparing to join his regiment, when General Degear, who commanded the artillery of "the army of Italy," then encamped round the city, required his services and employed him in several delicate operations. Shortly after, the insurrection of Marseilles broke out – a movement consequent upon the arrest of the leaders of the Girondist party in the Convention, on the first Prairial [31st May], and which extended with violence into the departments. The insurgents of Marseilles organised a force of 6,000 men, with which they took possession of Avignon, and thereby intercepted the communications of the army of Italy. The general-in-chief, being much embarrassed by this circumstance, sent Buonaparte to the insurgents to try to induce them to let the convoys pass. In July he went to Marseilles and Avignon, had interviews with the leaders, convinced them that it was in their own interest not to excite the resentment of the army of Italy, and secured the transit of the convoys.

During his residence at Marseilles, when sent to the insurgents, having, he says, an opportunity of observing all the weakness and incoherence of their means of resistance, he drew up a little pamphlet which he called "Le Souper de Beaucaire," which he published in that city. "He endeavoured," he says, "to open the eyes of these frantic people, and predicted that the only result of their revolt would be to furnish a pretext to the men of blood for sending the principal persons amongst them to the scaffold." "It produced," he adds, "a very powerful effect, and contributed to calm the agitation which prevailed." During these proceedings Toulon had surrendered to the English. Buonaparte was ordered on service to the siege of that town, and joined the army on the 12th September.

CHAPTER II

Lord Mulgrave, who commanded personally in the place, notwithstanding the motley character of the garrison and other discouraging circumstances, began the defence with spirit. Sir George Keith Elphinstone also defeated the Republicans at the mountain pass, called Ollioules. The English for some time retained possession of this important gorge, but were finally driven out from it. Cartaux, a republican general, now advanced on the west of Toulon at the head of a very considerable army, while General Lapoype blockaded the city on the east with a part of the army of Italy. It was the object of the French to approach Toulon on both sides of the mountainous ridge, called Pharon. But on the east the town was covered by the strong and regular fort of La Malgue, and on the west by a less formidable work, called Malbosquet. To support Malbosquet, and to protect the entrance to the roadstead and harbour, the English fortified with great skill an eminence called Hauteur de Grasse. The height bent into a sort of bay, the two promontories of which were secured by redoubts, named L'Eguillette and Balagnier, which communicated with and supported the new fortification, which the English had termed fort Mulgrave.

Several sallies and skirmishes took place, in most of which the Republicans were worsted. Lieutenant-General O'Hara arrived from Gibraltar with reinforcements, and assumed the chief command. Little could be said for the union of the commanders within Toulon; yet their enterprises were so successful that the French began to be alarmed at the slow progress of the siege. The dearth of provisions was daily increasing, the discontent of the people of Provence was augmented; and Barras and

Freron wrote from Marseilles [December 1st], to the Convention, suggesting that the siege of Toulon should be raised and the besieging army withdrawn beyond the Durance. But while weaker minds were despairing, talents of the first order were preparing to achieve the conquest of Toulon.

When Napoleon arrived at the scene of action and had visited the posts of the besieging army, he found so many marks of incapacity that he could not conceal his astonishment. Batteries had been erected for destroying the English shipping, but they were three gun-shots' distance from the point which they were designed to command; red-hot balls were preparing, but they were not heated in furnaces beside the guns, but in the country-houses in the neighbourhood at the most ridiculous distance. Buonaparte with difficulty obtained General Cartaux's permission to make a shot or two by way of experiment; and when they fell more than half-way short of the mark, the general had no excuse but to rail against the aristocrats, who had, he said, spoiled the quality of the powder with which he was supplied. The young officer of artillery, with prudence, and at the same time with spirit, made his remonstrances to the member of Convention, Gasparin, who witnessed the experiment, and explained the necessity of proceeding more systematically if any successful result was expected.

At a council of war, where Gasparin presided, the instructions of the Committee of Public Safety were read, directing that the siege should be commenced according to the usual forms, by investing the city itself. The orders of the Committee of Public Safety were no safe subject of criticism for those who were to act under them; yet Buonaparte ventured to recommend their being departed from on this important occasion. His comprehensive genius had at once discovered a less direct, yet more certain manner, of obtaining the surrender of the place. He advised that, neglecting the body of the town, the attention of the besiegers should be turned to attaining possession of the promontory called Hauteur de Grasse, by driving the besiegers from fort Mulgrave, and the two redoubts of L'Eguillette and Balagnier, by means of which the English had established the line of defence necessary to protect the fleet and harbour. The fortress of Malbosquet, on the same point, he also recommended as a principal object of attack. He argued that if the besiegers succeeded in possessing themselves of these fortifications, they must obtain a complete command of the roads where the English fleet lay and oblige them to put to sea. They would, in the same manner, prevent supplies or provisions from being thrown into the city. If the garrison were thus in danger of being totally cut off, it was natural to suppose that the English would rather evacuate Toulon, than remain within, blockaded on all sides, until they might be compelled to surrender by famine.

The plan was adopted by the council of war after much hesitation, and the young officer by whom it was projected received full powers to carry it on. He rallied round him a number of excellent artillery officers and soldiers; assembled against Toulon more than 200 pieces of cannon, well served; and stationed them so advantageously that he annoyed considerably the English vessels in the roads, even before he had constructed the batteries on which he depended for reducing forts Mulgrave and Malbosquet.

From this time the commandant of artillery, having the complete concurrence of his general, had no doubt of success. To ensure it, however, he used the utmost vigilance and exertion, and exposed his person to every risk. One of the dangers which he incurred was of a singular character. An artilleryman being shot while Napoleon was visiting a battery, he took up the dead man's rammer, and, to give encouragement to the soldiers, charged the gun repeatedly with his own hands. In consequence of using this implement he caught an infectious cutaneous complaint, which, being injudiciously treated and thrown inward, was of great prejudice to his health until after his Italian campaigns, when he was completely cured by Dr. Corvissart; after which, for the first time, he showed that tendency to *embonpoint* which marked the latter part of his life.

Upon another occasion, while Napoleon was overlooking the construction of a battery, which the enemy endeavoured to interrupt by their fire, he called for some person who could write that he might dictate an order. A young soldier stepped out of the ranks, and resting the paper on the breast-work, began to write accordingly. A shot from the enemy's battery covered the letter with earth the instant it was finished. "Thank you – we shall have no occasion for sand this bout," said the military secretary. The gaiety and courage of the remark drew Buonaparte's attention on the young man, who was the celebrated General Junot, afterwards created

Duke d'Abrantes. During this siege, also, he discovered the talents of Duroc, afterwards one of his most faithful adherents.

Notwithstanding the influence which the commandant of artillery had acquired, he found himself occasionally thwarted by the members of the Convention upon mission to the siege, who latterly were Fréron, Ricord, Salicetti, and the younger Robespierre. These representatives of the people, knowing that their commission gave them supreme power over generals and armies, never seem to have paused to consider whether nature or education had qualified them to exercise it. They criticised Buonaparte's plan of attack, finding it impossible to conceive how his operations, being directed against detached fortifications at a distance from Toulon, could be eventually the means of placing the town itself with facility in their hands. But Napoleon was patient and temporising; and having the good opinion of Salicetti and some intimacy with young Robespierre, he contrived to have the works conducted according to his plan.

The presumption of these dignitaries became the means of precipitating his operations. It was his intention to complete his proposed works against fort Mulgrave before opening a large and powerful battery, which he had constructed with great silence and secrecy against Malbosquet, so that the whole of his meditated assault might confound the enemy by commencing at the same time. The operations, being shrouded by an olive plantation, had been completed without being observed by the English. Messrs. Fréron and Robespierre, however, in visiting the military posts, stumbled upon this masked battery; and having no notion why 4 mortars and 8 twenty-four pounders should remain inactive, commanded the fire to be opened on Malbosquet without any delay.

General O'Hara, confounded at finding this important post exposed to a fire so formidable and unexpected, determined by a strong effort to carry the French battery at once. 3000 men were employed in this sally; and the general resolved to put himself at their head. The sally was at first completely successful; but while the English pursued the enemy too far, in all the confidence of what they considered as assured victory, Buonaparte availed himself of some broken ground and a covered way, to rally a strong body of troops, bring up reserves, and attack the scattered English both in flank and rear. There was a warm skirmish, in which Napoleon himself received a bayonet wound in the thigh, by which, though a serious injury, he was not, however, disabled. The English were thrown into irretrievable confusion and retreated, leaving their general wounded and a prisoner in the hands of the enemy.

The loss of their commandant, added to the discouragement which began to prevail among the defenders of Toulon, together with the vivacity of the attack which ensued, seemed finally to have disheartened the garrison. Five batteries were opened on fort Mulgrave, the possession of which Buonaparte considered as ensuring success. After a fire of 24 hours, Dugommier and Napoleon resolved to try the fate of a general attack. The attacking columns advanced before day, during a heavy shower of rain. They were at first driven back on every point by the most determined opposition; and Dugommier, as he saw the troops fly in confusion, exclaimed, well knowing the consequences of bad success to a general of the Republic, "I am a lost man!" Renewed efforts, however, at last prevailed, the fort fell [December 18th] into the possession of the French, who showed no mercy to its defenders.

The allied troops resolved to evacuate Toulon. It had been resolved that the arsenal and naval stores should be destroyed; and they were set on fire accordingly. The assistance of the Spaniards was offered and accepted; and they undertook the duty of scuttling and sinking two vessels used as powder magazines, and destroying some part of the disabled shipping. The rising conflagration growing redder and redder, seemed at length a great volcano, amid which were distinctly seen the masts and yards of the burning vessels, and which rendered obscurely visible the advancing Republican troops, who attempted on different points to push their way into the place. The Jacobins began to rise in the town upon the flying Royalists; horrid screams and yells of vengeance, and revolutionary choruses, were heard to mingle with the cries and plaintive entreaties of the remaining fugitives, who had not yet found means of embarkation. The guns from Malbosquet, now possessed by the French and turned on the bulwarks of the town, increased the uproar. At once a shock, like that of an earthquake, occasioned by the explosion of many hundred barrels of gunpowder, silenced all noise save its own and threw high into the midnight heaven a thousand blazing fragments, which descended, threatening ruin wherever they fell. A second explosion took place, as the other magazine blew up, with the same dreadful effects.

This tremendous addition to the terrors of the scene was owing to the Spaniards setting fire to those vessels used as magazines, instead of sinking them. It was upon this night of terror, conflagration, tears, and blood, that the star of Napoleon first ascended the horizon; and though it gleamed over many a scene of horror ere it set, it may be doubtful whether its light was ever blended with those of one more dreadful.

So many of the citizens of Toulon concerned in the late resistance had escaped, by the means provided by the English, that Republican vengeance could not collect its victims in the usual numbers. Many were shot, however, and it has been said that Buonaparte commanded the artillery, by which they were exterminated; and also that he wrote a letter to Fréron and the younger Robespierre, congratulating them and himself on the execution of these aristocrats, and signed Brutus Buonaparte, Sans-Culotte. If he actually commanded at this execution, he had the poor apology, that he must do so or himself perish; but, had the fact and the letter been genuine, there has been enough of time since his downfall to prove the truth of the accusation, and certainly enough of writers disposed to give these proofs publicity. He himself positively denied the charge; and alleged that the victims were shot by a detachment of what was called the Revolutionary Army. This we think highly probable.

In the meanwhile, the young general of artillery was rapidly rising in reputation. Buonaparte's name was placed on the list of those recommended for promotion, with the pointed addition, that if neglected, he would be sure to force his own way. He was accordingly confirmed in his provisional situation of chief of battalion,[8] and appointed to hold that rank in the army of Italy. Before joining that army, the genius of Napoleon was employed by the Convention in surveying and fortifying the sea-coast of the Mediterranean.

Buonaparte proceeded to join the Headquarters of the French army, then lying at Nice, straitened considerably and hemmed in by the Sardinians and Austrians, who had remained masters of the Col de Tende, and lower passes of the Alps, together with the road leading from Turin to Nice by Saorgio. Buonaparte had influence enough to recommend with success a plan for driving the enemy out of this position, forcing them to retreat beyond the higher Alps, and taking Saorgio; all of which succeeded as he had predicted, and the French army obtained possession of the chain of the higher Alps, which, being tenable by defending few and difficult passes, placed a great part of the army of Italy at disposal for actual service.

In the remainder of 1794, there was little service of consequence in the army of Italy, and the 9th and 10th Thermidor [27th and 28th July] of that year, brought the downfall of Robespierre, and threatened unfavourable consequences to Buonaparte, who had been in close communication with the tyrant's brother, and was understood to have participated in the tone of exaggerated patriotism affected by his party. He endeavoured to shelter himself under his ignorance of the real tendency of the proceedings of those who had fallen – an apology which resolves itself into the ordinary excuse, that he found his late friends had not been the persons he took them for. "I am somewhat affected," he wrote to a correspondent, "at the fate of the younger Robespierre; but, had he been my brother, I would have poniarded him with my own hand, had I been aware that he was forming schemes of tyranny."

Buonaparte's disclamations do not seem at first to have been favourably received. His situation was now precarious; and when those members were restored to the Convention, who had been expelled and proscribed by the Jacobins, it became still more so. The reaction of the moderate party, accompanied by horrible recollections of the past, and fears for the future, began now to be more strongly felt. Those officers who had attached themselves to the Jacobin party were the objects of their animosity; and, besides, they were desirous to purify the armies, as far as possible, of those whom they considered as their own enemies; the rather, that the Jacobinical principles still continued to be more favoured in the armies than in the interior.

Before the downfall of Robespierre took place, Buonaparte had received regular but secret instructions to examine the fortifications of Genoa. Ricord, by whom these instructions had been signed, having now been superseded, and the younger Robespierre guillotined, Albitte, Salicetti, and Laporte, the new superintendents of the army of Italy, were pleased to suspect that Buonaparte had engaged in some plot of betraying Genoa to the enemy: he was arrested early in August but his papers established his innocence and after the lapse of a fortnight, he was released.

In March 1795, he was sent to Toulon to take command of the artillery in an expedition destined against Rome; but this scheme was not persevered in. On his rejoining the troops in the Maritime Alps, near the end of March, he found the army about to be altered, and placed under the command of General Kellerman. A recent arrangement had recalled to the service many officers of high rank who had of late been unemployed; and he, as the youngest of the list of generals, could not only not be allowed to retain his command of the artillery in the army of Kellerman, but was removed to the infantry. He repaired therefore to Paris, with the view of soliciting professional employment elsewhere. On reaching Paris in May, he found his pretensions thwarted by Aubry, the President of the Military Committee. When, in the heat of discussion, Aubry objected his youth, Buonaparte replied, that presence in the field of battle ought to anticipate the claim of years. The president, who had not been much in action, considered his reply as a personal insult; and Napoleon, disdaining further answer, tendered his resignation. It was not, however, accepted; and he still remained in the rank of expectants, but among those whose hopes were entirely dependent upon their merits.

Meantime, his situation becoming daily more unpleasant, Buonaparte solicited Barras and Fréron, who, as Thermidoriens, had preserved their credit, for occupation in almost any line of his profession, and even negotiated for permission to go into the Turkish service, to train the Mussulmans in the use of artillery. A fanciful imagination may pursue him to the rank of pacha, or higher; for, go where he would, he could not have remained in mediocrity. His own ideas had a similar tendency. "How strange," he said, "it would be, if a little Corsican officer of artillery were to become King of Jerusalem!" He was offered a command in La Vendée, which he declined to accept, and was finally named to command a brigade of artillery in Holland. But it was in a land where there still existed so many separate and conflicting factions that he was doomed to be raised, amid the struggles of his contending countrymen, and upon their shoulders and over their heads, to the very highest eminence to which fortune can exalt an individual. The times required such talents as his, and the opportunity for exercising them soon arose.

Scott describes the settlement adopted by the Convention in 1795 — the Constitution of the Year Three – which gave rise to the Directory. The Thermidoriens of the Convention, who were keen to retain power in their own hands, attempted to pass unpopular decrees which gave deputies of the Convention the power to effectively select themselves and their successors, 'continuing the exercise of their own arbitrary authority'. The citizens of Paris responded by making moves to defend the liberties of France and defy the new legislation.

The Convention, unpopular themselves, and embarked in an unpopular cause, began to look anxiously around for assistance. They chiefly relied on the aid of about 5000 regular troops, who were assembled in and around Paris. These declared for government with the greater readiness, that the insurrection was of a character decidedly aristocratic, and that the French armies were attached to the Republic. The Convention had also the assistance of several hundred artillerymen, who, since the taking of the Bastille, had been always zealous democrats. Still apprehensive of the result, they added to this force another of a more ominous description. It was a body of volunteers, consisting of about 1500 men, whom they chose to denominate the Sacred Band, or the Patriots of 1789. They were gleaned out of the suburbs, and from the jails, the remnants of the insurrectional battalions which had formed the body-guard of Hébert and Robespierre, and had been the instruments by which they executed their atrocities. The Convention proclaimed them men of the 10th of August – undoubtedly, they were also men of the massacres of September. It was conceived that beholding such a pack of bloodhounds, ready to be let loose, might inspire horror into the citizens of Paris. It did so, but it also inspired hatred; and the number and zeal of the citizens, compensating for the fury of the Terrorists, and for the superior discipline of the regular troops to be employed against them, promised an arduous and doubtful conflict.

The sections employed, as their commander-in-chief, General Danican, an old officer of no high reputation, but otherwise a worthy and sincere man. The Convention at first made choice of Menou, and directed him to march into the section Le Pelletier, and disarm the national guards of that district. This section is one of the most wealthy in Paris, being inhabited by bankers, merchants, the wealthiest class of tradesmen, and the better orders in general. Its inhabitants had formerly composed the battalion of national guards des Filles Saint Thomas, the only one which, taking part in the defence of the Tuileries, shared the fate of the Swiss Guards upon the memorable 10th of August. The section continued to entertain sentiments of the same character, and when Menou appeared at the head of his forces, he found the citizens under arms, and exhibiting such a show of resistance as induced him, after a parley, to retreat without venturing an attack upon them.

The direction of the Conventional forces was then committed to Barras; but the utmost anxiety prevailed to find a general of nerve and decision enough to act under Barras, in the actual command of the military force. It was then that a few words from Barras, addressed to Carnot and Tallien, decided the fate of Europe for well nigh 20 years, "I have the man," he said, "whom you want, a little Corsican officer, who will not stand upon ceremony."

Buonaparte was sent for. He had witnessed the retreat of Menou, and explained with much simplicity the causes of that check, and the modes of resistance which ought to be adopted in case of the apprehended attack. His explanations gave satisfaction. Buonaparte was placed at the head of the Conventional forces, and took all the necessary precautions to defend the palace. He had 200 pieces of cannon, which his high military skill enabled him to distribute to the utmost advantage. He had more than 5000 regular forces, and about 1500 volunteers. He was thus enabled to defend the whole circuit of the Tuileries; to establish posts in all the avenues by which it could be approached; to possess himself of the bridges, so as to prevent co-operation between the sections which lay on the opposite banks of the river; and finally, to establish a strong reserve in the Place Louis Quinze, or, as it was then called, Place de la Révolution.

A merely civic army, having no cannon, ought to have respected so strong a position. Their policy should have been to have barricaded the streets at every point, and cooped up the Conventional troops till want of provisions obliged them to sally at disadvantage, or to surrender. But a popular force is generally impatient of delay. The retreat of Menou had given them spirit, and they apprehended, with some show of reason, that the sections, if they did not unite their forces, might be attacked and disarmed separately. They therefore resolved to invest the Convention, require of the members to recall the obnoxious decrees, and allow the nation to make a free and undictated election of its representatives.

On the thirteenth Vendémiaire,[9] the Day of the Sections took place. The national guards assembled to the number of 30,000 men and upwards. They advanced by different avenues, in close columns, but everywhere found the most formidable resistance. One large force occupied the quays on the left bank of the Seine, threatening the palace from that side of the river. Another strong division advanced on the Tuileries, through the Rue St. Honoré, designing to debouche on the palace, where the Convention was sitting, by the Rue de l'Echelle. They did so, without duly reflecting that they were flanked on most points by strong posts in the lanes and crossings, defended by artillery.

The contest began in the Rue St. Honoré. Buonaparte had established a strong post with two guns at the cul-de-sac Dauphine, opposite to the church of St. Roche. He permitted the imprudent Parisians to involve their long and dense columns in the narrow street without interruption, until they established a body of grenadiers in the front of the church, and opposite the cul-de-sac. Each party, as usual, throws on the other the blame of commencing the civil contest for which both were prepared. But all agree the firing commenced with musketry. It was instantly followed by discharges of grape-shot and canister, which, pointed as the guns were, upon thick columns of the national guards, made an astounding carnage. The national guards offered a brave resistance, and even attempted to rush on the artillery, and carry the guns by main force. But a measure which is desperate enough in the open field becomes impossible when the road to assault lies through narrow streets, which are swept by the cannon at every discharge. The citizens were compelled to give way. The affair, in which several hundred men were killed and wounded, was terminated as a general action in about an hour; and the victorious troops of the Convention, marching into the different sections, completed the dispersion and disarming of their opponents.

Five days after the battle, Barras solicited the attention of the Convention to the young officer, by whose prompt and skilful dispositions the Tuileries had been protected, and proposed that they should approve of General Buonaparte's appointment as second in command of the army of the interior, Barras himself still remaining commander-in-chief. The proposal was adopted by acclamation. From second in command, the new general soon became general-in-chief of the army of the interior. He employed his genius in improving the state of the military forces; and, in order to prevent the recurrence of such insurrections as that of the 13th Vendemaire, and the many others by which it was preceded, he appointed and organised a guard for the protection of the representative body.

As the dearth of bread and other causes of disaffection continued to produce commotions in Paris, the general of the interior was sometimes obliged to oppose them with a military force. On one occasion, when Buonaparte was anxiously admonishing the multitude to disperse, a very bulky woman exhorted them to keep their ground. "Never mind these coxcombs with the epaulets," she said, "they do not care if we are all starved, so they themselves feed and get fat."-"Look at me, good woman," said Buonaparte, who was then as thin as a shadow, "and tell me which is the fatter of us two." This turned the laugh against the Amazon, and the rabble dispersed in good-humour. If not among the most distinguished of Napoleons victories, this is certainly worthy of record, as achieved at the least cost.

Meantime, circumstances introduced Buonaparte to an acquaintance which was destined to have much influence on his future fate. A fine boy of ten or twelve years old presented himself at the levee of the general of the interior with a request of a nature unusually interesting. He stated his name to be Eugene Beauharnais, son of the ci-devant Vicomte de Beauharnais, who, adhering to the revolutionary party, had been a general in the Republican service upon the Rhine, and falling under the causeless suspicion of the Committee of Public Safety, was delivered to the Revolutionary Tribunal, and fell by its sentence just four days before the overthrow of Robespierre. Eugene was come to request of Buonaparte that his father's sword might be restored to him. The prayer of the young supplicant was as interesting as his manners were engaging, and Napoleon felt so much interest in him that he was induced to cultivate the acquaintance of Eugene's mother, afterwards the Empress Josephine.

This lady was a Creolian, the daughter of a planter in St. Domingo. Her name was Marie-Joseph Rose Detacher de la Pagérie.[10] She had suffered her share of revolutionary miseries. After her husband had been deprived of his command, she was arrested as a suspected person, and detained in prison till the general liberation. While in confinement, Madame Beauharnais had formed an intimacy with a companion in distress, Madame Fontenay, now Madame Tallien, from which she derived great advantages after her friend's marriage. With a remarkably graceful person, amiable manners, and an inexhaustible fund of good humour, Madame Beauharnais was formed to be an ornament to society. Barras, the Thermidorien hero, himself an ex-noble, was fond of society, desirous of enjoying it on an agreeable scale. At the apartments which he occupied as one of the directory in the Luxemburg palace, he gave its free course to his natural taste, and assembled an agreeable society of both sexes. Madame Tallien and her friend formed the soul of these assemblies, and it was supposed that Barras was not insensible to the charms of Madame Beauharnais – a rumour which was likely to arise, whether with or without foundation.

When Madame Beauharnais and General Buonaparte became intimate, the latter assures us, and we see no reason to doubt him, that although the lady was two or three years older than himself,[11] yet being still in the full bloom of beauty and extremely agreeable in her manners, he was induced, solely by her personal charms, to make her an offer of his hand, heart, and fortunes – little supposing, of course, to what a pitch the latter were to arise.

Although he himself is said to have been a fatalist, believing in destiny and in the influence of his star, he knew nothing, probably, of the prediction of a negro sorceress, who, while Marie-Joseph was but a child, prophesied she should rise to a dignity greater than that of a queen, yet fall from it before her death. This was one of those vague auguries, delivered at random by fools or imposters, which the caprice of Fortune sometimes matches with a corresponding and conforming event. But without trusting to the African sibyl's prediction, Buonaparte may have formed his match under the auspices of ambition as well as love. The marrying of Madame Beauharnais was a means of uniting his fortune with those of Barras and Tallien, the first of whom governed France as one of the directors; and the last, from talents and political connections, had scarcely inferior influence. He had already deserved well of them for his conduct on the Day of the Sections, but he required their countenance to rise still higher; and without derogating from the bride's merits, we may suppose her influence in their society corresponded with the views of her lover. It is, however, certain, that he always regarded her with peculiar affection; that he relied on her fate, which he considered as linked with and strengthening his own; and reposed, besides, considerable confidence in Josephine's tact and address in political business. She had at all times the art of mitigating his temper and turning aside the hasty determinations of his angry moments, not by directly opposing, but by gradually parrying and disarming them. It must be added, to her great praise, that she was always a willing, and often a successful advocate, in the cause of humanity.

They were married 9th March 1796; and the dowry of the bride was the chief command of the Italian armies, a scene which opened a full career to the ambition of the youthful general. Buonaparte remained with his wife only three days after his marriage, hastened to see his family, who were still at Marseilles, and having enjoyed the pleasure of exhibiting himself as a favourite of Fortune, proceeded rapidly to commence the career to which Fate called him.

Chapter III

It may be imagined with what delight the general, scarce aged 26, advanced to an independent field of glory and conquest, confident in his own powers, and in the perfect knowledge of the country, which he had acquired when he had enabled General Dumerbion to drive the Austrians back and obtain possession of the Col di Tende, Saorgio, and the gorges of the higher Alps. Buonaparte's achievements had hitherto been under the auspices of others. But if he reaped honour in Italy, the success would be exclusively his own.

No man ever possessed in a greater degree than Buonaparte the power of calculation and combination necessary for directing decisive manoeuvres. It constituted, indeed, his *secret* – as it was for some time called – and that secret consisted in an imagination fertile in expedients which would never have occurred to others; clearness and precision in forming his plans; a mode of directing with certainty the separate moving columns which were to execute them, by arranging so that each division should arrive on the destined position at the exact time when their service was necessary; and above all, in the knowledge which enabled such a master-spirit to choose the most fitting subordinate implements, to attach them to his person, and, by explaining to them so much of his plan as it was necessary each should execute, to secure the exertion of their utmost ability in carrying it into effect.

Thus, not only were his manoeuvres, however daring, executed with a precision which warlike operations had not attained before his time; but they were also performed with a celerity which gave them almost always the effect of surprise. Napoleon was like lightning in the eyes of his enemies; and when repeated experience had taught them to expect this portentous rapidity of movement, it sometimes induced his opponents to wait, in a dubious and hesitating posture, for attacks, which, with less apprehension of their antagonist, they would have thought it more prudent to frustrate and to anticipate.

Great sacrifices were necessary to enable the French troops to move with that degree of celerity which Buonaparte's combinations required. He made no allowance for impediments or unexpected obstacles; the time which he had calculated for execution of manœuvres, was on no account to be exceeded – every sacrifice was to be made of baggage, stragglers, even artillery, rather than the column should arrive too late. Hence, all that had hitherto been considered as essential not only to the health, but to the very existence of an army, was in a great measure dispensed with in the French service; and troops were seen to take the field without tents, without camp-equipage, without magazines of provisions, without military hospitals; the soldiers eating as they could, sleeping where they could, dying where they could; but still advancing, still combating, and still victorious.

It is true that the abandonment of every object, save success in the field, augmented frightfully all the usual horrors of war. The soldier, with arms in his hands and wanting bread, became a marauder in self-defence; and, in supplying his wants by rapine, did mischief to the inhabitants. Still, though purchased at a high rate, that advantage was gained by this rapid system of tactics, which, in a slower progress, might have been rendered doubtful. It wasted the army through all the consequences of want and toil; but still the victory was attained, and that was enough to make the survivors forget their hardships. Patient of labours, light of heart and temper, and elated by success beyond all painful recollections, the French soldiers were the very men calculated to execute this desperate species of service under a chief, who, their sagacity soon discovered, was sure to lead to victory all those who could sustain the hardships by which it was to be won.

The character of the mountainous countries, among which he was, for the first time, to exercise his system, was highly favourable to Buonaparte's views. Presenting many lines and defensible positions, it induced the Austrian generals to become stationary, and occupy a considerable extent of ground, according to their old system of tactics. But though abounding in such positions as might at first sight seem absolutely impregnable, the mountains also exhibited to a great captain gorges, defiles, and unsuspected points of access, by which he could turn the positions that appeared formidable; and, by threatening them on the flank and on the rear, compel the enemy to a battle at disadvantage, or to a retreat with loss.

The plan of crossing the Alps suited in every respect the ambitious and self-confident character of the general to whom it was entrusted. The young general's mind was made up to the alternative of conquest or ruin, as may be judged from his words to a friend at taking leave of him. "In three months," he said, "I will be either at Milan or at Paris;" intimating at once his desperate resolution to succeed, and his sense that the disappointment of all his prospects must be the consequence of a failure.

On the 27th March Buonaparte reached Nice. The army before him was even worse than he had formed any idea of. The supply of bread was very uncertain; distributions of meat had long ceased; and for means of conveyance there were only mules, and not above 500 of these.

The headquarters had never been removed from Nice: they were instantly ordered to be transferred to Albenga. On the 3rd April, the army reached port Maunie, near Oneglia, and on the 4th arrived at Albenga; where, with the view of animating his followers to ambitious hopes, he addressed the army of Italy to the following purpose: "Soldiers, you are hungry and naked. The Republic owes you much, but she has not the means to acquit herself of her debts. The patience with which you support your hardships among these barren rocks is admirable, but it cannot procure you glory. I am come to lead you into the most fertile plains that the sun beholds – Rich provinces, opulent towns, all shall be at your disposal – Soldiers, with such a prospect before you, can you fail in courage and constancy?" This was showing the deer to the hound when the leash is about to be slipped.

Buonaparte's plan for entering Italy differed from that of former conquerors and invaders, who had approached that country by penetrating or surmounting at some point or other her Alpine barriers. This inventive warrior resolved to attain the same object, by turning round the southern extremity of the Alpine range, keeping as close as possible to the shores of the Mediterranean and passing through the Genoese territory by the narrow pass called the Boccheta. Thus he proposed to penetrate into Italy by the lowest level which the surface of the country presented, which must be of course where the range of the Alps unites with that of the Apennines.

To attain his object of turning the Alps, it was necessary that Buonaparte should totally change the situation of his army. Speaking of an army as of a battalion, he was to form into column upon the right of the line which he had hitherto occupied. This was an extremely delicate operation, to be undertaken in presence of an active enemy, his superior in numbers; nor was he permitted to execute it uninterrupted.

No sooner did Beaulieu [the commander of the Austro-Sardinian forces] learn that the French general was concentrating his forces and about to change his position, than he hastened to preserve Genoa, without possession of which, or at least of the adjacent territory, Buonaparte's scheme of advance could scarce have been accomplished. The Austrian divided his army into three bodies. Colli, at the head of a Sardinian division, he stationed on the extreme right at Ceva; his centre division, under d'Argenteau, having its head at Sasiello, had directions to march on a mountain called Montenotte, near to which was a strong position at a place called Montelegino, which the French had occupied in order to cover their flank during their march towards the east. At the head of his left wing, Beaulieu himself moved upon Voltri, a small town within ten miles of Genoa. Thus it appears, that while the French were endeavouring to penetrate into Italy by an advance from Sardinia by the way of

Genoa, their line of march was threatened by three armies of Austro-Sardinians, descending from the skirts of the Alps, and menacing to attack their flank. But though a skilful disposition, Beaulieu's had, from the very mountainous character of the country, the great disadvantage of wanting connection between the three separate divisions; neither, if needful, could they be easily united on any point desired, while the lower line, on which the French moved, permitted constant communication and co-operation.

On the 10th of April, d'Argenteau, with the central division, marched on Montenotte, while Beaulieu attacked the van of the French army, which had come as far as Voltri. General Cervoni, commanding the French division which sustained the attack of Beaulieu, was compelled to fall back on the main body of his countrymen; and had the assault of d'Argenteau been equally successful, the fame of Buonaparte might have been stifled in the birth. But Colonel Rampon, a French officer, who commanded the redoubts near Montelegino, stopped the progress of d'Argenteau by the most determined resistance. At the head of not more than 1500 men, whom he caused to swear either to maintain their post or die there, he continued to defend the redoubts, during the whole of the 11th, until d'Argenteau, whose conduct was afterwards greatly blamed, drew off his forces, intending to renew the attack next morning.

But, on the morning of the 12th, the Austrian general found himself surrounded with enemies. Cervoni, who retreated before Beaulieu, had united himself with La Harpe, and both advancing northward during the night of the 11th, established themselves in the rear of the redoubts of Montelegino. This was not all. The divisions of Augereau and Massena had marched, by different routes, on the flank and on the rear of d'Argenteau's column; so that next morning, instead of renewing his attack, the Austrian general was obliged to extricate himself by a disastrous retreat, leaving behind him colours and cannon, 1000 slain, and 2000 prisoners. /

Such was the battle of Montenotte, the first of Buonaparte's victories; eminently displaying that truth and mathematical certainty of combination, which enabled him on many more memorable occasions, even when his forces were inferior in numbers, and apparently disunited, suddenly to concentrate them and defeat his enemy, by overpowering him on the very point where he thought himself strongest. He had accumulated a superior force on the Austrian centre, and destroyed it, while Colli, on the right, and Beaulieu himself, on the left, each at the head of numerous forces, did not even hear of the action till it was fought and won.

In consequence of Montenotte, and the close pursuit of the defeated Austrians, the French obtained possession of Cairo, which placed them on that side of the Alps which slopes towards Lombardy.

Beaulieu had now to retreat northward with all haste to Dego, in the valley of the river Bormida, in order to resume communication with the right wing of his army, from which he was now nearly separated by the defeat of the centre. General Colli, by a corresponding movement on the right, occupied Millesimo, a small town about nine miles from Dego, with which he resumed and maintained communication by a brigade stationed on the heights of Biastro. From the strength of this position, though his forces were scarce sufficiently concentrated, Beaulieu hoped to maintain his ground till he should receive supplies from Lombardy, and recover the consequences of Montenotte. But the antagonist whom he had in front had no purpose of permitting him such respite.

Determined upon a general attack on all points of the Austrian position, the French army advanced in three bodies upon a space of four leagues in extent. The defeat was decisive; and the Sardinians, after the loss of the best of their troops, their cannon, baggage, and appointments, were now totally divided from their Austrian allies, and liable to be overpowered by the united forces of the French army. Buonaparte, pursuing his victory, took possession of Cherasco, within ten leagues of the Piedmontese capital.

Thus Fortune, in the course of a campaign of scarce a month, placed her favourite in full possession of the desired road to Italy by command of the mountain-passes, which had been invaded and conquered with so much military skill. He had gained three battles over forces far superior to his own; inflicted on the enemy a loss of 25,000 men in killed, wounded, and prisoners; taken eighty pieces of cannon, and 21 stand of colours; reduced to inaction the Austrian army; almost annihilated that of Sardinia; and stood in full communication with France upon the eastern side of the Alps, with Italy lying open before him, as if to invite his invasion.

Under these afflicting circumstances, a suspension of hostilities was requested by the King of Sardinia; and, on the 24th April, conferences were held at Carru, the headquarters of the French, but an armistice could only be purchased by placing two of the King's strongest fortresses – Coni and Tortona, in the hands of the French, and thus acknowledging that he surrendered at discretion. The armistice was agreed on [April 28th] at Cherasco.

*C*HAPTER IV

A general with less extraordinary talent would perhaps have thought it sufficient to have obtained possession of Piedmont, and would have awaited fresh supplies and reinforcements from France before advancing to further and more distant conquests, and leaving the Alps under the dominion of a hostile, though for the present a subdued and disarmed monarchy. But Buonaparte had studied the campaign of Villars in these regions, and was of the opinion that it was by that general's hesitation to advance boldly into Italy, after the victories which the Marshal de Coigni had obtained at Parma and Guastalla, that the enemy had been enabled to assemble an accumulating force, before which the French were compelled to retreat. He determined, therefore, to give the Republic of Venice, the Grand Duke of Tuscany, and other states in Italy, no time to muster forces, and to oppose a French invasion. A speedy resolution was the more necessary, as Austria, alarmed for her Italian possessions, was about to make every effort for their defence. Orders had already been sent by the Aulic Council of War to detach an army of 30,000 men, under Wurmser, from the Army of the Rhine to the frontiers of Italy. These were to be strengthened by other reinforcements from the interior, and by such forces as could be raised in the mountainous district of the Tyrol, which furnishes perhaps the most experienced and most formidable sharpshooters in the world. The whole was to be united to the fragments of Beaulieu's defeated troops. If suffered to form a junction, and arrange their plans for attack or defence, an army, of force so superior to the French in numbers, veterans in discipline, and commanded by a general like Wurmser, was likely to prevent all the advantages which the French might gain by a sudden irruption, ere an opposition so formidable was collected and organised. But the daring scheme which Napoleon contemplated, required to be executed with caution, united with secrecy and celerity. These were the more necessary, as, although the thanks of the French Government had been voted to the army of Italy five times in the course of a month, yet the Directory, alarmed at the more doubtful state of hostilities upon the Rhine, had turned their exertions chiefly in that direction; and, trusting to the skill of their general and the courage of his troops, had not transmitted recruits and supplies upon the scale necessary for the great undertakings which he meditated.

The fortress of Tortona was surrendered to the French by the King of Sardinia and Buonaparte's headquarters were fixed there [May 4th]. Massena concentrated another part of the army at Alexandria, menacing Milan, and threatening, by the passage of the Po, to invade the territories belonging to Austria on the northern bank of that stream. As Buonaparte himself observed, the passage of a great river is one of the most critical operations in modern war; and Beaulieu had collected his forces to cover Milan, and prevent the French from crossing the Po. But Buonaparte's subtle genius had already prepared the means for deceiving the old Austrian.

Valenza appeared to be the point of passage proposed by the French; it is one of those fortresses which cover the eastern frontier of Piedmont. During the conferences previous to the armistice of Cherasco, Buonaparte had thrown out hints as if he were particularly desirous to be possessed of this place, and it was actually stipulated in the terms of the treaty, that the French should occupy it for the purpose of effecting their passage over the river. Beaulieu did not fail to learn what had passed, which coincided with his own ideas of the route by which Buonaparte meant to advance upon Milan. He hastened to concentrate his army on the opposite bank, at a place called Valeggio, about eighteen miles from Valenza, from which he could move easily in any direction towards the river, before the French could send over any considerable force. Massena also countenanced this report by pushing strong reconnoitring parties in the direction of that fortress.

But it was never Buonaparte's intention to cross the Po at Valenza. The proposal was a feint to draw Beaulieu's attention to that point, while the French accomplished the desired passage at Placenza,[12] nearly fifty miles lower down the river than Valeggio. Marching for this purpose with incredible celerity, Buonaparte, on the 7th of May, assembled his forces at Placenza, when their presence was least expected, and where there were none to defend the opposite bank, except two or three squadrons of Austrians, stationed there merely for the purpose of reconnoitring. General Andréossi commanded an advanced guard of 500 men. They had to pass in the common ferry-boats, and the crossing required nearly half an hour; so that the impossibility of achieving the operation, had they been seriously opposed, appears to demonstration. Colonel Lannes threw himself ashore first with a body of grenadiers, and speedily dispersed the Austrian hussars. The vanguard having thus opened the passage, the other divisions of the army were enabled to cross, and in two days the whole were in the Milanese territory and on the left bank of the Po. The military manoeuvres, by means of which Buonaparte achieved an operation of so much consequence, and which, without such address as he displayed, must have been attended with great loss, and risk of failure, have often been considered as among his most masterly movements.

Beaulieu, informed too late of the real plans of the French general, moved his advanced guard, composed of the division of General Liptay, in the direction of Placenza. But here also the alert general of the French had been too rapid in his movements for the aged German. Buonaparte had no intention to wait for an attack from the enemy with such a river as the Po in his rear, which he had no means of recrossing if the day should go against him. He was, therefore, pushing forward in order to gain ground on which to manœuvre, and the advanced divisions of the two armies met at a village called Fombio, on the 8th of May. The Austrians threw themselves into the place, fortified and manned the steeples, and whatever posts else could be made effectual for defence, and reckoned upon defending themselves until the main body of Beaulieu's army should come up to support them. But they were unable to sustain the vivacity of the French onset, to which so many successive victories had now given a double impulse. The village was carried at the bayonet's point; the Austrians lost their cannon, and left behind one-third of their men in slain, wounded, and prisoners. The wreck of Liptay's division saved them-selves by crossing the Adda at Pizzighitone, while they protected their retreat by a hasty defence of that fortress.

Buonaparte calculated that, if he could accomplish the passage of the Adda at Lodi, he might overtake and disperse the remainder of Beaulieu's army, without allowing the veteran time to concentrate them for further resistance in Milan, or even for rallying under the walls of the strong fortress of Mantua.

Upon the 10th day of May, attended by his best generals, and heading the choicest of his troops, Napoleon pressed forward towards Lodi. About a league from Casal, he encountered the Austrian rear-guard, who had been left, it would appear, at too great a distance from the main body. The French had no difficulty in driving these troops before them into Lodi, which was but slightly defended by the few soldiers whom Beaulieu had left on the western side of the Adda. He had also neglected to destroy the bridge. But though left standing, it was swept by 20 or 30 Austrian pieces of artillery, whose thunders menaced death to any who should attempt that pass of peril. The French, with great alertness, got as many guns in position on the left bank, and answered this tremendous fire with equal spirit. The Austrian army now completely gave way, and lost in their retreat, annoyed as it was by the French cavalry, upwards of 20 guns, 1000 prisoners, and perhaps 2000 more wounded and slain.

On the 15th of May, Buonaparte made his public entry into Milan, under a triumphal arch prepared for the occasion, surrounded by his guards, and took up his residence in the archiepiscopal palace. The same evening a splendid entertainment was given, and the Tree of Liberty, (of which the aristocrats observed that it was a bare pole without either leaves or fruit, roots or branches,) was erected with great form in the principal square. All this affectation of popular joy did not disarm the purpose of the French general, to make Milan contribute to the relief of his army. He imposed a requisition of 20 million livres, but offered to accept goods of any sort in kind, and at a rateable valuation. The public funds of every description, even those dedicated to the support of hospitals, went into the French military chest; the church-plate was seized as a part of the requisition; and, when all this was done, the citizens were burdened with the charge of finding rations for 15,000 men, by which force the citadel, with its Austrian garrison, was instantly to be blockaded.

Napoleon imposed similarly brutal exactions upon the technically neutral states of Modena and Parma.

CHAPTER V

Buonaparte permitted his forces only the repose of four or five days, ere he again summoned them to active exertion. He advanced to Brescia, and manoeuvred in such a manner as induced Beaulieu, whom repeated surprises of the same kind had not put upon his guard, to believe, that either the French general intended to attempt the passage of the Mincio at the small but strong town of Peschiera, where that river issues from the lago di Guarda, or else that, marching northward along the eastern bank, he designed to come round the head of the lake, and thus turn the right of the Austrian position. While Beaulieu disposed his forces as expecting an attack on the right of his line, Buonaparte, with his usual celerity, proposed to attack him on the centre, at Borghetto, a town situated on the Mincio, and commanding a bridge over it, above ten miles lower than Peschiera.

On the 30th May, the French general attacked with superior force and repulsed across the Mincio an Austrian corps who endeavoured to cover the town. Beaulieu hastened to retreat, and, evacuating Peschiera, marched his dismayed forces behind the Adige, leaving 500 prisoners, with other trophies of victory, in the hands of the French.

The left of the Austrian line, cut off from the centre by the passage of the French, had been stationed lower on the Mincio. When Sebottendorf, who commanded the troops stationed on the left bank, heard the cannonade, he immediately ascended the river, to assist his commander-in-chief to repel the French, or to take them in flank if it was already crossed. The retreat of Beaulieu made both purposes impossible; and yet this march of Sebottendorf had almost produced a result of greater consequence than would have been the most complete victory.

The French division which first crossed the Mincio had passed through Valeggio without halting in pursuit of Beaulieu. Buonaparte with a small retinue remained in the place, and Massena's division were still on the right bank of the Mincio, preparing their dinner. At this moment, the advanced guard of Sebottendorf pushed into Valeggio. There was but barely time to cry to arms, and, shutting the gates of the inn, to employ the general's small escort in its defence, while Buonaparte, escaping by the garden, mounted his horse and galloped towards Massena's division. The soldiers threw aside their cookery, and marched instantly against Sebottendorf, who, with much difficulty, and not without loss, effected a retreat in the same direction as his commander-in-chief Beaulieu. This personal risk induced Buonaparte to form what he called the corps of guides, veterans of ten years' service at least, who were perpetually near his person, and, like the *Triarii* of the Romans, were employed only when the most desperate efforts of courage were necessary. Bessières, afterwards Duke of Istria and Marshal of France, was placed at the head of this chosen body, which gave rise to the formation of the celebrated Imperial Guards of Napoleon.

The passage of the Mincio obliged the Austrians to retire within the frontier of the Tyrol; and they might have been considered as completely expelled from Italy, had not Mantua and the citadel of Milan still continued to display the Imperial banners.

Napoleon blockaded Mantua [June 4th] with a large force. The garrison was numerous, amounting to 12,000 to 14,000 men; and the deficiencies of the fortifications, which the Austrians had neglected in security, were made up for by the natural strength of the place.

To complete the blockade, it was necessary to come to some arrangement with the ancient republic of Venice. With this venerable government Napoleon had the power of working his own pleasure. He contented himself for the time with occupying Verona, and other dependencies of Venice upon the line of the Adige. "You are too weak," he said to the Proveditore Foscarelli, "to pretend to enforce neutrality, with a few hundred Sclavonians, on two such nations as France and Austria. The Austrians have not respected your territory where it suited their purpose, and I must, in requital, occupy such part as falls within the line of the Adige." Having disposed his army in its position, and prepared some of its divisions for service as moveable columns, he returned to Milan to reap the harvest of his successes.

Naples pulled out of the conflict while the Papal states, despite the French occupation of Ferrara and Bologna, sued for what turned out to be an expensive peace. Tuscany was summarily deprived of Livorno, leaving Austria standing alone in the way of French hegemony in Italy.

Beaulieu, aged and unlucky, was no longer considered as a fit opponent to his inventive, young, and active adversary. He was recalled, therefore, in that species of disgrace which misfortune never fails to infer, and the command of his remaining forces, now drawn back and secured within the passes of the Tyrol, was provisionally assigned to the veteran Melas.

*C*HAPTER VI

The thunder-cloud which had been so long blackening on the mountains of the Tyrol, seemed now about to discharge its fury. Wurmser, having perhaps 80,000 men, was about to march from Trent against the French, whose forces, amounting to scarce half so many, were partly engaged in the siege of Mantua, and partly dispersed on the Adige and Chiese, covering the division of Serrurier, which carried on the siege. The Austrian veteran, confident in his numbers, was only anxious so to regulate his advance, as to derive the most conclusive consequences from the victory which he doubted not to obtain. With an imprudence which the misfortunes of Beaulieu ought to have warned him against, he endeavoured to occupy so large an extent of country, as rendered it very difficult for them to maintain their communications. This was particularly the case with his right wing under Quasdonowich, the Prince of Reuss, and General Ocskay, who were detached down the valley of the river Chiese, with orders to occupy Brescia, and cut off the retreat of the French in the direction of Milan. The left wing of Wurmser's army, under Melas, was to descend the Adige by both banks at once, and manoeuvre on Verona, while the centre, commanded by the field-marshal in person, was to march southward by the left bank of the lago di Guarda, take possession of Peschiera, which the French occupied, and, descending the Mincio, relieve the siege of Mantua. There was this radical error in the plan, that, by sending the right wing by the valley of Chiese, Wurmser placed lake Guarda, occupied by a French flotilla, between that division and the rest of his army, and of course made it impossible for the centre and left to support Quasdonowich, or even to have intelligence of his fate.

The active invention of Buonaparte, sure as he was to be seconded by the zeal and rapidity of the French army, speedily devised the means to draw advantage from this dislocation of the Austrian forces. He resolved not to await the arrival of Wurmser and Melas, but, concentrating his whole strength, to march into the valley of Chiese, and availing himself of the local superiority thus obtained, to attack and overpower the Austrian division under Quasdonowich. The plan inevitably involved the raising of the siege of Mantua. Napoleon did not hesitate to relinquish this great object, at whatever loss, as it was his uniform system to sacrifice all secondary views, and to incur all lesser hazards, to secure what he considered the main object. Serrurier was hastily ordered to destroy as much as possible of the cannon and stores which had been collected for the siege. 100 guns were abandoned, and Wurmser, on arriving at Mantua, found that Buonaparte had retired with a precipitation resembling that of fear.

On the night of the 31st July this operation took place, and, leaving the division of Augereau at Borghetto, and that of Massena at Peschiera, to protect, while it was possible, the line of the Mincio, Buonaparte rushed, at the head of an army which his combinations had rendered superior, upon the right wing of the Austrians, which had directed its march to Lonato, near the bottom of the lago di Guarda, in order to resume its communication with Wurmser. But Buonaparte, placed by the celerity of his movements between the two hostile armies, defeated one division of the Austrian right at Salo and another at Lonato. At the same time, Augereau and Massena, leaving just enough of men at their posts of Borghetto and Peschiera to maintain a respectable defence against Wurmser, made a forced march to Brescia, which they supposed to be still occupied by a third division of the Austrian right wing. But that body, finding itself insulated, and conceiving that the whole French army was debouching on them, was already in full retreat towards the Tyrol. Some French troops were left to accelerate their flight, while Massena and Augereau, rapidly countermarching, returned to the banks of the Mincio to support their respective rear-guards.

They received intelligence, however, which induced them to halt upon this counter-march. Both rear-guards had been compelled to retire from the line of the Mincio, of which river the Austrians had forced the passage. The rear-guard of Massena, under General Pigeon, had fallen back in good order, so as to occupy Lonato; that of Augereau fled with precipitation and confusion, and failed to make a stand at Castiglione, which was occupied by Austrians, who entrenched themselves there.

Wurmser became now seriously anxious about the fate of his right wing, and determined to force a communication with Quasdonowich at all risks. But he could only attain the valley of the Chiese, and the right bank of the lago di Guarda, by breaking a passage through the divisions of Massena and Augereau. On the 3rd of August, at break of day, two divisions of Austrians, who had crossed the Mincio in pursuit of Pigeon and Valette, now directed themselves, with the most determined resolution, on the French troops, in order to clear the way between the commander-in-chief and his right wing.

The late rear-guard of Massena, which, by his counter-march, had now become his advanced-guard, was defeated, and Lonato taken. But the Austrian general, thus far successful, fell into the great error of extending his line too much towards the right, in order, if possible, to turn the French position on their left flank, thereby the sooner to open a communication with his own troops on the right bank of the lago di Guarda. In thus manoeuvring he weakened his centre, an error of which Massena instantly availed himself. He formed two strong columns under Augereau, with which he redeemed the victory by breaking through and dividing the Austrian line, and retaking Lonato at the point of the bayonet. The Austrians, finding their line cut asunder, and their flanks pressed by the victorious columns of the French, fell into total disorder. Some, who were farthest to the right, pushed forward, in hopes to unite themselves to Quasdonowich; but these were attacked in front by General Soret, who had been active in defeating Quasdonowich upon the 30th July, and were at the same time pursued by another detachment of the French, which had broken through their centre.

Such was the fate of the Austrian right at the battle of Lonato, while that of the left was no less unfavourable. They were attacked by Augereau with the utmost bravery, and driven from Castiglione. Augereau achieved this important result at the price of many brave men's lives; but it was always remembered as an essential service by Buonaparte, who afterwards, when such dignities came in use, bestowed on Augereau the title of Duke of Castiglione.

When Wurmser learned the disasters of his right wing, and the destruction of the troops despatched to form a communication with it, he advanced against the French position between Lonato and Castiglione, with an army still numerous, notwithstanding the reverses which it had sustained. But Buonaparte had not left the interval unimproved. He had recalled Serrurier, to assail the left wing and the flank of the Austrian. The opening of Serrurier's fire was a signal for a general attack on all points of Wurmser's line. He was defeated, and nearly made prisoner; and it was not till after suffering great losses in the retreat, that he gained Trent and Roveredo, the positions adjacent to the Tyrol, from which he had so lately sallied with such confidence of victory. He had lost perhaps one half of his fine army, and the only consolation which remained was, that he had thrown supplies into the fortress of Mantua.

The Austrians are supposed to have lost nearly 40,000 men in these disastrous battles. The French must have at least suffered the loss of one-fourth of the number, though Buonaparte confesses only to 7000 men; and their army, desperately fatigued by so many marches, such constant fighting, and the hardships of a campaign, where even the general for seven days never laid aside his clothes, or took any regular repose, required some time to recover their physical strength. Meantime, Napoleon resumed his position before Mantua; but the want of battering cannon, and the commencement of the unhealthy heats of autumn, amid lakes, besides the great chance of a second attack, induced him to limit his measures to a simple blockade.

Nothing is more remarkable, during these campaigns, than the inflexibility of Austria, which, reduced to the extremity of distress by extraordinary exertions again recruited Wurmser with fresh troops, to the amount of 20,000 men; which reinforcement enabled that general, though under no more propitious star, again to resume the offensive, by advancing from the Tyrol. Wurmser, with less confidence than before, hoped now to relieve the siege of Mantua a second time, and at a less desperate cost, by moving from Trent towards Mantua, through the defiles formed by the river Brenta. This manoeuvre he proposed to execute with 30,000 men, while he left 20,000 under General Davidowich in a strong position at or near Roveredo for the purpose of covering the Tyrol; an invasion of which district must have added much to the general panic which already astounded Germany, from the apprehended advance of Moreau and Jourdan from the banks of the Rhine.

Buonaparte penetrated the design of the veteran general, and suffered him without disturbance to march towards Bassano upon the Brenta, with the secret intention that he would himself assume the offensive and overwhelm Davidowich as soon as the distance betwixt them precluded communication. He left General Kilmaine with about 3000 men, to cover the siege of Mantua, while, concentrating a strong body of forces, Napoleon marched upon Roveredo, situated in the valley of the Adige, and having in its rear the strong position of Calliano.

The battle of Roveredo, fought upon the 4th of September, was one of that great general's splendid days. Before he could approach the town, one of his divisions had to force the strongly entrenched camp of Mori, where the enemy made a desperate defence. Another attacked the Austrians on the opposite bank of the Adige, until the enemy at length retreated, still fighting desperately.

The retreating enemy were driven through the town of Roveredo, without having it in their power to make a stand. The extreme strength of the position of Calliano seemed to afford them rallying ground. The Adige is there bordered by precipitous mountains, approaching so near its course, as only to leave a pass of forty toises'[13] breadth between the river and the precipice, which opening was defended by a village, a castle, and a strong defensive wall resting upon the rock, all well garnished with artillery. The French, in their enthusiasm of victory, could not be stopped even by these obstacles. Eight pieces of light artillery were brought forward, under cover of which the infantry charged and carried this strong position; so little do natural advantages avail when the minds of the assailants are influenced with an opinion that they are irresistible, and those of the defenders are depressed by a uniform and uninterrupted course of defeat. 6000 or 7000 prisoners, and 15 pieces of cannon captured, were the fruits of this splendid victory; and Massena the next morning took possession of Trent in the Tyrol.

Buonaparte had no sooner disposed of Davidowich and his army, than he began his operations against Wurmser. The Austrian field-marshal immediately conceived that the French general, in consequence of his successes, would be disposed to leave Italy behind, and advance to Innsbruck, in order to communicate with the armies of Moreau and Jourdan, which were now on the full advance into Germany. Instead, therefore, of renouncing his own scheme of relieving Mantua, Wurmser thought the time favourable for carrying it into execution; and in place of falling back with his army on Friuli, and thus keeping open his communication with Vienna, he committed the great error of involving himself still deeper in the Italian passes to the southward, by an attempt, with a diminished force, to execute a purpose, which he had been unable to accomplish when his army was double the strength of the French. With this ill-chosen plan, he detached Mezaros with a division of his forces, to manœuvre on Verona, where Buonaparte had stationed Kilmaine to cover the blockade of Mantua. Mezaros departed accordingly, and marched south-westward towards the valley of the Adige, and attacked Kilmaine, who, by drawing his men under cover of the fortifications of Verona, made a resolute defence. The Austrian general, finding it impossible to carry the place by a coup-de-main, was meditating to cross the Adige, when he was recalled to rejoin Wurmser with all possible despatch.

As soon as Buonaparte learned this new separation of Wurmser from a large division of his army, he anticipated the possibility of defeating the field-marshal himself, driving him from his position at Bassano, and of cutting off at his leisure the division of Mezaros. To execute this plan required the utmost rapidity of movement; for, should Wurmser learn that Buonaparte was advancing towards Bassano, in time to recall Mezaros, he might present a front too numerous to be attacked with hope of success. There are 20 leagues' distance betwixt Trent and Bassano, and that ground was to be traversed by means of very difficult roads, in the space of two days at farthest. But it was in such circumstances that the genius of Napoleon triumphed, through the enthusiastic power which he possessed over the soldiery, and by which he could urge them to the most incredible exertions. He left Trent on the 6th September, at break of day, and reached, in the course of the evening, Borgo di Val Lugano, a march of ten French leagues. A similar forced march of five leagues and upwards, brought him up with Wurmser's advanced-guard, which was strongly posted at Primolano.

The effect of the surprise and the impetuosity of the French attack surmounted all the advantages of position. The Austrian double lines were penetrated by a charge of three French columns – the cavalry occupied the high-road, and cut off the enemy's retreat on Bassano – in a word, Wurmser's vanguard was totally destroyed. From Primolano the French, dislodging whatever enemies they encountered, advanced to Cismone. There they halted exhausted; and on that evening no sentinel in the army endured more privations than Napoleon himself, who took up his quarters for the night without either staff officers or baggage, and was glad to accept a share of a private soldier's ration of bread, of which the poor fellow lived to remind his general when he became Emperor.

Cismone is only about four leagues from Bassano, and Wurmser heard with alarm, that the French leader, whom he conceived to be already deeply engaged in the Tyrolese passes, had destroyed his vanguard, and was menacing his own position. It was under this alarm that he despatched expresses to recall Mezaros. But it was too late; for that general was under the walls of Verona, nigh fifteen leagues from Wurmser's position, on the night of the 7th September, when the French army was at Cismone, within a third part of that distance. The utmost exertions of Mezaros could only bring his division as far as Montebello, upon the 8th September, when the battle of Bassano seemed to decide the fate of his unfortunate commander-in-chief.

This victory was as decisive as any which Buonaparte had hitherto obtained. The village of Salagna was first carried by main force, and then the French, continuing to descend the defiles of the Brenta, attacked Wurmser's main body, which still lay under his own command in the town of Bassano. Augereau penetrated the town upon the right, Massena upon the left. They bore down all opposition, and seized the cannon by which the bridge was defended, in spite of the efforts of the Austrian grenadiers, charged with the duty of protecting Wurmser and his staff, who were now in absolute flight. The field-marshal himself, with the military chest of his army, nearly fell into the hands of the French; and though he escaped for the time, it was after an almost general dispersion of his troops. 6000 Austrians surrendered to Buonaparte; Quasdonowich, with 3000 or 4000 men, effected a retreat to the north-east, and gained Friuli; while Wurmser, finding it impossible to escape otherwise, fled to Vicenza in the opposite direction, and there united with the division of Mezaros. When this junction was accomplished, the aged marshal had still the command of about 16,000 men, out of 60,000, with whom he had, scarce a week before, commenced the campaign. The material part of his army, guns and baggage, was all lost – his retreat upon the hereditary states of Austria was entirely cut off – the flower of his army was destroyed – there seemed no remedy but that he should lay down his arms to the youthful conqueror by whose forces he was now surrounded. Wurmser followed the gallant determination to throw himself and his remaining forces into Mantua, and share the fate of the beleaguered fortress which he had vainly striven to relieve.

When Wurmser threw himself into Mantua, the garrison might amount to 26,000 men; yet, ere October was far advanced, there were little above the half of the number fit for service. There were nearly 9000 sick in the hospitals – infectious diseases, privations of every kind, and the unhealthy air of the lakes and marshes, had cut off the remainder. The French also had lost great numbers; but the conquerors could reckon up their victories, and forget the price at which they had been purchased.

It was a proud vaunt, and a cure in itself for many losses, that the minister of war had a right to make the following speech to the Directory, at the formal introduction of Marmont, then aide-de-camp of Buonaparte, and commissioned to present on his part the colours and standards taken from the enemy: "In the course of a single campaign," he truly said, "Italy had been entirely conquered – three large armies had been entirely destroyed – more than fifty stand of colours had been taken by the victors – 40,000 Austrians had laid down their arms – and, what was not the least surprising part of the whole, these deeds had been accomplished by an army of only 30,000 Frenchmen, commanded by a general scarce 26 years old."

CHAPTER VII

Mantua still held out, and was likely to do so. Wurmser had caused about three-fourths of the horses belonging to his cavalry to be killed and salt-ed for the use of the garrison, and thus made a large addition, such as it was, to the provisions of the place. His character for courage and determination was completely established; and being now engaged in defending a fortress by ordinary rules of art, which he perfectly understood, he was in no danger of being over-reached and out-manoeuvred by the new system of tactics, which occasioned his misfortunes in the open field.

While the last pledge of Austria's dominions in Italy was confided to such safe custody, the Emperor and his ministers were eagerly engaged in making a new effort to recover their Italian territories. By orders of the Aulic Council, two armies were assembled on the Italian frontier; one at Friuli; the other was to be formed on the Tyrol. They were to operate in conjunction, and both were placed under the command of Marshal Alvinzi, an officer of high reputation, which was then thought merited.

Thus, for the 4th time, Buonaparte was to contest the same objects on the same ground, with new forces belonging to the same enemy. He had, indeed, himself, received from France, reinforcements to the number of twelve battalions. The army, in general, since victory had placed the resources of the rich country which they occupied at the command of their leader, had been well supplied with clothes, food, and provisions, and were devotedly attached to the chief who had conducted them from starving on the barren Alps into this land of plenty, and had directed their military efforts with such skill, that they could scarce ever be said to have failed of success in whatever they undertook under his direction.

Napoleon had also on his side the good wishes, if not of the Italians in general, of a considerable party, especially in Lombardy, and friends and enemies were alike impressed with belief in his predestined success. During the former attempts of Wurmser, a contrary opinion had prevailed, and the news that the Austrians were in motion, had given birth to insurrections against the French in many places, and to the publication of sentiments unfavourable to them almost everywhere. But now, when all predicted the certain success of Napoleon, the friends of Austria remained quiet, and the numerous party who desire in such cases to keep on the winning side, added weight to the actual friends of France by expressing their opinions in her favour. It seems, however, that Victory, as if displeased that mortals should presume to calculate the motives of so fickle a deity, was, on this occasion, disposed to be more coy than formerly even to her greatest favourite.

It was the plan of Alvinzi to descend from Friuli, and approach Vicenza, to which place he expected Davidowich might penetrate by a corresponding movement down the Adige. Having thus brought his united army into activity, his design was to advance on Mantua, the constant object of bloody contention. As soon as Buonaparte heard that Alvinzi was in motion, he sent orders to Vaubois to attack Davidowich, and to Massena to advance to Bassano upon the Brenta, and make head against the Austrian commander-in-chief.

The first battle of Arcola, famous for the obstinacy with which it was disputed, was attended with no decisive result. But it checked the inclination of Alvinzi to advance on Verona – it delayed all communication betwixt his army and that of the Tyrol – above all, it renewed the Austrians' apprehensions of the skill of Buonaparte and the bravery of his troops. The night approached without any thing effectual being decided. Both parties drew off, the French to Ronco, where they recrossed the Adige; the Austrians to a position behind Arcola.

The [next] was to be a day more decisive. It was now that, after a calculation of the losses sustained by the enemy, Napoleon conceived their numerical superiority so far diminished, and their spirit so much broken, that he need no longer confine his operations to the dikes, but meet his enemy on the firm plain which extended beyond the Alpon. He passed the brook by means of a temporary bridge, and the battle raged as fiercely on the dry level, as it had done on the dikes and amongst the marshes.

Alvinzi was eventually compelled to give way, and commence his retreat on Montebello. He disposed 7000 men in echelon to cover this movement, which was accomplished without very much loss; but his ranks had been much thinned by the slaughter of the battles of Arcola. 8000 men has been stated as the amount of his losses. The French who made so many sanguinary assaults upon the villages must also have suffered a great deal. Buonaparte acknowledges this in energetic terms. "Never," he writes to Carnot, "was field of battle so disputed. I have almost no generals remaining – I can assure you that the victory could not have been gained at a cheaper expense. The enemy were numerous, and desperately resolute." The truth is that Buonaparte's mode of striking terror by these bloody and desperate charges in front upon strong positions, was a blemish in his system. They cost many men, and were not uniformly successful.

Thus ended the 4th campaign undertaken for the Austrian possessions in Italy. The consequences were not so decidedly in Buonaparte's favour as those of the three former. Mantua, it is true, had received no relief; and so far the principal object of the Austrians had miscarried. But Wurmser was of a temper to continue the defence till the last moment. The armies of Friuli and the Tyrol had also, since the last campaign, retained possession of Bassano and Trent, and removed the French from the mountains through which access is gained to the Austrian hereditary dominions. Neither had Alvinzi suffered any such heavy defeat as his predecessors Beaulieu or Wurmser; while Davidowich, on the contrary, was uniformly successful, had he known how to avail himself of his victories. Still the Austrians were not likely, till reinforced again, to interrupt Buonaparte's quiet possession of Lombardy.

During two months following the battle of Arcola and the retreat of the Austrians, the war which had been so vigorously maintained in Italy experienced a short suspension.

Meantime Austria, who seemed to cling to Italy with the tenacity of a dying grasp, again, and now for the 5th time, recruited her armies on the frontier, and placing Alvinzi once more at the head of 60,000 men, commanded him to resume the offensive. But notwithstanding this display of zeal on the part of the Austrian nation, its councils do not appear to have derived wisdom from experience. The losses sustained by Wurmser and by Alvinzi, proceeded in a great measure from the radical error of having divided their forces. Yet they commenced this campaign on the same unhappy principles. One army descending from the Tyrol upon Montebaldo, the other was to march down by the Brenta on Paduan territory, and then to operate on the lower Adige, the line of which, of course, they were expected to force, for the purpose of relieving Mantua. The Aulic Council ordered that these two armies were to direct their course so as to meet, if possible, upon the beleaguered fortress. Should they succeed in raising the siege, there was little doubt that the French must be driven out of Italy; but even were the scheme only partially successful, still it might allow Wurmser with his cavalry to escape from that besieged city, and retreat into the Romagna, where it was designed that he should assume the command of the papal army. In the meantime, an intelligence agent was sent to communicate with Wurmser.

This man fell into the hands of the besiegers. It was in vain that he swallowed his despatches, which were enclosed in a ball of wax; means were found to make the stomach render up its trust, and the document which the wax enclosed was found to be a letter, signed by the Emperor's own hand, directing Wurmser to enter into no capitulation, but to hold out as long as possible in expectation of relief, and if compelled to leave Mantua, to accept of no conditions, but to cut his way into the Romagna. Thus Buonaparte became acquainted with the storm which was approaching, and which was not long of breaking.

Alvinzi, who commanded the principal army, advanced from Bassano to Roveredo upon the Adige. Provera commanded the divisions which were to act upon the lower Adige. He marched as far as Bevi l'Acqua, while his advanced guard, under Prince Hohenzollern, compelled a body of French to cross to the right bank of the Adige.

Buonaparte, uncertain which of these attacks he was to consider as the main one, concentrated his army at Verona, from which he might at pleasure march either up the Adige against Alvinzi, or descend the river to resist the attempts of Provera. He trusted that Joubert, whom he had placed in defence of La Corona, a little town which had been strongly fortified for the purpose, might be able to make a good temporary defence. He despatched troops for Joubert's support to Castel Nuovo, but hesitated to direct his principal force in that direction until ten in the evening of 13th January, when he received information that Joubert had been attacked at La Corona by an immense body, which he had resisted with difficulty during the day, and was now about to retreat, in order to secure the important eminence at Rivoli, which was the key of his whole position.

The field of Rivoli was one of the most desperate that Buonaparte ever won, and was gained entirely by superior military skill, and not by the overbearing system of mere force of numbers, to which he has been accused of being partial. He himself had his horses repeatedly wounded in the course of the action, and exerted to the utmost his personal influence to bring up the troops into action where their presence was most required.

Almost before this important and decisive victory was absolutely gained, news arrived which required the presence of Buonaparte elsewhere. On the very same day of the battle, Provera threw a bridge of pontoons over that river, where the French were not prepared to oppose his passage, and pushed forward to Mantua.

Buonaparte arrived at Roverbella, within twelve miles of Mantua, to which he had marched with incredible despatch from the field of battle at Rivoli, leaving to Massena, Murat, and Joubert, the task of completing his victory.

In the meanwhile, Provera communicated with the garrison of Mantua across the lake, and concerted the measures for its relief with Wurmser. On the 16th of January, the garrison of Mantua sallied from the place in strength, and took post at the causeway of La Favorita. Napoleon, returning at the head of his victorious forces, surrounded and attacked with fury the troops of Provera, while the blockading army compelled the garrison, at the bayonet's point, to re-enter the besieged city. Provera, who had in vain, though with much decision and gallantry, attempted the relief of Mantua, was compelled to lay down his arms with a division of about 5000 men. The detached corps which he had left to protect his bridge, and other passes in his rear, sustained a similar fate. Thus one division of the army, which had commenced the campaign of January only on the 7th of that month, were the prisoners of the destined conqueror before ten days had elapsed. The larger army, commanded by Alvinzi, had no better fortune.

Amid such extraordinary success, the ground which the French had lost in Italy was speedily resumed. Trent and Bassano were again occupied. They regained all the positions which they had possessed on the frontiers of Italy before Alvinzi's first descent, and might perhaps have penetrated deeper into the mountainous frontier of Germany, but for the snow which choked up the passes. One crowning consequence of the victories of Rivoli and of La Favorita, was the surrender of Mantua itself, that prize which had cost so much blood, and had been defended with such obstinacy.

For several days after the decisive actions which left him without a shadow of hope of relief, Wurmser continued the defence of the place in a sullen yet honourable despair, natural to the feelings of a gallant veteran, who, to the last, hesitated between the desire to resist, and the sense that, his means of subsistence being almost totally expended, resistance was absolutely hopeless. At length he sent his aide-de-camp, Klenau, to the headquarters of Serrurier, who commanded the blockade, to negotiate a surrender.

A French officer of distinction was present, muffled in his cloak, and remaining apart from the two officers, but within hearing of what had passed. When their discussion was finished, this unknown person stepped forward, and taking a pen wrote down the conditions of surrender to which Wurmser was to be admitted – conditions more honourable and favourable by far than what his extremity could have exacted. "These," said the unknown officer to Klenau, "are the terms which Wurmser may accept at present, and which will be equally tendered to him at any period when he finds further resistance impossible. We are aware he is too much a man of honour to give up the fortress and city, so long and honourably defended, while the means of resistance remain in his power. If he delays accepting the conditions for a week, for a month, for two months, they shall be equally his when he chooses to accept them. To-morrow I pass the Po, and march upon Rome." Klenau, perceiving that he spoke to the French commander-in-chief, frankly admitted that the garrison could not longer delay surrender, having scarce three days' provisions unconsummated.

This trait of generosity towards a gallant but unfortunate enemy was highly favourable to Buonaparte. The taste which dictated the stage-effect of the cloak may indeed be questioned; but the real current of his feeling towards the venerable object of his respect, and at the same time compassion, is ascertained otherwise. He wrote to the Directory, that he had afforded to Wurmser such conditions of surrender as became the generosity of the French nation towards an enemy, who, having lost his army by misfortune, was so little desirous to secure his personal safety, that he threw himself into Mantua; thus voluntarily undertaking the privations of a siege, which his gallantry protracted until almost the last morsel of provisions was exhausted.

CHAPTER VIII

The eyes of all Europe were now riveted on Napoleon Buonaparte, whose rise had been so sudden, that he had become the terror of empires and the founder of states – the conqueror of the best generals and most disciplined troops in Europe; within a few months after he had been a mere soldier of fortune, rather seeking for subsistence than expecting honourable distinction. Such sudden elevations have occasionally happened amid semi-barbarous nations, where great popular insurrections, desolating and decisive revolutions, are common occurrences, but were hitherto unheard of in civilised Europe. The pre-eminence which he had suddenly obtained had, besides, been subjected to so many trials, as to afford every proof of its permanence. Napoleon stood aloft, like a cliff on which successive tempests had expended their rage in vain. The means which raised him were equally competent to make good his greatness. He had infused into the armies which he commanded the firmest reliance on his genius, and the greatest love for his person; so that he could always find agents ready to execute his most difficult commands. He had even inspired them with a portion of his own indefatigable exertion and his commanding intelligence. The maxim which he inculcated upon them when practising those long and severe marches which formed one essential part of his system, was, "I would rather gain victory at the expense of your legs than at the price of your blood." The French, under his training, seemed to become the very men he wanted, and to forget in the excitation of war and the hope of victory, even the feelings of weariness and exhaustion.

To command this active, intelligent, and intrepid soldiery, Buonaparte possessed officers entirely worthy of the charge; men young, or at least not advanced in years, to whose ambition the Revolution, and the wars which it had brought on, had opened an unlimited career, and whose genius was inspired by the plans of their leader, and the success which attended them. Buonaparte, who had his eye on every man, never neglected to distribute rewards and punishments, praise and censure with a liberal hand, or omitted to press for the promotion of such officers as particularly distinguished themselves.

It should further be remarked, that Napoleon withstood, instantly and boldly, all the numerous attempts made by commissaries, and that description of persons, to encroach upon the fund destined for the use of the army. Much of his public, and more of his private correspondence, is filled with complaints against these agents, although he must have known that, in attacking them, he disobliged men of the highest influence, who had frequently some secret interest in their wealth. But his military fame made his services indispensable, and permitted him to set at defiance the enmity of such persons, who are generally as timid as they are sordid.

Towards the general officers there took place a gradual change of deportment, as the commander-in-chief began to feel more and more the increasing sense of his own personal importance. We have been informed by an officer of the highest rank that, during the earlier campaigns, Napoleon used to rejoice with and embrace them as associates, nearly on the same footing, engaged in the same tasks. After a period, his language and carriage became those of a frank soldier, who, sensible of the merit of his subordinate assistants, yet makes them sensible, by his manner, that he is their commander-in-chief.

Napoleon's conduct towards the Italians individually was, in most instances, in the highest degree prudent and political; while, at the same time, it coincided, as true policy usually does, with the rules of justice and moderation, and served, in a great measure, to counterbalance the odium which he incurred by despoiling Italy, and even by his infringements on the religious system of the Catholics.

On the latter subject, the general became particularly cautious, and his dislike or contempt of the Church of Rome was no longer shown in that gross species of satire which he had at first given loose to. On the contrary, it was veiled under philosophical indifference; and, while relieving the clergy of their worldly possessions, Napoleon took care to avoid the error of the Jacobins; never proposing their tenets as an object of persecution, but protecting their persons, and declaring himself a decided friend to general toleration on all points of conscience.

In point of politics the opinions of Buonaparte appear to have experienced a great change. It may be doubted, indeed, if he ever in his heart adopted those of the outrageous Jacobins. At all events, his clear and sound good sense speedily made him aware, that such violence on the established rules of reason and morality is too unnatural to remain long, or to become the basis of a well-regulated state. Being at present a Republican of the Thermidorien party, Buonaparte, even though he made use of the established phrases, Liberty and Equality, acknowledged no dignity superior to citizen, and *thee'd* and *thou'd* whomsoever he addressed, was permitted to mix many grains of liberality with those democratic forms. Indeed, the republican creed of the day began to resemble the leathern apron of the brazier, who founded a dynasty in the East – his descendants continued to display it as their banner, but enriched it so much with gems and embroidery, that there was little of the original stuff to be discovered.

The progress which Buonaparte made personally in the favour of the Italians, was, doubtless, a great assistance to the propagation of the new doctrines which were connected with the French Revolution, and was much aided by the trust which he seemed desirous to repose in the natives. He retained, no doubt, in his own hands, the ultimate decision of every thing of consequence; but in matters of ordinary importance, he permitted and encouraged the Italians to act for themselves, in a manner they had not been accustomed to under their German masters. The internal government of their towns was entrusted to provisional governors, chosen without respect to rank, and the maintenance of police was committed to the armed burghers, or national guards. Conscious of the importance annexed to these privileges, they already became impatient for national liberty. Napoleon could hardly rein back the intense ardour of the large party among time Lombards who desired an immediate declaration of independence, and he had no other expedient left than to amuse them with procrastinating excuses, which enhanced their desire of such an event, while they delayed its gratification. Other towns of Italy, for it was among the citizens of the towns that these sentiments were chiefly cultivated, began to evince the same wish to remodel their governments on the revolutionary system; and this ardour was chiefly shown on the southern side of the Po.

Napoleon founded the Cispadane Republic out of 'legations appertaining to the Papal See' and cities that had risen in revolt against the Duke of Modena, who was notionally at peace with France. Similar developments occurred further up the Po, leading to the establishment of the Transpadane Republic. The two were merged into the Cisalpine Republic in 1797. There remained the problem of Rome.

CHAPTER IX

By the direction of the Aulic Council, the Archduke Charles took up his position at Friuli, where it had been settled that the 6th Austrian army, designed to act against Buonaparte, should be assembled.

In the space of scarce 20 days, Napoleon defeated the Austrians in ten combats, in the course of which Prince Charles lost at least one fourth of his army. The French surmounted the southern chain of the Julian Alps, and the Archduke, the pride and hope of the Austrian armies, retired behind the river Meuhr, and seemed to be totally without the means of covering Vienna.

It was one of the most artful rules in Buonaparte's policy, that when he had his enemy at decided advantage, he seldom failed to offer peace, and peace upon conditions much more favourable than perhaps the opposite party expected. By doing this, he secured such immediate and undisputed fruits of his victory, as the treaty of peace contained; and he was sure of means to prosecute further advantages at some future opportunity. He obtained, moreover, the character of generosity; and, in the present instance, he avoided the great danger of urging to bay so formidable a power as Austria, whose despair might be capable of the most formidable efforts.

With this purpose, and assuming for the first time that disregard for the usual ceremony of courts, and etiquette of politics, he wrote a letter in person to the Archduke Charles on the subject of peace. This composition affects that abrupt laconic severity of style, which cuts short argument, by laying down general maxims of philosophy of a trite character, and breaks through the usual laboured periphrastic introductions with which ordinary politicians preface their proposals, when desirous of entering upon a treaty. "It is the part of a brave soldier," he said, "to make war, but to wish for peace. The present strife has lasted six years. Have we not yet slain enough of men, and sufficiently outraged humanity? Peace is demanded on all sides. Europe at large has laid down the arms assumed against the French Republic. Your nation remains alone in hostility, and yet blood flows faster than ever. This 6th campaign has commenced under ominous circumstances. End how it will, some thousands of men more will be slain on either side; and at length, after all, we must come to an agreement, for every thing must have an end at last, even the angry passions of men. The Executive Directory made known to the Emperor their desire to put a period to the war which desolates both countries, but the intervention of the Court of London opposed it. Is there then no means of coming to an understanding, and must we continue to cut each other's throats for the interests or passions of a nation, herself a stranger to the miseries of war? You, the general-in-chief, who approach by birth so near to the crown, and are above all those petty passions which agitate ministers, and the members of government, will you resolve to be the benefactor of mankind, and the true saviour of Germany? Do not suppose that I mean by that expression to intimate, that it is impossible for you to defend yourself by force of arms; but under the supposition, that fortune were to become favourable to you, Germany would be equally exposed to ravage. With respect to my own feelings, general, if this proposition should be the means of saving one single man's life, I should prefer a civic crown so merited, to the melancholy glory attending military success."

The whole tone of the letter is ingeniously calculated to give the proposition the character of moderation, and at the same time to avoid the appearance of too ready an advance towards his object. The Archduke returned this brief answer, in which he stripped Buonaparte's proposal of its gilding, and treated it upon the footing of an ordinary proposal for a treaty of peace, made by a party, who finds it convenient for his interest: "Unquestionably, sir, in making war, and in following the road prescribed by honour and duty, I desire as much as you the attainment of peace for the happiness of the people, and of humanity. Considering, however, that in the situation which I hold, it is no part of my business to enquire into and determine the quarrel of the belligerent powers; and that I am not furnished on the part of the Emperor with any plenipotentiary powers for treating, you will excuse me, general, if I do not enter into negotiation with you touching a matter of the highest importance, but which does not lie within my department. Whatever shall happen, either respecting the future chances of the war, or the prospect of peace, I request you to be equally convinced of my distinguished esteem."

The Archduke would willingly have made some advantage of this proposal, by obtaining an armistice of five hours, sufficient to enable him to form a junction with the corps of Kerpen, which, having left the Tyrol, was now within a short distance. But Buonaparte took care not to permit himself to be hampered by any such ill-timed engagement, and, after some sharp fighting, in which the French, as usual, were successful, he was able to interpose such a force as to prevent the junction taking place.

Two encounters followed at Neumark and at Unzmark – both gave rise to fresh disasters, and the continued retreat of the Archduke Charles and the Imperial army. The French general then pressed forward on the road to Vienna. Judenburg, the capital of Upper Styria, was abandoned to the French without a blow and, shortly after, Buonaparte entered Gratz, the principal town of Lower Styria, with the same facility.

The Court of Vienna finally accepted the alternative treaty. The preliminaries were proposed for signature on the 18th April. The articles in the treaty of Leoben remained long secret; the cause of which appears to have been, that the contracting parties were not willing for comparisons to be made between the preliminaries, and the strange and violent altercations which occurred in the definitive treaty of Campo Formio. These two treaties of pacification differed in relation to the degree and manner how a meditated partition of the territory of Venice, of the Cisalpine republic, and other smaller powers was to be accomplished.

Buonaparte was considerably blamed, by the Directory and others, for stopping short in the career of conquest, and allowing Austria terms which left her still formidable, when, said the censors, it would have cost him but another victory to blot the most constant and powerful enemy of the French Republic out of the map of Europe; or, at least, to confine her to her hereditary states in Germany. To such criticism he replied, in a despatch to the Directory from Leoben, "If, at the commencement of these Italian campaigns, I had made a point of going to Turin, I should never have passed the Po – had I insisted prematurely on advancing to Rome, I could never have secured Milan – and now, had I made an indispensable object of reaching Vienna, I might have destroyed the Republic."

Such was his judicious defence of a conduct, which, by stopping short of some ultimate and extreme point apparently within his grasp, extracted every advantage from fear, which despair perhaps might not have yielded him, if the enemy had been driven to extremity. And it is remarkable, that the catastrophe of Napoleon himself was a corollary of the doctrine which he now laid down; for, had he not insisted upon penetrating to Moscow, there is no judging how much longer he might have held the empire of France.

Napoleon delivered an ultimatum to Venice followed by a draconian treaty that effectively signified the end of the decadent Republic's independence.

*C*HAPTER X

Buonaparte was yet a bridegroom, though he had now been two years married, and upwards. A part of his correspondence with his bride has been preserved, and gives a curious picture of a temperament as fiery in love as in war. The language of the conqueror, who was disposing of states at his pleasure, and defeating the most celebrated commanders of the time, is as enthusiastic as that of an Arcadian. We cannot suppress the truth, that (in passages which we certainly shall not quote) it carries a tone of indelicacy, which, notwithstanding the intimacy of the married state, an English husband would not use, nor an English wife consider as the becoming expression of connubial affection. There seems no doubt, however, that the attachment was perfectly sincere, and on one occasion at least, it was chivalrously expressed; "Wurmser shall buy dearly the tears which he makes you shed."

Josephine had rejoined her husband, under the guardianship of Junot, when he returned from Paris, after having executed his mission of delivering to the Directory, and representatives of the French people, the banners and colours taken from Beaulieu. In December, 1796, Josephine was at Genoa, where she was received with studied magnificence, by those in that ancient state who adhered to the French interest. These, however, were probably only occasional visits; but after the signature of the treaty of Leoben, and during the various negotiations which took place before it was ratified at Campo Formio, Josephine lived in domestic society with her husband, at the beautiful palace of Montebello.

This villa is situated a few leagues from Milan, on a gently sloping hill, which commands an extensive prospect over the fertile plains of Lombardy. The ladies of the highest rank, as well as those celebrated for beauty and accomplishments – all, in short, who could add charms to society – were daily paying their homage to Josephine, who received them with a felicity of address which it seemed as if she had been born for. It was probably the happiest time of [Napoleon's] life. Honour, beyond that of a crowned head, was his own. Power was his, and he had not experienced its cares and risks; high hopes were formed of him by all around, and he had not yet disappointed them. He was in the flower of youth, and married to the woman of his heart.

The various objects which occupied Buonaparte's mind during this busy yet pleasing interval, were the affairs of Genoa, of Sardinia, of Naples, of the Cisalpine republic, of the Grisons, and lastly, and by far the most important of them, the definitive treaty with Austria, which involved the annihilation of Venice as an independent state. By the time the negotiators met for finally discussing the preliminaries, the Directory, either to thwart Buonaparte, whose superiority became too visible, or because they actually entertained the fears they expressed, were determined that Mantua, which had been taken with such difficulty, should remain the bulwark of the Cisalpine republic, instead of returning to be once more that of the Austrian territories in Italy. The Imperial plenipotentiaries insisted, on the other hand, that Mantua was absolutely necessary to the safety of their Italian possessions, and became more so from the peculiar character of their new neighbour, the Cisalpine republic, whose example was likely to be so perilous to the adjacent dependencies of an ancient monarchy. To get over this difficulty, the French general proposed that the remaining dominions of Venice should be also divided betwixt Austria and France, the latter obtaining possession of the Albanian territories and the Ionian islands belonging to the republic, of which the high contracting powers signed the death-warrant; while Istria, Dalmatia, Venice herself, and all her other dominions, should be appropriated to Austria. The latter power, through her minister, consented to this arrangement with as little scruple, as to the former appropriation of her forlorn ally's possessions on the Terra Firma.

But as fast as obstacles were removed on one side, they appeared to start up on another, and a sort of pause ensued in the deliberations, which neither party seemed to wish to push to a close. In fact, both Napoleon, and Count Cobentzel, on the part of Austria, were sufficiently aware that the French government, long disunited, was in the act of approaching a crisis. This accordingly took place on the eighteenth of Fructidor, creating, by a new revolutionary movement, a total change of administration. When this revolution was accomplished, the Directory, feeling themselves more strong, appeared to lay aside the idea of peace, and showed a strong disposition to push their advantages to the utmost.

Buonaparte was opposed to this. He knew that if war was resumed, the difficulties of the campaign would be thrown on him, and the blame also, if the results were not happy. He was determined, therefore, in virtue of his full powers, to bring the matter to a conclusion, whether the Directory would or not. For this purpose he confronted Cobentzel, who still saw his game in gaining delay. On the 16th October, the conferences were renewed, and Cobentzel went over the whole subject of the indemnifications – insisting that Mantua, and the line of the Adige, should be granted to the Emperor; threatening to bring down the Russians in case the war should be renewed; and insinuating that Buonaparte desired a renewal of the war. Napoleon, with stern but restrained indignation, took from a bracket an ornamental piece of china, on which Cobentzel set some value, as being a present from the Empress Catherine. "The truce," he said, "is then ended, and war declared. But beware – before the end of autumn, I will break your empire into as many fragments as this potsherd." He dashed the piece of china against the hearth, and withdrew abruptly.

The Austrian plenipotentiaries no longer hesitated to submit to all Napoleon's demands. The treaty of Campo Formio was signed on the following day; not the less promptly, perhaps, that the affairs at Paris appeared so doubtful as to invite an ambitious and aspiring man like Napoleon to approach the scene where honours and power were distributed, and where jarring factions seemed to await the influence of a character so distinguished and so determined.

Napoleon Buonaparte had finished for the present his career of destiny in Italy, which country first saw his rising talents, and was always a subject of peculiar interest to him. He took an affecting leave of the soldiers, who could scarce hope ever to see him replaced by a general of merits so transcendent, and made a moderate and judicious address to the Cisalpine republic. Finally, he departed, to return through Switzerland to Rastadt, where a congress was sitting for the settlement and pacification of the German empire, and where he was to act as a plenipotentiary on the part of France.

On the journey he was observed to be moody and deeply contemplative. The separation from 100,000 men whom he might call his own, and the uncertainty of the future destinies to which he might be summoned, are enough to account for this, without supposing, as some have done, that he already had distinctly formed any of those projects of ambition which Time opened to him. He must either be raised to a yet more distinguished height, or altogether broken down, levelled with the mass of subjects, and consigned to comparative obscurity. There was no middle station for the Conqueror and Liberator of Italy.

CHAPTER XI

The coup of 18th Fructidor IV (4th September 1797) was a palace revolution that preserved the Republic but further undermined its legitimacy. Like the bulk of the army, Napoleon supported the coup, although Scott maintains he would have liked to play a more prominent role in it.

During this whole revolution, the lower portion of the population, which used to be so much agitated upon like occasions, remained perfectly quiet; the struggle lay exclusively between the middle classes, who inclined to a government on the basis of royalty, and the Directory, who, without having any very tangible class of political principles, had become possessed of the supreme power, desired to retain it, and made their point good by the assistance of the military.

Buonaparte was much disappointed at the result of the 18th Fructidor, chiefly because, if less decisive, it would have added more to his consequence, and have given him an opportunity of crossing, as he termed it, the Rubicon. As it was, the majority of the directors – three men of no particular talent, undistinguished alike by birth, by services to their country, or even by accidental popularity, and cast as it were by chance, upon supreme power – remained by the issue of the struggle still the masters of the bold and ambitious conqueror, who probably already felt his own vocation to be for command rather than obedience.

It followed, from the doubtful terms on which Buonaparte stood with the Directory, that they must have viewed his return to Paris with some apprehension, when they considered the impression likely to be made on any capital, but especially on Paris, by the appearance of one who seemed to be the chosen favourite of Fortune. The mediocrity of such men as Barras never gives them so much embarrassment, as when, being raised to an elevation above their desert, they find themselves placed in comparison with one to whom nature has given the talents which their situation requires. The higher their condition, their demeanour is the more awkward; for the factious advantages which they possess cannot raise them to the natural dignity of character, unless in the sense in which a dwarf, by the assistance of crutches, may be said to be as tall as a giant. The Directory had already found Buonaparte, on several occasions, a spirit which would not be commanded. Undoubtedly they would have been well pleased had it been possible to have found him employment at a distance; but as that seemed difficult, they were obliged to look round for the means of employing him at home, or abide the tremendous risk of his finding occupation for himself.

It is surprising that it did not occur to the Directory to make at least the attempt of conciliating Buonaparte, by providing for his future fortune. He deserved that attention to his private affairs, for he had himself entirely neglected them. While he drew from the dominions which he conquered or overawed, immense sums on behalf of the French nation, which he applied in part to the support of the army, and in part remitted to the Directory, he kept no accounts, nor were any demanded of him; but according to his own account, he transmitted sixty million francs to Paris, and had not remaining of his own funds, when he returned from Italy, more than 300,000.

It is no doubt true, that Buonaparte had pillaged the old states, thus selling to the newly-formed commonwealths their liberty and equality at a very handsome rate, and probably leaving them in very little danger of corruption from that wealth which is said to be the bane of republican virtue. But on the other hand, it must be acknowledged, that if the French general plundered the Italians as Cortez did the Mexicans, he did not reserve any considerable share of the spoil for his own use, though the opportunity was often in his power. But, however free from the wish to obtain wealth by any indirect means, Napoleon appears to have expected that in return for public services of such an unusual magnitude, some provision ought to have been made for him. An attempt was made to procure a public grant of the domain of Chambord, and a large hotel in Paris, as an acknowledgment of the national gratitude for his brilliant successes; but the Directory thwarted the proposal.

Malibran, a member of the Council of Five Hundred, made a motion that Buonaparte should be endowed with a revenue of 50,000 livres annually, with a reversion to his wife of one half of that sum. It may be supposed that this motion had not been sufficiently considered and preconcerted, since it was very indifferently received, and was evaded by the swaggering declaration of a member, that such glorious deeds could not be rewarded by gold. So the Assembly adopted the reasonable principle, that because the debt of gratitude was too great to be paid in money, therefore he to whom it was due was to be suffered to remain in comparative indigence – an economical mode of calculation, and not unlike that high-sounding doctrine of the civil law, which states, that a free man being seized on, and forcibly sold for a slave, shall obtain no damages on that account, because the liberty of a citizen is too transcendently valuable to be put to estimation.

Whatever might be the motives of the Directory; whether they hoped that poverty might depress Buonaparte's ambition, render him more dependent on the government, and oblige him to remain in a private condition for want of means to put himself at the head of a party; or whether they acted with the indistinct and confused motives of little minds, who wish to injure those whom they fear, their conduct was alike ungracious and impolitic. They ought to have calculated, that a generous mind would have been attached by benefits, and that a selfish one might have been deterred from more doubtful and ambitious projects, by a prospect of sure and direct advantage; but that marked ill-will and distrust must in every case render him dangerous, who has the power to be so.

Their plan, instead of resting on an attempt to conciliate the ambitious conqueror, and soothe him to the repose of a tranquil indulgence and ease, seems to have been that of devising for him new labours, like the wife of Eurystheus for the juvenile Hercules. If he succeeded, they may have privately counted upon securing the advantages for themselves; if he failed, they were rid of a troublesome rival. It was with these views that they proposed to Napoleon to crown his glories, by assuming the command of the preparations made for the conquest of England.

CHAPTER XII

Towards the end of October 1797, the Directory announced that there should be instantly assembled an army, to be called the Army of England, and that the Citizen-General Buonaparte was named to the command. The intelligence was received in every part of France with all the triumph which attends the anticipation of certain victory. The address of the Directory numbered all the conquests which France had won, and prepared the French nation to expect the fruit of so many victories and sacrifices when they had punished England for her perfidy and maritime tyranny. "It is at London where the misfortunes of all Europe are forged and manufactured – It is in London that they must be terminated." In a solemn meeting held by the Directory, for the purpose of receiving the treaty of peace with Austria, which was presented to them by Berthier and Mongé on the part of Buonaparte, the latter, accepted, on the part of the army and general, the task imposed by the French rulers. "The Government of England and the French Republic cannot both continue to exist – you have given the word which shall fall – already our victorious troops brandish their arms and Scipio is at their head."

While this farce, for such it proved, was acting in Paris, the chief of the intended enterprise arrived there, and took up his abode in the same modest house which he had occupied before becoming the conqueror of palaces. The community of Paris, with much elegance, paid their successful general the compliment of changing the name of the street from Rue Chartereine to Rue de la Victoire. In a metropolis where all is welcome that can vary the tedium of human life, the arrival of any remarkable person is a species of holiday; but such an eminent character as Buonaparte, was no everyday wonder. His youth, too, added to the marvel, and still more the claim of general superiority over the society in which he mingled, though consisting of the most distinguished persons in France; a superiority cloaking itself with a species of reserve, which inferred, "You may look upon me, but you cannot penetrate or see through me." Napoleon's general manner in society, during this part of his life, has been described by an observer of first-rate power; according to whom, he was one for whom the admiration which could not be refused to him, was always mingled with a portion of fear. He was different in his manner from other men, and neither pleased nor angry, kind nor severe, after the common fashion of humanity. He appeared to live for the execution of his own plans, and to consider others only in so far as they were connected with, and could advance or oppose them; and, with a precision of intelligence which seemed intuitive from its rapidity, he penetrated the sentiments of those whom it was worth his while to study. Buonaparte did not then possess the ordinary tone of light conversation in society; probably his mind was too much burdened or too proud to stoop to adopt that mode of pleasing, and there was a stiffness and reserve of manner which was perhaps adopted for the purpose of keeping people at a distance. His look had the same character. When he thought himself closely observed, he had the power of discharging from his countenance all expression, save that of a vague and indefinite smile, and presenting to the curious investigator the fixed eyes and rigid features of a bust of marble.

When he talked with the purpose of pleasing, Buonaparte often told anecdotes of his life in a very pleasing manner; when silent, he had something disdainful in the expression of his face; when disposed to be quite at ease, he was, in Madame de Staël's opinion, rather vulgar. His natural tone of feeling seemed to be a sense of internal superiority, and of secret contempt for the world in which he lived. His character and manners were upon the whole strongly calculated to attract the attention of the French nation, and to excite a perpetual interest even from the very mystery which attached to him, as well as from the splendour of his triumphs. The supreme power was residing in the Luxembourg ostensibly; but Paris was aware, that the means which had raised, and which must support and extend that power, were to be found in the humble mansion of the newly-christened Rue de la Victoire.

Some of these features are perhaps harshly designed, as being drawn *recentibus odiis*. The disagreement between Buonaparte and Madame de Staël is well known. It originated about this time, when, as a first-rate woman of talent, she was naturally desirous to attract the notice of the Victor of Victors. They appear to have misunderstood each other; for the lady, who ought certainly to know best, has informed us, "that far from feeling her fear of Buonaparte removed by repeated meetings, it seemed to increase, and his best exertions to please could not overcome her invincible aversion for what she found in his character." His ironical contempt of excellence of every kind, operated like the sword in romance, which froze while it wounded. Buonaparte seems never to have suspected the secret and mysterious terror with which he impressed the ingenious author of Corinne; on the contrary, Las Cases tells us, that she combined all her means to make an impression on the general. She wrote to him when distant, and, as the Count ungallantly expresses it, tormented him when present. In truth they stood in a false position with respect to each other. Madame de Staël might be pardoned for thinking that it would be difficult to resist her wit and her talent; but Buonaparte was disposed to repel, rather than encourage the advances of one whose views were so shrewd, and her observations so keen, while her sex permitted her to push her inquiries further than one man might have dared to do in conversing with another. She certainly did desire to look into him "with considerate eyes," and on one occasion put his abilities to the proof, by asking him rather abruptly, "whom he esteemed the greatest woman in the world, alive or dead?" – "Her, madam, that has borne the most children," answered Buonaparte, with much appearance of simplicity. Disconcerted by the reply, she observed, that he was reported not to be a great admirer of the fair sex. "I am very fond of my wife, madam," he replied, with one of those brief and yet piquant observations, which adjourned a debate as promptly as one of his characteristic manoeuvres would have ended a battle. From this period there was enmity between Buonaparte and Madame de Staël; and at different times he treated her with a harshness which had some appearance of actual personal dislike, though perhaps rather directed against the female politician than the woman of literature.

In the meantime, while popular feeling and distinguished genius were thus seeking to pay court to the youthful conqueror, the Directory found themselves obliged to render to him that semblance of homage which could not have been withheld without giving much offence to general opinion, and injuring those who omitted to pay it. On the 10th of December, the Directory received Buonaparte with honours which the Republican government had not yet conferred on any subject, and which must have seemed incongruous to those who had any recollection of liberty and equality. The ceremony took place in the great court of the Luxembourg palace, where the Directory, surrounded by all that was officially important or distinguished by talent, received from Buonaparte's hand the treaty of Campo Formio. The delivery of this document was accompanied by a speech from Buonaparte, in which he told the Directory, that, in order to establish a constitution founded on reason, it was necessary that eighteen centuries of prejudices should be conquered – "The constitution of the year three, and you, have triumphed over all these obstacles." The triumph lasted exactly until the year eight, when the orator himself overthrew the constitution, destroyed the power of the rulers who had overcome the prejudices of eighteen centuries, and reigned in their stead.

The general, conducted by Barras, the president of the Directory, approached an erection, termed the Altar of the Country, where they went through various appropriate ceremonies, and at length dismissed a numerous assembly, much edified with what they had seen. The two Councils, or Representative Bodies, also gave a splendid banquet in honour of Buonaparte. And what he appeared to receive with more particular satisfaction than these marks of distinction, the Institute admitted him a member of its body in the room of his friend Carnot, (who was actually a fugitive,) while the poet Chenier promulgated his praises, and foretold his future triumphs, and his approaching conquest of England.

Buonaparte made a complete survey of the coast of the British channel. The result of his observations decided his opinion, that in the present case the undertaking ought to be abandoned. The demonstrations of invasion, however, were ostensibly continued, and every thing seemed arranged on either side for a desperate collision betwixt the two most powerful nations in Europe. But the proceedings of politicians resemble those of the Indian traders called Banians, who seem engaged in talking about ordinary and trifling affairs, while, with their hands concealed beneath a shawl that is spread between them, they are secretly debating and adjusting, by signs, bargains of the utmost importance. While all France and England had their eyes fixed on the fleets and armies destined against the latter country, the Directory and their general had no intention of using these preparations, except as a blind to cover their real object, which was the celebrated expedition to Egypt.

While yet in Italy, Buonaparte had suggested to the Directory [13th September, 1797,] the advantage which might be derived from seizing Malta. The knights, he said, were odious to the Maltese, and were almost starving; to augment which state of distress he had already confiscated their Italian property. He then proceeded to intimate, that being possessed of Corfu and Malta, it was natural to take possession of Egypt. 25,000 men, with 8 or 10 ships of the line, would be sufficient for the expedition.

Talleyrand, then minister for foreign affairs, (in his answer of 23rd September,) saw the utmost advantage in the design upon Egypt, which, as a colony, would attract the commerce of India to Europe, in preference to the circuitous route by the Cape of Good Hope. This proves that even before Buonaparte left Italy he had conceived the idea of the Egyptian expedition, though probably only as one of the vast and vague schemes of ambition which success in so many perilous enterprises had tended to foster. There was something of wild grandeur in the idea, calculated to please an ambitious imagination. He was to be placed far beyond the reach of any command superior to his own, and left at his own discretion to the extending conquests, and perhaps founding an empire, in a country long considered as the cradle of knowledge. The first specimens of early art were also to be found among the gigantic ruins of Egypt, and its time-defying monuments of antiquity. This had its effect upon Buonaparte, who affected so particularly the species of fame which attaches to the protector and extender of science, philosophy, and the fine arts. On this subject he had a ready and willing counsellor at hand. Mongé, the artist and virtuoso, was Buonaparte's confidant, and, there is no doubt, encouraged him to an undertaking which promised a rich harvest to the antiquarian among ruins hitherto imperfectly examined.

The Directory, eager to rid themselves of his perilous vicinity, hastened to accomplish the means of his expedition to Egypt, upon a scale far more formidable than any which had yet sailed from modern Europe, for the invasion and subjection of distant and peaceful realms. The public observed with astonishment a detachment of no less than 100 men, who had cultivated the arts and sciences, or, to use the French phrase, *Savans*, selected for the purpose of joining this expedition, of which the object still remained a secret; while all classes of people asked each other what new quarter of the world France had determined to colonise, since she seemed preparing at once to subdue it by her arms, and to enrich it with the treasures of her science and literature. This singular department of the expedition, the first of the kind which ever accompanied an invading army, was liberally supplied with books, philosophical instruments, and all means of prosecuting the several departments of knowledge. Buonaparte did not, however, trust to the superiority of science to ensure the conquest of Egypt. He was fully provided with more effectual means. 25,000 men, chiefly veterans from his own Italian army, had in their list of generals the names of Kleber, Desaix, Berthier, Regnier, Murat, Lannes, Andréossi, Menou, Belliard, and others well known in the revolutionary wars. 400 transports were assembled, 13 ships of the line and 4 frigates, commanded by Admiral Brueyes, formed the escort of the expedition. It is true, that, so far from dreading the English forces which were likely to be employed against them, the French regarded as a recommendation to the conquest of Egypt, that it was to be the first step to the destruction of the British power in India; and Napoleon continued to the last to consider the conquest of Egypt as the forerunner of that of universal Asia.

Meanwhile, the moment of departure approached. The blockading squadron, commanded by Nelson, was blown off the coast by a gale of wind, and so much damaged that they were obliged to run down to Sardinia. The various squadrons from Genoa, Civitavecchia, and Bastia, set sail and united with that which already lay at Toulon. At the moment of departure, Buonaparte made one of those singular harangues which evinces such a mixture of talent and energy with bad taste and bombast. He promised to introduce those who had warred on the mountains and in the plains, to maritime combat. He reminded them that the Romans combated Carthage by sea as well as by land – he proposed to conduct them, in the name of the Goddess of Liberty, to the most distant regions and oceans, and he concluded by promising to each individual of his army seven acres of land. Whether this distribution of property was to take place on the banks of the Nile, of the Bosphorus, or the Ganges, the soldiers had not the most distant guess, and the commander-in-chief himself would have had difficulty in informing them.

On the 19th of May, 1798, this magnificent armament set sail from Toulon, illuminated by a splendid sunrise. The line-of-battle ships extended for a league, and the semi-circle formed by the convoy was at least six leagues. A sufficient garrison was established in Malta, destined by Buonaparte to be an intermediate station between France and Egypt; and on the 16th June, the daring general resumed his expedition. On the coast of Candia, while the *Savans* were gazing on the rocks where Jupiter, it is said, was nurtured, and speculating concerning the existence of some vestiges of the celebrated labyrinth, Buonaparte learned that a new enemy was in his immediate vicinity. This was the English squadron. Nelson was now in full and anxious pursuit of his renowned contemporary. Reinforced by ten ships of the line, a meeting with Napoleon was the utmost wish of his heart. The French had been heard of at Malta, but as the British admiral was about to proceed thither, he received news of their departure; and concluding that Egypt must be unquestionably the object of their expedition, he made sail for Egypt. It singularly happened, that although Nelson anticipated the arrival of the French at Alexandria, and accordingly directed his course thither, yet, keeping a more direct path than Brueyes, when he arrived there on the 28th June, he heard nothing of the enemy, who, in the meanwhile, were proceeding to the very same port. The English set sail, therefore, for Rhodes and Syracuse; and thus were the two large and hostile fleets traversing the same narrow sea, without being able to attain any certain tidings of each other's movements.

Escaped from the risk of an encounter so perilous, Buonaparte's greatest danger seemed to be over on the 1st July, when the French fleet came in sight of Alexandria. The disembarkation took place [July 2nd] at an anchorage called Marabout. It was not accomplished without losing boats and men on the surf, though such risks were encountered with great joy by the troops, who had been so long confined on shipboard. As soon as 5000 or 6000 men were landed, Buonaparte marched toward Alexandria, when the Turks, incensed at this hostile invasion on the part of a nation with whom they were at peace, shut the gates, and manned the walls. But the walls were ruinous, and presented breaches in many places, and the chief weapons of resistance were musketry and stones. The conquerors of Italy forced their passage over such obstacles, but not easily or with impunity. 200 French were killed. There was severe military execution done upon the garrison, and the town was abandoned to plunder for three hours; which has been justly stigmatised as an act of unnecessary cruelty, perpetrated only to strike terror, and extend the fame of the victorious French general. But it was Napoleon's object to impress the highest idea of his power upon the various classes of natives.

Upon the 7th of July, the army marched from Alexandria against the Mamelukes. Their course was up the Nile, and a small flotilla of gun-boats ascended the river to protect their right flank, while the infantry traversed a desert of burning sands, at a distance from the stream, and without a drop of water to relieve their tormenting thirst. The army of Italy, accustomed to the enjoyments of that delicious country, were astonished at the desolation they saw around them. "Is this," they said, "the country in which we are to receive our farms of seven acres each? The general might have allowed us to take as much as we chose – no one would have abused the privilege." Their officers, too, expressed horror and disgust; and even generals of such celebrity as Murat and Lannes threw their hats on the sand, and trod on their cockades. It required all Buonaparte's authority to maintain order.

Meanwhile, the French were obliged to march with the utmost precaution. The whole plain was now covered with Mamelukes, mounted on the finest Arabian horses, and armed with pistols, carabines, and blunderbusses – their plumed turbans waving in the air, and their rich dresses and arms glittering in the sun. Entertaining a high contempt for the French force, as consisting almost entirely of infantry, this splendid barbaric chivalry watched every opportunity for charging them, nor did a single straggler escape the unrelenting edge of their sabres. Their charge was almost as swift as the wind, and as their severe bits enabled them to halt, or wheel their horses at full gallop, their retreat was as rapid as their advance. Even the practised veterans of Italy were at first embarrassed by this new mode of fighting, and lost several men; especially when fatigue caused anyone to fall out of the ranks, in which case his fate became certain. But they were soon reconciled to fighting the Mamelukes, when they discovered that each of these horsemen carried about him his fortune, and that it not uncommonly amounted to considerable sums in gold.

After fourteen days of marches, they arrived within six leagues of Cairo, and beheld at a distance the celebrated Pyramids, but learned, at the same time, that Murad Bey, with 22 of his brethren, at the head of their Mamelukes, had formed an entrenched camp at a place called Embabeh, with the purpose of covering Cairo and giving battle to the French. On the 21st of July, they saw their enemy in the field, and in full force. A splendid line of cavalry, under Murad, displayed the whole strength of the Mamelukes. Their right rested on the imperfectly entrenched camp, in which lay 20,000 infantry, defended by 40 pieces of cannon. But the infantry were undisciplined; the guns were mounted on clumsy wooden frames; and the fortifications of the camp were but commenced. Buonaparte made his dispositions. He extended his line to the right, in such a manner as to keep out of gunshot of the entrenched camp, and have only to encounter the line of cavalry.

Murad Bey saw this movement, and prepared to charge with his magnificent body of horse, declaring he would cut the French up like gourds. Buonaparte, as he directed the infantry to form squares, called out to his men, "From yonder Pyramids 20 centuries behold your actions." The Mamelukes advanced with utmost speed, and corresponding fury, and charged with horrible yells. They disordered one of the French squares of infantry, which would have been sabred in an instant, but that the mass of this fiery militia was a little behind the advanced guard. The French had a moment to restore order, and used it. The combat then in some degree resembled that which, nearly 20 years afterwards, took place at Waterloo; the hostile cavalry furiously charging the squares of infantry, and trying, by the most undaunted efforts of courage, to break in upon them at every practicable point, while a tremendous fire of musketry, grape-shot, and shells, crossing in various directions, repaid their audacity. Nothing in war was ever seen more desperate than the exertions of the Mamelukes. Failing to force their horses through the French squares, individuals were seen to wheel them round, and rein them back on the ranks, that they might disorder them by kicking. As they became frantic with despair, they hurled at the immoveable phalanxes their pistols, their poniards, and their carabines. Those who fell wounded to the ground dragged themselves on, to cut at the legs of the French with their crooked sabres. But their efforts were all vain.

The Mamelukes, after the most courageous efforts, were finally beaten off with great slaughter; and as they could not form or act in squadron, their retreat became a confused flight. The greater part attempted to return to their camp. By taking this route they placed themselves betwixt the French and the Nile; and the insupportable fire of the former soon obliged them to plunge into the river, in hopes to escape by swimming to the opposite bank – a desperate effort, in which few succeeded. Their infantry at the same time evacuated their camp without a show of resistance, precipitated themselves into boats, and endeavoured to cross the Nile. Very many of these also were destroyed. The French soldiers long afterwards occupied themselves in fishing for the drowned Mamelukes, and failed not to find money and valuables upon all whom they could recover. Murad Bey, with a part of his best Mamelukes, escaped the slaughter by a more regular movement to the left, and retreated into Upper Egypt.

Cairo surrendered without resistance. Lower Egypt was completely in the hands of the French, and thus far the expedition of Buonaparte had been perfectly successful. But it was not the will of Heaven, that even the most fortunate of men should escape reverses; and a severe one awaited Napoleon.

CHAPTER XIII

The severe reverse alluded to by Scott was the battle of Aboukir, on 1st August 1798, in which Nelson destroyed the French fleet off Alexandria, leaving Napoleon with no means of evacuating the army from Egypt. He was not discouraged, however, and set about restoring order over Lower Egypt.

His first care was to gather up the reins of government which had dropped from the hands of the defeated beys. With two classes of the Egyptian nation, it was easy to establish his authority. The Fellahs, or peasantry, sure to be squeezed to the last penny by one party or other, willingly submitted to the invaders as the strongest, and the most able to protect them. The Cophts, or men of business, were equally ready to serve the party which was in possession of the country. But the Turks were to be attached to the conqueror by other means, since their haughty national character, and the intolerance of the Mahometan religion rendered them alike inaccessible to profit, the hope of which swayed the Cophts, and to fear, which was the prevailing argument with the Fellahs. To gratify their vanity, and soothe their prejudices, seemed the only mode by which Napoleon could insinuate himself into favour. With this view, Buonaparte was far from assuming a title of conquest in Egypt, though he left few of its rights unexercised. On the contrary, he wisely continued to admit the pacha to that ostensible share of authority which was yielded to him by the beys, and spoke with as much seeming respect of the Sublime Porte, as if it had been his intention ever again to permit their having any effective power in Egypt. Their imams, or priests; their ulemats, or men of law; their cadis, or judges; their sheiks, or chiefs; their Janissaries, or privileged soldiers, were all treated by Napoleon with a certain degree of attention, and the Sultan Kebir, as they called him, affected to govern, like the Grand Signior, by the intervention of a divan.

This general council consisted of about forty sheiks, or Moslems of distinction by birth or office, who held their regular meetings at Cairo, and from which body emanated the authority of provincial divans. Napoleon affected to consult the superior council, and act in many cases according to their report of the law of the Prophet. On one occasion, he gave them a moral lesson which it would be great injustice to suppress. A tribe of roving Arabs had slain a peasant, and Buonaparte had given directions to search out and punish the murderers. One of his Oriental counsellors laughed at the zeal which the general manifested on so slight a cause:

"What have you to do with the death of this Fellah, Sultan Kebir?" said he, ironically; "was he your kinsman?"

"He was more," said Napoleon; "he was one for whose safety I am accountable to God, who placed him under my government."

"He speaks like an inspired person!" exclaimed the sheiks; who can admire the beauty of a just sentiment, though incapable, from the scope they allow their passions, to act up to the precepts of moral rectitude.

Thus far, the conduct of Buonaparte was admirable. He protected the people who were placed under his power, he respected their religious opinions, he administered justice to them according to their own laws, until they should be supplied with a better system. Unquestionably, his good administration did not amend the radical deficiency of his title. Yet in delivering Egypt from the tyrannical sway of the Mamelukes, and administering the government of the country with wisdom and comparative humanity, the mode in which he used the power which he had acquired, might be admitted in some measure to atone for his usurpation. Not contented with directing his soldiers to hold in respect the religious observances of the country, he showed equal justice and policy in collecting and protecting the scattered remains of the great caravan of the Mecca pilgrimage. So satisfactory was his conduct, that he contrived to obtain from the clergy of the Mosque an opinion, declaring that it was lawful to pay tribute to the French, though such a doctrine is diametrically inconsistent with the Koran. Thus far Napoleon's measures had proved rational and successful. But with this laudable course of conduct was mixed a species of artifice, which, while we are compelled to term it impious, has in it, at the same time, something ludicrous, and almost childish.

Buonaparte entertained the strange idea of persuading the Moslems that he pertained in some sort to their religion, being an envoy of the Deity, sent to earth, not to take away, but to confirm and complete, the doctrines of the Koran, and the mission of Mahomet. He used, in executing this purpose, the inflated language of the East, the more easily that it corresponded, in its allegorical and amplified style, with his own natural tone of composition; and he hesitated not to join in the external ceremonial of the Mahometan religion, that his actions might seem to confirm his words. The French general celebrated the feast of the prophet, with some sheik of eminence, and joined in the litanies and worship enjoined by the Koran. He affected, too, the language of an inspired follower of the faith.

On entering the sepulchral chamber in the pyramid of Cheops, "Glory be to Allah," said Buonaparte, "There is no God but God, and Mahomet is his prophet." A confession of faith which is, in itself, a declaration of Islamism.

"Thou hast spoken like the most learned of the prophets," said the mufti, who accompanied him.

"I can command a car of fire to descend from heaven," continued the French general, "and I can guide and direct its course upon earth."

"Thou art the great chief to whom Mahomet gives power and victory," said the mufti.

Napoleon closed the conversation with this not very pertinent Oriental proverb, "The bread which the wicked seizes upon by force, shall be turned to dust, in his mouth."

Though the mufti played his part in the above scene with becoming gravity, Buonaparte over-estimated his own theatrical powers, and did too little justice to the shrewdness of the Turks, if he supposed them really edified by his pretended proselytism. With them as with us, a renegade from the religious faith in which he was brought up, is like a deserter from the standard of his country; and though the services of either may be accepted and used, they remain objects of disregard and contempt.

The Turks and Arabs of Cairo soon showed Buonaparte, by a general and unexpected insurrection, (October 22nd,)[14] in which many Frenchmen were slain, how little they were moved by his pretended attachment to their faith. Yet, when the insurgents had been quelled by force, and the blood of 5000 Moslems had atoned for that of 300 Frenchmen, Napoleon, in an address to the inhabitants of Cairo, new-modelling the general council, held still the same language as before. "Sheriffs," he said, "Ulemats, Orators of the Mosque, teach the people that those who become my enemies shall have no refuge in this world or the next. Is there anyone blind enough not to see, that I am the agent of Destiny, or incredulous enough to call in question the power of Destiny over human affairs? Make the people understand, that since the world was a world, it was ordained, that having destroyed the enemies of Islamism, and broken down the Cross, I should come from the West to accomplish the task designed for me – show them, that in more than 20 passages of the Koran my coming is foretold. I could demand a reckoning from each of you for the most secret thoughts of his soul, since to me everything is known; but the day will come when all shall know from whom I have my commission, and that human efforts cannot prevail against me." It is plain from this strange proclamation, that Buonaparte was willing to be worshipped as a superior being, as soon as altars could be built, and worshippers collected together.

Two Turkish armies were gathered with the purpose of recovering Egypt; one at Rhodes, the other in Syria. Napoleon decided to anticipate the enemy and march into Syria across the desert separating Africa from Asia, which led him to Palestine.

Upon his entering the Holy Land, Buonaparte occupied without resistance Gaza. Jaffa, a celebrated city during the time of the Crusades, was the next object of attack. It was bravely assaulted, and fiercely defended. But French valour and discipline prevailed – the place was carried by storm – 3000 Turks were put to the sword, and the town was abandoned to the license of the soldiery, which, by Buonaparte's own admission, never assumed a shape more frightful. A large part of the garrison, estimated by Buonaparte at 1200 men, which Miot raises to betwixt 2000 and 3000, and others exaggerate still more, remained on the defensive, and held out in the mosques, and a sort of citadel, till despairing of succour, they surrendered, and were in appearance admitted to quarter. Of this body, the Egyptians were carefully separated from the Turks, Maugrabins, and Arnaouts; and while the first were restored to liberty, and sent back to their country, these last were placed under a strong guard. Provisions were distributed to them, and they were permitted to go by detachments in quest of water. According to all appearance they were considered and treated as prisoners of war. This was on the 7th of March. On the 9th this body of prisoners was marched out of Jaffa, in the centre of a large square battalion, commanded by General Bon. Miot assures us, that he himself accompanied the melancholy column, and witnessed the event. The Turks foresaw their fate, but used neither entreaties nor complaints to avert it. They marched on, silent and composed. Some of them, of higher rank, seemed to exhort the others to submit, like servants of the Prophet, to the decree, which, according to their belief, was written on their forehead. They were escorted to the sand-hills to the south-east of Jaffa, divided there into small bodies, and put to death by musketry. The execution lasted a considerable time, and the wounded were despatched with the bayonet. Their bodies were heaped together, and formed a pyramid which is still visible, consisting now of human bones.

The cruelty of this execution occasioned the fact itself to be doubted though never denied by the French themselves. Napoleon frankly admitted the truths of the statement to Lord Ebrington and to Dr. O'Meara. Buonaparte's defence was that the massacre was justified by the laws of war – that the head of his messenger had been cut off by the governor of Jaffa, when sent to summon him to surrender – that these Turks were a part of the garrison of El Arish, who had engaged not to serve against the French, and were found immediately afterwards defending Jaffa, in breach of the terms of their capitulation. They had incurred the doom of death, therefore, by the rules of war – Wellington, he said, would have, in his place, acted in the same manner.

To this plea the following obvious answers apply. If the Turkish governor had behaved like a barbarian, for which his country, and the religion which Napoleon meditated to embrace, might be some excuse, the French general had avenged himself by the storm and plunder of the town. If some of these unhappy Turks had broken their faith, and were found again in the ranks which they had sworn to abandon, it could not, according to the most severe construction of the rules of war, authorise the dreadful retaliation of indiscriminate massacre upon a multitude of prisoners, without inquiring whether they had been all equally guilty. Lastly, and admitting them all to stand in the same degree of criminality, although their breach of faith might have entitled Buonaparte to refuse these men quarter while they had arms in their hands, that right was ended when the French general received their submission on condition of safety for life at least.

This bloody deed must always remain a deep stain on the character of Napoleon. Yet we do not view it as the indulgence of an innate love of cruelty for nothing in Buonaparte's history shows the existence of that vice, and there are many things which intimate his disposition to have been naturally humane. But he was ambitious, aimed at gigantic undertakings, and easily learned to overlook the waste of human life, which the execution of his projects necessarily involved. He seems to have argued, not on the character of the action, but solely on the effect which it was to produce upon his own combinations. His army was small; it was his business to strike terror into his numerous enemies, and the measure seemed capable of making a deep impression on all who should hear of it. Besides, these men, if dismissed, would immediately rejoin his enemies. He had experienced their courage, and to disarm them would have been almost an unavailing precaution, where their national weapon, the sabre, was so easily attained. To detain them prisoners would have required a stronger force than Napoleon could afford, would have added difficulty and delay to the movement of his troops, and tended to exhaust his supplies. That sort of necessity, therefore, which men fancy to themselves when they are unwilling to forego a favourite object for the sake of obeying a moral precept – that necessity which might be more properly termed a temptation difficult to be resisted – that necessity which has been called the tyrant's plea, was the cause of the massacre at Jaffa, and must remain its sole apology.

It might almost seem that Heaven set its vindictive brand upon this deed of butchery; for about the time it was committed the plague broke out in the army. Buonaparte, with a moral courage deserving as much praise as his late cruelty deserved reprobation, went into the hospitals in person, and while exposing himself, without hesitation, to the infection, diminished the terror of the disease in the opinion of the soldiers generally, and of the patients themselves, who were thus enabled to keep up their spirits, and gained by doing so the fairest chance of recovery.

Meanwhile, determined to prosecute the conquest of Syria, Buonaparte resolved to advance to Saint Jean d'Acre. The Turkish Pacha, or governor of Syria, was Achmet; who, by his unrelenting cruelties and executions, had procured the terrible distinction of Djezzar, or the Butcher. Buonaparte addressed this chief in two letters, offering his alliance, and threatening him with his vengeance if it should be rejected. To neither did the pacha return any answer; in the second instance he put to death the messenger. The French general advanced against Acre, vowing revenge.

The pacha communicated the approach of Napoleon to Sir Sidney Smith, to whom had been committed the charge of assisting the Turks. He hastened to sail for Acre with the Tigre and Theseus, ships of the line; and, arriving there two days ere the French made their appearance, contributed greatly to place the town in a respectable state of defence.

On the 17th March, the French came in sight of Acre, which is built on a peninsula, and so conveniently situated that vessels can lie near the shore, and annoy with their fire whatever advances to assault the fortification. Notwithstanding the presence of two British ships of war, and the disappointment concerning his battering cannon, which were now pointed against him, Buonaparte, with a characteristic perseverance, which, on such an occasion, was pushed into obstinacy, refused to abandon his purpose, and proceeded to open trenches, although the guns which he had were only twelve pounders. The point of attack was a large tower which predominated over the rest of the fortifications. A mine at the same time was run under the extreme defences.

By the 28th March a breach was effected, the mine was sprung, and the French proceeded to the assault. They advanced at the charging step, under a murderous fire from the walls, but had the mortification to find a deep ditch betwixt them and the tower. They crossed it, nevertheless, by help of the scaling-ladders, and forced their way as far as the tower, from which it is said that the defenders impressed by the fate of Jaffa, were beginning to fly. They were checked by the example of Djezzar himself, who fired his own pistols at the French, and upbraided the Moslems who were retreating from the walls. The defences were again manned; the French, unable to support the renewed fire, were forced back; and the Turks falling upon them in their retreat with sabre in hand, killed a number of their best men. At length, Buonaparte, in spite of a bloody and obstinate opposition, forced his way to the disputed tower, and made a lodgement on the second story. It afforded, however, no access to the town; and the troops remained there as in a *cul-de-sac*, the lodgement being covered from the English and Turkish fire by a work constructed partly of packs of cotton, partly of the dead bodies of the slain.

Sir Sidney Smith in person proceeded to the disputed tower, at the head of a body of British seamen, armed with pikes. They united themselves to a corps of brave Turks, who defended the breach rather with heavy stones than with other weapons. The muzzles of the muskets touched each other, and the spear-heads of the standards were locked together. At this moment one of the Turkish regiments of Hassan's army, which had landed, made a sortie upon the French; and though they were driven back, yet the diversion occasioned the besiegers to be forced from their lodgement.

Abandoning the ill-omened tower, which had cost so many men, Buonaparte now turned his efforts towards a considerable breach that had been effected in the curtain and which promised a more easy entrance. It proved, indeed, but too easy; for Djezzar Pacha opposed to the assault on this occasion a new mode of tactic. Confiding in his superior numbers, he suffered the French, who were commanded by the intrepid General Lannes, to surmount the breach without opposition, by which they penetrated into the body of the place. They had no sooner entered, than a numerous body of Turks mingled among them with loud shouts; and ere they had time or room to avail themselves of their discipline, brought them into that state of close fighting, where strength and agility are superior to every other acquirement. The Turks, wielding the sabre in one hand, and the poniard in the other, cut to pieces almost all the French who had entered. The Turks gave no quarter; and instantly cutting the heads off of those whom they slew, carried them to the pacha, who sat in public distributing money to those who brought him these bloody trophies. This was the 6th assault upon these tottering and blood-stained ramparts. "Victory," said Napoleon, "is to the most persevering;" and, contrary to the advice of Kleber, he resolved upon another and yet more desperate attack. On the 21st May the final effort was made.[15] The attack of the morning failed, and Colonel Veneux renewed it at mid-day. "Be assured," said he to Buonaparte, "Acre shall be yours to-night, or Veneux will die on the breach." He kept his word at the cost of his life. The French now retreated, dispirited and despairing of success. The contest had been carried on at half a musket shot distance; and the bodies of the dead lying around, putrefied under the burning sun, spread disease among the survivors.

The siege of Acre had now continued sixty days. The besiegers had marched no less than eight times to the assault, while eleven desperate sallies were evidence of the obstinacy of the defence. Several of the best French generals were killed and the army was greatly reduced by the sword and the plague. Retreat became inevitable. Yet Buonaparte endeavoured to give it such a colouring as might make the measure seem voluntary. Sometimes he announced, that his purpose of going to Acre was sufficiently accomplished when he had battered down the palace of the pacha; at other times he affirmed he had left the whole town a heap of ruins; and finally, he informed the Directory that he could easily have taken the place, but the plague being raging within its walls, and it being impossible to prevent the troops from seizing on infected clothes for part of their booty, he had rather declined the capture of Acre. What his real feelings must have been may be conjectured from the following frank

avowal in Saint Helena. Speaking of the dependence of the most important affairs on the most trivial, he remarks, that the mistake of the captain
of a frigate, who bore away, instead of forcing his passage to his destination, had prevented the face of the world from being totally changed.
"Acre," he said, "would otherwise have been taken – the French army
would have flown to Damascus and Aleppo – in a twinkling of an eye
they would have been on the Euphrates – the Syrian Christians would
have joined us – the Druses, the Armenians would have united with us."
Some one replied, "We might have been reinforced to the number of
100,000 men." – "Say 600,000," said the Emperor, "who can calculate the
amount? I would have reached Constantinople and the Indies – I would
have changed the face of the world."

CHAPTER XIV

The siege being raised on the 21st of May, 1799, the French army retreated to Jaffa, where their military hospitals had been established. Upon the
27th, Buonaparte was under the necessity of continuing his retreat, and
such of the patients as were convalescent were sent forward on the road
to Egypt. Their disease was the plague, and to carry them onward, seemed
to threaten the army with infection; while to leave them behind, was abandoning them to the cruelty of the Turks, by whom all stragglers and prisoners were cruelly murdered, often with protracted torture. It was on this
occasion that Buonaparte submitted to Desgenettes, chief of the medical
staff, the propriety of ending the victims' misery by a dose of opium. The
physician answered, with the heroism belonging to his profession, that his
art taught him how to cure men, not to kill them.

A rear-guard was left to protect these unhappy men; and the English
found some of them alive, who, if Desgenettes had been more compliant,
would have been poisoned. If Buonaparte was guilty of entertaining such
a purpose, whether entertained from indifference to human life, or from
wild and misdirected ideas of humanity, he met an appropriate punishment in the general belief which long subsisted, that the deed had been
actually carried into execution, not in the persons of a few expiring

wretches, but upon several hundred men. Miot says the report was current in the French army – Sir Robert Wilson found it credited among their officers, when they became the English prisoners – and Count Las Cases admits it was generally believed by the soldiers. But though popular credulity eagerly receives whatever stories are marked by the horrible and wonderful, history, on the contrary, demands direct evidence, and the existence of powerful motives for whatever is beyond the ordinary bounds of credibility. The poisoning of 500 or 600 men is neither easily managed nor easily concealed and why should the French leader have had recourse to it, since, like many a retreating general before him, he had only to leave the patients for whom he had not the means of transportation? Had such a horrible expedient been had recourse to, it could not have escaped the knowledge of Sir Sidney Smith, who would not have failed to give the horrid fact publicity. But though he mentions various complaints which the prisoners made against their general, and though he states himself to have found seven men alive in the hospitals at Jaffa, (being apparently the very persons whom it had been proposed to despatch by opium,) he says not a word of what he would doubtless have told not unwillingly. Neither, among the numerous persons to whom the truth must be known, has anyone come forward since Buonaparte's fall, who could give the least evidence to authenticate the report otherwise than as a rumour, that had sprung out of the unjustifiable proposal which had indeed been made but never acted upon. The same patient and impartial investigation, therefore, which compels us to record that the massacre of the Turkish prisoners in cold blood is fully proved, induces us to declare, that the poisoning of the sick at Jaffa has been affirmed without sufficient evidence.

Buonaparte left Jaffa on the 28th May, and upon the 14th June re-entered Cairo. Three or four weeks after, Murad Bey, re-entering Upper Egypt with his Mamelukes and allies, descended the Nile in two bodies, one occupying each bank of the river. Ibrahim Bey, formerly his partner in the government of Egypt, made a corresponding movement towards the frontiers of Syria, as if to communicate with the right-hand division of Murad's army. La Grange was despatched against the Mamelukes who occupied the right bank, while Murat marched against those who, under the bey himself, were descending the Nile. The French were entertained at the idea of the two Murats, as they termed them, from the similarity of their names, encountering each other; but the Mameluke Murad retreated before *Le Beau Sabreur.*

Meantime, the cause of this incursion was explained by the appearance of a Turkish fleet off Alexandria, who disembarked 18,000 men at Aboukir. This Turkish army possessed themselves of the fort, and proceeded to fortify themselves, expecting the arrival of the Mamelukes, according to the plan for expelling the French from Egypt. This news reached Buonaparte near the Pyramids, to which he had advanced, to ensure the destruction of Murad Bey. The arrival of the Turks instantly recalled him to Alexandria, whence he marched to Aboukir. He joined his army, which had assembled from all points within a short distance of the Turkish camp, and was employed late in the night making preparations for the battle on the next morning. Murat was alone with Buonaparte, when the last suddenly made the oracular declaration, "Go how it will, this battle will decide the fate of the world." "The fate of this army, at least," replied Murat, who did not comprehend Buonaparte's secret meaning. "But the Turks are without horse, and if ever infantry were charged to the teeth by cavalry, they shall be so charged to-morrow by mine." Napoleon, however, referred not to Egypt alone, but to Europe; to which he probably already meditated an unexpected return, which must have been prevented had he not succeeded in obtaining the most complete triumph over the Turks.

In their first attack the French were eminently successful, and pursued the fugitive Turks to their entrenchments, doing great execution. But when the batteries opened upon them from the trenches, while they were at the same time exposed to the fire from the gun-boats in the bay, their impetuosity was checked, and the Turks sallying out upon them with their muskets slung at their backs, made such havoc among the French with their sabres, poniards, and pistols, as compelled them to retreat in their turn. The advantage was lost by the eagerness of the barbarians to possess themselves of the heads of their fallen enemies, for which they received a certain reward. They threw themselves confusedly out of the entrenchments to obtain these bloody testimonials, and were in considerable disorder, when the French suddenly rallied, charged them with great fury, drove them back into the works, and scaled the ramparts along with them.

Murat had made good his promise of the preceding evening, and had been ever in the front of the battle. When the French line surmounted the entrenchments, he formed a column which reversed the position of the Turks, and pressing them with the bayonet, threw them into utter and inextricable confusion. Fired upon and attacked on every point, they became, instead of an army, a confused rabble, who, in the impetuosity of animal terror, threw themselves by hundreds and by thousands into the sea, which at once seemed covered with turbans. It was no longer a battle, but a massacre; and it was only when wearied with slaughter that quarter was given to about 6000 men; the rest of the Turkish army, originally consisting of 18,000, perished on the field or in the waves.

This splendid and most decisive victory of Aboukir concluded Napoleon's career in the East. It was imperiously necessary, ere he could have ventured to quit the command of his army, with the hope of preserving his credit with the public; and it enabled him to plead that he left Egypt for the time in absolute security. His military views had, indeed, been uniformly successful; and Egypt was under the dominion of France as completely as the sword could subject it. For two years afterwards, like the strong man in the parable, they kept the house which they had won, until in there came a stronger one, by whom they were finally and forcibly expelled.

But, the situation of Buonaparte no longer permitted him those brilliant and immense prospects, in which his imagination loved to luxuriate. His troops were considerably weakened, and the miscarriage at Acre dwelt on the recollection of the survivors. The march upon Constantinople was now an impossibility – that to India an empty dream. To establish a French colony in Egypt, of which Buonaparte sometimes talked, and to restore the Indian traffic to the shores of the Red Sea, thus sapping British prosperity in India, was a work for the time of peace, when the necessary communication was not impeded by the naval superiority of England.

It follows, that if he remained in Egypt, his residence there must have resembled the situation of a governor in a large city, threatened indeed, but as yet in no danger of being besieged, where the only fame which can be acquired is that due to prudent and patient vigilance. This would be a post which no young or ambitious soldier would covet, providing he had the choice of being engaged in more active service. On the other hand, there opened a scene of ambition in France, which permitted an almost boundless extent of hopes and wishes. Thus, Napoleon had the choice either of becoming a candidate for one of the greatest prizes which the world afforded – the supreme authority in that fine country – or of remaining the governor of a defensive army in Egypt, waiting the arrival of some new invaders to dispute his conquest with him. Had he chosen this latter line of conduct, he might have soon found himself the vassal of Moreau, or some other military adventurer, who, venturing on the course from which he had himself withdrawn, had attained to the government of France, and might soon have been issuing orders from the Luxembourg or the Tuileries to General Buonaparte.

Admiral Gantheaume, who had been with the army ever since the destruction of the fleet, received the general's orders to make ready for sea, with all possible despatch, two frigates then lying in the harbour of Alexandria. Meantime, determined to preserve his credit with the Institute, and to bring evidence of what he had done for the cause of science, Buonaparte commanded Mongé, and the accomplished Denon, who became its historian, with Berthollet, to prepare to accompany him to Alexandria. Of military chiefs, he selected the Generals Berthier, Murat, Lannes, Marmont, Desaix, Andréossy, and Bessieres, the best and most attached of his officers. He left Cairo as soon as he heard the frigates were ready, making a visit to the Delta the pretext of his tour. Kleber and Menou, whom he meant to leave first and second in command, were appointed to meet him at Alexandria.

The general embarked, from an unfrequented part of the beach, on the 22nd August. Menou came to Denon and others, who had attended the rendezvous without knowing exactly its purpose, and informed them with agitation, that Buonaparte waited for them. They followed, as in a dream; but Denon had already secured that mass of measurements, drawings, manuscripts, and objects of antiquarian and scientific curiosity, which afterwards enabled him to complete the splendid work, which now contains almost the only permanent or useful fruits of the memorable expedition to Egypt.

To avoid the English cruisers, the vessels coasted the shores of Africa, and the wind was so contrary, that they made but 100 leagues in 20 days.

During this time, Buonaparte studied alternately the Bible and the Koran; more solicitous, it seemed, about the history of the countries which he had left behind, than the part which he was to play in that to which he was hastening. On the 9th October, at ten in the morning, he on whose fate the world so long seemed to depend, landed at St. Rapheau, near Fréjus. He had departed at the head of a powerful fleet, and a victorious army, on an expedition designed to alter the destinies of the most ancient nations of the world. The result had been far from commensurate to the means employed. The fleet had perished – the army was blockaded in a distant province, when their arms were most necessary at home. He returned clandestinely, and almost alone; yet Providence designed that, in this apparently deserted condition, he should be the instrument of more extensive and more astonishing changes, than the efforts of the greatest conquerors had ever before been able to effect upon the civilised world.

CHAPTER XV

When Napoleon accepted what was to be considered as a doom of honourable banishment, in the command of the Egyptian expedition, he answered to those friends who advised him rather to stay and assert a pre-eminent station in the government, "that the fruit was not ripe." The seventeen months, or thereabouts, of his absence had done much to complete the maturity. The French Government had ceased to be invariably victorious, and had suffered internal changes, which, instead of restoring the national confidence, had only induced a general expectation of some further and decisive revolution, that should forever overthrow the Directorial system.

When Buonaparte sailed for Egypt, he left France at peace with Austria, and negotiations proceeding, which no one doubted would settle on a pacific footing the affairs of Germany. England alone remained hostile to France; but the former being victorious on the sea, and the latter upon the land, it seemed as if the war must languish and die of itself, unless there had been a third element, of which the rivals might have disputed the possession. But, though the interests of France peremptorily demanded peace, her rulers, feeling that their own tottering condition would be rendered still more precarious by the disbanding of their numerous armies, resolved to continue the war in a new quarter.

The Directory invaded 'unoffending' Switzerland, annexed Turin, founded the Roman Republic and managed to conquer Naples. Russia was subsequently drawn into the war on Austria's side. The French were then expelled from Italy by the allies, who made significant gains on the Rhine and in Switzerland. The Directory's military failures encouraged factions within and without government to plot its downfall.

But as if the calamities of France had attained their height of tide, affairs began all of a sudden to assume a more favourable aspect. The success of General Brune in Holland against the Anglo-Russian army, had obliged the invaders of Holland to retreat. A dispute, or misunderstanding, having occurred between the Emperors of Austria and Russia, the Archduke Charles withdrew a great part of his army from the line of the Limmat, which was taken up by the Russians under Korsakow. Massena took the advantage of this imprudent step, crossed the Limmat, and defeated Korsakow, whilst the formidable Suwarrow, who had already advanced to communicate with that general, found his right flank uncovered by his defeat, and had the greatest difficulty in executing a retrograde movement.

The news of these successes induced the Republicans to defer their attack upon the moderate party; and on so nice a point do the greatest events hang, that had a longer period intervened between these victories and the arrival of Buonaparte, it is most probable that he would have found the situation of military chief of the approaching revolution filled up by some one of those generals. But he landed at the happy crisis, when the presence of a chief of first-rate talents was indispensable, and when no favourite name had yet been found, to fill the public voice with half such loud acclaim as his own.

*C*HAPTER XVI

Buonaparte had caused himself to be preceded by an account of his cam-

paigns in Africa, and Asia, in which the splendid victory over the Turks at
Aboukir enabled him to gloss over his bad success in Syria, the total loss
of his fleet, and the danger of Malta, which was closely besieged by the
English. Still, however, these despatches could never have led anyone to
expect the sudden return of a general engaged on a foreign service of the
utmost importance, who, without having a better reason than his own
opinion that his talents were more essential to his country in France than
in Egypt, left his army to its fate, and came, without either order or permission from his government, to volunteer his services where they were
not expected, or perhaps wished for. Another in the same circumstances,
or perhaps the same general at another period of the Revolution, would
have been received by the public with alienated favour, and by the government with severe inquiry, if not with denunciation.

On the contrary, such was the general reliance on the talents of
Buonaparte, that, delighted to see him arrive, no one thought of asking
wherefore, or by whose authority he had returned. He was received like a
victorious monarch re-entering his dominions. Bells were everywhere
rung, illuminations made, a delirium of joy agitated the public mind, and
the messenger who carried the news of his disembarkation to Paris, was
received as if he had brought news of a battle gained. The members of
Government, it must be supposed, felt alarm and anxiety, which they
endeavoured to conceal under the appearance of sharing in the general
joy. The arrival of a person so influential by his fame, so decided in his
character, engaged with no faction, and pledged to no political system,
was likely to give victory to one or the other party who were contending
for superiority, as he should himself determine. The eyes of all men were
upon Napoleon, while his reserved and retired mode of life prevented any
accurate anticipation being formed of the part which he was likely to take.
While both parties might hope for his participation and succour, they
courted him as the arbiter, whose decision was likely to have most influence.

Napoleon, meanwhile, seemed to give his exclusive attention to literature, and, having exchanged the usual visits of form with ministers, he was
more frequently to be found at the Institute, or discussing with men of
letters, the information which he had acquired in Egypt on science and
antiquities, than in the haunts of politicians, or the society of the leaders

of either party. Neither was he to be seen at the places of popular resort: he went into no general company, seldom attended the theatres, and, when he did, took his seat in a private box. To the military, his conduct seemed equally reserved – he held no levees, and attended no reviews. While all ranks contended in offering their tribute of applause, he turned in silence from receiving them.

In all this there was deep policy. No one knew better how much popular applause depends on the gloss of novelty, and how great is the difference in public estimation, betwixt him who appears to hunt and court acclamations, and the wiser and more dignified favourite of the multitude. Yet under this apparently indifferent demeanour, Napoleon was in secret employed in collecting all the information necessary concerning the purposes and the powers of the various parties in the state. The violent Republicans, who possessed the majority in the Council of five hundred, made advances to him; and the generals Jourdan, Augereau, and Bernadotte, offered to place him at the head of that party, provided he would maintain the democratic constitution of the year three. In uniting with this active and violent party, Buonaparte saw every chance of instant and immediate success; but, by succeeding in the outset, he would probably have marred the further projects of ambition which he nourished. Military leaders at the head of a party so furious as the Republicans, could not have been thrown aside without danger: and it being unquestionably the ultimate intention of Buonaparte to usurp the supreme power, it was most natural for him to seek adherents among those, who, though differing concerning the kind of government which should be finally established, concurred in desiring a change from the republican model.

A union with Sièyes, and the party whom he influenced, promised greater advantages. Under this speculative politician were united for the time all who, though differing in other points, joined in desiring a final change from a revolutionary to a moderate and efficient government, bearing something of a monarchical character. Their number rendered this party powerful. In the Directory it was espoused by Sièyes and Ducos; it possessed a large majority in the Council of Ancients, and a respectable minority in that of the Five Hundred. The greater part of the middling classes throughout France embraced with more or less zeal the principles of moderation; and agreed that an executive government of some strength was necessary to save them from the evils of revolutionary movements. Thus Buonaparte saw himself encouraged to hope for victory over the existing government and the Republicans by the united strength of the Moderates of every class, whilst their difference in opinion concerning the ultimate measures to be adopted, afforded him the best opportunity of advancing, during the competition, his own pretensions to the larger share of the spoil.

Napoleon communicated with Siêyes, upon the understanding that he was to be raised to the principal administration of affairs; that the constitution of the year Three, which he himself had once pronounced "the masterpiece of legislation, which had abolished the errors of eighteen centuries," was to be done away; and that a constitution was to be adopted in its stead, of which he knew nothing more, than that it was ready drawn up, and lay in the portfolio of Siêyes. No doubt, the general mentally reserved the right of altering and adjusting it as it should best suit his own views. When these preliminaries had been adjusted, it was agreed that it should be executed between the 15th and 20th Brumaire.

A sufficient military force was next to be provided; and this was not difficult, for the reputation of Buonaparte ensured the conspirators unlimited influence among the soldiery. Three regiments of dragoons were enthusiastically petitioning for the honour of being reviewed by Napoleon. The adherence of these troops might be counted upon. The officers of the garrison of Paris were desirous to pay their respects to him; so were the forty adjutants of the national guard, whom he himself had appointed when general of the troops in the interior. Many other officers desired to see the celebrated general, that they might express their devotion to his person, and adherence to his fortunes. All these introductions had been artfully postponed. Two men of more renowned name, Moreau and Macdonald, had made tenders of service to Buonaparte. These both favoured the moderate party, and had no suspicion of the ultimate design of Napoleon or the final result of his undertaking. A final resolution on 15th Brumaire determined the 18th [9th November] for the attempt. The secret was well kept; yet being unavoidably entrusted to many persons, some floating and vague rumours did get abroad, and gave alarm.

Meanwhile, all the generals and officers whom we have named, were invited to repair to Napoleon's house at six o'clock on the morning of the 18th Brumaire, and the three regiments of cavalry already mentioned were appointed to be ready and mounted in the Champs Elysées, to receive the honour of being reviewed by Buonaparte. As an excuse for assigning so unusual an hour of rendezvous, it is said that the general was obliged to set out upon a journey. Many officers, however, understood or guessed what was to be done, and came armed with pistols as well as with swords. Bernadotte, unacquainted with the project, and attached to the Republican faction, was brought to Buonaparte's house by his brother Joseph.

The surprise of some, and the anxious curiosity of all, may be supposed, when they found a military levee so numerous and so brilliant assembled at a house incapable of containing half of them. Buonaparte was obliged to receive them in the open air.

Early as Buonaparte's levee had taken place, the Council of Ancients, secretly and hastily assembled, had met still earlier. The ears of all were filled by a report, generally circulated, that the Republican party had formed a daring plan for giving a new popular impulse to the government. It was said, that the resolution was taken to connect the two representative bodies into one National Assembly, and invest the powers of government in a Committee of Public Safety, after the model of what was called the Reign of Terror. Circulated hastily, and with such addition to the tale as rumours speedily acquire, the mind of the Council of Ancients was agitated with much fear and anxiety. Cornudet, Lebrun, and Fargues, made glowing speeches to the Assembly, in which the terror that their language inspired was rendered greater by the mysterious and indefinite manner in which they expressed themselves. They spoke of personal danger – of being overawed in their deliberations – of the fall of liberty, and of the approaching destruction of the Republic. "You have but an instant to save France," said Cornudet; "permit it to pass away, and the country will be a mere carcass, disputed by the vultures, whose prey it must become." Though the charge of conspiracy was not distinctly defined, the measures recommended to defeat it were sufficiently decisive.

By the 102nd, 103rd and 104th articles of the Constitution, it was provided, that the Council of Ancients might alter the place where the legislative bodies meet, and convoke them elsewhere. By one edict the sittings of the two councils were removed to St. Cloud; by another, the

Council delegated to General Buonaparte full power to see this measure carried into effect, and vested him for that purpose with the military command of the department. A state messenger was sent to communicate to the general these important measures, and require his presence in the Council of Ancients. A few words determined the numerous body of officers to concur with him without scruple.

When Buonaparte sallied forth on horseback, and at the head of such a gallant cavalcade of officers, his first movement was to assume the command of the three regiments of cavalry, drawn up in the Champs Elysées, and to lead them to the Tuileries, where the Council of Ancients expected him. He entered their hall surrounded by his military staff, and by those other generals, whose name carried the memory of so many victories. "You are the wisdom of the nation," he said to the Council: "At this crisis it belongs to you to point out the measures which may save the country. I come, surrounded by the generals of the Republic, to promise you their support. I name Lefebvre my lieutenant. Let us not lose time in looking for precedents. Nothing in history ever resembled the end of the eighteenth century – nothing in the eighteenth century resembled this moment. Your wisdom has devised the necessary measure, our arms shall put it into execution." He announced to the military the will of the Council, and the command with which they had entrusted him; and it was received with loud shouts.

In the meanwhile the three directors, Barras, Gohier, and Moulins, who were not in the secret of the morning, began too late to take the alarm. Moulins proposed to send a battalion to surround the house of Buonaparte, and make prisoner the general, and whomsoever else they found there. But they had no longer the least influence over the soldiery, and had the mortification to see their own personal guard, when summoned by an aide-de-camp of Buonaparte, march away to join the forces which he commanded, and leave them defenceless.

Barras sent his secretary, Rottot, to expostulate with Buonaparte. The general received him with great haughtiness, and publicly upbraided him with the reverses of the country; not in the tone of an ordinary citizen, possessing but his own individual interest in the fate of a great nation, but like a prince, who, returning from a distant expedition, finds that in his absence his deputies have abused their trust, and misruled his dominions.

"What have you done," he said, "for that fine France, which I left you in such a brilliant condition? I left you peace, I have found war – I left you the wealth of Italy, I have found taxation and misery. Where are the 100,000 Frenchmen whom I have known? – all of them my companions in glory? – They are dead."

Barras, overwhelmed and stunned, and afraid, perhaps, of impeachment for his alleged peculations, belied the courage which he was once supposed to possess, and sent in his resignation. His colleagues, Gohier and Moulins also resigned; Sièyes and Ducos had already set the example; and thus, the whole Constitutional Executive Council was dissolved while the real power was vested in Buonaparte's single person. Cambacérès, minister of justice, Fouché, minister of police, with all the rest of the administration, acknowledged his authority; and he was thus placed in full possession as well of the civil as of the military power.

The Council of Five Hundred, or rather the Republican majority of that body, showed a more stubborn temper; and if, instead of resigning, Barras, Gohier, and Moulins, had united themselves to its leaders, they might perhaps have given trouble to Buonaparte. This hostile Council only met at ten o'clock on that day, when they received, to their surprise, the message intimating that the Council of Ancients had changed the place of meeting from Paris to St. Cloud; and thus removed their debates from the neighbourhood of the populace, over whom the old Jacobinical principles might have retained influence. The laws as they stood afforded the young Council no means of evading compliance, and they accordingly adjourned to meet the next day at St. Cloud, with unabated resolution to maintain the democratic part of the constitution.

The contending parties held counsel all the evening and deep into the night to prepare for the final contest. Sièyes advised, that forty leaders of the opposition should be arrested; but Buonaparte esteemed himself strong enough to obtain a decisive victory, without resorting to any such obnoxious violence. They adjusted their plan of operations in both Councils, and agreed that the government to be established should be provisionally entrusted to three Consuls, Buonaparte, Sièyes, and Ducos. Proper arrangements were made of the armed force at St. Cloud; and the command was confided to the zeal and fidelity of Murat. Buonaparte used some interest to prevent Bernadotte, Jourdan, and Augereau, from attending at St. Cloud the next day, as he did not expect them to take his part in the approaching crisis. The last of these seemed rather hurt at the want of confidence which this caution implied, and said, "What, general! Dare you not trust your own little Augereau?" He went to St. Cloud accordingly.

In the Council of Ancients, the Modérés, having the majority, were prepared to carry forward and complete their measures for a change of government and constitution. But the minority, having rallied after the surprise of the preceding day, were neither silent nor passive. The Commission of Inspectors, whose duty it was to convene the Council, were inculpated severely for having omitted to give information to several leading members of the minority, of the extraordinary convocation which took place at such an unwonted hour on the morning preceding. The legality of the transference of the legislative bodies to St. Cloud was also challenged. A sharp debate took place, which was terminated by the appearance of Napoleon, who entered the hall, and harangued the members by permission of the president. "Citizen representatives," said he, "you are placed upon a volcano. Let me tell you the truth with the frankness of a soldier. I was remaining tranquil with my family, when the commands of the Council of Ancients called me to arms. I collected my brave military companions, and brought forward the arms of the country in obedience to you who are the head. We are rewarded with calumny – they compare me to Caesar – to Cromwell. Had I desired to usurp the supreme authority, I have had opportunities to do so before now. But I swear to you the country has not a more disinterested patriot. We are surrounded by dangers and by civil war. Let us not hazard the loss of those advantages for which we have made such sacrifices – Liberty and Equality."

"And the Constitution!" exclaimed Linglet, a democratic member, interrupting a speech which seemed to be designedly vague and inexplicit.

"The Constitution!" answered Buonaparte, giving way to a more natural expression of his feelings, and avowing his object more clearly than he had yet dared to do – "It was violated on the eighteenth Fructidor – violated on the twenty-second Floreal – violated on the thirtieth Prairial. All parties have invoked it – all have disregarded it in turn. It can be no longer a means of safety to anyone, since it obtains the respect of no one. Since we cannot preserve the Constitution, let us at least save Liberty and

Equality, the foundations on which it is erected." He went on to assure them, that for the safety of the Republic he relied only on the wisdom and power of the Council of Ancients, since in the Council of Five Hundred were found those men who desired to bring back the Convention, with its revolutionary committees, its scaffolds, its popular insurrections. "But I," he said, "will save you from such horrors – I and my brave comrades at arms, whose swords and caps I see at the door of the hall; and if any hired orator shall talk of outlawry, I will appeal to the valour of my comrades, with whom I have fought and conquered for liberty."

The Assembly invited the general to detail the particulars of the conspiracy, but he confined himself to a reference to the testimony of Sièyes and Ducos; and again reiterating that the Constitution could not save the country, and inviting the Council of Ancients to adopt some course which might enable them to do so, he left them, amid cries of "Vive Buonaparte!" loudly echoed by the military in the courtyard, to try the effect of his eloquence on the more unmanageable Council of Five Hundred.

The deputies of the younger Council having found the place designed for their meeting filled with workmen, were for some time in a situation which seemed to resemble the predicament of the National Assembly at Versailles, when they took refuge in a tennis-court. The recollection was of such a nature as inflamed their resolution, and they entered the Orangerie, when at length admitted, in no good humour with the Council of Ancients, or with Buonaparte. Proposals of accommodation had been circulated among them ineffectually. They would have admitted Buonaparte into the Directory, but refused to consent to any radical change in the constitution.

The debate of the day, remarkable as the last in which the Republican party enjoyed the full freedom of speech in France, was opened on 19th Brumaire, at two o'clock, Lucien Buonaparte being president. Gaudin, a member of the moderate party, began by moving, that a committee of seven members should be formed, to report upon the state of the Republic; and that measures should be taken for opening a correspondence with the Council of Ancients. He was interrupted by exclamations and clamour on the part of the majority.

"The Constitution! The Constitution or Death!" was echoed and re-echoed on every side. "Bayonets frighten us not," said Delbrel; "we are free men." – "Down with the Dictatorship – no Dictators!" cried other members.

Lucien in vain endeavoured to restore order. Gaudin was dragged from the tribune; the voice of other Moderates was overpowered by clamour – never had the party of democracy shown itself fiercer or more tenacious than when about to receive the death-blow.

"Let us swear to preserve the Constitution of the year Three!" exclaimed Delbrel; and the applause which followed was so general, that it silenced all resistance. Even the members of the moderate party – nay, Lucien Buonaparte himself were compelled to take the oath of fidelity to the Constitution, which they were leagued to destroy.

In the midst of this fermentation, the letter containing the resignation of Barras was read, and received with marks of contempt, as the act of a soldier deserting his post in the time of danger. The moderate party seemed overpowered and on the point of coalescing with the majority of the Council, when the clash of arms was heard at the entrance. All eyes were turned to that quarter. Bayonets, drawn sabres, the plumed hats of general officers, and the caps of grenadiers, were visible without, while Napoleon entered the Orangerie, attended by four grenadiers belonging to the constitutional guard. The soldiers remained at the bottom of the hall, while he advanced with a measured step and uncovered, about one-third up the room.

He was received with loud "What! Drawn weapons, armed men, soldiers in the sanctuary of the laws!" exclaimed the members, whose courage seemed to rise against the display of force with which they were menaced. All the deputies arose, some rushed on Buonaparte, and seized him by the collar; others called out – "Outlawry – outlawry – let him be proclaimed a traitor!" It is said that Arena, a native of Corsica, aimed a dagger at his breast, which was only averted by the interposition of one of the grenadiers. The fact seems extremely doubtful, though it is certain that Buonaparte was seized by two or three members, while others exclaimed, "Was it for this you gained so many victories?" and loaded him with reproaches. At this crisis a party of grenadiers rushed into the hall with drawn swords; and extricating Buonaparte from the deputies, bore him off in their arms breathless with the scuffle.

The Council remained in the highest state of commotion, accusing Buonaparte of having usurped the supreme authority, calling for a sentence of outlawry, or demanding that he should be brought to the bar. "Can you ask me to put the outlawry of my own brother to the vote?" said Lucien. But this appeal to his personal situation and feelings made no impression upon the Assembly, who continued to demand the question. At length Lucien flung on the desk his hat, scarf, and other parts of his official dress. "Let me be rather heard," he said, "as the advocate of him whom you falsely and rashly accuse." But this request only added to the tumult. At this moment a small body of grenadiers, sent by Napoleon to his brother's assistance, marched into the hall. They were at first received with applause; for the Council did not doubt that they were deserting their general to range themselves on the side of the deputies. Their appearance was but momentary – they instantly left the hall, carrying Lucien in the centre of the detachment.

Matters were now come to extremity on either side. The Council, thrown into the greatest disorder by these repeated military incursions, remained in violent agitation, furious against Buonaparte, but without the calmness necessary to adopt decisive measures. Meantime, the sight of Napoleon, almost breathless, and bearing marks of personal violence, excited to the highest the indignation of the military. In broken words he told them, that when he wished to show them the road to lead the country to victory and fame, "they had answered him with daggers."

Cries of resentment arose from the soldiery. Lucien, who seconded his brother admirably, or rather who led the way in this perilous adventure, mounted on horseback instantly, and called out, in a voice naturally deep and sonorous, "General, and you, soldiers! the President of the Council of Five Hundred proclaims to you, that factious men, with drawn daggers, have interrupted the deliberations of the Assembly. He authorises you to employ force against these disturbers – The Assembly of Five Hundred is dissolved!"

Murat, deputed by Buonaparte to execute the commands of Lucien, entered the Orangerie with drums beating, at the head of a detachment with fixed bayonets. He summoned the deputies to disperse on their peril, while an officer of the constitutional guard called out, he could be no longer answerable for their safety. Cries of fear became now mingled with vociferations of rage, execrations of abhorrence, and shouts of *Vive la République.* An officer mounted the president's seat, and summoned the representatives to retire. "The General" said he, "has given orders." Some of the deputies and spectators began now to leave the hall; the greater part continued firm, and sustained the shouts by which they reprobated this military intrusion. The drums at length struck up and drowned further remonstrance.

"Forward, grenadiers," said the officer who commanded the party. They levelled their muskets, and advanced as if to the charge. The deputies seem hitherto to have retained a lingering hope that their persons would be regarded as inviolable. They now fled on all sides, most of them jumping from the windows of the Orangerie, and leaving behind them their official caps, scarves, and gowns. In a very few minutes the apartments were entirely clear; and thus terminated the last democratic assembly of France.

Both councils adjourned till the 19th February, 1800, after each had devolved their powers upon a committee of 25 persons, who were instructed to prepare a civil code against the meeting of the legislative bodies. A provisional consular government was appointed, consisting of Buonaparte, Siêyes, and Roger Ducos. The victory, therefore, of the 18th and 19th Brumaire, was, by dint of sword and bayonet, completely secured. It remained for the conquerors to consider the uses which were to be made of it.

CHAPTER XVII

The victory obtained over the Directory and the democrats was generally acceptable to the French nation. The feverish desire of liberty, which had been the characteristic of all descriptions of persons in the year 1792, was quenched by the blood shed during the Reign of Terror; and even just and liberal ideas of freedom had so far fallen into disrepute, from their resemblance to those which had been used as a pretext for the disgusting cruelties perpetrated at that terrible period, that they excited from association a kind of loathing as well as dread. The great mass of the nation sought no longer guarantees for metaphysical rights, but, broken down by suffering, desired repose, and were willing to submit to any government which promised to secure to them the ordinary benefits of civilisation.

Buonaparte and Sièyes – for, though only during a brief space, they may still be regarded as joint authorities – were enabled to profit by this general acquiescence, in many important particulars. It put in their power to dispense with the necessity of pursuing and crushing their scattered adversaries; and the French saw a revolution effected in their system, and that by military force, in which not a drop of blood was spilt. Yet lists of proscription were prepared; and without previous trial or legal sentence, fifty-nine of those who had chiefly opposed the new Consulate on the 18th and 19th Brumaire were condemned to deportation by the sole *fiat* of the consuls. Sièyes is said to have suggested this unjust and arbitrary measure, which, bearing a colour of revenge and persecution, was highly unpopular. It was not carried into execution. Exceptions were at first made in favour of such of the condemned persons disposed to be tractable; and at length the sentence was altogether dispensed with, and the more obnoxious partisans of democracy were only placed under the superintendence of the police. This conduct showed at once conscious strength, and a spirit of clemency, which no attributes can contribute more to the popularity of a new government; since the spirit of the opposition, deprived of hope of success, and yet not urged on by despair, gradually becomes disposed to sink into acquiescence. The democrats, or, as they were now termed, the anarchists, became intimidated, or cooled in their zeal; and only a few of the more enthusiastic continued yet to avow those principles.

Two of the most oppressive measures of the directors were repealed without delay. The first referred to the finances, which were found in a state of ruinous exhaustion, and were only maintained by a system of compulsory and progressive loans, according to rates of assessment on the property of the citizens. The new minister of finance, Gaudin, would not even go to bed, or sleep a single night, until he had produced a substitute for this ruinous resource, for which he levied an additional rise of 25% on all contributions, direct and indirect, which produced a large sum. He carried order and regularity into all the departments of finance, improved the collection and income of the funds of the Republic, and

inspired so much confidence by the moderation and success of his measures, that credit began to revive, and several loans were attained on easy
terms. The repeal of the law of hostages was a measure equally popular.
This cruel enactment, which rendered the aged and weak, unprotected
females, and helpless children of emigrants, or armed royalists, responsible for the actions of their relatives, was immediately mitigated. Couriers
were despatched to open the prisons; and this act of justice and humanity was hailed as a pledge of returning moderation and liberality.

Important measures were also taken for tranquillising the religious discord by which the country had been so long agitated. Buonaparte, who,
had lately professed himself more than half persuaded of the truth of
Mahommed's mission, became now – such was the decree of Providence
– the means of restoring to France the free exercise of the Christian faith.
The churches were restored to public worship; pensions were allowed to
such religious persons as took an oath of fidelity to the government; and
more than 20,000 clergymen, with whom the prisons had been filled, in
consequence of intolerant laws, were set at liberty upon taking the vow.
Public and domestic rites of worship in every form were tolerated and
protected; and the law of the decades was abolished. Even the earthly
relics of Pope Pius VI, who had died at Valence, in exile, were not neglected, but received the rites of sepulture with the solemnity due to his
high office, by command of Buonaparte, who had first shaken the Papal
authority.

The part taken by Cambacérès, the minister of justice, in Brumaire,
had been agreeable to Buonaparte; and his moderation now aided him in
the lenient measures which he had determined to adopt. He was a good
lawyer, and a man of sense and information, and under his administration
means were taken to relax the severity of the laws against the emigrants.
Nine of them, noblemen of the most ancient families in France, had been
thrown on the coast near Calais by shipwreck, and the directors had meditated bringing to trial those whom the winds and waves had spared, as
fallen under the class of emigrants returned to France without permission, against whom the laws denounced the penalty of death. Buonaparte
more liberally considered their being found within the prohibited territory, as an act, not of violation, but of inevitable necessity, and they were
dismissed accordingly. From the same spirit of politic clemency, La

Fayette, Latour Maubourg and others, who, although revolutionists, had been expelled from France for not carrying their principles of freedom sufficiently high and far, were permitted to return to their native country.

Napoleon showed no less talent in closing the wounds of internal war. The Chouans had disturbed the western provinces; but the despair of pardon, which drove so many malcontents to their standard, began to subside, and the liberal and accommodating measures adopted by the new Consular government, induced most to make peace with Buonaparte. This they did the more readily, that many of them believed the chief consul intended when the opportunity offered to accomplish the restoration of the Bourbons. Many of the chiefs of the Chouans submitted to him, and afterwards supported his government. Châtillon, Suzannet, d'Autichamp, nobles and chiefs of the Royalist army, submitted at Montluçon, and their reconciliation with the government was sincerely observed by them.

While Buonaparte was thus busied in adopting measures for composing internal discord, and renewing the wasted resources of the country, those discussions were at the same time privately carrying forward, which were to determine by whom and in what way it should be governed. There is little doubt that when Sièyes undertook the revolution of Brumaire, he would have desired for his military assistant a very different character from Buonaparte. Some general would have best suited him who possessed no knowledge beyond that of his profession, and whose ambition would have been contented to accept such share of power as corresponded to his limited views. The wily priest, however, saw that no other coadjutor save Buonaparte could have availed him and was not long of experiencing that Napoleon would not be satisfied with any thing short of the lion's share of the spoil.

At the very first meeting of the consuls, the defection of Roger Ducos to the side of Buonaparte convinced Sièyes, that he would be unable to support those pretensions to the first place in the government. He had reckoned on Ducos's vote; but Ducos saw better where the force and talent of the Consulate reposed, "General," said he to Napoleon, at the first meeting, "the presidency belongs to you as a matter of right." Buonaparte took the chair as a thing of course. In the course of the deliberations, Sièyes had hoped to find that the general's opinions and interference would have been limited to military affairs; whereas, on the contrary, he heard him express distinctly, and support firmly, propositions on policy and finance, religion and jurisprudence. He showed, in short, so little occasion for an independent coadjutor that Siêyes appears from this first interview, to have given up all hope of establishing a separate interest of his own, and to have seen that the Revolution was, from that moment, ended. On his return home, he said to those statesmen with whom he had consulted and acted preceding the eighteenth Brumaire, as Talleyrand, Boulay, Roederer, Cabanis, &c. "Gentlemen, you have a Master – give yourself no further concern about the affairs of the state – Buonaparte can and will manage them all at his own pleasure."

Three Consuls were appointed; the first to hold the sole power of nominating to public offices, and right of determining on public measures; the other two were to be his indispensable counsellors. The first of these offices was designed to bring back the constitution of France to a monarchical system, while the second and third were added to conciliate the Republicans, who were not yet prepared for a retrograde movement. The office of one of these supplementary consuls was offered to Siêyes, but he declined to accept of it, and expressed his wish to retire from public life.

Every species of power was heaped upon the chief consul. He possessed the sole right of nominating counsellors of state, ministers, ambassadors, officers, civil and military, and almost all functionaries. He was to propose all new laws, and take all measures for internal and external defence of the state. He commanded all the forces, of whatever description, superintended all the national relations at home and abroad, and coined the public money. In these high duties he had the advice of his brother consuls, and also of a Council of State. But he was recognised to be independent of them all. The consuls were to be elected for the space of ten years, and to be re-eligible.

The new constitution of France also adopted the Legislative Body and the Tribunate proposed by the Abbé Siêyes. The duty of the Legislative Body was to take into consideration such laws as should be approved by the Tribunate and pass or refuse them by vote, but without any debate, or even an expression of their opinion. The Tribunate, on the contrary, was a deliberative body, to whom the chief consul and his Council of State were to propose such laws as appeared to them desirable. These, when discussed by the Tribunate, and approved of by the assent of the Legislative Body, passed into decrees, and became binding upon the community.

Buonaparte selected exactly as much of the ingenious constitution of Sièyes as was applicable to his own object of acquiring supreme and despotic authority, while he got rid of all, the Tribunate excepted, which contained, directly or indirectly, any check or balance affecting the executive power. But the members of the Tribunate were selected by the Senate, not by the people, whom, except in metaphysical mockery, it could not be said to represent any more than a bottle of distilled liquor can be said to represent the sheaf of grain which it was originally drawn from. What chance was there that, in 100 men so chosen, there should be courage and independence enough found to oppose that primary power, by which, like a steam-engine, the whole constitution was put in motion?

The spirit of France must have been much broken when this arbitrary system was adopted without debate or contradiction. Personal safety was now a principal object with most. They saw no alternative between absolute submission to a military chief of talent and power, and the return to anarchy and new revolutionary excesses. Thus were lost at once the fruits of the virtues, the crimes, the blood, the treasure, the mass of human misery, which, flowing from the Revolution, had agitated France for ten years; and thus, having sacrificed almost all that men hold dear, the rights of humanity themselves included, in order to obtain national liberty, her inhabitants, without having enjoyed rational freedom, or the advantages which it ensures, for a single day, returned to be the vassals of a despotic government, administered by a chief whose right was only in his sword.

CHAPTER XVIII

In availing himself of the privileges he had usurped, the first consul showed a moderation as artful as it was conciliatory. The consular government seemed a general place of refuge and sanctuary to persons of all various opinions, and in all various predicaments. It was only required of them, in return for the safety which it afforded, that they should pay homage to the presiding deity.

So artfully was the system of Buonaparte contrived, that each of the numerous classes of Frenchmen found something in it congenial, providing only he was willing to sacrifice to it the essential part of his political principles. To the Royalist, it restored monarchical forms, a court, and a sovereign – but he must acknowledge that sovereign in Buonaparte. To the churchman, it opened the gates of the temples – promised in course of time a national church – but by the altar must be placed the image of Buonaparte. The Jacobin, dyed double red in murder and massacre, was welcome to safety and security from the aristocratic vengeance which he had so lately dreaded. The regicide was guaranteed against the return of the Bourbons – they who had profited by the Revolution as purchasers of national domains, were ensured against their being resumed. But it was under the implied condition, that not a word was to be mentioned of liberty or equality: the principles for which forfeitures had been made, and revolutionary tribunals erected, were henceforth never to be named. To all these parties, as to others, Buonaparte held out the same hopes under the same conditions. – "All these things will I give you, if you will kneel down and worship me." Shortly afterwards, he was enabled to place before those to whom the choice was submitted, the original temptation in its full extent – a display of the kingdoms of the earth, over which he offered to extend the empire of France, providing always he was himself acknowledged as the object of general obedience, and almost adoration.

The system, as it combined great art with an apparent generosity and liberality, proved eminently successful when subjected to the semblance of a popular vote. The constitution of the year Eight was approved by the suffrages of nearly four million citizens – a more general approbation than any preceding system had been received with. The vote was doubtless a farce in itself, considering how many constitutions had been adopted and sworn to within so short a space; but still the numbers who expressed assent, more than doubling those votes which were obtained by the constitution of 1792 and of the year Three, indicate the superior popularity of Buonaparte's system.

For second and third consuls, Buonaparte chose Cambacérès, a member of the moderate party, with Lebrun, who had formerly co-operated with the Chancellor Maupeou. The former was employed by the chief consul as his organ of communication with the Revolutionists, while Lebrun rendered him the same service with the Royal party; and although, as Madame de Staël observes, they preached very different sermons on the same texts, yet they were both eminently successful in detaching from their original factions many of either class, and uniting them with this third, or government party. In the ministry, Buonaparte acted upon the same principle, selecting and making his own the men whose talents were most distinguished, without reference to their former conduct. Two were particularly distinguished, as men of the most eminent talents, and extensive experience. These were Talleyrand and Fouché. The former, noble by birth, and Bishop of Autun, notwithstanding his high rank in church and state, had been deeply engaged in the Revolution. He had been placed on the list of emigrants, from which his name was erased on the establishment of the Directorial government, under which he became minister of foreign affairs. He resigned that office in the summer preceding 18th Brumaire and Buonaparte, finding him at variance with the Directory, readily passed over some personal grounds of complaint which he had against him, and enlisted in his service a supple and dexterous politician, and an experienced minister.

If the character of Talleyrand bore no strong traces of public virtue or inflexible morality, that of Fouché was marked with still darker shades. He had been dipt in some of the worst transactions of the Terror. In the days of the Directory, he is stated to have profited by the universal peculation which was then practised and to have amassed large sums by shares in contracts and brokerage in the public funds. To atone for the imperfections of a character stained with perfidy, venality, and indifference to human suffering, Fouché brought to Buonaparte's service a devotion, never like to fail the first consul unless his fortunes should happen to change; and a perfect experience with all the weapons of revolutionary war. He had managed under Barras's administration the department of police; and had become better acquainted perhaps than any man in France with all the various parties in that distracted country. Formidable by his extensive knowledge of the revolutionary springs and the address with which he could either put them into motion, or prevent them from operating, Fouché, in the latter part of his life, displayed a species of wisdom which came in place of morality and benevolence.

It was scarcely three months since the President of the Directory had said to the people, on the anniversary of the taking of the Bastille, "Royalty shall never raise its head again." Yet now the national oath, expressing hatred to royalty, was annulled, under the pretext that the Republic, being universally acknowledged, had no occasion for the guard of such disclamations. In like manner, the public observance of the day on which Louis XVI had suffered decapitation, was formally abolished. Buonaparte, declining to pass a judgment on the action as just, politic, or useful, pronounced that, in any event, it could only be regarded as a national calamity, and was therefore in a moral, as well as a political sense, an unfit epoch for festive celebration.

The first measures of Buonaparte's new government had already gone some length in restoring domestic quiet; but he was well aware that the external relations of France must be attended to without delay and that the French expected from him either the conclusion of an honourable peace, or the restoration of victory to their national banners. It was necessary, too, that advances towards peace should in the first place be made, in order, if they were unsuccessful, that the national spirit should be excited, which might reconcile the French to the renewal of the war with fresh energy.

Buonaparte addressed the King of England in a personal epistle. This letter[ii] intimates Buonaparte's affectation of superiority to the usual forms of diplomacy and his pretence to a character determined to emancipate itself from rules only designed for mere ordinary men. But the manner of the address was in bad taste and ill calculated to obtain credit for his being sincere in the proposal of peace. The answer transmitted by Lord Grenville to the Minister for Foreign Affairs dwelt on the aggressions of France, declared that the restoration of the Bourbons would have been the best security for their sincerity, but disavowed all right to dictate to France in her internal concerns. Some advances were made to a pacific treaty; and it is probable that England might at that period have obtained the same or better terms than she afterwards got. But the possession of Egypt, which Buonaparte must have insisted on, were it only for his own reputation, was likely to be an insuperable difficulty. The conjuncture also appeared to the English ministers propitious for carrying on the war. Italy had been recovered and the Austrian army, to the number of 140,000, were menacing Savoy, and mustering on the Rhine. Buonaparte, in the check received before Acre, had been found not absolutely invincible. The exploits of Suwarrow over the French were recent, and had been decisive. The state of the interior of France was well known; and it was conceived that, though this successful general had climbed into the seat of supreme power which he found unoccupied, yet that two strong parties, of which the Royalists objected to his person, the Republicans to his form of government, could not fail, the one or other, to deprive him of his influence. The treaty was finally broken off. There may be a difference of opinion in regard to Buonaparte's sincerity in the negotiation, but there can be none as to the reality of his joy at its being defeated. The voice which summoned him to war was that which sounded sweetest in his ears, since it was always followed by exertion and by victory.

Austria's principal force was in Italy, and it was on the Italian frontier that they meditated a grand effort, by which, supported by the British fleet, they proposed to reduce Genoa and penetrate across the Var into Provence, where existed a strong body of Royalists ready to take arms. To execute this plan, Melas was placed at the head of an army of 140,000 men quartered for the winter in Piedmont, and waited but the approach of spring to commence operations. Opposed to them, and occupying the country betwixt Genoa and the Var, lay a French army of 20,000 men; the relics of those who had been defeated in Italy by Suwarrow. They were quartered in a poor country, and the English squadron, which blockaded the coast, was vigilant in preventing any supplies from being sent to them. Distress was therefore considerable, and the troops were in proportion dispirited and disorganised. Whole corps abandoned their position, contrary to orders; and, with drums beating, and colours flying, returned into France. A proclamation from Napoleon was almost alone sufficient to remedy these disorders. He called on the soldiers, and particularly those corps who had formerly distinguished themselves under his command, to remember the confidence he had once placed in them. The scattered troops returned to their duty, as war-horses when dispersed are said to rally and form ranks at the mere sound of the trumpet. Massena was entrusted with the command of the Italian army, which Buonoparte resolved to support in person with the army of reserve.

Napoleon rather surprisingly chose Moreau, his closest rival, to command French forces on the Rhine and carry the war into Germany.

In committing the charge of the campaign upon the Rhine to Moreau, the first consul had reserved for himself the task of bringing back victory to the French standards, on the fields in which he won his earliest laurels. His plan of victory again included a passage of the Alps, as boldly as in 1795, but in a different direction. On both occasions, the Austrians menaced Genoa; but in 1800, Switzerland, formerly neutral, was now as open to French troops as any of their own provinces, and of this Buonaparte determined to avail himself. He was aware of the Austrian plan of taking Genoa and entering Provence; and he formed the daring resolution to put himself at the head of the army of reserve, surmount the line of the Alps, and, descending into Italy, place himself in the rear of the Austrian army, interrupt their communications, coop them up betwixt his own army and that of Massena, and compel them to battle, in a situation where defeat must be destruction. But to accomplish this daring movement, it was necessary to march a whole army over the highest chain of mountains in Europe, by roads which afford but a dangerous passage to the solitary traveller, and through passes where one man can do more to defend, than ten to force their way. Artillery was to be carried through sheep-paths and over precipices impracticable to wheel-carriages; ammunition and baggage were to be transported at the same disadvantages; and provisions were to be conveyed through a country poor in itself, and inhabited by a nation which had every cause to be hostile to France.

The strictest secrecy was necessary, to procure even the opportunity of attempting this audacious plan. It was made as public as possible, by orders, proclamations, and the like, that the first consul was to place himself at the head of the army of reserve, and that it was to assemble at Dijon. Accordingly, a numerous staff was sent, and much apparent hustle took place in assembling there 6000 or 7000 men. These, as the spies of Austria truly reported, were either conscripts, or veterans unfit for service; and caricatures were published of the first consul reviewing troops composed of children and disabled soldiers. When an army so composed was reviewed by the first consul himself with great ceremony, it impressed a general belief that Buonaparte was only endeavouring, by making a show of force, to divert the Austrians from their design upon Genoa, and thus his real purpose was effectually concealed.

*C*HAPTER XIX

On the 6th of May 1800, seeking to renew the fortunes of France, now united with his own, the chief consul left Paris, and, having reviewed the pretended army of reserve at Dijon on the 7th, arrived on the 8th at Geneva. On the 13th, arriving at Lausanne, Buonaparte joined the van of his real army of reserve, which consisted of six effective regiments, commanded by the celebrated Lannes. The whole army, in its various divisions, was now united under the command of Berthier nominally, as general-in-chief, though in reality under that of the first consul himself.

The army made the difficult journey across the Alps, while the Austrians, under Melas, marched eastward, invading Genoa and advancing into the Var. Melas, believing that Napoleon was only at the head of an army of reserve, divided his forces, making his way back into Italy while persisting with the siege of Genoa and leaving an army of observation on the French border. He misjudged Napoleon's intentions entirely and thus allowed him to seize Milan with relative ease.

Buonaparte, fixing his residence in the ducal palace of Milan, employed himself in receiving the deputations of various public bodies and in re-organising the Cisalpine government, while he waited impatiently to be joined by Moncey and his division from Mont Saint Gothard. They arrived at length, but marching more slowly than accorded with the fiery promptitude of the first consul, who was impatient to relieve the blockade of Genoa. He issued a proclamation to his troops in which he described, as the result of the efforts he expected from them, "Cloudless glory and solid peace." On the 9th of June, his armies were again in motion.

Buonaparte resolved to force his passage over the Po and move against the Austrians, who were found to occupy in strength the villages of Casteggio and Montebello. These troops proved to be the greater part of the very army which he expected to find before Genoa and which was commanded by Ott, but which had moved westward, in conformity to the orders of Melas.

General Lannes, who led the vanguard of the French, as usual, was attacked early in the morning of 9th June by a superior force, which he had much difficulty in resisting. The nature of the ground gave advantage to the Austrian cavalry, and the French were barely able to support their charges. At length, the division of Victor came up to support Lannes, and the victory became no longer doubtful, though the Austrians fought most obstinately. The fields being covered with tall crops of grain, and especially of rye, the different bodies were frequently hid until they found themselves at the bayonet's point, without having had any previous opportunity to estimate each other's force; a circumstance which led to much close fighting, and necessarily to much slaughter. At length the Austrians retreated, leaving the field of battle covered with their dead, and above 5000 prisoners in the hands of their enemies.

General Ott rallied the remains of his army under the walls of Tortona. From the prisoners taken at the battle of Montebello, as this action was called, Buonaparte learned, for the first time, of the surrender of Genoa, which apprised him that he was too late for the enterprise which he had meditated.

In the meanwhile, the headquarters of Melas had been removed from Turin, and fixed at Alexandria for the space of two days, so that the first consul was obliged to advance towards them, apprehensive lest the Austrians should escape from him. Both armies were in high spirits, determined to fight, and each confident in their general – the Austrians in the bravery and experience of Melas, the French in the genius and talents of Buonaparte. The immediate stake was the possession of Italy, but it was impossible to guess how many yet more important consequences the event of the day might involve.

Early in the morning the Austrians crossed the Bormida in three columns, by three military bridges, and advanced in the same order. Buonaparte, by several desperate charges of cavalry, endeavoured in vain to arrest the progress of the enemy. His left wing was put completely to flight; his centre was in great disorder, and it was only his right wing, which, by strong support, had been enabled to stand their ground. At this time, and when victory seemed within his grasp, the strength of General Melas, eighty years old, and who had been many hours on horseback, failed entirely; and he was obliged to leave the field, committing to General Zach the charge of completing a victory which appeared to be already gained.

The French soldier understands better perhaps than any other in the world the art of rallying, after having been dispersed. The Austrians were forced back at all points and pursued along the plain, suffering immense loss; nor were they again able to make a stand until driven back over the Bormida. It is evident, in perusing the accounts of this battle, that victory was wrested out of the hands of the Austrians, after they had become, by the fatigues of the day, too weary to hold it.

Melas resolved to save the remains of his army, by entering, upon the 15th June, 1800, into a convention, or rather capitulation, by which he agreed, on receiving permission to retire behind Mantua, to yield up Genoa, and all the fortified places which the Austrians possessed in Piedmont, Lombardy, and the Legations. Buonaparte the more readily granted these terms, that an English army was in the act of arriving on the coast. His wisdom taught him not to drive a powerful enemy to despair, and to be satisfied with the glory of having regained, in the affairs of Montebello and of Marengo, almost all the loss sustained by the French in the disastrous campaign of 1799. An armistice was also agreed upon, which it was supposed might afford time for the conclusion of a victorious peace with Austria; and Buonaparte extended this truce to the armies on the Rhine, as well as those in Italy.

The presence of Napoleon was now eagerly desired at Paris. He set out from Milan on the 24th June, and returned to Paris upon the 2nd July. He had left it on the 6th of May; yet, in the space of not quite two months, how many hopes had he realised! All that the most sanguine partisans had ventured to anticipate of his success had been exceeded. It seemed that his mere presence in Italy was of itself sufficient at once to obliterate the misfortunes of a disastrous campaign, and restore the fruits of his own brilliant victories, which had been lost during his absence.

CHAPTER XX

Napoleon offered Austria generous terms. She nevertheless felt compelled to honour her alliance with Britain and would therefore only enter into a treaty in which the latter power was included. Negotiations between France and Britain took place but failed. War was resumed and, on 3rd December 1800, the Austrians were decisively beaten by Moreau at Hohenlinden. The Austrians had no alternative but to negotiate a peace separate from their allies.

There were two conditions of the treaty, which were peculiarly galling to the Emperor. Buonaparte peremptorily exacted the cession of Tuscany, the hereditary dominions of the brother of Francis, which were to be given up to a prince of the House of Parma, while the archduke was to obtain an indemnity in Germany. The French Consul demanded, with no less pertinacity, that Francis (though not empowered to do so by the Germanic constitution) should confirm the peace, as well in his capacity of Emperor of Germany, as in that of sovereign of his own hereditary dominions. This demand involved a point of great difficulty and delicacy. One of the principal clauses of the treaty included the cession of the whole territories on the left bank of the Rhine to the French Republic; thereby depriving not only Austria, but Prussia, and various other princes of the German empire, of their possessions in the districts.

Buonaparte was determined to make peace on no other terms. Francis was compelled to submit, and, as the necessity of the case pleaded its apology, the act of the Emperor was afterwards ratified by the Diet. Except in these mortifying claims, the submission to which plainly intimated the want of power to resist compulsion, the treaty of Luneville was not much more advantageous to France than that of Campo Formio; and the moderation of the first consul indicated at once his desire of peace upon the continent, and considerable respect for the bravery and strength of Austria.

Naples, which had entered the fray on the Austrian side, was rapidly despatched, and owed her independent survival to the intercession of Tsar Paul, who by now was an admirer of Napoleon.

While all the continent appeared thus willing to submit to one so ready to avail himself of their subjection, Britain alone remained at war; without allies, without, it might seem, a direct object; yet on the grand and unalterable principle, that no partial distress should induce her to submit to the system of degradation, which seemed preparing for all nations under the yoke of France. On every point the English squadrons annihilated the commerce of France, crippled her revenues, blockaded her ports, and prevented those combinations which would have crowned the total conquest of Europe, could the master, as he might now be called, of the land, have enjoyed, at the same time, communication by sea.

It was in vain that Buonaparte, who, besides his natural hardiness of perseverance, connected a part of his own glory with the preservation of Egypt, endeavoured by various means to send supplies to that distant province. His convoys were driven back into harbour by the English fleets; and he directed against his admirals, who could not achieve impossibilities, the unavailing resentment natural to one who was so little accustomed to disappointment. The chance of relieving Egypt was rendered yet more precarious by the loss of Malta, which, after a distressing blockade of two years, was obliged to submit to the English arms on the 5th of September, 1800. The English were thus in possession of a strong and almost impregnable citadel, in the midst of the Mediterranean, with an excellent harbour; above all, they had obtained the very spot which Buonaparte had fixed upon for maintaining the communication with Egypt, which was now in greater danger than ever.

CHAPTER XXI

We return to the internal government of France under the chief consul.

The events subsequent to the revolution of the 18th Brumaire seemed to work a miraculous change on the French nation. The superior talents of

Napoleon, with the policy exercised by Talleyrand and Fouché, and the other statesmen of ability whom he had called into administration – but, above all, the victory of Marengo, had at once created and attached to the person of the chief consul an immense party, which might be said to comprehend all those, who, being neither decided Royalists nor determined Republicans, were indifferent about the form of the government, so they found ease and protection while living under it.

But, on the other hand, the heads of the two factions continued to exist; and, as the power of the first consul became at once more absolute and more consolidated, it grew doubly hateful and formidable to them. His political existence was a total obstruction to the system of both parties, and yet one which it was impossible to remove. There was no national council left, in which the authority of the first consul could be disputed, or his measures impeached. The strength of his military power bid defiance alike to popular commotions. What chance remained for ridding themselves of the autocrat, in whom the Republicans saw a dictator, the Royalists a usurper? None, save that, being mortal, Napoleon was subject to being taken off by assassination.

It is no wonder that some obscure Jacobins should have early nourished the purpose of assassinating Napoleon; but it is singular, that most of the conspirators against his person were Italians. Arena, brother of the deputy who was said to have aimed a dagger at Buonaparte in the Council of Five Hundred, was at the head of the conspiracy. He was a Corsican. With him, Ceracchi and Diana, two Italian refugees; a painter called Topino-Lebrun; and two or three enthusiasts of low condition, formed a plot for the purpose of assassinating the chief consul at the Opera-house. Their intention was detected by the police; Ceracchi and Diana were arrested in the lobby, armed, it was said, and prepared for the attempt.

The Royalists for some time entertained a good opinion of Buonaparte, and conceived that he intended, in his own time and in his own way, to act on behalf of the exiled royal family. So general was the belief among this class, that several agents of the family made their way so far as to sound his own mind upon the subject. Louis himself, afterwards XVIII, addressed to the first consul a letter of the following tenor – "You cannot achieve the happiness of France without my restoration, any more than I can ascend the throne which is my right, without your co-operation. Hasten then to complete the good work, which none but you can accomplish, and name the rewards which you claim for your friends." Buonaparte answered the letter with cold civility. He esteemed the person, he said, and pitied the misfortunes, of his Royal Highness the Comte de Provence, and should be glad to assist him, did an opportunity permit. But as his royal highness could not be restored to France, save at the expense of 100,000 lives, it was an enterprise in which he, Buonaparte, must decline to aid him.

As soon as the Royalists discovered, by the failure of these and similar applications, as well as by the gradual tendency of Buonaparte's measures, that the restoration of the Bourbons was the thing farthest from his purpose, their disappointment exasperated them against the audacious individual, whose single person seemed now the only obstacle to that event. A horrible invention, first hatched, it is said, by the Jacobins, was adopted by certain Royalists of a low description, of whom the leaders were named Carbon and St. Regent. It was a machine consisting of a barrel of gunpowder, placed on a cart, and charged with grape-shot so disposed as to be dispersed in every direction by the explosion. The fire was to be communicated by a slow match. It was the purpose of the conspirators, undeterred by the indiscriminate slaughter which such a discharge must occasion, to place the machine in the street through which the first consul was to go to the opera, having contrived that it should explode, exactly as his carriage should pass the spot; and, strange to say, this stratagem, which seemed as uncertain as it was atrocious, was within a hair's-breadth of success.

On the evening of the 24th December, 1800, Buonaparte has informed us that, though he himself felt a strong desire to remain at home, his wife and one or two intimate friends insisted that he should go to the opera. He was slumbering under a canopy when they awakened him. One brought his hat, another his sword. He was in a manner forced into his carriage, where he again slumbered, and was dreaming of the danger which he had escaped in an attempt to pass the Tagliamento some years before. On a sudden he awoke amidst thunder and flame.

The cart bearing the engine, which was placed in the street St. Nicaise, intercepted the progress of the chief consul's coach, which passed it with some difficulty. St. Regent had fired the match at the appointed instant;

but the coachman, who chanced to be somewhat intoxicated, driving unusually fast, the carriage had passed the machine two seconds before the explosion took place. The explosion was terrible. Two or three houses were greatly damaged – 20 persons killed, and about fifty-three wounded; among the latter the incendiary St. Regent. The report was heard several leagues from Paris. Buonaparte instantly exclaimed to Lannes and Bessières, who were in the carriage, "We are blown up!" The attendants would have stopped the coach, but with more presence of mind he commanded them to drive on, and arrived in safety at the opera; his coachman during the whole time never discovering what had happened, but conceiving the consul had only received a salute of artillery.

A public officer, escaped from such a peril, became an object of yet deeper interest than formerly to the citizens in general; and the reception of the consul at the opera, and elsewhere, was more enthusiastic than ever. Relief was ostentatiously distributed amongst the wounded, and the relatives of the slain; and everyone, shocked with the wild atrocity of such a reckless plot, became, while they execrated the perpetrators, attached in proportion to the object of their cruelty. A disappointed conspiracy always adds strength to the government against which it is directed; and Buonaparte did not fail to push this advantage to the uttermost.

Notwithstanding that the infernal machine (for so it was not inappropriately termed) had in fact been managed by the hands of Royalists, the first suspicion fell on the Republicans; and Buonaparte took the opportunity, before the public were undeceived, of dealing that party a blow, from which they did not recover during his reign. An arbitrary decree of the Senate was readily obtained for the transportation beyond seas of nearly 130 of the chiefs of the Jacobins, among whom were several names which belonged to the celebrated Reign of Terror, and had figured in the rolls of the National Convention. These men were so generally hated, that the unpopularity of their characters excused the irregularity of the proceedings against them, and their fate was viewed with complacency by many, and with indifference by all. The actual conspirators were proceeded against with severity. Chevalier and Veycer, Jacobins, said to have constructed the original model of the infernal machine, were tried before a military commission, condemned to be shot, and suffered death accordingly. Arena, Ceracchi, Topino-Lebrun, and Demerville, were tried before the ordinary court of criminal judicature, and condemned by the voice of a jury; although there was little evidence against them, save that of their accomplice Harel. They also were executed. At a later period, Carbon and St. Regent, Royalists, the agents in the actual attempt of 24th December, were also tried, condemned, and put to death. Some persons tried for the same offence were acquitted; and justice seems to have been distributed with an impartiality unusual in France since the Revolution.

But Buonaparte did not design that the consequences of these plots should end with the deaths of the wretches engaged in them. It afforded an opportunity to advance his principal object, which was the erection of France into a despotic kingdom, and the possessing himself of uncontrolled power over the lives, properties, thoughts, and opinions, of those who were born his fellow subjects, and of whom the very meanest but lately boasted himself his equal. He has himself expressed his purpose respecting the Constitution of the year Eight, in words dictated to General Gourgaud:

"The ideas of Napoleon were fixed; but the aid of time and events were necessary for their realisation. The organisation of the Consulate had presented nothing in contradiction to them; it taught unanimity, and that was the first step. This point gained, Napoleon was quite indifferent as to the form and denominations of the several constituted bodies. He was a stranger to the Revolution. It was natural that the will of these men, who had followed it through all its phases, should prevail in questions as difficult as they were abstract. The wisest plan was to go on from day to day – by the polar star by which Napoleon meant to guide the Revolution to the haven he desired."

If there is any thing obscure in this passage, it received but too luminous a commentary from Buonaparte's actions; all of which tend to show that he embraced the Consular government as a mere temporary arrangement, calculated to prepare the minds of the French nation for his ulterior views of ambition. He tells us in plain terms, he let the revolutionary sages take their own way in arranging the constitution; determined, without regarding the rules they laid down on the chart, to steer his course by one fixed point to one desired haven. That polar star was his own selfish interest – that haven was despotic power. What he considered as most for his own interest, he was determined to consider as the government most suited for France also. Perhaps he may have persuaded himself that he was actually serving his country as well as himself; and, indeed, justly considered, he was in both instances equally grievously mistaken.

These repeated attacks on the Head of the state made it desirable that some mode should be introduced of trying such offences, briefer and more arbitrary than the slow forms required by ordinary jurisprudence. The court which Government now proposed to establish was to consist of eight members thus qualified: 1. The president and two judges of the ordinary criminal tribunal; 2. Three military men, bearing at least the rank of a captain; 3. Two citizens, to be suggested by Government, who should be selected from such as were by the constitution qualified to act as judges. Thus, five out of eight judges were directly named by the Government for the occasion. The court was to decide without jury, without appeal, and without revision of any kind. As a boon to the accused, the court were to have at least six members present, and there was to be no casting vote; so that the party would have his acquittal, unless six members out of eight, or four members out of six, should unite in finding him guilty; whereas in other courts, a bare majority is sufficient for condemnation. With this poor boon to public opinion, the special Commission Court was to be the jurisdiction before whom armed insurgents, conspirators, and in general men guilty of crimes against the social compact, were to undergo their trial.

The counsellor of state, Portalis, laid this plan before the Legislative Body, by whom it was referred to the consideration of the Tribunate. It was in this body that those who continued to entertain free sentiments could have any opportunity of expressing them. Benjamin Constant, Daunon, Chenier, and others, the gleanings as it were of the liberal party, made an honourable but unavailing defence against this invasion of the constitution, studying at the same time to express their opposition in language and by arguments least likely to give offence to the Government. To the honour of the Tribunate, the project had nearly made shipwreck, and was only passed by a small majority of forty-nine over forty-one. In the Legislative Body there was also a strong minority. It seemed as if the friends of liberty, however deprived of direct popular representation, and of the means of influencing public opinion, were yet determined to maintain in opposition to the first consul.

It was [also] announced that there were a set of persons, who were to be regarded rather as public enemies than as criminals, and who ought to be provided against by anticipating and defeating their schemes. These consisted of Republicans, Royalists, or any others entertaining, or supposed to entertain, opinions inimical to the present state of affairs; and the law now passed entitled the government to treat them as suspected persons, and as such, to banish them from Paris or from France. Thus was the chief consul invested with full power over the personal liberty of every person whom he chose to consider as the enemy of his government.

Buonaparte was enabled to avail himself to the uttermost of the powers which he had thus extracted from the constitutional bodies, by the frightful agency of the police. This institution may, even in its mildest form, be regarded as a necessary evil; for although, while great cities continue to afford obscure retreats for vice and crime of every description, there must be men, whose profession it is to discover and bring criminals to justice, as while there are vermin in the animal world, there must be kites and carrion-crows to diminish their number; yet, as the excellence of these guardians of the public depends in a great measure on their familiarity with the arts, haunts, and practices of culprits, they cannot be expected to feel the same horror for crimes, or criminals, which is common to other men. On the contrary, they have a sympathy with them of the same kind which hunters entertain for the game which is the object of their pursuit. Besides, as much of their business is carried on by the medium of spies, they must be able to personate the manners and opinions of these whom they detect; and are frequently induced, by their own interest, to direct, encourage, nay suggest crimes, that they may obtain the reward due for conviction of the offenders.

Applied to state offences, the agency of such persons, though sometimes unavoidable, is yet more frightfully dangerous. Moral delinquencies can be hardly with any probability attributed to worthy or innocent persons; but there is no character so pure, that he who bears it may not be supposed capable of entertaining false and exaggerated opinions in politics, and, as such, become the victim of treachery and delation. In France, the power of the police had become overwhelming; indeed, the very existence of the government seemed in some measure dependent upon the accuracy of their intelligence; and for this purpose their numbers had been enlarged, and their discipline perfected, under the administration of the sagacious and crafty Fouché. He was totally without principle; but his nature was not of that last degree of depravity, which delights in evil for its own sake, and his good sense told him, that an unnecessary crime was a political blunder. The lenity with which he exercised his terrible office, when left in any degree to his own discretion, while it never prevented his implicit execution of Buonaparte's commands, made the abominable system over which he presided to a certain extent endurable.

By combining the reports of his agents, the minister of police arrived at so accurate a knowledge of the purpose, disposition, adherents, and tools of the different parties in France, that he could anticipate their mode of acting upon all occasions that were likely to occur; and when any particular accident took place, was able, from his previous general information, to assign it to the real cause, and the true actors.

An unlimited system of espial, and that stretching through society, was necessary to the perfection of this system, which had not arrived to its utmost height, till Napoleon ascended the throne. The expense of maintaining this establishment was immense; for Fouché comprehended amongst his spies and informers, persons whom no ordinary gratuity would have moved. But this expense was provided for by the large sums which the minister of police received for the toleration yielded to brothels, gambling houses, and other places of profligacy to which he granted licenses, in consideration of their observing certain regulations. His system of espial was also extended, by the information which was collected in these haunts of debauchery; and thus the vices of the capital were made to support the means by which it was subjected to a despotic government. His autobiography contains a boast, that the private secretary of the chief consul was his pensioner, and that the lavish profusion of Josephine made even her willing to exchange intelligence concerning the chief consul. Thus was Fouché not only a spy upon the people in behalf of Buonaparte, but a spy also on Buonaparte himself.

It was the duty of the police to watch the progress of public opinion, whether it was expressed in general society, and confidential communication, or by the medium of the press. Buonaparte entertained a feverish apprehension of the effects of literature on the general mind, and in doing so acknowledged the weak points in his government. The public journals were under the daily superintendence of the police, and their editors were summoned before Fouché when any thing was inserted which could be considered as disrespectful. Threats and promises were liberally employed, and such journalists as proved refractory, were soon made to feel that the former were no vain menaces. The suppression of the offensive newspaper was often accompanied by the banishment or imprisonment of the editor. The same measure was dealt to authors, booksellers, and publishers, respecting whom the jealousy of Buonaparte amounted to a species of disease.

The interference of Buonaparte's police went much further, and frequently required from those authors who wrote only on general topics, some express recognisance of his authority. The ancient Christians would not attend the theatre, because it was necessary that, previous to enjoying the beauties of the scene, they should sacrifice some grains of incense to the false deity, supposed to preside over the place. In like manner, men of generous minds in France were often obliged to suppress works on subjects the most alien to politics, because they could not easily obtain a road to the public unless they consented to recognise the right of the individual who had usurped the supreme authority, and extinguished the liberties of his country. The circumstances which subjected Madame de Staël to a long persecution by the police of Buonaparte, may be quoted as originating in this busy desire, of connecting his government with the publications of all persons of genius.

Another support of a very different kind, and grounded on the most opposite principles, was afforded to the rising power of Napoleon, through the re-establishment of religion in France, by his treaty with the Pope, called the Concordat. Two great steps had been taken towards this important point, by the edict opening the churches, and renewing the exercise of the Christian religion, and by the restoration of the Pope to his temporal dominions, after the battle of Marengo. The further objects to be attained were the sanction of the first consul's government by the Pontiff on the one hand, and, on the other, the re-establishment of the rights of the Church in France, so far as should be found consistent with the new order of things.

This important treaty was managed by Joseph Buonaparte. The ratifications were exchanged on the 18th of September 1801; and when they were published it was singular to behold how submissively the once proud See of Rome had prostrated before the power of Buonaparte, and how absolutely he must have dictated all the terms of the treaty. Every article innovated on some of those rights and claims, which the Church of Rome had for ages asserted as the unalienable privileges of her infallible head: I. It was provided, that the Catholic religion should be freely exercised in France, acknowledged as the national faith, and its service openly practised, subject to such regulations of police as the French Government should judge necessary; II. The Pope, in concert with the French Government, was to make a new division of dioceses, and to require of the existing bishops even the resignation of their sees, should that be found necessary; III. The sees which should become vacant by such resignation, or by deprivation, in case a voluntary abdication was refused, as also all future vacancies, were to be filled up by the Pope, on nominations proceeding from the French Government; IV. The new bishops were to take an oath of fidelity to the Government, and to observe a ritual, in which there were to be especial forms of prayer for the consuls; V. The church-livings were to undergo a new division, and the bishops were to nominate to them, but only such persons as should be approved by the Government; VI. The Government was to make suitable provision for the national clergy, while the Pope expressly renounced all right competent to him and his successors, to challenge or dispute the sales of church property which had been made since the Revolution.

Such was the celebrated compact, by which Pius VII surrendered to a soldier, whose name was five or six years before unheard of in Europe, those high claims to supremacy in spiritual affairs, which his predecessors had maintained for so many ages against the whole potentates of Europe. A puritan might have said of the power seated on the Seven Hills – "Babylon is fallen – it is fallen that great city!" The more rigid Catholics were of the same opinion. The Concordat, they alleged, showed rather the abasement of the Roman hierarchy than the re-erection of the Gallic Church. Others of that faith there were, who, though they considered the new system as very imperfect, yet thought it might have the effect of preserving in France some sense of the Christian religion, which, under the total disuse of public worship, stood a chance of being entirely extinguished in the minds of the rising generation. They granted, that the countenance shown by Buonaparte to the religious establishment, was entirely from motives of self-interest; but still they hoped that God, who works his own will by the selfish passions of individuals, was now using those of the first consul to recall some sense of religion to France; and they anticipated that religion, as the best friend of all that is good and graceful in humanity, was likely, in the course of time, to bring back and encourage a sense of rational liberty.

The revolutionary part of France beheld the Concordat with very different eyes. The Christian religion was, as to the Jews and Greeks of old, a stumbling-block to the Jacobins, and foolishness to the philosophers. Buonaparte defended himself among the philosophers, by comparing his Concordat to a sort of vaccination of religion, which, by introducing a slighter kind into the system of the state, would gradually prepare for its entire extinction.

In the meantime, he proceeded to renew the ancient league betwixt the church and crown, with as much solemnity as possible. The Concordat was inaugurated at Notre Dame, [April 1802] with the utmost magnificence. Buonaparte attended in person, with all the badges and pomp of royalty, and in the style resembling as nearly as possible that of the former Kings of France. The Archbishop of Aix was appointed to preach upon the occasion, being the very individual prelate who had delivered the sermon upon the coronation of Louis XVI. Some address, it was said, was employed to procure the attendance of the old republican generals. They were invited by Berthier to breakfast, and thence carried to the first consul's levee; after which it became impossible for them to decline attending him to Notre Dame. As he returned from the ceremony, surrounded by these military functionaries, Buonaparte remarked with complacency, that the former order of things was fast returning. One of his generals boldly answered, "Yes! All returns – excepting the two million Frenchmen, who have died to procure the proscription of the very system now in the act of being restored."

It is said that Buonaparte, when he found the Pope and the clergy less tractable than he desired, regretted having taken the step of re-establishing religion, and termed the Concordat the greatest error of his reign. But such observations could only escape him in a moment of pique or provocation. He well knew the advantage which a government must derive from a national church; and at Saint Helena, he himself at once acknowledged the advantage of his compact with the Pope as a measure of state, and his indifference to it in a religious point of view. "I never regretted the Concordat," he said. "I must have had either that or something equivalent. Had the Pope never before existed, he should have been made for the occasion." The first consul took care, accordingly, to make his full advantage of the Concordat, by introducing his own name as much as possible into the catechism. To honour Napoleon, the catechumen that was taught, was the same as to honour and serve God himself – to oppose his will, was to incur the penalty of eternal damnation.

An ordinance, eminently well qualified to heal the civil wounds of France, next manifested the talents of Buonaparte, and, as men hoped, his moderation. This was the general amnesty granted to the emigrants. A decree of 26th April, 1802, permitted the return of these unfortunate persons to France, providing they did so, and took the oath of fidelity to Government, within a certain period. There were, however, five classes of exceptions, containing such as seemed too deeply pledged to the house of Bourbon. Such were, 1st, those who had been chiefs of bodies of armed royalists; 2nd, who had held rank in the armies of the allies; 3rd, who had belonged to the household of the princes of the blood; 4th, who had been agents or encouragers of foreign or domestic war; 5th, the generals and admirals, together with the representatives of the people, who had been guilty of treason against the Republic, together with the prelates, who declined to resign their sees in terms of the Concordat. It was at the same time declared that not more than 500 in all should be excepted from the amnesty. Buonaparte truly judged, that the mass of emigrants, thus winnowed and purified from all who had been leaders, exhausted in fortune and wearied out by exile, would in general be grateful for permission to return, passive, and attached subjects of his dominion; and the event in a great measure, if not fully, justified his expectations. Such part of their property as had not been sold was directed to be restored to them; but they were subjected to the special superintendence of the police for the space of ten years after their return.

With similar and most laudable attention to the duties of his high office, Buonaparte founded plans of education, and particularly, with Mongé's assistance, established the Polytechnic school, which has produced so many men of talent. He inquired anxiously into abuses and was particularly active in correcting those which had crept into the prisons during the Revolution. In amending such evils, Buonaparte, though not of kingly birth, showed a mind worthy of the rank to which he had ascended. It is only to be regretted, that in what interfered with his personal wishes or interest, he uniformly failed to manifest the sound and correct views, which on abstract questions he could form so clearly.

Other schemes of a public character were held out as occupying the attention of the chief consul. Like Augustus, whose situation his own in some measure resembled, Napoleon endeavoured, by the magnificence of his projects for the improvement of the state, to withdraw attention from his inroads upon public freedom. The inland navigation of Languedoc was to be completed, and a canal, joining the river Yonne to the Saône, was to connect the south part of the Republic so completely with the north, as to establish a communication by water between Marseilles and Amsterdam. Bridges were also to be built, roads to be laid out and improved, museums founded in the principal towns of France, and many other public labours undertaken, on a scale which should put to shame even the boasted days of Louis XIV. Buonaparte knew the French nation well, and was aware that he should best reconcile them to his government, by indulging his own genius for bold and magnificent undertakings.

But although these splendid proposals filled the public ear, and flattered the national pride, commerce continued to languish, under the effects of a constant blockade, provisions became dear, and discontent against the Consulate began to gain ground. The effectual cure for these heart-burnings was only to be found in a general peace.

CHAPTER XXII

Having thus given a glance at the internal affairs of France during the commencement of Buonaparte's domination, we return to her external relations, which, since the peace of Luneville, had assumed the appearance of universal ascendency, so much had the current of human affairs been altered by the talents and fortunes of one man. Not only was France in secure possession, by the treaty of Luneville, of territories extending to the banks of the Rhine, but Holland, Switzerland, and Italy, were all in a state of subjection to her will; Spain, like a puppet, moved but at her signal; Austria was broken-spirited and dejected; Prussia still remembered her losses in the first revolutionary war; and Russia, who alone could be considered as unmoved by any fear of France, was yet in a situation to be easily managed, by flattering and cajoling the peculiar temper of the Emperor Paul.

Paul's admiration for Napoleon, coupled with the Northern States' irritation at Britain's arrogation of the right of search at sea, gave Napoleon hope of being able to prosecute the war against Britain as well as to embark on more conquests. Prompt British action in the form of the battle of Copenhagen, as well as Paul's assassination, put paid to this possibility and left Napoleon with no option but to invade Britain or seek a settlement. Britain was all the more willing to negotiate as she had liberated Egypt, thus removing the French threat to her Indian trade.

The conquest of Egypt excited a strong sensation both in France and Britain; but the news of the contest being finally closed by Menon's submission, are believed to have reached the former country some time before the English received them. Buonaparte, on learning the tidings, is reported to have said, "Well, there remains no alternative but to make the descent on Britain." But it seems to have occurred to him presently afterwards, that the loss of this disputed province might, instead of being an argument for carrying the war to extremity, be considered as the removal of an obstacle to a treaty of peace.

CHAPTER XXIII

As the words of the first consul appeared to intimate, preparations were resumed on the French coast for the invasion of Great Britain. The British naval preparations were very great, and what gave yet more confidence than the number of vessels and guns, Nelson was put into command of the sea. Under his management, it soon became the question, not whether the French flotilla was to invade the British shores, but whether it was to remain in safety in the French harbours.

The British attack in some degree failed, owing to the several divisions of boats missing each other in the dark; some French vessels were taken, but they could not be brought off; and the French chose to consider this result as a victory, on their part. Meantime, the changes which had taken place in the British administration, were preparing public expectation for that peace which all the world now longed for.

Mr. Pitt left the Ministry, [February 1801,] and was succeeded by Mr. Addington, now Lord Sidmouth. The change was justly considered as friendly to pacific measures. Buonaparte himself was disposed to peace. It was necessary to France, and no less necessary to him, since he otherwise must remain pledged to undertake the hazardous alternative of invasion, in which chances stood incalculably against his success; while a failure might have inferred the total ruin of his power. All parties were, therefore, in a great degree inclined to treat with sincerity; and Buonaparte was with little difficulty brought to consent to the evacuation of Egypt. It was also stipulated, that the French should evacuate Rome and Naples; a condition of little consequence, as they were always able to reoccupy these countries when their interest required it. The Dutch colony of the Cape of Good Hope was to be restored to the Batavian republic.

In respect of the settlements which the British arms had conquered, England underwent a punishment not unmerited. The important possessions of Ceylon in the East, and Trinidad in the West Indies, were the only part of her conquests which England retained. The integrity of her ancient ally, Portugal, was, however, recognised, and the independence of the Ionian islands was stipulated for and guaranteed. Britain restored what places she had occupied on the Italian coast; but the occupation of Malta for some time threatened to prove an obstacle to the treaty. The English considered it as of the last consequence that this strong island should remain in their possession, and intimated that they regarded the pertinacious resistance which the first consul testified to this proposal, as implying a private desire of renewing his designs on Egypt, to which Malta might be considered a key. After much discussion, it was at length agreed that the independence of the island should be secured by its being garrisoned by a neutral power, and placed under its guarantee and protection.

The preliminaries of peace were signed 10th October, 1801. Amiens was appointed for the meeting of commissioners, who were finally to adjust the treaty, which was not ended till five months after the preliminaries had been agreed on. The isle of Malta, according to this agreement, was to be occupied by a garrison of Neapolitan troops, while, besides Britain and France, Austria, Spain, Russia, and Prussia, were to guarantee its neutrality. The Knights of St. John were to be the sovereigns, but neither French nor English were in future to be members of that order. The harbours were to be free to the commerce of all nations, and the order was to be neutral towards all nations save the Algerines and other piratical states.

Napoleon, had he chosen to examine the feelings of the English, must have seen plainly that this treaty, unwillingly acceded to by them, and only by way of experiment, was to have a duration long or short, in proportion to their confidence in his own good faith. His ambition, and the little scruple which he showed in gratifying it, was the terror of Europe; and until the fears he had excited were disarmed by a tract of peaceful and moderate conduct, the suspicions of England must have been constantly awake, and the peace must have been considered as precarious as an armed truce. Yet these considerations could not induce him to lay aside, or even postpone, a train of measures, tending directly to his own personal aggrandisement, and confirming the jealousies which his character already inspired. These measures were partly of a nature adapted to consolidate and prolong his own power in France; partly to extend the predominating influence of that country over her neighbours.

By the treaty of Luneville, and by that of Tolentino, the independent existence of the Cisalpine and Helvetian republics had been expressly stipulated; but this independence, according to Buonaparte, did not exclude their being reduced to mere satellites, whose motions were to be regulated by France, and by himself. When, therefore, the Directory was overthrown, it was not his purpose that a directorial form of government should continue to subsist in Italy. For this purpose, in the beginning of January, 1802, a convention of 450 deputies from the Cisalpine states arrived at Lyons, (for they were not trusted to deliberate within the limits of their own country,) to contrive for themselves a new political system. In that period, when the modelling of constitutions was so common, there was no difficulty in drawing up one; which consisted of a president, a deputy-president, a legislative council, and three electoral colleges, composed, first, of proprietors; second, of persons of learning; and, third, of commercial persons. If the Italians had been awkward upon the occasion, they had the assistance of Talleyrand; and soon after, the arrival of Buonaparte himself at Lyons gave countenance to their operations. His presence was necessary for the exhibition of a most singular farce.

A committee of thirty, to whom had been entrusted the principal duty of suggesting the new model of government, gave in a report, in which it was stated, that, from the want of any man of sufficient influence amongst themselves to fill the office of president, upon whom devolved all the executive duties of the state, the new system could not be considered as secure, unless Buonaparte should be prevailed upon to fill that situation, not, as it was carefully explained, in his character of head of the French government, but in his individual capacity. Napoleon graciously inclined to their suit. He informed them, that he concurred in the modest opinion they had formed, that their republic did not at present possess an individual sufficiently gifted to take charge of their affairs, which he should, therefore, retain under his own chief management, while circumstances required him to do so.

Having thus established his power in Italy as firmly as in France, Buonaparte proceeded to take measures for extending his dominions. By a treaty with Spain, now made public, the duchy of Parma was to devolve on France, together with the island of Elba, upon the death of the present duke – an event at no distant date to be expected. The Spanish part of the province of Louisiana, in North America, was to be ceded to France. Portugal, too, though the integrity of her dominions had been guaranteed by the preliminaries of the peace with England, had been induced, by a treaty kept studiously private from the British court, to cede her province of Guiana to France. These stipulations served to show that there was no quarter of the world in which France and her present ruler did not entertain views of aggrandisement, and that questions of national faith would not be considered too curiously when they interfered with their purpose.

While Europe was stunned and astonished at the spirit of conquest and accumulation manifested by this insatiable conqueror, France was made aware that he was equally desirous to consolidate and to prolong his power. He was all, and more than all, that sovereign had ever been; but he still wanted the title and the permanence which royalty requires. To attain these was no difficult matter, when the first consul was the prime mover of each act; nor was he long of discovering proper agents eager to gratify his wishes.

Chabot de L'Allier took the lead in the race of adulation. Arising in the Tribunate, he pronounced a long eulogium on Buonaparte, enhancing the gratitude due to the hero by whom France had been preserved and restored to victory. He therefore proposed that the Tribunate should transmit to the Conservative Senate a resolution, to consider the manner of bestowing on Napoleon Buonaparte a splendid mark of the national gratitude. There was no misunderstanding this hint. The motion was unanimously adopted, and transmitted to the Senate, to the Legislative Body, and to the Consuls. The Senate conceived they should best meet the demand, by electing Napoleon first consul for a second space of ten years, to commence when the date of the original period should expire. The proposition being reduced into the form of a decree, was intimated to Buonaparte, but fell short of his wishes; as it assigned to him, however distant it was, a period at which he must be removed from authority. It is true, that the space of seventeen years, to which the edict proposed to extend his power, seemed to guarantee a very ample duration. But still there was a termination, and that was enough to mortify his ambition.

He thanked the Senate, therefore, for this fresh mark of their confidence, but eluded accepting it in express terms, by referring to the pleasure of the people. Their suffrages, he said, had invested him with power, and he could not think it right to accept of the prolongation of that power but by their consent. It might have been thought that there was now nothing left but to present the decree of the Senate to the people. But the second and third consuls took it upon them, though the constitution gave then no warrant for such a manœuvre, to alter the question of the Senate, and to propose to the people one more acceptable to Buonaparte's ambition, requesting their judgment, whether the chief consul should retain his office, not for ten years longer, but for the term of his life. By thus juggling the proposal of the Senate was set aside, and the assembly soon found it wisest to adopt the more liberal views suggested by the consuls, to whom they returned thanks, for having taught them (we suppose) how to appreciate a hint.

The question was sent to the departments. The registers were opened with great form, as if the people had really some constitutional right to exercise. As the subscriptions were received at the offices of the various functionaries of government, it is no wonder, considering the nature of the question, that the ministers were enabled to report a majority of three million citizens who gave votes in the affirmative. It was much more surprising, that there should have been an actual minority of a few hundred determined Republicans, with Carnot at their head, who answered the question in the negative. This statesman observed, as he signed his vote, that he was subscribing his sentence of deportation; from which we may conjecture his opinion concerning the fairness of this mode of consulting the people. He was mistaken notwithstanding. Buonaparte found himself so strong, that he could afford to be merciful, and to assume a show of impartiality, by suffering those to go unpunished who had declined to vote for the increase of his power.

He did not, however, venture to propose to the people another innovation, which extended beyond his death the power which their liberal gift had continued during his life. A simple decree of the Senate assigned to Buonaparte the right of nominating his successor, by a testamentary deed. So that Napoleon might call his children or relatives to the succession, as to a private inheritance. To such a pass had the domination of a military chief, reduced the fierce democracy and stubborn loyalty of the two factions, which seemed before that period to combat for the possession of France. Napoleon had stooped on them both, like the hawk in the fable.

The period at which we close this chapter was a most important one in Napoleon's life, and seemed a crisis on which his fate, and that of France, depended. In his personal capacity, the first consul possessed all the power which he desired, and a great deal more than, whether his own or the country's welfare was regarded, he ought to have wished for.

CHAPTERS XXIV, XXV

The bulk of this chapter is devoted to Switzerland. Although her independence had been guaranteed by the Treaty of Luneville, Napoleon took advantage of unrest between the cantons to invade her and impose a settlement establishing him as Grand Mediator of Helvetian Republic, thus transforming the country into little more than a French appanage.

These advances towards universal empire, made during the very period when the pacific measures adopted by the preliminaries, and afterwards confirmed by the treaty of Amiens, were in the act of being carried into execution, excited the natural jealousy of the people of Britain. They had not been accustomed to rely much on the sincerity of the French nation; nor did the character of its present chief, so full of ambition, and so bold and successful in his enterprises, incline them to feelings of greater security. On the other hand, Buonaparte seems to have felt as a matter of personal offence the jealousy which the British entertained; and instead of soothing it, as policy dictated, he showed a disposition to punish it, by measures which indicated anger and irritation. There ceased to be any cordiality in the intercourse betwixt the two nations, and they began to look into the conduct of each other for causes of offence, rather than for the means of removing it.

France had innovated upon the state of things which existed when the treaty with Britain was made, and England might, therefore, in justice, claim an equitable right to innovate upon the treaty itself, by refusing to make surrender of what had been promised in very different circumstances. Perhaps it had been better to fix upon this obvious principle, as the ground of declining to surrender such British conquests as were not yet given up, unless France consented to relinquish the power which she had usurped upon the continent.

While things were thus rapidly approaching a rupture, the chief consul adopted the unusual resolution of entering personally into conference with the British ambassador. He probably took this determination upon the same grounds which dictated his contempt for customary forms, in entering into direct correspondence with the princes whom he had occasion to treat with.

Their first interview of a political nature took place in the Tuileries, 17th February, 1803. Buonaparte, having announced that this meeting was for the purpose of "making his sentiments known to the King of England in a clear and authentic manner," proceeded to talk incessantly for the space of nearly two hours, not without considerable incoherence, his temper rising as he dwelt on the alleged causes of complaint, though not so much or so incautiously as to make him drop the usual tone of courtesy to the ambassador. He complained of the delay of the British in evacuating Alexandria and Malta; cutting short all discussion on the latter subject, by declaring he would as soon agree to Britain's possessing the suburb of St. Antoine as that island. He then referred to the abuse thrown upon him by the English papers, but more especially by those French journals published in London. He affirmed that Georges and other Chouan chiefs, whom he accused of designs against his life, received relief or shelter in England; and that two assassins had been apprehended in Normandy, sent over by the French emigrants to murder him. This, he said, would be publicly proved in a court of justice. From this point he diverged to Egypt, of which he affirmed he could make himself master whenever he had a mind; but that he considered it too paltry a stake to renew the war for. Yet, while on this subject, he suffered it to escape him, that the idea of recovering this favourite colony was only postponed: "Egypt, must sooner or later belong to France, either by the falling to pieces of the Turkish government, or in consequence of some agreement with the Porte." In evidence of his peaceable intentions, he asked what he should gain by going to war, since he had no means of acting offensively against England, except by a descent, of which he acknowledged the hazard in the strongest terms. The chances, he said, were a hundred to one against him; and yet he declared that the attempt should be made if he were now obliged to go to war. He extolled the power of both countries. The army of France, he said, should be soon recruited to 480,000 men; and the fleets of England were such as he could not propose to match within the space of ten years at least. United, the two countries might govern the world, would they but understand each other. Had he found, he said, the least cordiality on the part of England, she should have had indemnities assigned her upon the continent, treaties of commerce, all that she could wish for or desire. But he confessed that his irritation increased daily, "since every gale that blew from England, brought nothing but enmity and hatred against him." He then made an excursive digression, in which, taking a review of the nations of Europe, he contended that England could hope for assistance from none of them in a war with France. In the total result, he demanded the instant implement of the treaty of Amiens, and the suppression of the abuse in the English papers. War was the alternative.

During this declamation, which the first consul delivered with great rapidity, Lord Whitworth, notwithstanding the interview lasted two hours, had scarcely time to slide in a few words in reply or explanation. As he endeavoured to state the new grounds of mistrust which induced the King of England to demand more advantageous terms, in consequence of the accession of territory and influence which France had lately made, Napoleon interrupted him – "I suppose you mean Piedmont and Switzerland – they are trifling occurrences, which must have been foreseen while the negotiation was in dependence. You have no right to recur to them at this time of day." To the hint of indemnities which might be allotted to England out of Europe, if she would cultivate the friendship of Buonaparte, Lord Whitworth nobly answered, that the King of Britain's ambition led him to preserve what was his, not to acquire that which belonged to others. They parted with civility, but with a conviction on Lord Whitworth's part, that Buonaparte would never resign his claim to Malta.

The British Ministry were of the same opinion; for a message was sent down by his Majesty to the House of Commons, stating, that he had occasion for additional aid to enable him to defend his dominions, in case of an encroachment on the part of France. A reason was given, which injured the cause of the Ministers, by placing the vindication of their measures upon simulated grounds; it was stated, that these apprehensions arose from "military preparations carrying on in the ports of France and Holland." No such preparations had been complained of during the intercourse between the ministers of France and England – in truth, none such existed to any considerable extent. All, however, were sensible of the real merits of the dispute, which were grounded on the grasping and inordinate ambition of the French ruler, and the sentiments of dislike and irritation with which he seemed to regard Great Britain.

The charge of the pretended naval preparations being triumphantly refuted by France, Talleyrand was next employed to place before Lord Whitworth the means which France possessed of wounding England, not directly indeed, but through those states of Europe whom she would most wish to see, if not absolutely independent, yet unoppressed by military exactions. "It was natural," a note of this statesman asserted, "that Britain being armed in consequence of the King's message, France should arm also – that she should send an army into Holland – form an encampment on the frontiers of Hanover – continue to maintain troops in Switzerland – march others to the south of Italy, and, finally, form encampments upon the coast." All these threats, excepting the last, referred to neutral nations, who were not alleged to have given any cause of complaint to France. It was an entirely new principle of warlike policy, which introduced the oppression of unoffending and neutral neighbours as a legitimate mode of carrying on war against a hostile power, against whom there was little possibility of using measures directly offensive.

Shortly after this note had been lodged, Buonaparte seems to have formed the scheme of bringing the protracted negotiations betwixt France and England to a point, in a time, place, and manner, equally extraordinary. At a public court held at the Tuileries, on the 13th March, the chief consul came up to Lord Whitworth in considerable agitation, and observed aloud, and within hearing of the circle, "You are then determined on war?" and, without attending to the disclamations of the English ambassador, proceeded, "We have been at war for fifteen years – you are determined on hostility for fifteen years more – and you force me to it." He then addressed Count Marrow and the Chevalier Azara – "The English wish for war; but if they draw the sword first, I will be the last to return it to the scabbard. They do not respect treaties, which henceforth we must cover with black crape." He then again addressed Lord Whitworth – "To what purpose are these armaments? Against whom do you take these measures of precaution? I have not a single ship of the line in any port in France: But if you arm, I too will take up arms – if you fight, I will fight – you may destroy France, but you cannot intimidate her."

"We desire neither the one nor the other," answered Lord Whitworth, calmly: "We desire to live with her on terms of good intelligence."

"You must respect treaties, then," said Buonaparte, sternly. "Woe to those by whom they are not respected! They will be accountable for the consequences to all Europe."

So saying, and repeating his last remark twice over, he retired from the levee.

This remarkable explosion may be easily explained, if we refer it entirely to the impatience of a fiery temper, rendered, by the most extraordinary train of success, morbidly sensitive to any obstacle which interfered with a favourite plan. But it has been averred by those who had best opportunity to know Buonaparte that the fits of violent passion which he sometimes displayed, were less the bursts of unrepressed and constitutional irritability, than means previously calculated upon to intimidate and astound those with whom he was treating at the time. There may, therefore, have been policy amid the first consul's indignation.

Talleyrand, to whom Lord Whitworth applied for an explanation of the scene, only answered, that the first consul, publicly affronted, as he conceived himself, desired to exculpate himself in presence of the ministers of all the powers of Europe. The question of peace or war came now to turn on the subject of Malta. The English lowered their claim of retaining Malta in perpetuity to their right of holding it for ten years. Buonaparte, on the other hand, would listen to no modification of Amiens, but offered, as the guarantee afforded by the occupation of Neapolitan troops was objected to, that the garrison should consist of Russians or Austrians. To this proposal Britain would not accede. Lord Whitworth left Paris, and, on the 18th May, 1803, Britain declared war against France.

CHAPTER XXVI

This chapter begins with Napoleon's disastrous attempt, while at peace, to re-establish French control over St. Domingo, the subsequent betrayal of Toussaint L'Ouverture, and the permanent loss of what had once been France's richest colony.

While Buonaparte made these strong efforts for repossessing France of this fine colony, it was not to be supposed that he was neglecting the establishment of his own power upon a more firm basis. His present situation was – like every other in life – considerably short of what he could have desired, though infinitely superior to all that his most unreasonable wishes could at one time have aspired to. He had all the real power, and, since the settlement of his authority for life, he had daily assumed more of the pomp and circumstance with which sovereignty is usually invested. The Tuileries were once more surrounded with guards without, and filled by levees within. The ceremonial of a court was revived, and Buonaparte, judging of mankind with accuracy, neglected no minute observance by which princes are wont to enforce their authority. Still there remained much to be done. He held the sovereignty only in the nature of a life-rent. He could, indeed, dispose of it by will, but the last wills even of kings have been frequently set aside; and, at any rate, the privilege comes short of that belonging to an hereditary crown, which, in one sense, may be said to confer on the dynasty a species of immortality.

Buonaparte knew also the virtue of names. The title of chief consul did not necessarily infer sovereign rights – it might signify every thing, or it might signify nothing – in common language, it inferred alike one of the annual executive governors of the Roman Republic, whose *fasces* swayed the world, or the petty resident who presides over commercial affairs in a foreign seaport. There were no precise ideas of power or rights necessarily and inalienably connected with it. Besides, Buonaparte had other objections to his present title. The title of first consul implied that there were two others. Again, the word reminded the hearer that it belonged to a government of recent establishment, and of revolutionary origin, and Napoleon did not wish to present such ideas to the public mind; since that which last arose out of the revolutionary cauldron might, like the phantoms which had preceded it, give place in its turn to an apparition more potent. Policy seemed to recommend, to have recourse to the ancient model which Europe had been long accustomed to reverence; to adopt the form of government best known and longest established through the greater part of the world; and, assuming the title and rights of a monarch, to take his place among the ancient and recognised authorities of Europe.

Before he could venture on this bold measure, in which, were it but for very shame's sake, he must be certain of great opposition, Buonaparte endeavoured, by every means in his power, to strengthen himself in his government. The army was carefully new-modelled, so as to make it as much as possible his own; and the French soldiers, who regarded the power of Buonaparte as the fruit of their own victories, were in general devoted to his cause, notwithstanding Moreau, to whom a certain part of their number still adhered. The consular guard, a highly privileged body of select forces, was augmented to the number of 6000 men. These formidable legions, which included troops of every species of arms, had been gradually formed and increased upon the plan of the corps of guides. But the guards, as now increased in numbers, had a duty much more extended. They were chosen men, taught to consider themselves as superior to the rest of the army, and enjoying advantages in pay and privileges. When the other troops were subject to privations, care was taken that the guards should experience as little of them as possible, and that by every possible exertion they should be kept in the highest degree of readiness for action. They were only employed upon service of the utmost importance, and seldom in the beginning of an engagement, when they remained in reserve under the eye of Napoleon himself. It was usually by means of his guard that the final and decisive exertion was made which marked Buonaparte's tactics, and so often achieved victory at the very crisis when it seemed inclining to the enemy. Regarding themselves as considerably superior to the other soldiers, and accustomed also to be under Napoleon's immediate command, his guards were devotedly attached to him; and a body of troops of such high character might be considered as a formidable bulwark around the throne which he meditated ascending.

The attachment of these chosen legions, and of his soldiers in general, formed the foundation of Buonaparte's power, who, of all sovereigns that ever mounted to authority, might be said to reign by dint of victory and of his sword. But he surrounded himself by another species of partisan. The Legion of Honour was destined to form a distinct and particular class of privileged individuals, whom, by honours and bounties, he resolved to bind to his own interest.

This institution, which attained considerable political importance, originated in the custom which Napoleon had early introduced, of conferring on soldiers, of whatever rank, a sword, fusée, or other military weapon, in the name of the state, as acknowledging and commemorating some act of peculiar gallantry. The influence of such public rewards was of course very great. They encouraged those who had received them to make every effort to preserve the character which they had thus gained, while they awakened the emulation of hundreds and thousands who desired similar marks of distinction. Buonaparte now formed the project of embodying the persons who had merited such rewards into an association, similar in many respects to those orders of chivalry, with which, during the Middle Ages, the sovereigns of Europe surrounded themselves. These, however, have been uniformly created on the feudal principles, and the honour they confer was supposed to be limited, to persons of some rank and condition; but the scheme of Buonaparte was to extend this species of honourable distinction through all ranks, in the quality proper to each, as medals to be distributed among various classes of the community are struck upon metals of different value, but are all stamped with the same dye. The outlines of the institution were these:

The Legion of Honour was to consist of a great council of administration and fifteen cohorts, each of which was to have its own separate headquarters, in some distinguished town of the Republic. The council was to consist of the three consuls, and four other members; a senator, a member of the Legislative Body, a member of the Tribunate, and one of the Council of State, each chosen by the body to which he belonged. The order might be acquired by distinguished merit, either of a civil or a military nature. The first consul was captain-general of the legion, and president of the council of administration. Every cohort was to consist of 7 grand officers, 20 commanders, 30 subaltern officers, 350 legionaries. Their nomination was for life, and their appointments considerable. They were to swear upon their honour to defend the government of France, and maintain the inviolability of her empire; to combat, by every lawful means, against the re-establishment of the feudal institutions; and to concur in maintaining the principles of liberty and equality.

Notwithstanding these last words, the friends of liberty were not to be blinded, regarding the purpose of this new institution. Their number was now much limited; but amidst their weakness they had listened to the lessons of prudence and experience, and seem to have set themselves seriously, and at the same time moderately to work, to protect the cause of practical and useful freedom, by such resistance as the constitution still permitted, by means of the Tribunate and the Legislative Body.

The institution of the Legion of Honour was at length carried in the Tribunate, by a majority of fifty-six voices over thirty-eight, and sanctioned in the Legislative Body by 166 over 110. The strong divisions of the opposition on this trying question, showed high spirit in those who composed that party; but they were placed in a situation so insulated and separated from the public, so utterly deprived of all constitutional guarantees for the protection of freedom, that their resistance, however honourable to themselves, was totally ineffectual.

CHAPTERS XXVII, XXVIII

Hostilities between Britain and France resumed. The Royal Navy swept up France's overseas possessions and commercial shipping, while France occupied Hanover and illegally detained, in the event for up to twelve years, British travellers in France. Napoleon's best chance to invade Britain occurred immediately on the resumption of said hostilities, before Britain's defences were prepared, but France was equally unprepared at the time.

While Buonaparte was meditating the regeneration of Europe, by means of conquering first Britain, and then the northern powers, a course of opposition to his government was beginning to arise even among the soldiers themselves. The consulate for life was naturally considered as a death-blow to the Republic; and to that name many of the principal officers of the army, who had advanced themselves to promotion by means of the Revolution, still held a grateful attachment. The dissatisfaction of these men was the more natural, as some of them might see in Buonaparte nothing more than a successful adventurer, who had raised himself high above the heads of his comrade, and now exacted their homage. The discontent spread wide, and was secretly augmented by the agents of the house of Bourbon; and, besides the constitutional Opposition, there existed malcontents without doors, composed of two parties, and the most eager partisans of both began to meditate on the practicability of removing him by any means, the most violent not excepted.

These zealots, however, bore no proportion to the great body of Frenchmen, who, displeased with the usurpation of Buonaparte, and disposed to overthrow it, if possible, held themselves yet obliged to refrain from all practices against his life. Proposing to destroy his power in the same way in which it had been built, the first and most necessary task of the discontented party was to find some military chief, whose reputation might bear to be balanced against that of Napoleon; and no one could claim such distinction excepting Moreau. If his campaigns were inferior to those of his great rival in lightning-like brilliancy and celerity, and in boldness of combination, they were executed at smaller loss to his troops, and were less calculated to expose him to disastrous consequences if they chanced to miscarry. Moreau was no less celebrated for his retreat through the defiles of the Black Forest, in 1796, than for the splendid and decisive victory of Hohenlinden.

Moreau's natural temper was mild, gentle, and accessible to persuasion – a man of great abilities certainly, but scarcely displaying the bold and decisive character which he ought to possess, who aspires to place himself at the head of a faction in the state. Indeed, it rather would seem that he was forced into that situation by the influence of general opinion, joined to concurring circumstances, than that he deliberately aspired to place himself there. He was in every respect a man who had risen by the Revolution. He was not, therefore, naturally inclined towards the Bourbons; yet when Pichegru's communications with the exiled family in 1795 became known to him by the correspondence which he intercepted, Moreau kept the secret until some months after, when Pichegru had, with the rest of his party, fallen under the Revolution of 18th Fructidor. After this period, Moreau's marriage with a lady who entertained sentiments favourable to the Bourbons, seems to have gone some length in deciding his own political opinions.

Moreau had lent Buonaparte his sword and countenance on 18th Brumaire; but he was soon dissatisfied with the engrossing ambition of the new ruler of France, and they became gradually estranged from each other. This was not the fault of Buonaparte, who, naturally desirous of attaching to himself so great a general, showed him considerable attention, and complained that it was received with coldness. Upon the institution of the Legion of Honour, one of the grand crosses was offered to him. "The fool!" said Moreau, "does he not know that I have belonged to the ranks of honour for these twelve years?" Another pleasantry on this topic, upon which Buonaparte was very sensitive, was a company of officers, who dined together with Moreau, voting a sauce-pan of honour to the general's cook, on account of his merits in dressing some particular dish. Thus, living estranged from Buonaparte, Moreau came to be gradually regarded as the head of the disaffected party in France; and the eyes of all those who disliked Napoleon or his government, were fixed upon him.

Meantime, the peace of Amiens being broken, the British Government resolved once more to avail themselves of the state of public feeling in France, and engage the partisans of royalty in a fresh attack upon the Consular Government. They were probably in some degree deceived concerning the strength of that party, and had listened too implicitly to the promises and projects of agents who exaggerated even their own hopes in communicating them to the British ministers. It seems to have been acknowledged, that little success was to be hoped for, unless Moreau could be brought to join the conspiracy. This, however, was esteemed possible; and notwithstanding the disagreement, personal as well as political, which had subsisted betwixt him and Pichegru, the latter seems to have undertaken to become the medium of communication betwixt Moreau and the Royalists. Escaped from the deserts of Cayenne, to which he had been exiled, Pichegru had for some time found refuge and support in London, and there openly professed his principles as a Royalist.

A scheme was in agitation for raising the Royalists in the west, and the Duke de Berri was to make a descent on the coast of Picardy, to favour the insurrection. The Duke d'Enghien, grandson of the Prince of Condé, fixed his residence under the protection of the Margrave of Baden, at the chateau of Ettenheim, with the purpose, doubtless, of being ready to put himself at the head of the Royalists in the east of France, or, if occasion should offer, in Paris itself. This prince of the house of Bourbon was in the flower of youth, handsome, brave, and high-minded. He had been distinguished for his courage in the emigrant army, which his grandfather commanded. He gained by his valour the battle of Bortsheim; and when his army, to whom the French Republicans showed no quarter, desired to execute reprisals on their prisoners, he threw himself among them to prevent their violence. "These men," he said "are Frenchmen – they are unfortunate – I place them under the guardianship of your honour and your humanity." Such was the princely youth, whose name must now be written in bloody characters in this part of Napoleon's history.

Pichegru, Georges Cadoudal, and about thirty other Royalists of the most determined character, were secretly landed in France, made their way to the metropolis, and contrived to find lurking places invisible to the all-seeing police. There can be no reason to doubt that a part of those agents, and Georges in particular, saw the greatest obstacle in the existence of Buonaparte, and were resolved to commence by his assassination. Pichegru, who was constantly in company with Georges, cannot well be supposed ignorant of this purpose.

Pichegru effected the desired communication with Moreau. They met at least twice; and it is certain that on one of these occasions Pichegru carried with him Georges Cadoudal, at whose person and plans Moreau expressed horror, and desired that Pichegru would not again bring that irrational savage into his company. The cause of his dislike we must naturally suppose to have been the nature of the measures Georges proposed, being the last to which Moreau would willingly have resorted; but Buonaparte, when pretending to give an exact account of what passed betwixt Moreau and Pichegru, represents the conduct of the former in a very different point of view. Moreau, according to this account, informed Pichegru, that while the first consul lived, he had not the slightest interest in the army; but, were Napoleon removed, all eyes would be fixed on himself alone – that he would then become first consul. But we give no credit whatever to this story. Though nothing could have been so important to the first consul at the time as to produce proof of Moreau's direct accession to the plot on his life, no such proof was ever brought forward.

The police were speedily in action. Notice had been received that a band of Royalists had introduced themselves into the capital, though it was for some time very difficult to apprehend them. Georges, meanwhile, prosecuted his attempt against the chief consul, and is believed at one time to have insinuated himself in the disguise of a menial into Buonaparte's apartment; but without finding any opportunity to strike the blow, which his uncommon strength and desperate resolution might otherwise have rendered decisive. All the barriers were closed, and a division of Buonaparte's guards maintained the closest watch, to prevent anyone escaping from the city. By degrees sufficient light was obtained to arrest Moreau himself. This took place on the 15th February, 1804. He was seized without difficulty or resistance, while residing quietly at his country-house. On the day following, an order of the day announced the fact to the citizens, with the additional information, that Moreau was engaged in a conspiracy with Pichegru, Georges, and others, who were closely pursued by the police.

The news of Moreau's imprisonment produced the deepest sensation in Paris; and the reports which were circulated on the subject were by no means favourable to Buonaparte. Upon the 17th February, the great judge of police denounced Pichegru, Georges, and others, as having returned to France, with the purpose of overthrowing the government, and assassinating the chief consul, and implicated Moreau as having held communication with them.

Meanwhile the vigilance of the police accomplished the arrest of almost all the persons concerned in the plot. A false friend, whom Pichegru had trusted to the highest degree, betrayed his confidence for a large bribe, and introduced the gendarmes into his apartment while he was asleep. Georges Cadoudal, perhaps a yet more important capture, fell into the hands of the police soon after. He had been traced so closely, that at length he dared not enter a house, but spent many hours of the day and night in driving about Paris in a cabriolet. On being arrested, he shot one of the gendarmes dead, and mortally wounded another. The other conspirators were arrested to the number of forty persons, some followers or associates of Georges, and others belonging to the ancient nobility.

It might have been supposed, that among so many prisoners, enough of victims might have been selected to atone with their lives for the attempt which was alleged to be designed against the person of the first consul. Most unhappily for his fame, Napoleon thought otherwise; and sought to give a fuller scope to the gratification of his revenge. We have observed, that the residence of the Duke d'Enghien upon the French frontier was to a certain degree connected with the enterprise undertaken by Pichegru, so far as concerned the proposed insurrection of the royalists in Paris. This we infer from the duke's admission that he resided at Ettenheim in the expectation of having soon a part of importance to play in France. But that the duke participated in, or countenanced in the slightest degree, the meditated attempt on Buonaparte's life, has never even been alleged, and is contrary to all the proof led in the case.

On the evening of the 14th March, a body of French soldiers and gendarmes, commanded by Colonel Ordonner, acting under the direction of Caulaincourt, afterwards Duke of Vicenza, suddenly entered the territory of Baden, a power with whom France was in profound peace, and surrounded the chateau in which the unfortunate prince resided. The descendant of Condé sprung to his arms, but was prevented from using them by one of his attendants, who represented the force of the assailants as too great to be resisted. The soldiers rushed into the apartment, and, presenting their pistols, demanded to know which was the Duke d'Enghien. "If you desire to arrest him," said the Duke, "you ought to have his description in your warrant." – "Then we must seize on you all," replied the officer in command; and the prince, with his little household, was arrested and carried to a mill at some distance from the house, where he was permitted to receive some clothes and necessaries. Being now recognised, he was transferred, with his attendants, to the citadel of Strasburg, and separated from the gentlemen of his household, with the exception of his aid-de-camp, the Baron de St. Jacques. He was allowed to communicate with no one. He remained a close prisoner for three days; but on the 18th, betwixt one and two in the morning, he was obliged to rise and dress himself hastily, being only informed that he was about to commence a journey. He requested the attendance of his valet-de-chambre, but was answered that it was unnecessary. The linen which he was permitted to take with him amounted to two shirts only; so nicely had his worldly wants been ascertained. He was transported with the utmost speed and secrecy towards Paris, where he arrived on the 20th; and, after having been committed for a few hours to the Temple, was transferred to the ancient Gothic castle of Vincennes, about a mile from the city, long used as a state prison, but whose walls never received a more illustrious or a more innocent victim. There he was permitted to take some repose; and, as if the favour had only been granted for the purpose of being withdrawn, he was awaked at midnight, and called upon to sustain an interrogatory on which his life depended, and to which he replied with the utmost composure. On the ensuing night, at the same dead hour, he was brought before the pretended court. The law enjoined that he should have had a defender appointed to plead his cause. But none such was allotted to him.

The inquisitors, before whom he was hurried, formed a military commission of eight officers, having General Hulin as their president. They were, as the proceedings express it, named by Buonaparte's brother-in-law Murat, then governor of Paris. Though necessarily exhausted with fatigue and want of rest, the Duke d'Enghien performed in this melancholy scene a part worthy of the last descendant of the great Condé. He avowed his name and rank, and the share which he had taken in the war against France, but denied all knowledge of Pichegru or of his conspiracy. The interrogations ended by his demanding an audience of the chief consul. "My name," he said, "my rank, my sentiments, and the peculiar distress of my situation, lead me to hope that my request will not be refused."

The military commissioners paused and hesitated – nay, though selected doubtless as fitted for the office, they were even affected by the whole behaviour, and especially by the intrepidity, of the unhappy prince. But Savary, then chief of the police, stood behind the president's chair, and controlled their sentiments of compassion. When they proposed to further the prisoner's request, Savary cut the discussion short. At length they reported their opinion, that the Duke d'Enghien was guilty of having fought against the Republic, intrigued with England, and maintained intelligence in Strasburg, for the purpose of seizing the place; great part of which allegations, and especially the last, was in express contradiction to the only proof adduced, the admission of the prisoner himself. The report being sent to Buonaparte to know his further pleasure, the court received for answer their own letter, marked with the emphatic words, "Condemned to death." The sentence was pronounced, and the prisoner received it with the same intrepid gallantry which distinguished him through the whole of the bloody scene. He requested the aid of a confessor. "Would you die like a monk!" is said to have been the insulting reply. The duke, without noticing the insult, knelt down for a minute, and seemed absorbed in profound devotion.

"Let us go," he said, when he arose. All was in readiness for the execution; and, as if to stamp the trial as a mere mockery, the grave had been prepared ere the judgment pronounced. Upon quitting the apartment in which the pretended trial had taken place, the prince was conducted by torch-light down a winding-stair, which seemed to descend to the dungeons of the ancient castle.

"Am I to be immured in an oubliette?" he said, naturally recollecting the use which had sometimes been made of those tombs for the living. – "No, Monseigneur," answered the soldier he addressed, in a voice interrupted by sobs, "be tranquil on that subject." The stair led to a postern, which opened into the castle ditch, where, as we have already said, a grave was dug, beside which were drawn up a party of the *gendarme d'élite*. It was near six o'clock in the morning, and day had dawned. But as there was a heavy mist on the ground, several torches and lamps mixed their pale and ominous light with that afforded by the heavens – a circumstance which seems to have given rise to the inaccurate report, that a lantern was tied to the button of the victim, that his slayers might take the more certain aim. Savary was again in attendance, and had taken his place upon a parapet which commanded the place of execution. The victim was placed, the fatal word was given by the future Duke de Rovigo, the party fired, and the prisoner fell. The body, dressed as it was, and without the slightest attention to the usual decencies of sepulture, was huddled into the grave with as little ceremony as common robbers use towards the carcases of the murdered.

Paris learned with astonishment and fear the singular deed which had been perpetrated so near her walls. No act had ever excited more universal horror, both in France and in foreign countries, and none has left so deep a stain on the memory of Napoleon. If there were further proof necessary of the general opinion of mankind on the subject, the anxiety displayed by Savary, Hulin, and the other subaltern agents in this shameful transaction to diminish their own share in it, or transfer it to others, would be sufficient evidence of the deep responsibility to which they felt themselves subjected.

There is but justice, however, in listening to the defence which Buonaparte set up for himself. His exculpation seems to have assumed a different character, according to the audience to whom it was stated. Among his intimate friends and followers, he appears to have represented the whole transaction as an affair not of his own device, but which was pressed upon him by surprise by his ministers. "I was seated," he said, "alone, and engaged in finishing my coffee, when they came to announce to me the discovery of some new machination. They represented it was time to put an end to such horrible attempts, by washing myself in the blood of one amongst the Bourbons; and they suggested the Duke d'Enghien as the most proper victim." Buonaparte proceeds to say that he did not know exactly who the Duke d'Enghien was, far less that he resided so near France. This was explained. "In that case," said Napoleon, "he ought to be arrested." His prudent ministers had foreseen this conclusion. They had the whole scheme laid, and the orders ready drawn up for Buonaparte's signature; so that, according to this account, he was hurried into the enormity by the zeal of those about him, or perhaps in consequence of their private views and mysterious intrigues. He also charged Talleyrand with concealing from him a letter, written by the unfortunate prisoner, in which he offered his services to Buonaparte. If this had reached him in time, he intimates that he would have spared the prince's life.

It is unfortunate for the truth of this statement and the soundness of the defence which it contains, that neither Talleyrand, nor any human being save Buonaparte himself, could have the least interest in the death of the Duke d'Enghien. That Napoleon should be furious at the conspiracies of Georges and Pichegru, and should be willing to avenge the personal dangers he incurred; and that he should be desirous to intimidate the family of Bourbon, by "washing himself," as he expresses it, "in the blood of one of their House," was much in character. But that the sagacious Talleyrand should have hurried on a cruel proceeding, in which he had no earthly interest, is as unlikely, as that, if he had desired to do so, he could have been able to elicit from Buonaparte the powers necessary for an act of so much consequence, without his master having given the affair, in all its bearings, the most full and ample consideration. It may also be noticed, that besides transferring a part at least of the guilt from himself, Buonaparte might be disposed to gratify his revenge against Talleyrand, by stigmatising him, from St. Helena, with a crime the most odious to his new sovereigns of the House of Bourbon. Lastly, the existence of the letter has never been proved, and it is inconsistent with every thought and sentiment of the Duke d'Enghien. It is besides said to have been dated from Strasburg; and the duke's aide-de-camp, the Baron de St. Jacques, has given his testimony, that he was never an instant separated from his patron during his confinement in that citadel; and that the duke neither wrote a letter to Buonaparte nor to anyone else. But, after all, if Buonaparte had actually proceeded in this bloody matter upon the instigation of Talleyrand, it cannot be denied, that, as a man knowing right from wrong, he could not hope to transfer to his counsellor the guilt of the measures which he executed at his recommendation. The murder, like the rebellion of Absalom, was not less a crime, even supposing it recommended and facilitated by the unconscientious counsels of a modern Achitophel.

Accordingly, Napoleon has not chosen to trust to this defence; but, inconsistently with this pretence, he has, upon other occasions, broadly and boldly avowed that it was in itself just and necessary; that the Duke d'Enghien was condemned by the laws, and suffered execution accordingly.

It is an easy task to show, that even according to the law of France, jealous and severe as it was in its application to such subjects, there existed no right to take the life of the Duke. It is true he was an emigrant, and the law denounced the penalty of death against any of these as should return to France with arms in their hands. But the Duke did not so return – nay, his returning at all was not an act of his own, but the consequence of violence exercised on his person. He was in a more favourable case than even those emigrants whom storms had cast on their native shore, and whom Buonaparte himself considered as objects of pity, not of punishment. He had indeed born arms against France; but as a member of the house of Bourbon, he was not and could not be accounted, a subject of Buonaparte, having left the country before his name was heard of; nor could he be considered as in contumacy against the state of France, for he, like the rest of the royal family, was specially excluded from the benefits of the amnesty which invited the return of the less distinguished emigrants. The act by which he was trepanned, and brought within the compass of French power, not of French law, was as much a violation of the rights of nations, as the precipitation with which the pretended trial followed the arrest, and the execution the trial, was an outrage upon humanity. On the trial no witnesses were produced, nor did any investigation take place, saving by the interrogation of the prisoner. Whatever points of accusation, therefore, are not established by the admission of the Duke himself, must be considered as totally unproved. Yet this unconscientious tribunal not only found their prisoner guilty of having borne arms against the Republic, which he readily admitted, but of having placed himself at the head of a party of French emigrants in the pay of England, and carried on machinations for surprising the city of Strasburg; charges which he himself positively denied, and which were supported by no proof whatever.

Buonaparte, well aware of the total irregularity of the proceedings, seems, on some occasions, to have wisely renounced any attempt to defend what he must have been convinced was indefensible, and vindicated his conduct upon general grounds, of a nature well worthy of notice. It seems that, when he spoke of the death of the Duke d'Enghien among his attendants, he always chose to represent it as a case falling under the ordinary forms of law, in which all regularity was observed, and where, though he might be accused of severity, he could not be charged with violation of justice. This was safe language to hearers from whom he was sure to receive neither objection nor contradiction and is just an instance of an attempt, on the part of a conscientiously guilty party, to establish, by repeated asseverations, an innocence which was inconsistent with fact. But with strangers, from whom replies and argument might be expected, Napoleon took broader grounds. He alleged the death of the Duke d'Enghien to be an act of self-defence, a measure of state policy, arising out of the natural rights of humanity, by which a man, to save his own life, is entitled to take away that of another. "I was assailed," he said, "on all hands by the enemies whom the Bourbons raised up against me; threatened with air-guns, infernal machines, and deadly stratagems of every kind. I had no tribunal on earth to which I could appeal for protection, therefore I had a right to protect myself; and by putting to death one of those whose followers threatened my life, I was entitled to strike a salutary terror into the others."

We have no doubt that, in this argument, Buonaparte explained his real motives; at least we can only add to them the stimulus of obstinate resentment, and implacable revenge. But the whole resolves itself into an allegation of that state necessity, which has been justly called the Tyrant's plea, and which has always been at hand to defend, or rather to palliate the worst crimes of sovereigns. In every point of view, the act was a murder; and the stain of the Duke d'Enghien's blood must remain indelibly upon Napoleon Buonaparte.

The Duke d'Enghien's execution took place on the 21st March; on the 7th April following, General Pichegru was found dead in his prison. A black handkerchief was wrapped round his neck, which had been tightened by twisting round a short stick inserted through one of the folds. It was asserted that he had turned this stick with his own hands, until he lost the power of respiring, and then, by laying his head of the pillow, had secured the stick in its position. It did not escape the public, that this was a mode of terminating life far more likely to be inflicted by the hands of others. Surgeons were found, but men, it is said, of small reputation, to sign a report upon the state of the body, in which they affirm that Pichegru had died by suicide; yet as he must have lost animation and sense so soon as he had twisted the stick to the point of strangulation, it seems strange he should not have then unclosed his grasp on the fatal tourniquet. In that case the pressure must have relaxed, and the fatal purpose have remained unaccomplished. No human eye could see into the dark recesses of a state prison, but there were not wanting many who entertained a total disbelief of Pichegru's suicide. It was argued that the first consul did not dare to bring before a public tribunal, and subject to a personal interrogatory, a man of Pichegru's boldness and presence of mind – it was said, also, that his evidence would have been decisively favourable to Moreau – that the citizens of Paris were many of them attached to Pichegru's person – that the soldiers had not forgotten his military fame – and that in consideration of these circumstances, it was judged most expedient to take away his life in prison.

Buonaparte's government was now left to deal with Georges and his comrades, as well as Moreau. With the first it was an easy task, for the Chouan chief retained, in the court before which he was conveyed, the same fearless tone of defiance which he had displayed from the beginning. He acknowledged that he came to Paris for the sake of making war personally on Napoleon, and seemed only to regret his captivity, as it had disconcerted his enterprise. There was no difficulty in obtaining sentence of death against Georges and nineteen of his associates.

The discovery and suppression of this conspiracy seems to have produced, in a great degree, the effect expected by Buonaparte. The Royal party became silent and submissive, and, but that their aversion to the reign of Napoleon showed itself in lampoons, satires, and witticisms, which were circulated in their evening parties, it could hardly have been known to exist. Offers were made to Buonaparte to rid him of the remaining Bourbons, in consideration of a large sum of money; but with better judgment than had dictated his conduct of late, he rejected the proposal. His interest, he was now convinced, would be better consulted by a line of policy which would reduce the exiled family to a state of insignificance, than by any rash and violent proceedings, which must necessarily draw men's attention, and, in doing so, were likely to interest them on behalf of the sufferers, and animate them against their powerful oppressor. With this purpose, the names of the exiled family were, shortly after this period, carefully suppressed in all periodical publications, and, with one or two exceptions, little allusion to their existence can be traced in the pages of the official journal of France; and, unquestionably, the policy was wisely adopted towards a people so light, and animated so intensely with the interest of the moment, as the French, to whom the present is a great deal, the future much less, and the past nothing at all.

Though George's part of the conspiracy was disposed of thus easily, the trial of Moreau involved a much more dangerous task. It was found impossible to procure evidence against him, beyond his own admission that he had seen Pichegru twice; and this admission was coupled with a positive denial that he had engaged to be participant in his schemes. A majority of the judges seemed disposed to acquit him entirely, but were cautioned by the president Hemart, that, by doing so, they would force the government upon violent measures. Adopting this hint, and willing to compromise matters, they declared Moreau guilty, but not to the extent of a capital crime. He was subjected to imprisonment for two years; but the soldiers continuing to interest themselves in his fate, Fouché, who about this time was restored to the administration of police, interceded warmly in his favour, and seconded the applications of Madame Moreau, for a commutation of her husband's sentence. His doom of imprisonment was therefore exchanged for that of exile; a mode of punishment safer for Moreau, considering the late incidents in the prisons of state; and more advantageous for Buonaparte, as removing entirely from the thoughts of the republican party, and of the soldiers, a leader, whose military talents brooked comparison with his own, and to whom the public eye would naturally be turned when any cause of discontent with their present government might incline them to look elsewhere.

*C*HAPTER XXIX

Buonaparte, as we have seen, gained a great accession of power by the event of Pichegru's conspiracy. But this was, in some measure, counterbalanced by the diminution of character which attached to the kidnapping and murdering the Duke d'Enghien, and by the foul suspicions arising from the mysterious fate of Pichegru and Wright. He possessed no longer the respect which might be claimed by a victor and legislator, but had distinctly shown that either the sudden tempest of ungoverned passion, or the rankling feelings of personal hatred, could induce him to take the readiest means of wreaking the basest, as well as the bloodiest vengeance. Deep indignation was felt through every country on the Continent, though Russia and Sweden alone ventured to express their dissatisfaction with a proceeding so contrary to the law of nations.

Aware of the unpopularity which attached to his late cruel proceedings, Buonaparte became desirous to counterbalance it by filling the public mind with a terrific idea of the schemes of England, which, in framing and encouraging attempts upon his life, drove him to those unusual and extraordinary acts, which he desired to represent as measures of retaliation.

This chapter goes on to relate Lord Elgin's misadventures at the hands of the French police as further evidence of Napoleonic knavery.

*C*HAPTER XXX

The death of the Duke d'Enghien and of Pichegru had intimidated the Royalists, while the exile of Moreau had left the Republicans without a leader.

These events, while they greatly injured Buonaparte's character as a man, extended, in a like proportion, the idea of his power, and of his determination to employ it to the utmost extremity against whoever might oppose him. This moment, therefore, of general submission and intimidation was the fittest to be used for transmuting the military baton of the first consul into a sceptre, resembling those of the ancient and established sovereignties of Europe. The title of King most obviously presented itself; but it was connected with the claims of the Bourbons, which it was not Buonaparte's policy to recall to remembrance. That of Emperor implied a yet higher power of sovereignty, and there existed no competitor who could challenge a claim to it. It was a novelty also, and flattered the French love of change; and though, in fact, the establishment of an empire was inconsistent with the various oaths taken against royalty, it was not, in terms, so directly contradictory to them. To Napoleon's own ear, the word King might sound as if it restricted his power within the limits of the ancient kingdom; while that of Emperor might comprise dominions equal to the wide sweep of ancient Rome herself, and the bounds of the habitable earth alone could be considered as circumscribing their extent.

The main body of the nation being passive or intimidated, there was no occasion to stand upon much ceremony with the constitutional bodies, the members of which were selected and paid by Buonaparte himself, held their posts at his pleasure, had every species of advancement to hope if they promoted his schemes, and every evil, of which the least would be deprivation of office, to expect, should they thwart him. On the 30th of April, 1804, Curée, an orator of no great note, (and who was perhaps selected on that very account, that his proposal might be disavowed, should it meet with unexpected opposition,) took the lead in this measure, which was to destroy the slight and nominal remains of a free constitution which France retained.

The Senate, to whom the Tribunate hastened to present their project of establishing despotism under its own undisguised title, hastened to form a senatus consultum, which established the new constitution of France. The outline was as follows:

1st, Napoleon Buonaparte was declared hereditary Emperor of the French nation. The empire was made hereditary, first in the male line of the Emperor's direct descendants. Failing these, Napoleon might adopt the sons or grandsons of his brothers, to succeed him in such order as he might point out. In default of such adoptive heirs, Joseph and Louis Buonaparte were declared the lawful heirs of the empire. Lucien and Jerome Buonaparte were excluded from this rich inheritance, as they had both disobliged Napoleon by marrying without his consent. 2nd, The members of the Imperial family were declared Princes of the Blood, and by the decree of the Senate, the offices of Grand Elector, Arch-chancellor of the Empire, Arch-chancellor of State, High Constable, and Great Admiral of the Empire, were established as necessary appendages of the empire. These dignitaries, named of course by the Emperor himself, consisting of his relatives, connections, and most faithful adherents, formed his Grand Council. The rank of Marshal of the Empire was conferred upon seventeen of the most distinguished generals, comprehending Jourdan, Augereau, and others, formerly zealous Republicans. Duroc was named Grand Marshal of the Palace; Caulaincourt, Master of the Horse; Berthier, Grand Huntsman, and the Comte de Ségur, a nobleman of the old court, Master of Ceremonies.

Measures were taken to preserve appearances, by obtaining, in show at least, the opinion of the people, on this radical change. Government, however, were already confident of their approbation, which, indeed, had never been refused to any of the various constitutions, however inconsistent, that had succeeded each other with such rapidity. Secure in this point, Buonaparte's accession to the empire was proclaimed with the greatest pomp, without waiting to inquire whether the people approved. The proclamation was coldly received, even by the populace.

The Emperor, accompanied by his Empress, who bore her honours both gracefully and meekly, visited Aix-la-Chapelle, and the frontiers of Germany. They received the congratulations of all the powers of Europe, excepting England, Russia, and Sweden, upon their new exaltation; and the German princes, who had every thing to hope and fear from so powerful a neighbour, hastened to pay their compliments to Napoleon. But the most splendid and public recognition of his new rank was yet to be made, by the formal act of coronation, which Napoleon determined should take place with circumstances of solemnity, which had been beyond the reach of any temporal prince, however powerful, for many ages. His policy was often marked by a wish to revive, imitate, and connect his own titles and interest with some ancient observance of former days; as if the novelty of his claims could have been rendered more venerable by investing them with antiquated forms. Pope Leo had placed a golden crown on the head of Charlemagne, and proclaimed him Emperor of the Romans. Pius VII, he determined, should do the same for a successor to much more than the actual power of Charlemagne. But though Charlemagne had repaired to Rome to receive inauguration from the hands of the Pontiff, Napoleon resolved that he who now owned the proud, and in Protestant eyes profane, title of Vicar of Christ, should travel to France to perform the coronation of the successful chief.

Humiliating as the compliance with Buonaparte's request must have seemed to the more devoted Catholics, Pius VII had already sacrificed, to obtain the Concordat, so much of the power and privileges of the Roman See, that he could hardly have been justified if he had run the risk of losing the advantages of a treaty so dearly purchased, by declining to incur some personal trouble, or, it might be termed, some direct self-abasement. The Pope, and the cardinals whom he consulted implored the illumination of Heaven upon their councils; but it was the stern voice of necessity which assured them, that except at the risk of dividing the Church by a schism, they could not refuse to comply.

On the 2nd December, the ceremony of the coronation took place in Notre Dame, with the addition of every ceremony which could be devised to add to its solemnity. The Emperor took his coronation oath, as usual on such occasions, with his hands upon the Scripture, and in the form in which it was repeated to him by the Pope. But in the act of coronation itself, there was a marked deviation from the universal custom, characteristic of the man, the age, and the conjuncture. In all other similar solemnities, the crown had been placed on the sovereign's head by the presiding spiritual person, as representing the Deity, by whom princes rule. But not even from the Head of the Catholic Church would Buonaparte consent to receive the golden symbol of sovereignty, which he was sensible he owed solely to his own unparalleled train of military and civil successes. The crown having been blessed by the Pope, Napoleon took it from the altar with his own hands, and placed it on his brows. He then put the diadem on the head of his Empress, as if determined to show that his authority was the child of his own actions.

The very day before the ceremony, the Senate had waited upon the Emperor with the result of the votes, which, till that time, had been taken for granted. Upwards of 3, 500,000 citizens had given their votes on this occasion; of whom only about 3500 had declared against the proposition. The vice-president, Neufchateau, declared, "this report was the unbiased expression of the people's choice. No government could plead a title more authentic."

We will not stop to inquire how the registers, in which the votes of the citizens were enrolled, were managed by the functionaries who had the charge of them; it is only necessary to state in passing, that these returning officers were in general accessible to the influence of government, and that there was no possibility of instituting any scrutiny into the authenticity of the returns. Neither will we repeat, that instead of waiting for the event of the popular vote, he had accepted of the empire from the Senate, and had been proclaimed Emperor accordingly. Waiving those circumstances entirely, let it be remembered, that France is usually reckoned to contain upwards of thirty million inhabitants, and that 3, 500,000 only gave their votes. This was not a third part, deducing women and children, of those who had a title to express their opinion, where it was to be held decisive of the greatest change which the state could undergo; and it must be allowed that the authority of so limited a portion of the people is far too small to bind the remainder. We have heard it indeed argued, that the question having been formally put to the nation at large, everyone was under an obligation to make a specific reply; and they who did not vote, must be held to have acquiesced in the opinion expressed by the majority of such as did. This argument, being directly contrary to the presumption of law in all similar cases, is not more valid than the defence of the soldier, who, accused of having stolen a necklace from an image of the Virgin, replied to the charge, that he had first asked the Madonna's permission, and, receiving no answer, had taken silence for consent. But we leave those considerations; nor do we stop to inquire how many, amid the three million and upwards of voters, gave an unwilling signature, which they would have refused if they had dared.

In much of his administration, Buonaparte showed that he desired to have no advantage separate from that of France; that he conceived her interests to be connected with his own glory; that he expended his wealth in ornamenting the empire, and not upon objects more immediately personal to himself. We have no doubt that he had more pleasure in seeing treasures of art added to the Museum, than in hanging them on the walls of his own palace; and that he spoke truly, when asserting that he grudged Josephine the expensive plants with which she decorated her residence at Malmaison, because her taste interfered with the prosperity of the public botanical garden of Paris. We allow, therefore, that Buonaparte fully identified himself with the country which he had rendered his patrimony; and that while it should be called by his name, he was desirous of investing it with as much external splendour, and as much internal prosperity as his gigantic schemes were able to compass. No doubt it may be said, so completely was the country identified with its ruler, that as France had nothing but what belonged to its Emperor, he was in fact improving his own estate when he advanced her public works, and could no more be said to lose sight of his own interest, than a private gentleman does, who neglects his garden to ornament his park. But it is not fair to press the motives of human nature to their last retreat, in which something like a taint of self-interest may so often be discovered. It is enough to reply, that the selfishness which embraces the interests of a whole kingdom, is of a kind so liberal, so extended, and so refined, as to be closely allied to patriotism; and that the good intentions of Buonaparte towards that France, over which he ruled with despotic sway, can be no more doubted, than the affections of an arbitrary father whose object it is to make his son prosperous and happy, to which he annexes as the only condition, that he shall be implicitly obedient to every tittle of his will. The misfortune is, however, that arbitrary power is in itself a faculty, which, whether exercised over a kingdom, or in the bosom of a family, is apt to be used with caprice rather than judgment, and becomes a snare to those who possess it, as well as a burden to those over whom it extends. A father, for example, seeks the happiness of his son, while he endeavours to assure his fortunes, by compelling him to enter into a mercenary and reluctant marriage; and Buonaparte conceived himself to be benefiting as well as aggrandising France, when, preferring the splendour of conquest to the blessings of peace, he led the flower of her young men to perish in foreign fields, and finally was the means of her being delivered up, drained of her population, to the mercy of the foreign invaders.

Where France showed the way, Italy could but follow, and Napoleon was duly invited to assume the Italian crown, which he accepted on 17th March 1805. His coronation, in Milan, was followed by the annexation of Genoa to France.

*C*HAPTER XXXI

Buonaparte, Consul, had affected to give a direct testimony of his desire to make peace, by opening a communication immediately and personally with the King of Great Britain. Buonaparte, Emperor, had, according to his own interpretation of his proceedings, expiated by his elevation all the crimes of the Revolution which had alarmed such governments as continued to rest their authority on the ancient basis of legitimacy. He had, according to his own belief, preserved in his system all that the Republic had produced of good, and done away all the memory of that which was evil. With such pretensions, he hastened to claim admission among the Princes of Europe. By a letter addressed to King George III, personally, under the title of "Sir my Brother," he endeavoured to prove that the hostilities between the nations ought to be ended.

The answer to his letter, addressed by the Secretary of State to M. Talleyrand, declared, that Britain could not make a precise reply to the proposal of peace, until she had communicated with her allies on the continent, and in particular with the Emperor of Russia. These expressions indicated, what was already well known to Buonaparte, the darkening of another continental storm, about to be directed against his power. On this occasion, Russia was the soul of the confederacy. Since the death of the unfortunate Paul had placed that mighty country under the government of a wise and prudent prince, her counsels had been dignified, wise, and moderate. She had offered her mediation betwixt the belligerent powers, which, accepted willingly by Great Britain, had been somewhat haughtily declined by France. Russia and England had engaged in an alliance, the general purpose of which was to form a league, to compel the French Government to consent to the re-establishment of the balance of Europe. The objects proposed were briefly the independence of Holland and Switzerland; the evacuation of Hanover and the north of Germany by the French; the restoration of Piedmont to the King of Sardinia; and the complete evacuation of Italy by the French. 500,000 men were to be employed; and Britain, besides affording the assistance of her forces by sea and land, was to pay large subsidies for supporting the armies of the coalition.

Great Britain and Russia were the animating sources of this new coalition against France; but it was impossible that they alone, without the concurrence of the Emperor of Austria and the King of Prussia, should be able to assail France with any prospect of making a successful impression. Every effort, therefore, was used to awaken those states to a sense of the extreme danger to which they were respectively exposed by the rapidly increasing extent of his empire. But since the unsuccessful campaign of the year 1792, Prussia had observed a cautious and wary neutrality. She had seen, not perhaps without secret pleasure, the humiliation of Austria, her natural rival in Germany, and she had taken many opportunities to make acquisition of petty objects of advantage, in consequence of the various changes upon the continent; so that she seemed to find her own interest in the successes of France. It is imagined, also, that Buonaparte had found some of her leading statesmen not altogether inaccessible to influence of a different kind, by the liberal exercise of which he was enabled to maintain a strong interest in the Prussian councils. But the principles of these ministers were far from being shared by the nation at large. The encroachments on the German Empire intimately concerned the safety of Prussia, and the nation saw, in the decay of the Austrian influence, the creation and increase of a strong German party in favour of France, to whom Bavaria, Wirtemberg, and almost all the petty princes upon the Rhine, and its vicinity, began now to look up with the devotion and reverence which had hitherto been paid to Austria and Prussia. The subjects of the Great Frederick also remembered his numerous victories, and, proud of the army which he had created and bequeathed to his successor, felt neither apprehension nor unwillingness at the thought of measuring forces with the Dictator of Europe. The councils, therefore, of

Prussia were divided; and though those which were favourable to France prevailed so far as to prevent her immediately becoming a member of the coalition, yet, by increasing her army to the war establishment, and marching forces towards the country which appeared about to become the scene of hostilities, Prussia gave plain intimation that the continuance of her neutrality depended upon the events of war.

Austria was more accessible to the application of the allies. The disasters of the last two wars, the extent and military character of her population, and, above all, the haughty determination of a Cabinet remarkable for the tenacity with which they retain and act upon the principles which they have once adopted, induced her Government to accede to the alliance. She increased her force in every quarter; and while the Archduke Charles took command of 80,000 men in Italy, on which country Austria always kept a wishful eye, 80,000 more, destined to act upon the Lech, and it was hoped upon the Rhine, were placed under the charge of General Mack. The Archduke Ferdinand, a prince of great courage and hopes, was the nominal commander of the last-mentioned army, while the real authority was lodged in this old and empty professor of tactics. The Archduke John was appointed to command in the Tyrol.

It remained only to try the event of negotiation, ere finally proceeding to military extremities. It was not difficult to state the causes of the war. By the peace of Luneville, the independence of the Italian, Helvetian, and Batavian republics had been stipulated; but instead of such terms being complied with, Napoleon, rendering himself Grand Mediator of Switzerland and King of Italy, had at the same time filled Holland with troops, and occupied the three countries in such a manner, as made them virtually, and almost avowedly, the absolute dependencies of France. Complaints on these heads, warmly urged by Austria, were sharply answered by France, who in her turn accused Austria of want of confidence, and of assuming arms in the midst of peace. The Emperor of Russia interfered, and sent a special ambassador to Paris, with the purpose of coming, if possible, to an amicable accommodation, which might even yet preserve the tranquillity of Europe. But ere Novosiltzoff had reached his destination, the union of Genoa with the French empire was announced; an encroachment which, joined to Napoleon's influence in Switzerland, rendered the whole north-western frontier of Italy open for the march of French armies, and precluded the possible hope of that fine country assuming any character of independence, even if, at a future time, its crown should be vested in a person different from the ruler of France. Russia countermanded her ambassador; and Austria, after the exchange of some more angry notes, began her daring enterprise by marching a large army upon Bavaria.

While General Mack expected the approach of the French upon his front, Buonaparte had formed the daring resolution to turn the flank of the Austrian general, cut him off from his country and his resources, and reduce him to the necessity, either of surrender, or of giving battle without a hope of success. To execute this great conception, the French army was parted into six grand divisions. The direction of the divisions intimated that it was the object of the French Emperor to move round the right wing of the Austrians, by keeping on the north or left side of the Danube, and then by crossing that river, to put themselves in the rear of Mack's army, and interpose betwixt him and Vienna.

A defeat at Guntzburg induced Mack at length to concentrate his army around Ulm; but Bavaria and Swabia were now fully in possession of the French and Bavarians; and the Austrian General Spangenberg, surrounded in Memmingen, was compelled to lay down his arms with 5000 men. The French had crossed the Rhine about the 26th September; it was now the 13th October, and they could scarcely be said to have begun the campaign, when they had made, on various points, not fewer than 20,000 prisoners. Napoleon, however, expected that resistance from Mack's despair, which no other motive had yet engaged him to offer; and he announced to his army the prospect of a general action.

No general action, however, took place, though several sanguinary affairs of a partial nature were fought, and terminated uniformly to the misfortune of the Austrians. In the meantime, disunion took place among their generals. The Archduke Ferdinand, Schwartzenberg, afterwards destined to play a remarkable part in this changeful history, with Collowrath and others, resolved to leave Mack and his army, and cut their way into Bohemia at the head of the cavalry. Meanwhile, Mack found himself, with the remains of his army, cooped up in Ulm, as Wurmser had been in Mantua. He published an order of the day, which intimated an intention to imitate the persevering defence of that heroic veteran. He forbade the word surrender to be used by anyone – he announced the arrival of two powerful armies, one of Austrians, one of Russians, whose appearance would presently raise the blockade – he declared his determination to eat horse-flesh rather than listen to any terms of capitulation. This bravado appeared on the 16th October, and the conditions of surrender were sub-scribed by Mack on the next day, having been probably in the course of adjustment when he was making these notable professions of resistance.

The effects of Mack's poltroonery, want of skill, and probable treach-ery, were equal to the results of a great victory. Artillery, baggage, and mil-itary stores, were given up to an immense extent. Eight general officers surrendered upon parole and upwards of 20,000 men became prisoners of war, and were marched into France. The numbers of the prisoners taken in this campaign were so great, that Buonaparte distributed them amongst the agriculturalists, so that their work in the fields might make up for the absence of the conscripts, whom he had withdrawn from such labour.

CHAPTER XXXII

The tide of war now rolled eastward, having surmounted and utterly demolished the formidable barrier which was opposed to it. Napoleon placed himself at the head of his central army. Ney, upon his right, was ready to repel any descent which might be made from the passes of the Tyrol. Murat, on his left, watched the motions of the Austrians, under the Archduke Ferdinand, who had cut their way into Bohemia. Lastly, the divi-sion of Augereau, (who had recently advanced from France at the head of an army of reserve,) occupying part of Swabia, served to protect the rear of the French army against any movement from the Vorarlberg; and at the same time menaced the Prussians, in case they should have crossed the Danube, and engaged in the war.

If, however, the weight of Prussia had been thrown into the scale with sufficient energy at this decisive moment, it would not probably have been a tiny resistance which Augereau could have offered that could have saved Napoleon from a perilous situation, since the large armies of the new enemy would have been placed in his rear, and, of course, his communications with France entirely cut off.

Trusting to the vacillating and timid policy of Prussia, Napoleon continued to push forward with his central forces towards Vienna, whose fate seemed decided after the disaster of Ulm. It is true, that an army, partly consisting of Russians and partly of Austrians, had pressed forward to prevent that disgraceful calamity, and, finding that the capitulation had taken place, were now retreating step by step in front of the advancing French; but, not exceeding 45,000 men, they were unable to make any effectual stand upon any position which might have covered Vienna. They halted, indeed, repeatedly, and fought some severe though partial actions; but always ended by continuing their retreat, which was now directed upon Moravia, where the grand Russian army had already assembled, under the command of the Emperor Alexander, and were expecting still further reinforcements under General Buxhowden.

Some attempts were made to place Vienna in a state of defence, and the inhabitants were called upon to rise in mass for that purpose. But as the fortifications were ancient and in disrepair, an effort at resistance could only have occasioned the destruction of the city. The Emperor Francis saw himself, therefore, under the necessity of endeavouring to provide for the safety of his capital by negotiation, and for that of his person by leaving it. On the 7th November, he departed from Vienna for Brunn in Moravia, in order to place himself under the protection of the Russian forces. On the same day, but late in the evening, Count Giulay arrived at Buonaparte's headquarters, then at Lintz, with a proposal for an armistice, previous to a general negotiation for peace. Napoleon refused to listen to the proposal, unless Venice and the Tyrol were put into his hands. These terms were too hard to be accepted. Vienna, therefore, was left to its fate; and that proud capital of the proud House of Austria remained an unresisting prize to the invader.

On the 13th November the French took possession of Vienna, where they obtained an immense quantity of military stores, arms, and clothing and by a change as rapid as if it had taken place on the stage, the new Emperor of France occupied Schönbrunn, the splendid palace of the long-descended Emperor of Austria. But though such signal successes had crowned the commencement of the campaign, it was necessary to defeat the haughty Russians, before the object of the war could be considered as attained. The broken and shattered remnant of the Austrian forces had rallied from different quarters around the yet untouched army of Alexander; and although the latter retreated from Brunn towards Olmutz, it was only with the purpose of forming a junction with Buxhowden, before they hazarded a general battle.

Napoleon sent Savary to the Russian camp, under pretence of compliment to the Emperor Alexander, but in reality as a spy upon that monarch and his generals. He returned, having discovered, or affected to discover, that the Russian sovereign was surrounded by counsellors, whom their youth and rank rendered confident and presumptuous, and who, he concluded, might be easily misguided into some fatal act of rashness. Buonaparte acted on the hint, and upon the first movement of the Austro-Russian army in advance, withdrew his forces from the position they had occupied. Prince Dolgorucki, aide-de-camp of the Emperor Alexander, was despatched by him to return the compliments which had been brought him. He too was, doubtless, expected to use his powers of observation, but they were not so acute as those of the old officer of police. Buonaparte, as if the interior of his camp displayed scenes which he did not desire Dolgorucki to witness, met the prince at the outposts, which the soldiers were in the act of hastily covering with field-works, like an army which seeks to shelter conscious weakness under entrenchments. Encouraged by what he thought he saw, Dolgorucki entered upon politics, and demanded in plain terms the cession of the crown of Italy. To this proposal Buonaparte listened with a patience which seemed to be the effect of his present situation. In short, Dolgorucki carried back to his imperial master the hastily conceived opinion, that the French Emperor felt himself in a precarious posture. On this false ground the Russian council of war determined to act. Their plan was to extend their own left wing, with the purpose of turning the right of the French army, and taking them upon the flank and rear.

It was upon the 1st December at noon that the Russians commenced this movement, by which, in confidence of success, they abandoned a chain of heights where they might have received an attack with great advantage, descended into ground more favourable to the enemy, and, finally, placed their left wing at too great a distance from the centre. The

French general no sooner witnessed this rash manoeuvre, than he exclaimed, "Before tomorrow is over, that army is my own." In the meantime, withdrawing his outposts, and concentrating his forces, he continued to intimate a conscious inferiority, which was far from existing.

The Battle of Austerlitz, fought against an enemy of great valour but slender experience, was not of a very complicated character. The Russians, we have seen, were extending their line to surround the French flank. The sun rose with unclouded brilliancy; it was that sun of Austerlitz which Napoleon, upon so many succeeding occasions apostrophised, and recalled to the minds of his soldiers. As its first beams rose above the horizon, Buonaparte appeared in front of the army, surrounded by his marshals, to whom he issued his last directions, and they departed at full gallop to their different posts.

The encounter was desperate, and the Russians displayed the utmost valour before they at length gave way to the discipline and steadiness of Buonaparte's veterans. The centre of the French army advanced to complete the victory, and the cavalry of Murat made repeated charges with such success, that the Emperors of Russia and Austria, from the heights of Austerlitz, beheld their centre and left completely defeated. The fate of the right wing could no longer be protracted, and it was disastrous even beyond the usual consequences of defeat. They had been actively pressed during the whole battle by Lannes, but now the troops on their left being routed, they were surrounded on all sides, and, unable to make longer resistance, were forced down into a hollow, where they were exposed to the fire of twenty pieces of cannon. Many attempted to escape across a lake, which was partially frozen; but the ice proving too weak gave way under them, or was broken by the hostile cannonade. This fatality renewed, according to Buonaparte, the appearance of the battle with the Turks at Aboukir, where so many thousand men, flying from the battle, perished by drowning. It was with the greatest difficulty, that, rallying the remains of their routed forces around them, and retiring in the best manner they could, the Emperors effected their personal retreat. Only the devoted bravery of the Russians, and the loyalty of the Austrian cavalry, who charged repeatedly to protect the retrograde movement, could have rendered it possible, since the sole passage to the rear lay along a causeway, extending between two lakes. The retreat was, however, accomplished, and the Emperors escaped without sustaining the loss in the pursuit which might have been expected. But in the battle, at least 20,000 men had remained, killed, wounded, and prisoners; and forty standards, with a great proportion of the hostile artillery, were the trophies of Napoleon, whose army had thus amply redeemed their pledge. It was, however, at a high rate that they had purchased the promised bouquet. Their own ranks had lost probably 5000 men, though the bulletin diminishes the numbers to 2500.

The Austrian Emperor considered his last hope of successful opposition to Napoleon as extinguished by this defeat, and conceived, therefore, that he had nothing remaining save to throw himself upon the discretion of the victor. A personal interview took place betwixt the Emperor of Austria and Napoleon, and the Austrian monarch, left to his fate, obtained from Buonaparte an armistice. A small part of the price was imposed in the shape of a military contribution of 100,000,000 francs, to be raised in the territories occupied by the French armies. The treaties of Campo Formio and Luneville, though granted to Austria by Napoleon in the hour of victory, were highly advantageous compared to that of Presburgh, which was signed on the 26th of December, 1805. By this negotiation, Francis ceded to Bavaria the oldest possession of his house, the mountains of Tyrol and of the Vorarlberg, filled with the best, bravest, and most attached of his subjects, and which, by their situation, had hitherto given Austria influence at once in Germany and Italy. Venice, Austria's most recent possession, and which had not been very honourably obtained, was also yielded up, and added to the kingdom of Italy. She was again reduced to the solitary seaport of Trieste.

By the same treaty, the Germanic allies of Buonaparte were to be remunerated. Wirtemberg, as well as Bavaria, received large additions at the expense of Austria and of the other princes of the empire, and Francis consented that both electors should be promoted to the kingly dignity. By the treaty of Presburgh, Austria is said to have lost upwards of 20,000 square miles of territory, two million and a half subjects, and a revenue to the amount of ten million and a half of florins. And this momentous surrender was made in consequence of one unfortunate campaign, which lasted but six months, and was distinguished by only one general action.

CHAPTER XXXIII

The triumphs of Napoleon had been greater at this period of his reign, than had ever before been recorded in history as achieved by a single man. Yet even these, like every thing earthly, had their limit.

Napoleon persisted to the last in asserting that he saw clearly the means of utterly destroying the English superiority at sea. This he proposed to achieve by evading the blockades of the several ports of France and Spain, which, while weather permitted, were each hermetically sealed by the presence of a British squadron, and by finally assembling in the Channel that overwhelming force, which, according to his statement, was to reduce England to a dependency on France.

As a landsman, Napoleon did not make sufficient allowance for the action of contrary winds and waves; as indeed it was perhaps his fault, even in land operations, where their influence is less essential, to admit too little consequence to the opposition of the elements. There was also a great difference betwixt the land and the sea service, to which Buonaparte did not give sufficient weight. Upon land, the excellence of the French troops, their discipline, and the enthusiasm arising from uninterrupted success, might be safely reckoned upon as likely to bear down any obstacle which they might unexpectedly meet with. The situation of the French seamen was diametrically the contrary. Their only chance of safety consisted in their being able to elude a recontre with a British squadron, even of very inferior force.

A squadron of ten French vessels escaped from Rochefort on the 11th of January, 1805; and another, under Villeneuve, got out of Toulon on the 18th by a similarly favourable opportunity. The combined fleets escaped into Vigo, where they refitted; and, venturing to sail from that port, they proceeded to Ferrol, and united themselves with the squadron which was lying there, and continued their course for Cadiz, which they entered in safety. This did not consist with the plans of Buonaparte, who would have had the whole naval force united at Brest to be in readiness to cover the descent upon England.

When the certainty was known that the French fleets were actually in Cadiz, Nelson was put at the head of the British naval force in the Mediterranean, which was reinforced with an alertness and secrecy that did the highest honour to the Admiralty.

What principally determined the French admiral on putting to sea, was his ignorance of the reinforcements received by the English, and it was another and especial point of encouragement, that circumstances led him to disbelieve the report that Nelson commanded the British Fleet. Under the influence of these united motives, and confiding in a plan of tactics which he had formed for resisting the favourite mode of attack practised by the English, the French admiral sailed from Cadiz on the 19th October, 1805, in an evil hour for himself and for his country.

The hostile fleets were not long in meeting, and the wind never impelled along the ocean two more gallant armaments. Admiral Collingwood, who led the van, went down on the French with all his sails set, and, disdaining to furl them in the usual manner, cut the sheets, and let his canvass fly loose in the wind, as if he needed it no longer after it had borne him amidst the thickest of the enemy. Nelson ran his vessel, the Victory, on board the French Redoutable; the Temeraire, a second British ship, fell on board the same vessel on the other side; another enemy's ship fell on board the Temeraire, and the action was fiercely maintained betwixt these four vessels, which lay as close as if they had been moored together in some friendly harbour. The example of the admiral was universally followed by the British captains; they broke into the enemy's line on every side, engaged two or three ships at the same time, and maintained the battle at the very muzzles of the cannon. The superiority which we have claimed for our countrymen was soon made manifest. Seven out of the vessels which escaped into Cadiz were rendered unserviceable. The whole combined fleet was almost totally destroyed.

Nelson, the darling of Britain, bought with his life this last and decided triumph over his country's enemies. The good servant of his country slept not before his task was fulfilled; for, by the victory in which he fell, the naval force of the enemy was altogether destroyed, and the threat of invasion silenced forever.

It is a remarkable coincidence that, Mack's surrender having taken place the 20th October, Napoleon was probably entering Ulm in triumph upon the very day, when the united remains of his maritime force, and the means on which he relied for the subjugation of England, were flying, striking, and sinking, before the banners of Nelson. What his feeling may have been on learning the news, we have no certain means of ascertaining. The Memoirs of Fouché say, upon the alleged authority of Berthier, that his emotion was extreme, and that his first exclamation was, "I cannot be everywhere!" implying, certainly, that his own presence would have changed the scenes. The same idea occurs in his conversations with Las Cases.

The unfortunate event of the battle of Trafalgar was not permitted to darken the brilliant picture, which the extraordinary campaign of Ulm and Austerlitz enabled the victor to present to the empire. "His armies," he said, addressing the Legislative Body, the cession of which he opened with great pomp on 2nd March, 1806, "had never ceased to conquer until he commanded them to cease to combat. His enemies were humbled ... the entire peninsula of Italy now made a part of the Great Empire – his generosity had permitted the return of the defeated Russians to their own country, and had re-established the throne of Austria, after punishing her by the privation of a part of her dominions." Trafalgar was then touched upon. "A tempest," he said, "had deprived him of some few vessels, after a combat imprudently entered into;" – and thus he glossed over a calamitous and decisive defeat, in which so many of his hopes were shipwrecked.

Despite Trafalgar, Napoleon set about consolidating his extraordinary triumph and ascendance over the Continent. He bought Prussia off with Hanover. Bavaria ceded the Grand Duchy of Berg, which was conferred upon Murat. In return, she received Anspach and Bayreuth from Prussia as well as the Tyrol and Voralberg from Austria. Napoleon placed his brothers Joseph on the throne of Naples and Louis on that of Holland. His sister Eliza, already endowed with the principality of Lucca, saw it augmented.

The public opinion was less favourable to Lucca's younger sister, Pauline, who was one of the most beautiful women in France, and perhaps in Europe. Leclerc, her first husband, died in the fatal expedition to St. Domingo, and she was afterwards married to the Prince Borghese. Her encouragement of the fine arts was so little limited by the ordinary ideas of decorum, that the celebrated Canova was permitted to model from her person a naked Venus, the most beautiful, it is said, of his works. Scandal went the horrible length of imputing to Pauline an intrigue with her own brother; which we willingly reject as a crime too hideous to be imputed to anyone, without the most satisfactory evidence. The gross and guilty enormities practised by the ancient Roman emperors do not belong to the character of Buonaparte, though such foul aspersions have been cast upon him. Pauline Borghese received the principality of Guastalla, in the distribution of honours among the family of Napoleon. At this period, also, Buonaparte began first to display a desire of engrafting his own family upon the ancient dynasties of Europe, with whom he had been so long at war, and the ruin of most of whom had contributed to his elevation. The Elector of Bavaria had to repay the patronage which raised him to the rank of king, and enlarged his territories, by forming an alliance which should mix his ancient blood with that of the family connections of the fortunate soldier. Eugene Beauharnais, Viceroy of Italy, the son of Josephine by her first husband, and now the adopted son of Napoleon, was wedded to the eldest daughter of the King of Bavaria.

These various kingdoms and principalities, erected in favour of his nearest relations, imposed on the mind a most impressive image of Buonaparte's unlimited authority, who distributed crowns among his kinsfolk as ordinary men give veils to their domestics. But the sound policy of his conduct may be greatly doubted. Authority is a plant of a slow growth, and to obtain the full veneration which renders it most effectual, must have arisen by degrees in the place which it overshadows and protects. Suddenly transferred to new regions, it is apt to pine and to perish. The theoretical evils of a long-established government are generally mitigated by some practicable remedy, or those who suffer by them have grown callous from habit. The reverse is the case with a newly-established domination, which has no claim to the veneration due to antiquity, and to which the subjects are not attached by the strong though invisible chains of long habit.

Other and more special objections arise to Buonaparte's system of erecting thrones all through Europe for the members of his family. It was particularly impolitic, as marking too strongly his determination to be satisfied with nothing less than the dominion of the world, for while he governed France in his own person, the disposing of other countries to his brothers and near relations, feudatories of France, and his dependents as well by blood as by allegiance, what else could be expected than that the independence of such kingdoms must be merely nominal, and their monarchs bound to act in every respect as the agents of Buonaparte's pleasure? This did not remain concealed from the Dutch, from the Italians, or other foreigners, subjected to these pageant monarchs; and as it naturally incensed them against Napoleon's government, so it prevented the authority which he had delegated from obtaining either affection or reverence, and disposed the nations who were subjected to it to take the first opportunity of casting the yoke aside.

The erection of these kindred monarchies was not the only mode by which Napoleon endeavoured to maintain an ascendency in the countries which he had conquered, and which he desired to retain in dependence upon France, though not nominally or directly making parts of the French empire. Buonaparte had already proposed to his council the question of whether the creation of Grandees of the Empire, a species of nobility whose titles were to depend, not on their descents, but on their talents and services to the state, was to be considered as a violation of the laws of liberty and equality. He was universally answered in the negative; for, having now acquired an hereditary monarch, it seemed a natural, if not an indispensable consequence, that France should have peers of the kingdom, and great officers of the crown. Such an establishment, according to Buonaparte's view, would at once place his dignity on the same footing with those of the other courts of Europe, (an assimilation to which he attached a greater degree of consequence than was consistent with policy,) and by blending the new nobles of the empire with those of the ancient kingly government, would tend to reconcile the modern state of things with such relics of the old court as yet existed.

From respect, perhaps, to the republican opinions which had so long predominated, the titles and appanages of these grand feudatories were not chosen within the bounds of France herself, but from provinces which had experienced the sword of the ruler. Fifteen dukedoms, grand fiefs, not of France, but of the French empire, were created. The income attached to each amounted to the fifteenth part of the revenue of the province, which gave title to the dignitary. The Emperor invested with these endowments those who had best served him in war and in state affairs. Princedoms also were erected, and while marshals and ministers were created dukes, the superior rank of prince was bestowed on Talleyrand, Bernadotte, and Berthier, by the titles of Beneventum, Ponte-Corvo, and Neufchatel. The system of the new noblesse was settled by imperial edict, which was communicated to the Senate 30th March, 1806, not for the purpose of deliberation or acceptance, but merely that, like the old Parliament of Paris, they might enter it upon their register.

For the power of recompensing his soldiers, statesmen, and adherents, the conquered countries were again the Emperor's resource. National domains were reserved to a large amount throughout those countries, and formed funds, out of which gratifications and annuities were, at Napoleon's sole leisure, assigned to the generals, officers, and soldiers of the French army, who might in this way be said to have all Europe for their paymaster. Thus, every conquest increased his means of rewarding his soldiers; and that army, which was the most formidable instrument of his ambition, was encouraged and maintained at the expense of those states which had suffered most from his arms.

We have not yet concluded the important change; introduced into Europe by the consequences of the fatal campaign of Austerlitz. The Confederation of the Rhine, which withdrew from the German empire so large a portion of its princes, and, transferring them from the influence of Austria, placed them under the protection of France, was an event which tended directly to the dissolution of the Germanic League, which had subsisted since the year 800, when Charlemagne received the Imperial Crown.

By the new Federation of the Rhine, the courts of Wirtemberg and Bavaria, of Hesse-Darmstadt with some petty princes of the right bank of the Rhine, formed among themselves an alliance offensive and defensive, and renounced their dependence upon the Germanic Body, of which they declared they no longer recognised the constitution. The reasons assigned for this league had considerable weight. It was urged, that the countries governed by these princes were, in every case of war betwixt France and Austria, exposed to all the evils of invasion, from which the Germanic Body had no longer power to defend them. Therefore, being obliged to seek for more effectual protection, they placed themselves directly under the guardianship of France. Napoleon, on his part, did not hesitate to accept the title of Protector of the Confederation of the Rhine. It is true, that he had engaged to his subjects that he would not extend the limits of his empire beyond that river, which he acknowledged as the natural boundary of France; but this engagement was not held to exclude the sort of seigniory attached to the new Protectorate, in virtue of which he plunged the German states who composed the Confederacy into every war in which France herself engaged.

Francis of Austria, seeing the empire, of which his house had been so long the head, going to pieces like a parting wreck, had no other resource than to lay aside the Imperial Crown of Germany, and to declare that league dissolved which he now saw no sufficient means of enforcing. He declared the ties dissevered which bound the various princes to him as Emperor, to each other as allies; and although he reserved the Imperial title, it was only as the Sovereign of Austria, and his other hereditary states.

France became therefore in a great measure the successor to the Holy Roman Empire; and the Empire of Napoleon gained a still nearer resemblance to that of Charlemagne. Austria, stunned by her misfortunes, was passive and unresisting. Prussia, in the north of Germany, was halting between two very opposite sets of counsellors; one of which, with too much confidence in the military resources of the country, advised war with France, for which the favourable opportunity had been permitted to escape; while the other recommended that, like the jackal in the train of the lion, Prussia should continue to avail herself of the spoils which Napoleon might permit her to seize upon, without presuming to place herself in opposition to his will. In either case, the course recommended was sufficiently perilous; but to vacillate, as the Cabinet of Berlin did, betwixt the one and the other, inferred almost certain ruin.

CHAPTER XXXIV

One way remained to balance the new species of power which France had

acquired. It was possible, by forming the northern princes of the German empire into a league of the same character with the Confederacy of the Rhine, having Prussia instead of France for its protector, to create such an equilibrium as might render it difficult or dangerous for Buonaparte to use his means, however greatly enlarged, to disturb the peace of the north of Europe. It was, therefore, determined in the Prussian Cabinet to form a league on this principle.

This proposed Northern Confederacy, however, could not well be established without communication with France; and Buonaparte, though offering no direct opposition to the formation of a league, started such obstacles to the project in detail, as were likely to render its establishment on an effectual footing impossible. It was said by his ministers, that Napoleon was to take the Hanseatic towns under his own immediate protection; that the wise prince who governed Saxony showed no desire to become a member of the proposed Confederacy; and that France would permit no power to be forced into such a measure.

By this partial interruption and opposition, Napoleon rendered it impossible for Prussia to make any effectual efforts for combining together those remaining fragments of the German empire, over which her military power and geographical position gave her natural influence. This disappointment, with the sense of having been outwitted, excited feelings of chagrin and resentment in the Prussian Cabinet, which corresponded with the sentiments expressed by the nation at large. The people of Prussia were clamorous for war. They, too, were sensible that the late versatile conduct of their Cabinet had exposed them to the censure, and even the scorn of Europe; and that Buonaparte, seeing the crisis ended in which the firmness of Prussia might have preserved the balance of Europe, retained no longer any respect for those whom he had made his dupes.

Another circumstance of a very exasperating character took place at this time. One Palm, a bookseller at Nuremberg, had exposed to sale a pamphlet, containing remarks on the conduct of Napoleon, in which the Emperor and his policy were treated with considerable severity. The book seller was seized upon for this offence by the French gendarmes, and transferred to Braunau, where he was brought before a military commission, tried for a libel on the Emperor of France, found guilty, and shot [August 26th]. The murder of this poor man, for such it literally was, whether immediately flowing from Buonaparte's mandate, or the effects of the furious zeal of some of his officers, excited deep and general indignation. Amidst the ferment of the public mind, Alexander once more appeared in person at the court of Berlin, and prevailed on the King of Prussia at length to unsheath the sword. The support of the powerful hosts of Russia was promised. About the middle of August, Prussia began to arm. Perhaps there are few examples of a war declared with the almost unanimous consent of a great and warlike people, which was brought to an earlier and more unhappy termination.

The King of Prussia placed at the head of his armies the Duke of Brunswick. In his youth, this general had gained renown under his uncle Prince Ferdinand. But it had been lost in the retreat from Champagne in 1792, where he had suffered himself to be out-manœuvred. He was seventy-two years old, and is said to have added the obstinacy of age to others of the infirmities which naturally attend it. He was not communicative, nor accessible to any of the other generals, excepting Mollendorf; and this generated a disunion of councils in the Prussian camp and the personal dislike of the army.

The united force of the Prussian army, with its auxiliaries, amounted to 150,000 men, confident in their own courage, in the rigid discipline which continued to distinguish their service, and in the animating recollections of the victorious career of the Great Frederick.

While Buonaparte assembled in Franconia an army considerably superior in number to that of the Prussians, the latter occupied the country in the vicinity of the river Saale, and seemed, in doing so, to renounce all the advantage of making the attack on the enemy ere he had collected his forces. It might be partly owing to the difficulty of obtaining forage and subsistence that the Prussian army was extended upon a line by far too much prolonged to admit of mutual support. Indeed, they may be considered rather as disposed in cantonments than as occupying a military position; and as they remained strictly on the defensive, an opportunity was gratuitously afforded to Buonaparte to attack their divisions in detail.

The French advanced, in three divisions, upon the dislocated and extended disposition of the large but ill-arranged Prussian army. It was the object of this grand combined movement to overwhelm the Prussian right wing, which was extended further than prudence permitted; and, having beaten this part of the army, to turn their whole position, and possess themselves of their magazines. After some previous skirmishes, a serious action took place at Saalfield, where Prince Louis of Prussia commanded the advanced guard of the Prussian left wing.

In the ardour and inexperience of youth, the brave prince, instead of being contented with defending the bridge on the Saale, quitted that advantageous position, to advance with unequal forces against Lannes. If bravery could have atoned for imprudence, the battle of Saaifield would not have been lost. Prince Louis showed the utmost gallantry in leading his men when they advanced, and in rallying them when they fled. He was killed fighting hand to hand with a French subaltern, who required him to surrender, and, receiving a sabre-wound for reply, plunged his sword into the prince's body. The victory opened the course of the Saale to the French, who instantly advanced on Naumburg.

Naumburg and its magazines were consigned to the flames, which first announced to the Prussians that the French army had gotten completely into their rear, had destroyed their magazines, and, being now interposed betwixt them and Saxony, left them no alternative save that of battle, which was to be waged at the greatest disadvantage with an alert enemy, to whom their supineness had already given the choice of time and place for it. There was also this ominous consideration, that, in case of disaster, the Prussians had neither principle, nor order, nor line of retreat. The enemy were betwixt them and Magdeburg, which ought to have been their rallying point; and the army of the Great Frederick was, it must be owned, brought to combat with as little reflection or military science, as a herd of school-boys might have displayed in a mutiny.

Still the Prussian monarch, endeavouring to supply the want of professional experience by courage, brought up his last reserves, and encouraged his broken troops rather to make a final stand for victory, than to retreat in the face of a conquering army. This effort proved in vain. The Prussian line was attacked everywhere at once; centre and wings were broken through by the French at the bayonet's point; and the retreat, after so many fruitless efforts, in which no division had been left unengaged, was of the most disorderly character. But the confusion was increased tenfold, when, as the defeated troops reached Weimar, they fell in with the right wing of their own army, fugitives like themselves, and who were attempting to retreat in the same direction. The disorder of two routed armies meeting in opposing currents, soon became inextricable. The roads were choked up with artillery and baggage wagons; the retreat became a hurried flight; and the King himself, who had shown the utmost courage during the battle, was at length, for personal safety, compelled to leave the high-roads, and escape across the fields, escorted by a small body of cavalry.

While the left of the Prussian army were in the act of combating Davoust at Auerstadt, their right, as we have hinted, were with equally bad fortune engaged at Jena. This second action, though the least important of the two, has always given the name to the double battle; because it was at Jena that Napoleon was engaged in person.

The French Emperor had arrived at this town, which is situated upon the Saale, on the 13th of October, and had lost no time in issuing those orders, which produced the demonstrations of Davoust, and the victory of Auerstadt. With his usual activity, he formed or enlarged, in the course of the night, the roads by which he proposed to bring up his artillery on the succeeding day, and by hewing the solid rock, made a path practicable for guns to the elevated plain in the front of Jena, where his centre was established. In the morning [Oct 14th] he harangued his soldiers, and recommended to them to stand firm against the charges of the Prussian cavalry, which had been represented as very redoubtable. The Emperor ordered the columns destined for the attack to descend into the plain. His centre consisted of the Imperial Guard, and two divisions of Lannes. Augereau commanded the right, which rested on a village and a forest; and Soult's division, with a part of Ney's, were upon the left.

General Mollendorf advanced on his side, and both armies, as at Auerstadt, were hid from each other by the mist, until suddenly the atmosphere cleared, and showed them to each other within the distance of half-cannon shot. The conflict instantly commenced. It began on the French right, where the Prussians attacked with the purpose of driving Augereau from the village on which he rested his extreme flank. The battle then became general; and the Prussians showed themselves such masters of discipline, that it was long impossible to gain any advantage over men, who advanced, retired, or moved to either flank, with the regularity of machines. Soult at length, by the most desperate efforts, dispossessed the Prussians opposed to him of the woods from which they had annoyed the French left; and at the same conjuncture the division of Ney, and a large reserve of cavalry, appeared upon the field of battle. Napoleon, thus strengthened, advanced the centre, consisting in a great measure of the Imperial Guard, who, being fresh and in time highest spirits, compelled the Prussian army to give way. Their retreat was at first orderly; but it was a part of Buonaparte's tactics to pour attack after attack upon a worsted enemy, as the billows of a tempestuous ocean follow each other in succession, till the last waves totally disperse the fragments of the bulwark which the first have breached. All leading and following seemed now lost in this army, so lately confiding in its numbers and discipline. There was scarcely a general left to issue orders, scarcely a soldier disposed to obey them; and it seems to have been by a sort of instinct that several broken regiments were directed, or directed themselves, upon Magdeburg, where Prince Hohenloe endeavoured to rally them.

The French accounts state that 20,000 Prussians were killed and taken in the course of this fatal day; that 300 guns fell into their power, with twenty generals, and standards and colours to the number of sixty. The troops also, according to Buonaparte's evidence, scarcely maintained their high character, oppressed probably by a sense of the disadvantages under which they combated.

The fall of Prussia was so sudden and so total, as to excite the general astonishment of Europe. Its prince was compared to the rash and inexperienced gambler, who risks his whole fortune on one desperate cast, and rises from the table totally ruined. The King, driven to the extremity of his dominions, could only be considered as a fugitive, whose precarious chance of restoration depended on the doubtful success of his ally of Russia, who now, as after the capture of Vienna, had upon his hands, strong as those hands were, not the task of aiding an ally, but the far more difficult one of raising from the ground a prince who was totally powerless and prostrate. The French crossed the Oder – Glogau and Breslau were invested. Their defence was respectable; but it seemed not the less certain that their fall involved almost the last hopes of Prussia, and that a name raised so high by the reign of one wise monarch, was like to be blotted from the map of Europe by the events of a single day.

CHAPTER XXXV

At Potsdam and at Berlin, Napoleon showed himself as the sworn and implacable enemy, rather than as the generous conqueror. At Potsdam he seized on the sword, belt, and hat of the Great Frederick, and at Berlin he appropriated and removed to Paris the monument of Victory, erected by the same monarch, in consequence of the defeat of the French at Rosbach. The finest paintings and works of art in Prussia were seized upon for the benefit of the French National Museum.

Saxony had joined her arms to those of Prussia – forced by the arguments which a powerful neighbour can always apply to a weaker – still she *had* joined her, and fought on her side at the battle of Jena. The apology of compulsion was admitted Buonaparte; the Saxon troops were dismissed upon their parole, and their prince raised to the rank of a King, shortly afterwards admitted as a member of the Confederacy of the Rhine, and treated by Buonaparte with much personal consideration. The Dukes of Saxe-Weimar and Saxe-Gotha also were permitted to retain their dominions, on acknowledging a similar vassalage to the French empire.

The Landgrave, or Elector, of Hesse-Cassel, might have expected a still more favourable acceptance in the eyes of the victor; for he had refused to join Prussia, and, in spite of threats and persuasions, had observed neutrality during the brief contest. But Napoleon remembered, to the prejudice of the landgrave, that he had resisted all previous temptations to enter into the Confederation of the Rhine. He imputed his neutrality to fear, not choice. He alleged, that it had not been strictly observed; and, treating the inaction of Hesse, whose inclinations were with Prussia, as a greater crime than the actual hostilities of Saxony, whose will was with France, he declared, according to his usual form of dethronement, that the House of Hesse-Cassel had ceased to reign. The doom was executed even before it was pronounced. Louis Buonaparte, with Marshal Mortier, had possessed himself of Hesse-Cassel by the 1st of November.

The real cause of seizing the territories of an unoffending prince, who was totally helpless, unless in so far as right or justice could afford him protection, was Buonaparte's resolution to incorporate Hesse-Cassel with the adjacent territories, for the purpose of forming a kingdom to be conferred on his youngest brother Jerome. This young person had married an American young lady, distinguished for her beauty and her talents, and had thus lost the countenance of Napoleon, who maintained the principle, that segregated as his kindred were from the nation at large, by their connection with him, they were not entitled to enter into alliances according to the dictates of their own feelings, but were bound to form such as were most suitable to his policy. Jerome was tempted by ambition finally to acquiesce in this reasoning, and sacrificed the connection which his heart had chosen, to become the tool of his brother's ever-extending schemes of ambition. The reward was the kingdom of Westphalia, to which was united Hesse-Cassel, with the various provinces which Prussia had possessed in Franconia, Westphalia Proper, and Lower Saxony; as also the territories of the unfortunate Duke of Brunswick. Security could be scarcely supposed to attend upon a sovereignty, where the materials were acquired by public rapine, and the crown purchased by domestic infidelity.

The celebrated Decrees of Berlin appeared on the 21st November, 1806, interdicting all commerce betwixt Great Britain and the continent; which interdiction was declared a fundamental law of the French empire, until the English should consent to certain alterations in the mode of conducting hostilities by sea, which should render her naval superiority less useful to herself, and less detrimental to the enemy. This measure was justified upon the following grounds: That England had either introduced new customs into her maritime code, or revived those of a barbarous age; that she seized on merchant vessels, and made their crews prisoners, just as if they had been found on board ships of war; declared harbours blockaded which were not so in reality; and extended the evils of war to the peaceful and unarmed citizen. This induction to the celebrated project, afterwards called the Continental System of the Emperor, was false in the original proposition, and sophistical in those by which it was supported. It was positively false that Great Britain had introduced into her maritime law, either by new enact or by the revival of obsolete and barbarous customs, any alteration by which the rights of neutrals were infringed, or the unarmed citizen prejudiced, more than necessarily arose out of the usual customs of war. The law respecting the blockade of ports, and the capture of vessels at sea was the same on which every nation had acted for three centuries past, France herself not excepted. It is true that the maritime code seemed at this period to be peculiarly that of England, because no nation save herself had the means of enforcing them; but she did not in this respect possess any greater advantage by sea than Napoleon enjoyed by land.

Napoleon introduced the following Decrees, unheard of hitherto among belligerent powers, and tending greatly to augment the general distress, which must, under all circumstances, attend a state of war:

I. The British isles were declared in a state of blockade. II. All commerce and correspondence with England was forbidden. All English letters were to be seized in the post-houses. III. Every Englishman, of whatever rank or quality, found in France, or the countries allied with her, was declared a prisoner of war. IV. All merchandise, or property of any kind, belonging to English subjects, was declared lawful prize. V. All articles of English manufacture, and articles produced in her colonies, were in like manner declared contraband and lawful prize. VI. Half of the produce of the above confiscations was to be employed in the relief of those merchants whose vessels had been captured by the English cruisers. VII. All vessels coming from England, or the English colonies, were to be refused admission into any harbour.

This was the first link of a long chain of arbitrary decrees and ordinances, by which Napoleon, aiming at the destruction of British finance, interrupted the whole commerce of Europe, and destroyed for a season, and as far as lay in his power, that connection between distant nations which unites them by the most natural and advantageous means, the supply of the wants of the one country by the superfluous produce of the other. The extent of public inconvenience and distress, which was occasioned, may be judged of by reflecting, how many of the most ordinary articles of consumption are brought from foreign countries, in how many instances the use of these articles have brought them into the list of necessaries and how, before an ordinary mechanic or peasant sits down to breakfast, distant climes must be taxed to raise the coffee and sugar which he consumes.

The painful embarrassment of those deprived of their habitual comforts, was yet exceeded by the clamour and despair of the whole commercial world on the continent, who were thus, under pretext of relieving them from the vexation of the English cruisers, threatened with a total abrogation of their profession. Hamburg, Bordeaux, Nantes, and other continental towns, solicited, by petitions and deputations, some relaxation of decrees which inferred their general ruin. They pleaded the prospect of universal bankruptcy, which this prohibitory system must occasion. "Let it be so," answered the Emperor; "the more insolvency on the continent, the greater will be the distress of the merchants in London. The fewer traders in Hamburg, the less will be the temptation to carry on commerce with England. Britain must be humbled, were it at the expense of throwing civilisation back for centuries, and returning to the original mode of trading by barter."

But, great as was Buonaparte's power, he had overrated it in supposing, that, by a mere expression of his will, he could put an end to an intercourse, in the existence of which the whole world possessed an interest. The attempt to annihilate commerce resembled that of a child who tries to stop with his hand the stream of an artificial fountain, which escapes in a hundred partial jets from his palm and between his fingers. The Genius of Commerce, like a second Proteus, assumed every variety of shape, in order to elude the imperial interdiction, and all manner of evasions was practised for that purpose. False papers, false certificates, false bills of lading, were devised, and these frauds were overlooked in the seaports, by the very agents to whom the execution of the decrees was committed. Douaniers, magistrates, generals, and prefects, nay, some of the kindred princes of the House of Napoleon, were well pleased to listen to the small still voice of their interest, rather than to his authoritative commands; and British commerce, though charged with heavy expenses, continued to flourish in spite of the Continental System. Meantime such acts of increasing severity had the natural consequence of rendering his person and power more and more unpopular: so that, while he was sacrificing the interests and the comforts of the nations under his authority to his hope of destroying England, he was, in fact, digging a mine under his own feet, which exploded to his destruction long before the security of England was materially affected.

CHAPTER XXXVI

Napoleon was politically justified in the harsh terms which he was desirous to impose on Prussia, by having now brought his victorious armies to the neighbourhood of Poland, in which he had a good right to conceive himself sure to find numerous followers and a friendly reception.

The partition of this fine kingdom by its powerful neighbours, Russia, Austria, and Prussia, was the first open and audacious transgression of the law of nations, which disgraced the annals of civilised Europe. It was executed by a combination of three of the most powerful states of Europe against one too unhappy in the nature of its constitution, and too much divided by factions to offer any effectual resistance. The kingdom had appealed in vain to the code of nations for protection against an outrage, to which, after a desultory and uncombined, and therefore a vain defence, she saw herself under the necessity of submitting. The Poles retained, too, a secret sense of their fruitless attempt to recover freedom in 1791, and an animated recollection of the violence by which it had been suppressed by Russian arms. They waited with hope and exultation the approach of the French armies; and candour must allow, that, unlawfully subjected as they had been to a foreign yoke, they had a right to avail themselves of the assistance, not only of Napoleon, but of Mahomet, or of Satan himself; had he proposed to aid them in regaining the independence of which they had been oppressively and unjustly deprived.

Buonaparte received addresses from that country, which endeavoured to prevail on him to aid them in their views of regaining their independence. Their application was of a nature to embarrass him considerably. To have declared himself the patron of Polish independence, might have, indeed, brought large forces to his standard, might have consummated the disasters of Prussia, and greatly embarrassed even Russia herself. But Austria had been a large sharer in the various partitions of Poland, and Austria, humbled as she had been, was still a powerful state, whose enmity might have proved formidable, if, by bereaving her of her Polish

dominions, or encouraging her subjects to rebel, Buonaparte had provoked her to hostilities, at the time when the best part of his forces were
engaged in the North of Europe. The same attempt would have given a
very different character to the war, which Russia at present waged only in
the capacity of the auxiliary of Prussia. The safety and integrity of the
Russian empire, south of the Volga, depends almost entirely upon the
preservation of those territories which she has acquired in Poland; and, if
she had engaged in the war as a principal, Buonaparte was scarcely yet prepared to enter upon a contest with the immense power of that empire,
which must be waged as near to their resources as he was distant from his
own.

While Napoleon declined binding himself by any express stipulations
to the Polish delegates, the language he used was cautiously worded, so as
to keep up their zeal and animate their exertions. Dombrowski, a Polish
exile in the French army, was employed to raise men for Napoleon's service, and the enthusiasm of those who entered, as well as the expectations
of the kingdom at large, were excited by such oracular passages as the following, which appeared in the 36th bulletin: "Is the throne of Poland to
be re-established, and will that great nation regain her existence and independence? Will she be recalled to life, as if summoned to arise from the
tomb? God only, the great disposer of events, can be the arbiter of this
great political problem."

The continuance of war was now to be determined upon; a war to be
waged with circumstances of more than usual horror, as it involved the
sufferings of a winter campaign in the northern latitudes. The French
army at length advanced in full force, and crossed successively the Vistula
and Bug, forcing a passage wherever it was disputed. But it was not the
object of Bennigsen to give battle to forces superior to his own, and he
therefore retreated behind the Wkra, and was joined by the large bodies
of troops commanded by Generals Buxhowden and Kaminskoy.

Napoleon was himself sensible that he was approaching a conflict of
a different kind from that which he had maintained with Austria, and
more lately against Prussia. The common soldier in both those services
was too much levelled into a mere moving piece of machinery, the hun-
dred-thousandth part of the great machine called an army, to have any
confidence in himself, or zeal beyond the mere discharge of the task

entrusted to him. These troops, however highly disciplined, wanted that powerful and individual feeling, which in armies possessing a strong national character, (by which the Russians are peculiarly distinguished,) induces the soldier to resist to the last moment, even when resistance can only assure him of revenge. They were still the same Russians, of whom Frederick the Great said, "that he could kill, but could not defeat them;" – they were also strong of constitution, and inured to the iron climate in which Frenchmen were now making war for the first time; they were accustomed from their earliest life to spare nourishment and hardship; in a word, they formed then, as they do now, the sole instance in Europe of an army, the privates of which are semi-barbarians, with the passions, courage, love of war, and devotion to their country, which is found in the earlier periods of society, while the education received by their superior officers places them on a level with those of any other nation. That of the inferior regimental officers is too much neglected; but they are naturally brave, kind to the common soldier, and united among themselves like a family of brothers – attributes which go far to compensate the want of information.

The Russian army was at this period deficient in its military staff, and thence imperfect in the execution of combined movements; and their generals were better accustomed to lead an army in the day of actual battle, than to prepare for victory by a skilful combination of previous manœuvres. But this disadvantage was balanced by their zealous and unhesitating devotion to their Emperor and their country. Their infantry was confessedly excellent, composed of men in the prime of life, and carefully selected. Their artillery was of the first description, so far as the men, guns, carriages, and appointments were concerned; but the rank of General of Artillery had not the predominant weight in the Russian army, which ought to be possessed by those particularly dedicated to the direction of that arm, by which, according to Napoleon, modern battles must be usually decided. The direction of their guns was too often entrusted to general officers of the line. The service of cavalry is less natural to the Russians than that of the infantry, but their horse regiments are nevertheless excellently trained, and have uniformly behaved well.

But the Cossacks are a species of force belonging to Russia exclusively. The natives on the banks of the Don and the Volga hold their lands by

military service, and enjoy certain immunities and prescriptions, in consequence of which each individual is obliged to serve four years in the
Russian armies. They are trained from early childhood to the use of the
lance and sword, and familiarised to the management of a horse peculiar
to the country – far from handsome in appearance, but tractable, hardy,
swift, and sure-footed, beyond any breed perhaps in the world. At home,
and with his family and children, the Cossack is kind, gentle, generous,
and simple; but when in arms, and in a foreign country, he resumes the
predatory, and sometimes ferocious habits of his ancestors, the roving
Scythians. As the Cossacks receive no pay, plunder is generally their
object; and as prisoners were esteemed a useless encumbrance, they granted no quarter, until Alexander promised a ducat for every Frenchman
whom they brought in alive. In the actual field of battle, their mode of
attack is singular. Instead of acting in line, a body of Cossacks about to
charge, disperse at the word of command very much in the manner of a
fan suddenly flung open, and, joining in a loud yell, or *hourra*, rush, each
acting individually, upon the object of attack, whether infantry, cavalry, or
artillery, to all which they have been formidable assailants. But it is as light
cavalry that the Cossacks are perhaps unrivalled. They and their horses
have been known to march 100 miles in 24 hours without halting. They
plunge into woods, swim rivers, thread passes, cross deep morasses, and
penetrate through deserts of snow, without undergoing material loss or
suffering from fatigue. No Russian army, with a large body of Cossacks in
front, can be liable to surprise; nor, on the other hand, can an enemy surrounded by them ever be confident against it. In covering the retreat of
their own army, their velocity and courage, render pursuit by the enemy's
cavalry peculiarly dangerous; and pursuing a flying enemy, these qualities
are still more redoubtable. In the campaign of 1806-7 the Cossacks took
the field in great numbers, under their celebrated Hettman, or Attaman,
Platow.

The two armies clashed on 26th December in Pultusk and Golymin, to the disadvan-
tage of the French. As a result, Napoleon retreated for the winter to Warsaw.

Bennigsen, in supreme command of 90,000 men, was resolved not to wait
for Buonaparte's onset, but determined to anticipate his motions; wisely

concluding, that the desire of desisting from active operations, which the French Emperor had evinced, ought to be a signal to the Russians again to take the field.

Buonaparte saw himself forced into a winter campaign, and issued general orders for drawing out his forces, with the purpose of concentrating them at Willenberg, in the rear of the Russians, (then stationed at Mohrungen,) and betwixt them and their own country. He proposed, in short, to force his enemies towards the Vistula, as at Jena he had compelled the Prussians to fight with their rear turned to the Rhine. The Russian learned Buonaparte's intention from an intercepted despatch, and changed his purpose of advancing. Marches and counter-marches took place, through a country at all times difficult, and now covered with snow. The experience and dexterity of the French secured some advantages; but these were fully counterbalanced by the daily annoyance and loss which they in turn sustained from Platow and his Cossacks.

Bennigsen was aware that it was the interest of Russia to protract the campaign in this manner. He was near his reinforcements, the French were distant from theirs; every loss, therefore, told more in proportion on the enemy. On the other hand, the Russian army became clamorous for battle; for the hardships of their situation were such as to give them every desire to bring the war to a crisis. The distresses of the army were so extreme, that it induced General Bennigsen, against his judgment, to give battle at all risks, and for this purpose to concentrate his forces at Preuss-Eylau.

The action commenced with daybreak on the 8th of February. Two strong columns of the French advanced, with the purpose of turning the right, and storming the centre, of the Russians. But they were driven back in great disorder by the heavy and sustained fire of Russian artillery. An attack on the Russian left was equally unsuccessful. The Russian infantry stood like stone ramparts – they repulsed the enemy – their cavalry came to their support, pursued the retiring assailants, and took standards and eagles. About mid-day, a heavy storm of snow began to fall, which the wind drove right in the face of the Russians, which added to the obscurity caused by the smoke of the burning village of Serpallen.

Under cover of the darkness, six columns of the French advanced with artillery and cavalry, and were close on the Russian position ere they were opposed. Bennigsen, at the head of his staff, brought up the reserves in person, who, uniting with the first line, bore the French back at the point of the bayonet. Their columns, partly broken, were driven again to their own position, where they rallied with difficulty. A French regiment of cuirassiers, which, during this part of the action, had gained an interval in the Russian army, were charged by the Cossacks, and found their defensive armour no protection against the lance. They were all slain except eighteen.

At the moment when victory appeared to declare for the Russians, it was on the point of being wrested from them. Davoust's division had been manœuvring since the beginning of the action to turn the left, and gain the rear, of the Russian line. They now made their appearance on the field of battle with such effect, that Serpallen was lost, the Russian left wing, and a part of their centre, were thrown into disorder, and forced to retire and change their front, so as to form almost at right angles with the right, and that part of the centre which retained their original position.

At this crisis, and while the French were gaining ground on the rear of the Russians, L'Estocq appeared in his turn suddenly on the field, and, passing the left of the French, and the right of the Russians, pushed down in three columns to redeem the battle on the Russian centre and rear.

50,000 men perished in this dreadful battle – the best contested in which Buonaparte had yet engaged, and by far the most unsuccessful. He retired to the heights from which he had advanced in the morning, without having gained one point for which he had struggled, and after having suffered a loss considerably greater than that which he had inflicted on the enemy. But the condition of the Russian army was also extremely calamitous. Their generals held a council of war upon the field of battle, without dismounting from their horses. The general sentiment which prevailed among them was a desire to renew the battle on the next day at all hazards. Tolstoy undertook to move forward on the French lines – L'Estocq urged the same counsel. They offered to pledge their lives, that, would Bennigsen advance, Napoleon must necessarily retire; and they urged the moral effect which would be produced, not on their army only, but on Germany and on Europe, by such an admission of weakness.

Safe behind the Vistula, Napoleon concentrated on bringing the siege of Danzig to a successful close and replenishing his force following its losses.

The Russian army had received reinforcements, but they were deficient in numerical amount, and only made up their strength, at the utmost, to their original computation of 90,000 men. This proved unpardonable negligence in the Russian Government, considering the ease with which men can there be levied, and the vital importance of the war which they were now waging. It is said, however, that the poverty of the Russian Administration was the cause of this failure to recruit their forces.

Napoleon, so much more remote from his own territories, had already, by exertions unparalleled in the history of Europe, assembled 280,000 men between the Vistula and Memel. With such unequal forces, the war recommenced. On the 13th, the Russian army reached Friedland, a considerable town on the west side of the Aller, communicating with the eastern, or right bank of the river, by a long wooden bridge. It was the object of Napoleon to induce the Russian general to pass by this narrow bridge to the left bank, and then to decoy him into a general action, in a position where the difficulty of defiling through the town, and over the bridge, must render retreat almost impossible. For this purpose he showed such a proportion only of his forces, as induced General Bennigsen to believe that the French troops on the western side of the Aller consisted only of Oudinot's division. Under this deception he ordered a Russian division to pass the bridge, defile through the town, and march to the assault. The French took care to offer no such resistance as should intimate their real strength. Bennigsen was thus led to reinforce this division with another – the battle thickened, and the Russian general at length transported all his army, one division excepted, to the left bank, by means of the wooden bridge and three pontoons, and arrayed them in front of the town of Friedland, to overpower, as he supposed, the crippled division of the French.

But no sooner had he taken this irretrievable step than the mask was dropped. The French skirmishers advanced in force; heavy columns of infantry began to show themselves; batteries of cannon were got into position; and all circumstances concurred to assure Bennigsen that he, with his enfeebled forces, was in presence of the grand French army. His position, a sort of plain, surrounded by woods and broken ground, was difficult to defend; with the town and a large river in his rear, it was dangerous to attempt a retreat, and to advance was prevented by the inequality of his force.

The French advanced to the attack about ten o'clock. The broken and wooded country which they occupied enabled them to maintain and renew their efforts at pleasure, while the Russians, in their exposed situation, could not make the slightest movement without being observed. Yet they fought with such obstinate valour that at noon the French seemed sickening of the contest, and about to retire. But this was only a feint, to repose such of their forces as had been engaged, and to bring up reinforcements. The cannonade continued till about half past four, when Buonaparte brought up his full force in person, for the purpose of one of those desperate and generally irresistible efforts to which he was wont to trust the decision of a doubtful day. Columns of enormous power, and extensive depth, appeared partially visible among the interstices of the wooded country, and, seen from the town of Friedland, the hapless Russian army looked as if surrounded by a deep semicircle of glittering steel. The attack upon all the line, with cavalry, infantry, and artillery, was general and simultaneous, the French advancing with shouts of assured victory; while the Russians, weakened by the loss of at least 12,000 killed and wounded, were obliged to attempt that most dispiriting and dangerous of movements – a retreat through encumbered defiles, in front of a superior enemy. The principal attack was on the left wing, where the Russian position was at length forced. The troops which composed it streamed into the town, and crowded the bridge and pontoons; the enemy thundered on their rear, and without the valour of Alexander's Imperial Guard, the Russians would have been utterly destroyed. These brave soldiers charged with the bayonet the corps of Ney, who led the French vanguard, disordered his column, and, though they were overpowered by numbers, prevented the total ruin of the left wing.

Meanwhile, the bridge and pontoons were set on fire, to prevent the French from taking possession of them. The smoke rolling over the combatants, increased the horror and confusion of the scene; yet a considerable part of the Russian infantry escaped through a ford close by the town, which was discovered in the moment of defeat. The Russian centre and right, who remained on the west bank of the Aller, effected a retreat by a circuitous route. Thus were the Russians once more united on the right bank of the Aller, and enabled to prosecute their march towards Wehlau. Amid the calamities of defeat, they had saved all their cannon except seventeen, and preserved their baggage. Indeed, the stubborn character of their defence seems to have paralysed the energies of the victor, who, after carrying the Russian position, showed little of that activity which usually characterised him upon such occasions. He pushed no troops over the Aller in pursuit of the retreating enemy, but suffered Bennigsen to rally his broken troops without interruption. In short, the battle of Friedland, according to the expression of a French general, was a battle gained, but a victory lost.

Yet, the most important consequences resulted from the action. Königsberg, which had been so long the refuge of the King of Prussia, was evacuated by his forces, as it became plain his Russian auxiliaries could no longer maintain the war in Poland. But the moral consequences of the defeat were far greater than could have been either the capture of guns and prisoners, or the acquisition of territory. It had the effect, evidently desired by Napoleon, of disposing the Emperor Alexander to peace. The former could not but feel that he was engaged with a more obstinate enemy in Russia, than any he had yet encountered. After so many bloody battles, he was scarce arrived on the frontiers of an immense empire, boundless in its extent, and almost inexhaustible in resources; while the French, after suffering extremely in defeating an army that was merely auxiliary, could scarce be supposed capable of undertaking a scheme of invasion so gigantic, as that of plunging into the vast regions of Muscovy. Such an enterprise would have been peculiarly hazardous in the situation in which the French Emperor now stood. The English expedition to the Baltic was daily expected. Gustavus was in Swedish Pomerania, at the head of a considerable army. A spirit of resistance was awakening in Prussia. Hesse, Hanover, Brunswick, and the other provinces of Germany, deprived of their ancient princes, and subjected to heavy exactions by the conquerors, were ripe for insurrection.

Moved by such considerations, Napoleon had fully kept open the door for reconciliation betwixt the Czar and himself, abstaining from all those personal reflections against him, which he usually showered upon those who thwarted his projects, and intimating more than once, by different modes of communication, that a peace, which should enable Russia and France to divide the world betwixt them, should be placed within Alexander's reach so soon as he was disposed to accept it. The time was now arrived when the Emperor of Russia was disposed to listen to terms of accommodation with France. He had been for some time dissatisfied with his allies. Against Frederick William, indeed, nothing could be objected, save his bad fortune. The King of Sweden was a feeble ally at best, and, had become so unpopular with his subjects, that his dethronement was anticipated; and it was probably remembered, that the Swedish province of Finland extended so near to St. Petersburg, as to be a desirable acquisition, which, in the course of a treaty with Buonaparte might be easily attained.

The armistice was no sooner agreed upon than preparations were made for a personal interview betwixt the two Emperors. It took place upon a raft moored in the midst of the Niemen, which bore an immense pavilion. At half-past nine, 25th June, 1807, the two Emperors, in the midst of thousands of spectators, embarked at the same moment from the opposite banks. Arriving on the raft, they embraced amid the shouts and acclamations of both armies and, entering the pavilion, held a private conference of two hours. Their officers, who remained at a distance during the interview, were then reciprocally introduced, and the fullest good understanding seemed to be established between the sovereigns, who had at their disposal so great a portion of the universe. It is not to be doubted, that on this momentous occasion Napoleon exerted all those personal powers of attraction, which, exercised on the part of one otherwise so distinguished, rarely failed to acquire the good-will of all with whom he had intercourse.

The town of Tilsit was declared neutral. Entertainments of every kind followed each other. The two Emperors were constantly together in public and in private, and on those occasions their intimacy approached to the character of that of two young men of rank, who are comrades in sport or frolic, as well as accustomed to be associates in affairs, and upon occasions, of graver moment. On the 28th, the unfortunate King of Prussia arrived. Buonaparte did not admit him to the footing of equality on which he treated Alexander, and made an early intimation that it would only be for the purpose of obliging his brother of the North, that he might consent to relax his grasp on the Prussian territories. Those in the King's own possession were reduced to the petty territory of Memel, with the fortresses of Colberg and Graudentz. It was soon plain that the terms on which he was to be restored to his dominions would deprive Prussia of almost all the accessions which had been made since 1773 and reduce her at once from a first-rate power in Europe to one of the second class.

That portion of Poland acquired by Prussia in the partition of 1773 was erected into a separate territory, to be called the Grand Duchy of Warsaw. It was to be held by the King of Saxony, under the character of Grand Duke; and it was stipulated that he was to have direct communication with this new acquisition by means of a military road across Silesia, a privilege likely to occasion constant jealousy betwixt the courts of Berlin and Warsaw. Thus ended the hope of the Poles to be restored to the condition of an independent nation. They merely exchanged the dominion of one German master for another – Frederick William for Augustus – the only difference being, that the latter was descended from the Kings of Poland.

By the treaty, so far as made public, Russia offered her mediation betwixt Britain and France, on condition that the first named kingdom should accept the proffer of her interference within a month. So far, therefore, the Czar appeared careful of the interest of his late ally. But it is now perfectly well understood, that among other private articles, there existed one by which the Emperor bound himself, in case of Britain's rejecting the proposed mediation, to recognise and enforce the Continental System, by shutting his ports against British vessels, and engaging the Northern Courts in a new coalition, having for its object the destruction of English maritime superiority. Denmark, smarting under the recollections of the battle of Copenhagen, only waited, it was thought, the signal to join such a coalition, and would willingly consent to lend her still powerful navy to its support; and Sweden was in too weak and distracted a state to resist the united will of France and Russia. But, as there is no country of Europe to which the commerce of England is so beneficial as Russia, whose gross produce she purchases almost exclusively, it was necessary to observe strict secrecy upon these further objects. The ostensible proposal of mediation was therefore resorted to, less in the hope, perhaps, of establishing peace betwixt France and England, than in the expectation of affording a pretext, which might justify in the eye of the Russian nation a rupture with the latter power.

If the reader should wonder how Buonaparte, able and astucious as he was, came to be over reached in the treaty of Tilsit, we believe the secret may be found in a piece of private history. Even at that early period Napoleon nourished the idea of fixing, as he supposed, the fate of his own family, or dynasty, by connecting it by marriage with the blood of one of the established monarchies of Europe. He had hopes, even then, that he might obtain the hand of one of the Archduchesses of Russia, nor did the Emperor throw any obstacle in the way of the scheme. It is well known that his suit was afterwards disappointed by the Empress Mother, who pleaded the difference of religion; but at the time of Tilsit, Napoleon was actually encouraged, or deceived himself into an idea that he received encouragement, to form a perpetual family connection with Russia. This induced him to deal easily with Alexander in the matters which they had to discuss together, and to act the generous, almost the prodigal friend. And this also seems to have been the reason why Napoleon frequently complained of Alexander's insincerity, and often termed him *The Greek,* according to the Italian sense of the name, which signifies a trickster or deceiver.

*C*HAPTERS XXXVII, XXXVIII

At this period of Buonaparte's elevation, when his power seemed best established, it seems proper to take a hasty view of the means by which his empire was maintained, and the nature of the relations which it established betwixt the sovereign and his subjects.

The ruling, almost the sole principle on which the government of Buonaparte rested, was the simple proposition upon which despotism of every kind has founded itself in every species of society; namely, that the individual who is to exercise the authority and power of the state, shall, on the one hand, dedicate himself and his talents exclusively to the public service of the empire, while, on the other, the nation subjected to his rule shall requite this self-devotion on his part by the most implicit obe-

dience to his will. Some despots have rested this claim to universal submission upon family descent, and upon their right, according to Filmer's
doctrine, of representing the original father of the tribe, and becoming
the legitimate inheritors of a patriarchal power. Others have strained
scripture and abused common sense, to establish in their own favour a
right through the especial decree of Providence. To the hereditary title
Buonaparte could of course assert no claim; but he founded not a little
on the second principle, often holding himself out to others, and no
doubt occasionally considering himself, as an individual destined by
Heaven to the high station which he held, and one who could not therefore be opposed in his career, without an express struggle being maintained against Destiny, who had guided him by paths as strange as perilous, to the post of eminence which he now occupied. No one had been
his tutor in the lessons which led the way to his preferment – no one had
been his guide in the dangerous ascent to power – scarce anyone had been
of so much consequence to his promotion, as to claim even the merit of
an ally, however humble. It seemed as if Napoleon had been wafted on to
this stupendous pitch of grandeur by a power more effectual than that of
any human assistance, nay, which surpassed what could have been expected from his own great talents, unassisted by the especial interposition of
destiny in his favour. Buonaparte understood the character of the French
nation so well, that he could offer them an acceptable indemnification for
servitude; first, in the height to which he proposed to raise their national
pre-eminence; secondly, in the municipal establishments, by means of
which he administered their government, and which, though miserably
defective in all which would have been demanded by a nation accustomed
to the administration of equal and just laws, afforded a protection to life
and property that was naturally most welcome to those who had been so
long, under the republican system, made the victims of cruelty, rapacity,
and the most extravagant and unlimited tyranny, rendered yet more odious as exercised under the pretext of liberty.

He held himself out as the individual upon whom the fate of France
depended – of whose hundred decisive victories France enjoyed the glory.
It was he whose sword, hewing down obstacles which her bravest monarchs had accounted insurmountable, had cut the way to her now undeniable supremacy over Europe. He alone could justly claim to be Absolute

Monarch of France, who, raising that nation from a perilous condition, had healed her discords, reconciled her factions, turned her defeats into victory, and, from a disunited people, about to become the prey to civil and external war, had elevated her to the situation of Queen of Europe. This had been all accomplished upon one condition; and, as we have stated elsewhere, it was that which the Tempter offered in the wilderness, after his ostentatious display of the kingdoms of the earth – "All these will I give thee, if thou wilt fall down and worship me."

Thus did Napoleon play upon the imagination of the French people. He gave them public festivals, victories, and extended dominion; and in return, claimed the right of carrying their children in successive swarms to yet more distant and yet more extended conquests, and of governing, according to his own pleasure, the bulk of the nation which remained behind him. To attain this purpose, one species of idolatry was gradually and ingeniously substituted for another, and the object of the public devotion was changed, while the worship was continued. France had been formerly governed by political maxims – she was now ruled by the name of an individual. Formerly the republic was everything – Fayette, Dumouriez, Pichegru, were nothing. Now, the name of a successful general was of more influence than the whole code of the Rights of Man. France had submitted to murder, spoliation, revolutionary tribunals, and every species of cruelty and oppression, while they were gilded by the then talismanic expressions – "Liberty and Equality – Fraternisation – the public welfare, and the happiness of the people." She was now found equally compliant, when the watchword was, "The honour of his Imperial and Royal Majesty – the interests of the Great Empire – the splendours of the Imperial Throne." It must be owned, that the sacrifices under the last form were less enormous; they were limited to taxes at the Imperial pleasure, and a perpetual anticipation of the conscription. The Republican tyrants claimed both life and property, the Emperor was satisfied with a tithe of the latter, and the unlimited disposal of that portion of the family who could best support the burden of arms, for augmenting the conquests of France.

It cannot be forgotten that Buonaparte, the heir of the Revolution, appropriated to himself the forms and modifications of the Directorial government, but they subsisted as forms only. The Senate and Legislative

Bodies became merely passive and pensioned creatures of the Emperor's will, whom he used as a medium for promulgating the laws which he was determined to establish.

The deliberative Council of the Emperor existed in his own personal Council of State, of whose consultations, in which he himself presided, he made frequent use during the course of his reign. Its functions were of an anomalous character, comprehending political legislation, or judicial business, according to the order of the day. It was, in short, Buonaparte's resource, when he wanted the advice, or opinion, or information, of others in aid of his own; and he often took the assistance of the Council of State, in order to form those resolutions which he afterwards executed by means of his ministers. We have no doubt that Buonaparte, on certain occasions, permitted his counsellors to take considerable freedoms, and that he sometimes yielded up his opinion to theirs without being convinced, in such cases, at least, where his own passions or interest were no way concerned.

But, that part of the organisation of the Imperial government, upon which Buonaparte most piqued himself, was the establishment of the Prefectures, which certainly gave facilities for the most effectual agency of despotism that was ever exercised. These prefects, it must be understood, were each the supreme governor of a department. The individuals were carefully selected, as persons whose attachment was either to be secured or rewarded. They were entirely dependent on the will of the Emperor, who removed or cashiered them at pleasure. It was by means of the prefects that an impulse, given from the centre of the government, was communicated without delay to the extremities of the kingdom, and that the influence of the crown, and the execution of its commands, were transmitted, as if by magic, through a population of forty million.

It was the further duty of the prefects to see that all honour was duly performed towards the head of the state, upon the days appointed for public rejoicings, and to remind the municipal authorities of the necessity of occasional addresses to the government, declaring their admiration of the talents, and devotion to the person of the Emperor. These effusions were duly published in the *Moniteur*, and, if examined closely, would afford some of the most extraordinary specimens of composition which the annals of flattery can produce. It is sufficient to say, that a mayor, we believe of Amiens, affirmed, in his ecstasy of loyal adoration, that the Deity, after making Buonaparte, must have reposed, as after the creation of the universe. Napoleon well knew the influence produced on the public mind, by ringing the changes to different time on the same unvaried subject. The ideas which are often repeated in all variety of language and expression will, at length, produce an effect on the public mind, especially if no contradiction is permitted to reach it.

But a far more important change introduced by the Emperor, though not originating with him, was the total alteration of the laws of the kingdom of France, and the introduction of that celebrated code to which Napoleon assigned his name, and on the execution of which his admirers have rested his claim to be considered as a great benefactor to the country. It had been the reproach of France before the Revolution, and it was one of the great evils which tended to produce that immense and violent change, that the various provinces, towns, and divisions of the kingdom, having been united in different periods to the general body of the country, had retained the exercise of their own particular laws and usages. The evils attending such a state of things had been long felt, and, at various periods before the Revolution, it had been proposed to institute a uniform system of legislation for the kingdom.

After the 18th Brumaire, Napoleon saw no way more certain of assuring the popularity of that event, and connecting his own authority with the public interests of France, than to resume a task which former rulers of the Republic had thought too heavy to be undertaken. An order of the Consuls, dated 24th Thermidor, in the year VIII., directed the minister of justice, with a committee of lawyers of eminence, to examine the several projects which had been made towards compiling the civil code, to give their opinion on the plan most desirable for accomplishing its formation, and to discuss the bases upon which legislation in civil matters ought to be rested.

It would be doing much injustice to Napoleon to suppress the great personal interest which, amid so many calls upon his time, he nevertheless took in the labours of the commission. He frequently attended their meetings, or those of the Council of State, in which their labours underwent revision and, though he must be supposed entirely ignorant of the jurisprudence as a science, yet his acute, calculating, and argumentative mind enabled him, by the broad views of genius and good sense, often to get rid of those subtleties by which professional persons are occasionally embarrassed, and to treat as cobwebs, difficulties of a technical or meta-physical character, which, to the jurisconsults, had the appearance of bonds and fetters.

The fiscal operations of Buonaparte were those of which the subjects complained the most. High taxes were imposed on the French people, rendered necessary by the expenses of the government, which, with all its accompaniments, were very considerable; and although Buonaparte did all in his power to throw the charge of the eternal wars upon the countries he overran or subdued, yet so far does the waste of war exceed any emol-ument which the armed hand can wrest from the sufferers, that after all the revenue which was derived from foreign countries, the continual cam-paigns proved a constant and severe drain upon the produce of French industry. So rich, however, is the soil of France, such are the extent of her resources, such the patience and activity of her inhabitants, that she is qualified, if not to produce at once the large capitals which England can raise upon her national credit, yet to support the payment of a train of heavy annual imposts for a much longer period, and with less practical inconvenience. The agriculture of France had been extremely improved since the breaking up of the great estates into smaller portions, and the abrogation of those feudal burdens which had pressed upon the cultiva-tors; and it might be considered as flourishing, in spite of war taxes, and, what was worse, the conscription itself. Under a fixed and secure, though a severe and despotic government, property was protected, and agricul-ture received the best encouragement, namely, the certainty conferred on the cultivator of reaping the crop which he sowed.

It was far otherwise with commerce, which the maritime war had very much injured, and the utter destruction of which was in a manner per-fected by Buonaparte's adherence to the continental system. This, indeed, was the instrument by which, in the long run, he hoped to ruin the com-merce of his rival, but the whole weight of which fell in the first instance on that of France.

It might be thought that the manufacturing interest must have per-ished in France, for the same reasons which afflicted the commerce of that country. In ceasing to import, there must indeed have been a corresponding diminution of the demand for goods to be exported. Accordingly, this result had, in a great degree taken place. But, though the real and legitimate stimulus to manufactures had thus ceased, Napoleon had substituted an artificial one, which had, to a certain extent, supplied the place of the natural trade. We must remark, that Napoleon was totally a stranger to the science of Political Economy. He had proceeded to act against the commerce of England, as, in a military capacity, he would have done in regard to the water which supplied a besieged city. He strove to cut it off, and altogether to destroy it, and to supply the absence of its productions, by such substitutes as France could furnish. Hence the factitious encouragement given to the French manufactures, not by the natural demand of the country, but by the bounties and prohibitions by which they were guarded. Hence the desperate efforts made to produce a species of sugar from various substances, especially from the beet-root. To this unnatural and unthrifty experiment, Buonaparte used to attach so much consequence, that a piece of the new composition, which, with much time and trouble, had been made to approximate the quality of ordinary loaf-sugar, was preserved in a glass-case over the Imperial mantel-piece; and a pound or two of beet-sugar, highly-refined, was sent to foreign courts, to illustrate the means by which Napoleon consoled his subjects for the evils incumbent on the continental system. No way of flattering or gratifying the Emperor was so certain, as to appear eager in supporting these views; and it is said that one of his generals, when tottering in the Imperial good graces, regained the favour of his master, by planting the whole of a considerable estate with beet-root. The various encouragements given to the cotton manufacturers, and others, in France, by which it was designed to supply the want of British goods, proceeded upon a system equally illiberal and impolitic. Still, however, the expensive bounties, and forced sales, which the influence of government afforded, enabled these manufacturers to proceed, and furnished employment to a certain number of men, who were naturally grateful for the protection which they received from the Emperor. It was thus, that the efforts of Napoleon at encouraging arts and manufactures, though proceeding on mistaken principles, produced, in the first instance, results apparently beneficial.

We have already had occasion to observe the immense public works which were undertaken at the expense of Buonaparte's government.

Temples, bridges, and aqueducts, are, indeed, the coin with which arbitrary princes, in all ages, have endeavoured to compensate for the liberty of which the people are deprived. Such monuments are popular with the citizens, because the enjoyment of them is common to all, and the monarch is partial to a style of expenditure promising more plausibly than any other, to extend the memory of his present greatness far into the bosom of futurity. Buonaparte was not insensible to either of these motives. His mind was too much enlarged to seek enjoyment in any of the ordinary objects of exclusive gratification; and undoubtedly, he who had done so much to distinguish himself during his life above ordinary mortals, must have naturally desired that his public works should preserve his fame to future ages. Accordingly, he undertook and executed some of the most splendid labours of modern times. The road over the Simplon and the basins at Antwerp may be always appealed to as gigantic specimens of his public spirit.

Buonaparte's habits of activity, his powers of deciding with a single glance upon most points of either military or civil engineering, were liberally drawn upon to strike his subjects with wonder and admiration. During the few peaceful intervals of his reign, his impatience of inaction found amusement in traversing, with great rapidity, and often on the shortest notice, the various departments in France. [He] had no sooner visited any town of consequence, than he threw himself on horseback and, followed only by his aide-de-camp and his Mameluke Rustan, who with difficulty kept him in view, he took a flying survey of the place, its capacities of improvement, or the inconveniences which attached to it. With this local knowledge thus rapidly acquired, he gave audience to the municipal authorities, and overwhelmed them very often with liberal and long details concerning the place round which he had galloped for the first time. Amazement at the extent and facility of the Emperor's powers of observation was thus universally excited, and his hints were recorded in the *Moniteur*, for the admiration of France. Some public work, solicited by the municipality, or suggested by the enlightened benevolence of the Emperor himself, was then projected, but which, in many, if not most cases, remained unexecuted; the imperial funds not being in all circumstances adequate to the splendour of Napoleon's undertakings, or, which the more frequent case, some new absorbing war, or project of ambition, occasioning every other object of expenditure to be postponed. Napoleon did that which he ridiculed the Directory for being unable to do – he wrought on the imagination of the French nation, which indeed had been already so dazzled by the extraordinary things he had accomplished, that, had he promised them still greater prodigies, they might still have been justified in expecting the performance of his predictions. And it must be admitted, looking around Paris, and travelling through the provinces, that Buonaparte has, in the works of peaceful grandeur, left a stamp of magnificence not unworthy of the soaring and at the same time profound spirit, which accomplished so many wonders in warfare.

The personal life of Napoleon was skilfully adapted to his pre-eminent station. If he had foibles connected with pleasure and passion, they were so carefully veiled to remain unknown to the world – at least, they were not manifested by any of those weaknesses which might serve to lower the Emperor to the stamp of common men. His conduct towards the Empress Josephine was regular and exemplary. From their accession to grandeur till the fatal divorce, as Napoleon once termed it, they shared the privacy of the same apartment, and for many years partook the same bed. Josephine is said, indeed, to have given her husband some annoyance by her jealousy, to which he patiently submitted, and escaped the reproach thrown on so many heroes and men of genius, that, proof to every thing else, they are not so against the allurements of female seduction. What amours he had were of a passing character. No woman, excepting Josephine and her successor, was ever known to possess any power over him.

The dignity of his throne was splendidly and magnificently maintained, but the expense was still limited by that love of order which arose out of Buonaparte's powers of calculation, habitually and constantly employed, and the trusting to which contributed to that external regularity and decorum which he always supported.

The Imperial Court was distinguished not only by a severe etiquette, but the grandees, by whom its principal duties were discharged, were also given to understand, that the utmost magnificence of dress and equipage was required from them upon public occasions. It was, indeed, a subject of complaint among the servants of the Crown, that though Buonaparte was in many respects attentive to their interests, gave them opportunities of acquiring wealth, invested them with large dotations and endowments, and frequently assisted them with an influence not easily withstood in the accomplishment of advantageous marriages; yet still the great expenditure at which they were required to support their appearance at the Imperial court, prevented their realising any fortune which could provide effectually for their family. This expense Buonaparte loved to represent as a tax which he made his courtiers pay to support the manufactures of France; but it was extended so far as to show plainly that, determined as he was to establish his nobility on such a scale as to grace his court, it was far from being his purpose to permit them to assume any real power, or to furnish an existing and influential barrier between the crown and the people.

Amid the gleam of embroidery, of orders, decorations, the person of the Emperor was to be distinguished by his extreme simplicity of dress and deportment. A plain uniform, with a hat having no other ornament than a small three-coloured cockade, was the dress of him who bestowed all these gorgeous decorations, and in honour of whom these costly robes of ceremonial had been exhibited. Perhaps Napoleon might be of opinion that a person under the common size, and in his latter days somewhat corpulent, was unfit for the display of rich dresses; or it is more likely he desired to intimate, that although he exacted from others the strict observance of etiquette, he held that the Imperial dignity placed him above any reciprocal obligation towards them.

The love of order, as a ruling principle of his government, must have rendered Buonaparte a severe censor of all public breaches of the decencies of society. Public morals are in themselves the accomplishment and fulfilment of all laws; they alone constitute a national code. Accordingly, the manners of the Imperial court were under such regulation as to escape public scandal, if they were not beyond secret suspicion. In the same manner, gambling, the natural and favourite vice of a court, was not practised in that of Buonaparte, who discountenanced high play by every means in his power. But he suffered it to be licensed to an immense and frightful extent by the minister of police; nor can we give him the least credit when he affirms that the gambling-houses which paid such immense rents to Fouché, existed without his knowledge.

In the public amusements, Buonaparte took a deep interest. He often attended the theatre, though commonly in private and without éclat. The strictest care was taken that nothing should be admitted on the stage which could awaken feelings unfavourable to the Government. When the acute wit of the Parisian audience seized on some expression or incident which had any analogy to public affairs, the greatest pains were taken, not only to prevent the circumstance from recurring, but even to hinder it from getting into general circulation. This secrecy respecting what occurred in public was easily accomplished where the public papers were under the strict and unremitted vigilance of the government.

There were periods when Buonaparte, in order to gain the approbation and sympathy of those who claim the exclusive title of lovers of liberty, was not unwilling to be thought the friend of liberal opinions, and was heard to express himself in favour of the liberty of the press, and other checks upon the executive authority. To reconcile his opinions (or rather what he threw out as his opinions) with a practice diametrically opposite was no easy matter, yet he sometimes attempted it. On observing one or two persons who had been his surprised auditors on such occasions, unable to suppress some appearance of incredulity, he immediately entered upon his defence "I am," he said, "at bottom, and naturally, for a fixed and limited government. You seem not to believe me, perhaps because you conceive my opinions and practice are at variance. But you do not consider the necessity arising out of persons and circumstances. Were I to relax the reins for an instant, you would see a general confusion. Neither you nor I, probably, would spend another night in the Tuileries." Such declarations have often been found in the mouths of those, who have seized an unlawful degree of authority. Cromwell was forced to dissolve the Parliament, though he besought the Lord rather to slay him. State necessity is the usual plea of tyrants; and, by resorting to such an apology, they pay that tribute to truth in their language, to which their practice is in the most decided opposition.

The press, at no time, and in no civilised country, was ever so completely enchained and fettered as at this period in France. The public journals were prohibited from inserting any article of public news which had not first appeared in the *Moniteur*, and this, on all momentous occasions, was personally examined by Buonaparte himself. Nor were the inferior papers permitted to publish a word, whether in the way of explanation, criticism, or otherwise, which did not accurately correspond with the tone observed in the leading journal. They might enhance the praise, or deepen the censure, which characterise the leading paragraph; but seizure of their paper, confiscation, imprisonment, and sometimes exile, were the unfailing reward of any attempt to correct what was erroneous in point of fact, or sophistical in point of reasoning. The *Moniteur*, therefore, was the sole guide of public opinion; and by his constant attention to its contents, it is plain that Napoleon relied as much on its influence to direct the general mind, as he did upon the power of his arms, military reputation, and extensive resources, to overawe the other nations of Europe.

*C*HAPTER XXXIX

The instruction of the youth of France had been the subject of several projects during the Republic; which was the more necessary as the Revolution had entirely destroyed all the colleges and seminaries of public instruction, most of which were more or less connected with the Church, and had left the nation almost destitute of any public means of education. These schemes had agreed that each commune should provide a school and teacher, for the purpose of communicating the primary principles of education. This plan had in a great measure failed, owing to the poverty of the communes on whom the expense was thrown. Secondary schools were such as qualified persons, or those who held themselves out as such, had established for teaching the learned and modern languages, geography, and mathematics. There was besides evinced on the part of the Catholic clergy, as soon as the Concordat had restored them, a desire to resume the task of public education.

Matters were upon this footing when Buonaparte brought forward his grand project of a National University,[16] composed of a Grand Master, a Chancellor, a treasurer, ten counsellors for life, twenty counsellors in ordinary, and thirty inspectors-general; the whole forming a sort of imperial council, whose supremacy was to be absolute on matters respecting education. All teachers, and all seminaries of education were subjected to the authority of the National University, nor could any school be opened without a brevet or diploma from the Grand Master, upon which a considerable tax was imposed. It was indeed the policy of the government to diminish as far as possible the number of Secondary and of Ecclesiastical Schools, in order that the public education might be conducted at the public seminaries, called Lyceums, or Academies.

In these Lyceums the discipline was partly military, partly monastic. The masters, censors, and teachers, were bound to celibacy; the professors might marry, but in that case were not permitted to reside within the precincts. The youth were entirely separated from their families, and allowed to correspond with no one save their parents, and then only under the inspection of the censor. The whole system was subjected to the strict and frequent investigation of the University. The Grand Master might dismiss any person he pleased, and such a sentence of dismissal disqualified the party receiving it from holding any civil employment.

In the general case, it is the object of a place of learning to remove from the eyes of youth that pomp and parade of war, by which at an early age they are so easily withdrawn from severe attention to their studies. The Lyceums of Buonaparte were conducted on a contrary principle; every thing was done by beat of drum, all the interior arrangements were upon a military footing. At a period when the soldierly profession held out the most splendid prospects, it was no wonder that young men soon learned to look forward to it as the only line worthy of a man of spirit. The devotion of the young students to the Emperor, carefully infused into them by their teachers, was further excited by the recollection, that he was their benefactor for all the means of instruction afforded them.

From these Lyceums, 250 of the most selected youth were yearly draughted into the more professional and special military schools maintained by the Emperor; and to be included in this chosen number, was the prime object of every student. Thus, every thing induced the young men, to look upon a military life as the most natural and enviable course they had to pursue; and thus Buonaparte accomplished that alteration on the existing generation, which he intimated, when he said, "The clergy regard this world as a mere diligence which is to convey us to the next – it must be my business to fill the public carriage with good recruits for my army."

Of the whole range of national education, that which was conducted at the Lyceums was alone supported by the state; and the courses there taught were generally limited to Latin and mathematics, the usual accomplishments of a military academy. Undoubtedly Brienne was in Napoleon's recollection; nor might he perhaps think a better, or a more enlarged course of education necessary for the subjects of France, than that which had advanced their sovereign to the supreme government. But there was a deeper reason in the limitation. Those who, under another system, might have advanced themselves to that degree of knowledge which becomes influential upon the mind of the public, or the fortunes of a state, by other means than those of violence, were disqualified for the task by that which they received in the Lyceums; and the gentle, studious, and peaceful youth, was formed, like all the rest of the generation, to the trade of war, to which he was probably soon to be called by the conscription.

CHAPTER XL

We have shown that the course of education practised in France was so directed as to turn the thoughts and hope of the youth to a military life, and prepare them to obey the call of the conscription. This means of recruiting the military force, the most formidable ever established in a civilised nation, was originally presented to the Council of Five Hundred in 1798.

The law has its general principle in the duty which everyone owes to his country. Nothing can be more true than that all men capable of bearing arms are liable to be employed in the defence of the state; and nothing can be more politic than that the obligation should be, in the first instance, imposed upon youth. But it is obvious that such a measure can only be vindicated in defensive war, and that Buonaparte, who applied the system to the conduct of distant offensive wars, not otherwise necessary than for the satisfaction of his own ambition, stands liable to the heavy charge of having drained the very life-blood of the people entrusted to his charge.

The French conscription was yet more severely felt by the extreme rigour of its conditions. No distinction was made betwixt the married man, whose absence might be the ruin of his family, and the single member of a numerous lineage, who could be easily spared. The son of the widow, the child of the decrepid and helpless, had no right to claim an exemption. Three sons might be carried off in three successive years from the same desolated parents; there was no allowance made for having already supplied a recruit. Those unable to serve were mulcted in a charge proportioned to the quota of taxes which they or their parents contributed, and which might vary from 50 to 1200 francs. Substitutes might indeed be offered, but then it was both difficult and expensive to procure them, as the law required that such substitutes should be domesticated within the same district as their principal, or come within the conscription of the year. Suitable persons were sure to know their own value, and had learned so well to profit by it, that they were not to be bribed to serve without excessive bounties. The substitutes also had the practice of deserting and thus cheated the principal, who remained answerable for them till they joined their colours. On the whole, the difficulty of obtaining exemption by substitution was so great, that very many young men, well educated, and of respectable families, were torn from all their more propitious prospects, to bear the life, discharge the duties, and die the death, of common soldiers.

There was no part of Napoleon's government enforced with such extreme rigour. The mayor, upon whom the duty devolved of seeing the number called for selected by lot, was compelled to avoid showing the slightest indulgence, the brand, the pillory, or the galleys, awaited the magistrate if he was found to have favoured any individuals on whom the law of conscription had claims. The same laws held out the utmost extent of their terrors against refractory conscripts, and the public functionaries were everywhere in search of them. When arrested, they were treated like convicts of the most infamous description. Clothed in a dress of infamy, loaded with chains, and dragging weights, they were condemned to work upon the public fortifications. Their relations did not escape, but were often rendered liable for fines and penalties.

The habits of the nation being strongly turned towards war, the French formed, upon the whole, the most orderly, most obedient, and best regulated troops, that ever took the field. They excelled especially in the art of shifting for themselves; and it was one in which the wars of Napoleon required them to be peculiarly adroit.

The French Revolution first introduced into Europe a mode of conducting hostilities which transferred almost the whole burden of the war to the country which had the ill-fortune to be the seat of its operations, and rendered it a resource rather than a drain to the successful belligerent. At the commencement of a campaign, a French army was formed into large bodies, called *corps d'armée,* each commanded by a king, viceroy, mareschal, or general officer of high pretensions. Each *corps d'armée* formed a complete army within itself, and had its allotted proportion of cavalry, infantry, artillery, and troops of every description. The *corps d'armée* consisted of from six to ten divisions, each commanded by a general of division. The divisions, again, were subdivided into brigades, of which each, comprehending two or three regiments, (consisting of two or more battalions,) was commanded by a general of brigade. A *corps d'armée* might vary in number from 50,000 to 80,000 men, and upwards; and the general of such a body exercised the full military authority over it, without the control of anyone excepting the Emperor.

Thus organised, the French army was poured into some foreign country by forced marches, without any stores or magazines, and with the purpose of maintaining them solely at the expense of the inhabitants. Buonaparte was exercised in this system; and the combination of great masses, by means of such forced marches, was one great principle of his tactics. This species of war was carried on at the least possible expense of money to his treasury; but it was necessarily at the greatest possible expenditure of human life, and the incalculable increase of human misery. Napoleon's usual object was to surprise the enemy by the rapidity of his marches, defeat him in some great battle, and then seize upon his capital, levy contributions, make a peace with such advantages as he could obtain, and finally return to Paris.

In these dazzling campaigns, the army usually began their march with bread or biscuit for a certain number of days, on the soldiers' backs. Cattle also were for a time driven along with them, and slaughtered as wanted. The horses were likewise loaded with forage, for the consumption of two or three days. Thus provided, the army set forward on its expedition by forced marches, in a very short time the soldiers became impatient of their burdens, and either wasted them, or actually threw them away. It was then that the officers, who soon entertained just apprehensions of the troops suffering scarcity, gave authority to secure supplies by what was called *la maraude,* in other words, by plunder. To ensure that these forced supplies should be collected and distributed systematically, a certain number of soldiers from each company were despatched to obtain provisions at the villages and farm-houses in the neighbourhood of the march, or of the ground upon which the army was encamped. These soldiers were authorised to compel the inhabitants to deliver their provisions without receipt or payment; and, such being their regular duty, it may be well supposed that they did not confine themselves to provisions, but exacted money and articles of value, and committed many other similar abuses.

The most hideous features of this system were shown when the army marched through a thinly-peopled country, or when the national character encouraged the natives to offer resistance. Then the soldiers became animated alike by the scarcity of provisions, and irritated at the danger which they sometimes incurred in collecting them. As their hardships increased, their temper became reckless, and, besides indulging in every other species of violence, they increased their own distresses by destroying what they could not use. Famine and sickness were not long in visiting an army which traversed a country exhausted of provisions. Without hospitals and without magazines, every straggler who could not regain his ranks fell a victim to hunger, to weather, to weariness, to the vengeance of an incensed peasantry. In this manner, the French army suffered woes, which, till these tremendous wars, had never been the lot of troops in hostilities carried on between civilised nations. Still Buonaparte's object was gained; he attained, amid these losses and sacrifices, and at the expense of them, the point which he had desired; displayed his masses to the terrified eyes of a surprised enemy; reaped the reward of his despatch in a general victory; and furnished new subjects of triumph to the *Moniteur.* So much did he rely upon the celerity of movement that if an officer asked time to execute any of his commands, it was frequently his remarkable answer, "Ask me for any thing except time."

Buonaparte observed, with respect to his army, an adroit species of policy. His officers of high rank were liberally honoured and rewarded by him; but he never treated them with personal familiarity. The forms of etiquette were, upon all occasions, strictly maintained. Perhaps he was of the opinion that the original equality in which they had stood would have been too strongly recalled by a more familiar mode of intercourse. But to the common soldier, who could not misconstrue or intrude upon his familiarity, Buonaparte observed a different line of conduct. He permitted himself to be addressed by them on all suitable occasions, and paid strict attention to their petitions, complaints, and even their remonstrances. What they complained of was, in all instances, inquired into and reformed, if the complaints were just. After a battle, he was accustomed to consult the regiments which had distinguished themselves, concerning the merits of those who had deserved distinction. In these moments of conscious importance, the sufferings of the whole campaign were forgotten; and Napoleon seemed, to the soldiery who surrounded him, not as the ambitious man who had dragged them from their homes, to waste their valour in foreign fields, but as the father of the war, to whom his soldiers were as children, and to whom the honour of the meanest private was as dear as his own.

But with all this encouragement, it was the remark of Buonaparte himself, that the army no longer produced, under the Empire, such distinguished soldiers as Pichegru, Kleber, Moreau, Massena, Desaix, Hoche, and he himself above all, who, starting from the ranks of obscurity, like runners to a race, had astonished the world by their progress. These men of the highest genius, had been produced, as Buonaparte thought, in and by the fervour of the Revolution; and he appears to have been of the opinion that, since things had returned more and more into the ordinary and restricted bounds of civil society, men of the same high class were no longer created.

CHAPTER XLI

Napoleon consolidated and enforced the Continental System. Holland and the Kingdom of Westphalia were appanages and Prussia, since her defeat, was closed to British commerce, as were the Hanseatic Towns. The decrees of Berlin, reinforced by those of Milan, were countered by British Orders in Council, giving rise to a new species of commercial warfare as well as epic smuggling.

It was chiefly the Spanish Peninsula which gave an extended vent to

British commerce. Buonaparte, indeed, had a large share of its profits, since Portugal paid him great sums to connive at her trade with England. But, at last, the weakness of Portugal, and the total disunion of the Royal Family in Spain, suggested to Napoleon the thoughts of appropriating to himself that noble portion of the continent of Europe. Hence arose the Spanish contest, of which he afterwards said in bitterness, "That wretched war was my ruin; it divided my forces – obliged me to multiply my efforts, and injured my character for morality." But could he expect better results from usurpation, executed under circumstances of treachery perfectly unexampled in the history of Europe?

Shortly after Tilsit, the Prince Regent of Portugal was required, by France and Spain jointly, to shut his ports against the English, to confiscate the property of Britain, and to arrest the persons of her subjects within his dominions. The Prince reluctantly acceded to the first part of this proposal; the last he peremptorily refused, as calling upon him at once to violate the faith of treaties and the rights of hospitality. In the meantime, a singular treaty was signed at Fontainebleau, for the partition of the ancient kingdom of Portugal.[17] By this agreement, a plan was laid for invading Portugal with French and Spanish armies and dividing it into three parts. By the treaty, Napoleon obtained two important advantages; the first, that Portugal should be conquered; the second, that a great part of the Spanish troops should be employed on the expedition, and their native country thus deprived of their assistance.

Junot, one of the most grasping, extravagant, and profligate of the French generals, a man whom Buonaparte himself has stigmatised as a monster of rapacity, was appointed to march upon Lisbon, and entrusted with the charge of reconciling to the yoke of the invaders, a nation who had neither provoked war, nor attempted resistance. Two additional armies, consisting partly of French and partly of Spaniards, supported the attack of Junot. A French army, amounting to 40,000 men, was formed at Bayonne, in terms of the treaty, destined, it was pretended, to act as an army of reserve, in case the English should land troops for the defence of Portugal, but which, it had been stipulated, was on no account to enter Spain, unless such a crisis should demand their presence.

Meantime, Junot advanced upon Lisbon with such extraordinary forced marches, and very much dislocated and exhausted his army. But this was of the less consequence, because, aware that he could not make an effectual resistance, the Prince Regent had determined that he would not, by an ineffectual show of defence, give the invaders a pretext to treat Portugal like a conquered country. He resolved at this late hour to comply even with the last and harshest of the terms dictated by France and Spain, by putting the restraint of a register on British subjects and British property; but he had purposely delayed compliance, till little was left that could be affected by the measure.

Junot and his army had by this time [18th November] crossed the frontiers of Portugal. Nothing retarded the celerity of his march; for he was well aware that it was his master's most anxious wish to seize the persons of the Portuguese royal family, and especially that of the Prince Regent. The British ambassador offered every facility which her squadron could afford, and, as is now known, granted the guarantee of Great Britain, that she would acknowledge no government which the invaders might establish in Portugal, to the prejudice of the House of Braganza. The Prince Regent, with the whole royal family, embarked on board Portuguese vessels of the line [27th November]. Junot, within a day's march of Lisbon, was almost frantic with rage when he heard this news. He well knew how much the escape of the Prince, and the resolution he had formed, would diminish the lustre of his own success in the eyes of his master. Once possessed of the Prince Regent's person, Buonaparte had hoped to get him to cede possession of the Brazils; and transmarine acquisitions had for Napoleon all the merit of novelty. The empire of the House of Braganza in the new world, was now effectually beyond his reach.

Upon the first of December, the French vanguard approached the city, and their general might see the retreating sails of the vessels which deprived him of so fair a portion of his prize. The extortions and rapacity practised in Lisbon seemed to leave all former excesses of the French army far behind. This led to quarrels betwixt the French and the natives; blood was shed; public executions took place, and the invaders, proceeding to reduce and disband the remnant of the Portuguese army, showed their positive intention to retain the kingdom under their own exclusive authority. This purpose was at last intimated by an official document or proclamation, issued by Junot [1st

February] under Buonaparte's orders. It declared that, by leaving his kingdom, the Prince of Brazil had abdicated the sovereignty and that Portugal, having become a part of the dominions of Napoleon, should, for the present, be governed by the French general-in-chief, in the name of the Emperor. The French flag was accordingly displayed, the arms of Portugal everywhere removed. The property of the Prince Regent, and of all who had followed him was sequestrated. The next demand upon the unhappy country, was for a contribution of forty million crusadoes, or four million and a half sterling; which, laid upon a population of something less than three million, came to about thirty shillings a head.

*C*HAPTERS XLII, XLIII, XLIV, XLV, XLVI

Portugal turned out to be a mere appetiser; Napoleon had his eye on Spain. Taking advantage, among other factors, of dissension between the Spanish monarch and his heir, the Emperor ordered the French troops stationed in Bayonne to enter Spain and take control of her border fortresses before marching on Madrid. The King contemplated retreating, as the Portuguese monarch had, to the Americas. Alarm at that prospect provoked unrest in Madrid that led to his abdication in favour of his son, Ferdinand, whom France deferred recognising. Probably disobeying his more politic master's orders to remain outside the capital, Murat entered Madrid with 10,000 troops, on 23rd March. Ferdinand and his father made their separate ways to Bayonne to meet Napoleon. Under French pressure, Charles abdicated once again, on 4th May, this time in favour of Napoleon. Ferdinand was compelled, in turn, to abdicate on 6th May. Napoleon appointed Joseph to the vacant throne, transferring Murat from the Grand Duchy of Berg to Naples in his stead.

The popular insurrection in Madrid, on 2nd May 1807, was crushed, but the spirit of rebellion spread to different parts of the kingdom. Though disorganised, and doomed to violent and costly failure in the first instance, the rebels achieved a notable victory against the French at Baylen, underwent a heroic siege at Saragossa, and even obliged Joseph to retreat from Madrid. More significantly, French discomfiture in the Peninsula gave Britain an opportunity to intervene on the Continent. An expeditionary force under Arthur Wellesley, the future Duke of Wellington, despatched to Portugal, defeated the French under Junot at the battle of Vimiero, on 21st August 1808 and might have turned victory into triumph had Wellesley not been superseded by Sir Hew Dalrymple, who signed the convention of Cintra with Junot, enabling the French to evacuate. No alternative was left to Napoleon but to intervene in person in the Peninsula. Before doing so, however, he had to ensure German passivity. Austria was, yet again, rearming.

Yet it was not alone the hostile preparations of Austria which seemed to trouble Germany. Napoleon had defeated her efforts when her force was still more imposing. But there was gradually awakening and extending through Germany, especially its northern provinces, a strain of opinion incompatible with the domination of France, or of any other foreign power within the ancient empire. The disappearance of various petty states, together with the general system of oppression under which the whole country suffered, had broken down the divisions which separated the nations of Germany from each other, and, like relations who renew an interrupted intimacy under the pressure of a common calamity, the mass of the people forgot that they were Hanoverians, Hessians, Saxons, or Prussians, to remember that they were all Germans, and had one common cause in which to struggle. Less fiery than the Spaniards, but not less accessible to deep and impassioned feeling, the youth of Germany, especially such as were engaged in the liberal studies, cherished in secret, and with caution, a deep hatred to the French invaders, amid a stern resolution to avail themselves of the first opportunity to achieve the national liberty.

The thousand presses of Germany could not be altogether silenced, though the police of Napoleon was unceasingly active in suppressing political publications. But the kind of feeling which now prevailed among the German youth did not require the support of exhortations or reasoning, directly and in express terms adapted to the subject. While a book existed, from the Holy Scriptures down to the most idle romance; while a line of poetry could be recited from the works of Schiller or Goethe, down to the most ordinary stall ballad – innuendoes, at once secret and stimulating, might be drawn from them, to serve as watch-words, or as war-cries. The prevailing opinions, as they spread wider and wider, began to give rise to mysterious associations, the object of which was the liberation of Germany. That most generally known was called the Bund, or

Alliance for Virtue and Justice. The young academicians entered with great zeal into these fraternities, the rather that they had been previously prepared for them by the Burschenschafts, or associations of students, and that the idea of secret councils, tribunals, or machinations, is familiar to the reader of German history, and deeply interesting to a people whose temper is easily impressed by the mysterious and the terrible. The professors of the Universities, in most cases, gave way to or guided these patriotic impressions, and in teaching their students the sciences or liberal arts, failed not to impress on them the duty of devoting themselves to the liberation of Germany, or, as it was now called, Teutonia.

The French, whose genius is in direct opposition to that of the Germans, saw all this with contempt and ridicule. They laughed at the mummery of boys affecting a new sort of national freemasonry, and they gave the principle of patriotic devotion to independence the name of Ideology; by which nickname the French ruler used to distinguish every species of theory, which, resting in no respect upon the practical basis of self-interest, could, he thought, prevail with none save hot-brained boys and crazed enthusiasts.

Napoleon, however, saw and estimated the increasing influence of these popular opinions, more justly than might have been inferred from his language. He knew that a government might be crushed, an army defeated, an inimical administration changed, by violence; but that the rooted principle of resistance to oppression diffuses itself the wider the more martyrs are made on its behalf. The Heir of the Revolution spoke on such subjects the language of the most legitimate of monarchs, and exclaimed against the system of the Tugendbund, as containing principles capable of disorganising the whole system of social society.

The menacing appearance of Austria, and the extension of anti-Gallican principles and feelings through Germany, made it more especially necessary for Buonaparte to secure his hold upon the Emperor of Russia. Buonaparte and Alexander met at Erfurt on 27th September 1808, with the same appearance of cordiality with which they had parted. The most splendid festivities celebrated their meeting, and the theatres of Paris sent their choicest performers to enliven the evenings. Amid all these gaieties politics were not neglected, and Buonaparte found his great ally as tractable as at Tilsit. Alexander ratified the transactions of Spain. The

Czar stipulated, however, on his own part, that Buonaparte should not in any shape interfere to prevent Russia from aggrandising herself at the expense of Turkey. He promised, also, to take an ally's share with Buonaparte, if the quarrel with Austria should come to arms. To this, indeed, he was bound by treaties. The conferences of Erfurt ended on the 14th October, amid the most splendid festivities. Among these was an entertainment given to the Emperor on the battle-ground of Jena, where Prussia, the hapless ally of Alexander, received such a dreadful blow.

It is probable that Alexander did not require the recollections which this battle-field was sure to inspire, to infuse into his mind some tacit jealousy of his powerful ally. He even already saw the possibility of a quarrel emerging between them, and was deeply desirous that Austria should not waste her national strength by rushing into a contest in which he would be under the reluctant necessity of acting against her. Neither did Napoleon return from Erfurt with the same undoubting confidence in his imperial ally. The subject of a match between the Emperor of France and one of the Russian Archduchesses had been resumed and had been evaded on account, as it was alleged, of the difference in their religions. The objections of the Empress Mother, as well as of the reigning Empress, were said to be the real reasons – objections founded on the character of Napoleon, and the nature of his right to the greatness which he enjoyed. Such a proposal could not be brought forward and rejected or evaded, with however much delicacy, without injury to the personal feelings of Napoleon; and as he must have been conscious that more than the alleged reason of religion entered into the cause of declining his proposal, he must have felt in proportion offended, if not affronted. Still, however, if their cordiality was in any degree diminished, the ties of mutual interest which bound together these two great autocrats were as yet sufficient to assure Napoleon of the present assistance of Russia.

Strongly posted within the position of Northern Spain, the French armies, about 60,000 men strong, awaited the approach of Napoleon with such a predominating force as should enable them to resume the offensive. The co-operation of a British auxiliary force became now an object of the first consequence; and the conduct of Britain had given every reason to expect that she would make in the Spanish cause, exertions to which she had been yet a stranger.

After some fighting, a French division, under Marshal Victor, brought the Spanish general to action at the position of Espinosa. The battle continued for three hours in the evening, and was renewed the next day, when the French turned the Spanish position, and Blake, totally defeated, withdrew from the field, with the purpose of making a stand at Reynosa, where he had his supplies and magazines. Meantime the activity of Buonaparte had struck another fatal blow on a different part of the Spanish defensive line. An army designed to cover Burgos, and support the right flank of Blake's army, had been formed under the command of the Count de Belvidere, a young nobleman of courage, but without experience. Burgos was taken, in consequence of Belvidere's defeat; and it was by the same calamity rendered easy for the Duke of Dalmatia[18] to co-operate with the French generals, who were operating against the unfortunate Blake, with a view to drive him from his place of refuge at Reynosa. Surrounded on every side, the Spanish general saw no safety for the remnant of his forces, excepting in a retreat to Saint Andero, accomplished under such circumstances of haste and confusion, that his army might be considered as totally disorganised and dispersed.

The whole left wing of the Spanish defence, which so lately stretched from Bilboa to Burgos, and in support of which the British forces were advancing, was now totally annihilated, and the central army, under Castanos, whose left flank was now completely uncovered, was exposed to imminent danger. A great number of Spaniards were killed; guns and baggage were taken; and, for the first, a considerable number of prisoners fell into the hands of the French. The road of the invader was now open to Madrid.

Madrid fell and the British force was evacuated. Napoleon had, meanwhile, hurriedly returned to France.

CHAPTER XLVII

The incredible rapidity with which Napoleon pressed his return to France, without again visiting Madrid or pausing to hear the fate of the English army, surprised those around him. Some conjectured that a conspiracy had been discovered against his authority at Paris; others, that a band of Spaniards had devoted themselves to assassinate him; but it was soon found that the despatch which he used had its cause in the approaching rupture with Austria.

This breach of friendship appears to have been sought by Austria without any of those plausible reasons of complaint, on which nations generally are desirous to bottom their quarrels. She did not allege that France had given her cause of offence. The Abbé de Pradt remarks upon the occasion, with his usual shrewdness, that if Napoleon was no religious observer of the faith of treaties, it could not be maintained that other states acted much more scrupulously in reference to him. Buonaparte himself has alleged, what, in one sense of the word was true, that many of his wars were, in respect to the immediate causes of quarrel, merely defensive on his side. But this was a natural consequence of the style and structure of his government, which, aiming directly at universal empire, caused him to be looked upon by all nations as a common enemy, the legitimate object of attack whenever he could be attacked with advantage.

This principle of constant war with Buonaparte, or rather with the progress of his ambition, guided and influenced every state in Europe, which had yet any claim for their independence. Buonaparte being engaged in a constant train of innovation upon the liberties of Europe, it followed that the states whom he had not been able entirely to deprive of independence, should, without further cause of war, be perpetually on the watch for opportunities to destroy or diminish his terrible authority. In this point of view, the question for Austria to consider was not the justice of the war but its expediency; not her right of resisting the common enemy of the freedom of Europe, but practically, whether she had the means of effectual opposition. The event served to show that Austria had over-estimated her own resources.

It is true that an opportunity now presented itself, which seemed in the highest degree tempting. Buonaparte was absent in Spain, in which, besides the general unpopularity of his cause, resistance had been offered of a nature so serious, as to shake the opinion hitherto entertained of his invincibility. On the other hand, Austria had instituted in her states organic laws, by which she secured herself the power of being able to call out to arms her immense and military population; and her chief error seems to have been, in not postponing the fatal struggle until these new levies had acquired a better disciplined and more consolidated form.

The exertions made by Austria on this important occasion were gigantic, and her forces were superior to those which she had been able to summon out at any former period. Including the army of reserve, they were computed as high as 550,000 men which the Archduke Charles once more commanded. It is said that this gallant prince did not heartily approve of the war, at least of the period chosen to commence it, but readily sacrificed his own opinion to the desire of contributing to the service of his brother and of his country. Six *corps d'armée*, each about 30,000 strong, were destined, under the archduke's immediate command, to maintain the principal weight of the war in Germany; a 7th, under the Archduke Ferdinand, was stationed in Galicia, and judged sufficient to oppose themselves to what forces Russia might find herself obliged to detach in that direction; and two divisions, under the Archduke John, were destined to awaken hostilities in the north of Italy.

Buonaparte had not sufficient numbers to oppose these formidable masses; but he had recourse to his old policy, and trusted to make up for deficiency by such rapidity of movement as should ensure a local superiority. He summoned out the auxiliary forces of the Confederation of the Rhine, and of the King of Saxony. He remanded many troops who were on their march for Spain and, by doing so, adjourned, as it proved forever, the subjugation of that country. He had already in Germany the corps of Davoust and of General Oudinot. The garrisons which France had established in Prussia and in the northern parts of Germany were drained for the purpose of reinforcing his ranks; but the total amount of his assembled forces was still greatly inferior to those of the Archduke Charles.

While the Austrian army moved slow, and with frequent halts, encumbered as they were with their baggage and supplies, Napoleon had no sooner learned by telegraph of the actual invasion of Bavaria, than he left Paris, [11th April] and hurried to Frankfurt; without guards, without equipage, almost without a companion, save the faithful Josephine, who accompanied him as far as Strasbourg, and there remained for some time watching the progress of the campaign, the event of which was destined to have such a melancholy influence on her own happiness.

The Archduke Charles's plan was to act upon the offensive. His talents were undoubted, his army greatly superior in numbers to the French, and favourably disposed; yet, by a series of combinations, the most beautiful and striking, perhaps, which occur in the life of one so famed for his power of forming such, Buonaparte was enabled, in the short space of five days, totally to defeat the formidable masses which were opposed to him.

Napoleon found his own force unfavourably disposed, on a long line, extending between the towns of Augsburg and Ratisbon, and presenting an alarming vacancy in the centre, by operating on which the enemy might have separated the French army into two and exposed each to a flank attack. Napoleon determined on the daring attempt to concentrate his army by a lateral march, to be accomplished by the two wings simultaneously. With this view he posted himself in the centre, where the danger was principally apprehended. The order for this daring operation was sent to Massena on the night of the 17th, and concluded with an earnest recommendation of speed and intelligence. When the time for executing these movements had been allowed [20th April], Buonaparte, at the head of the centre of his forces, made a sudden and desperate assault upon two Austrian divisions, commanded by the Archduke Louis and General Hiller. So judiciously was this timed, that the appearance of Davoust on the one flank kept in check those other Austrian *corps d'armée* by whom the divisions attacked ought to have been supported while the yet more formidable operations of Massena, in the rear of the Archduke Louis, achieved the defeat of the enemy. This victory, gained at Abensberg upon the 20th April, broke the line of the Austrians. The Emperor attacked the fugitives the next day at Landshut, where the Austrians lost 30 pieces of cannon, 9000 prisoners and much ammunition and baggage.

On the 22nd April, Buonaparte directed his whole force, scientifically arranged into different divisions, and moving by different routes, on the principal army of the Archduke Charles. The battle is said to have been one of the most splendid which the art of war could display. 100,000 men and upwards were dispossessed of all their positions by the combined attack of their scientific enemy, the divisions appearing on the field, each in its due place and order, as regularly as the movements of the various pieces in a game of chess. All the Austrian wounded, great part of their artillery and 20,000 prisoners remained in the power of the French. The retreat was attended with corresponding loss; and Austria, again baffled in her hopes of reacquiring her influence in Germany, was once more reduced to combat for her existence amongst nations.

Thus within five days the aspect of the war was entirely changed. At no period in his momentous career did the genius of Napoleon appear more completely to prostrate all opposition; at no time did the talents of a single individual exercise such an influence on the fate of the universe. The forces which he had in the field had been not only unequal to those of the enemy, but they were, in a military point of view, ill-placed, and imperfectly combined. Napoleon arrived alone, found himself under all these disadvantages and, we repeat, by his almost unassisted genius, came, in the course of five days, in complete triumph out of a struggle which bore a character so unpromising. It was no wonder that others should have annexed to his person the degree of superstitious influence claimed for the chosen in instruments of Destiny, whose path must not be crossed and whose arms cannot be arrested.

The Archduke Charles effected his retreat into the mountainous country of Bohemia, where he could remodel his broken army, receive reinforcements of every kind and make a protracted defence, should Napoleon press upon him in that direction. But the victories of these memorable five days had placed the French Emperor in full possession of the right bank of the Danube, and of the high-road to the city of Vienna, which is situated on the same side of the river. On the other hand, the Austrian General Hiller, defeated at Landshut and cut off from communication with the Archduke, had been able to unite himself with a considerable reserve and assumed the mien of defending the high-road to the capital. Buonaparte had thus an enemy of some consequence in front, while the army of Charles might operate from Bohemia upon his rear; and a universal national insurrection of the Tyrolese threatened not only entirely to expel the French and Bavarians from their mountains, but even to alarm Bavaria herself. Insurrections were also beginning to take place all through Germany, which showed that, had the tide of war turned against France, almost all the north of Germany would have been in arms against her. These dangers, which would have staggered a man of less determination, only confirmed Napoleon in his purpose of compelling Austria to make peace, by descending the Danube and effecting a second occupation of her capital.

CHAPTER XLVIII

Napoleon occupied Vienna [12th May], and the right bank of the Danube. The Archduke Charles now approached the left bank of the same river, which, swollen by the spring rains and the melting of snow, divided the two hostile armies as if by an impassable barrier. Buonaparte determined to pursue the most vigorous measures, by constructing a bridge over the Danube, and crossing it at the head of his army, with the purpose of giving battle to the Archduke.

The battle began about four in the afternoon; and when the evening approached, nothing decisive had been done. The Archduke brought his reserves, and poured them in successive bodies upon the disputed village of Asperne. Every garden, terrace, and farm-yard, was a scene of the most obstinate struggle. Wagons, carts, harrows and ploughs were employed to construct barricades. The Austrians gained possession of the church and churchyard and claimed the superiority on the left accordingly. The French could not in any sense be said to have been beaten; but it was an unusual thing for them, fighting under Napoleon's eye, to be less than completely victorious. The Austrians could as little be called victors; but even the circumstance of possessing themselves of the most important part of Asperne, showed that the advantage had been with them. The feeling of the Austrians was exultation; that of the French not certainly discouragement, but unpleasant surprise.

The carnage recommenced the following day and the French were ultimately forced to retreat.

The loss of both armies was dreadful and computed to exceed 20,000 men on each side, killed and wounded. General St. Hilaire, one of the best

French generals, was killed in the field, and Lannes, mortally wounded, was brought back into the island. He was much lamented by Buonaparte, who considered him as his own work. "I found him," he said, "a mere swordsman; I brought him up to the highest point of talent. I found him a dwarf; I raised him up into a giant." The death of this general, called the Roland of the army, had something in it inexpressibly shocking. With both his legs shot to pieces, he refused to die, and insisted that the surgeons should be hanged who were unable to cure a mareschal and Duke de Montebello. While he thus clung to life, he called upon the Emperor, with the instinctive hope that Napoleon at least could defer the dreadful hour, and repeated his name to the last, with the wild interest with which an Indian prays to the object of his superstition. Buonaparte showed much and creditable emotion at beholding his faithful follower in such a condition.

On the 6th July[19] was fought the dreadful battle of Wagram, in which, it is said, that the Archduke Charles committed the great military error of extending his lines and weakening his centre. His enemy was too alert not to turn such an error to profit. Lauriston, with 100 pieces of cannon, and Macdonald, at the head of a chosen division, charged the Austrians in the centre, and broke through it. Napoleon himself showed all his courage and talents, and was ever in the hottest of the action, though the appearance of his retinue drew on him showers of grape, by which he was repeatedly endangered. At length the Austrian army seems to have fallen into disorder; the left wing, in particular, conducted itself ill; cries of alarm were heard, and the example of precipitate flight was set by those who should have been the last to follow it. The French took 20,000 prisoners. All hope of further resistance was now abandoned by the Austrian princes and government and they concluded an armistice at Znaim.

*C*HAPTER XLIX

The conditions of the peace with Austria were not adjusted until the 14th October, 1809. We avail ourselves of the interval to notice other remarkable events, which happened during this eventful summer.

It must be allowed by the greatest admirers of Napoleon that his policy, depending less upon principle than upon existing circumstances, was too apt to be suddenly changed, as opportunity or emergency seemed to give occasion. There could, for example, be scarce a measure of his reign adopted on more deep and profound consideration than that of the Concordat. In reward for this great service, Pope Pius VII had the unusual complaisance to cross the Alps, and visit Paris, for the sake of adding religious solemnity to Napoleon's coronation. It might have been thought that a friendship thus cemented, and which, altogether essential to the safety of the Pope, was far from indifferent to the interests of Buonaparte, ought to have subsisted undisturbed, at least for some years. But the Emperor and Pontiff stood in a suspicious attitude with respect to each other. Pius VII felt that he had made, in his character of chief of the Church, very great concessions to Napoleon, and such as he could hardly reconcile to the tenderness of his own conscience. He, therefore, expected gratitude in proportion to the scruples which he had surmounted, while Buonaparte was far from rating the services of his Holiness so high, or sympathising with his conscientious scruples.

It is probable, however, that, had there been only spiritual matters in discussion between them, Napoleon would have avoided an open rupture with the Holy Father, to which he was conscious much scandal would attach. But in the present situation of Italy, the temporal states of the Pope furnished the only portion of the Italian peninsula which was not either directly, or indirectly, under the empire of France; and, as it divided the Neapolitan dominions from those of Napoleon, it afforded facilities for descents of British troops, and, what Buonaparte was not less anxious to prevent, great opportunities for the importation of English commodities. His ambassador, therefore, had instructions to press on the Pope the necessity of shutting his ports against British commerce, and adhering to the continental system; together with the further decisive measure, of acceding to the confederacy formed between the kingdom of Italy and that of Naples or, in other words becoming a party to the war against Austria and England. Pius VII reluctantly submitted to shut his ports, but he positively refused to become a party to the war. He was, he said, the father of all Christian nations; he could not, consistently with that character, become the enemy of any.

Upon receiving this refusal, Buonaparte caused the towns of Ancona and Civita Vecchia to be occupied by French troops. This act of aggression, to which the Pope might have seen it prudent to submit without remonstrance, would probably have sufficiently answered all the immediate purposes of Buonaparte; nor would he, it may be supposed, have incurred the further scandal of a direct and irreconcilable breach with Pius VII, but for recollections that Rome had been the seat of empire over the Christian world, and that the universal sovereignty to which he aspired, would hardly be thought to exist in the full extent of majesty which he desired to attach to it, unless the ancient capital of the world made up a part of his dominions.

On the 2nd February, 1809, General Miollis, with a body of French troops, took possession of Rome itself, disarmed and disbanded the Pope's guard of gentlemen, and sent his other soldiers to the north of Italy. The French cardinals, or those born in countries occupied by, or subjected to the French, were ordered to retire to the various lands of their birth, in order to prevent the Holy Father from finding support in the councils of the conclave. The proposal of his joining the Italian League, offensive and defensive, was again pressed on the Pope as the only means of reconciliation. He was also urged to cede some portion of the estates of the Church, as the price of securing the rest. On both points, Pius VII was resolute; he would neither enter into an alliance which he conceived injurious to his conscience, nor consent to spoil the See of any part of its territories. This excellent man knew that, though the temporal strength of the Popedom appeared to be gone, every thing depended on the courage to be manifested by the Pope personally.

At length, on the 17th May, Napoleon published a decree, in which, assuming the character of successor of Charlemagne, he set forth: first, that his August predecessor had granted Rome and certain other territories in feoff to the bishops of that city, but without parting with the sovereignty thereof; second, that the union of the religious and civil authority had proved the source of constant discord, of which many of the Pontiffs had availed themselves to extend their secular dominion, under pretext of maintaining their religious authority; third, that the temporal pretensions of the Pope were irreconcilable with the tranquillity and well-being of the nations whom Napoleon governed;

and that all proposals which he had made on the subject had been rejected. Therefore it was declared by the decree that the estates of the Church were reunited to the French empire. A few articles followed for the preservation of the classical monuments, for assigning to the Pope a free income of two million francs, and for declaring that the property and palace belonging to the See were free of all burdens or right of inspection. Lastly, the decree provided for the interior government of Rome by a Consultum, or Committee of Administrators to who was delegated the power of bringing the city under the Italian constitution.

It had doubtless been thought possible to persuade the Pope to acquiesce in the annihilation of his secular power, as the Spanish Bourbons were compelled to ratify the usurpation of their inheritance. But Pius VII had a mind of a firmer tenor. In the very night when the proclamation of the new functionaries finally divested him of his temporal principality, the Head of the Church assumed his spiritual weapons, and in the name of God, from whom he claimed authority, by missives drawn up by himself, and sealed with the seal of the Fisherman, declared Napoleon, Emperor of the French, with his adherents, to have incurred the solemn doom of excommunication. To the honour of Pius VII it must be added that, different from the bulls which his predecessors used to send forth, the present sentence was pronounced exclusively as a spiritual punishment, and contained a clause prohibiting all and anyone from so construing its import, as to hold it authority for any attack on the person either of Napoleon or any of his adherents.

The Emperor was incensed at the pertinacity and courage of the Pontiff, and determined on punishing him. In the night betwixt the 5th and 6th of July, the Quirinal palace was forcibly entered by soldiers, and General Radet, presenting himself before the Holy Father, demanded that he should instantly execute a renunciation of the temporal estates belonging to the See of Rome. "I ought not – I will not – I cannot make such a cession," said Pius VII "I have sworn to God to preserve inviolate the possessions of the Holy Church – I will not violate my oath." The general then informed his Holiness he must prepare to quit Rome. "This, then, is the gratitude of your Emperor," exclaimed the aged Pontiff, "for my great condescension towards the Gallican Church, and towards himself? Perhaps in that particular my conduct has been blame-worthy in the eyes of God, and he is now desirous to punish me. I humbly stoop to his divine pleasure."

At three o'clock in the morning, the Pope was placed in a carriage which one cardinal alone was permitted to share with him and thus forcibly carried from his capital. At Florence, Pius was separated from Cardinal Pacca; and the attendance of General Radet was replaced by that of an officer of gendarmes. After a toilsome journey, partly performed in a litter, and sometimes by torchlight, the aged Pontiff was embarked for Alexandria and transferred from thence to Mondovi, and then across the Alps to Grenoble. At the end of ten days, Grenoble no longer seemed a fitting place for his residence, probably because he excited too much interest, and he was again transported to the Italian side of the Alps, and quartered at Savona. Here, it is said, he was treated with considerable harshness, and for a time at least confined to his apartment. The prefect of Savoy, M. de Chabrol presented his Holiness with a letter from Napoleon, upbraiding him in strong terms for his wilful obstinacy and threatening to convoke at Paris a Council of Bishops with a view to his deposition. "I will lay his threats," said Pius VII, with the firmness which sustained him through his sufferings, "at the foot of the crucifix, and I leave with God the care of avenging my cause, since it has become his own."

The feelings of the Catholics were doubtless enhanced by their belief in the sacred and, it may he said, divine character, indissolubly united with the Head of the Church. But the world, Papist and Protestant, were alike sensible to the outrageous indecency with which an old man, a priest and a sovereign, so lately the friend and guest of Buonaparte, was treated, for no other reason that could be alleged, than to compel him to despoil himself of the territories of the Church, which he had sworn to transmit inviolate to his successors. Upon reflection, Napoleon seems to have become ashamed of the transaction, which he endeavoured to shift from his own shoulders, while in the same breath he apologised for it, as the act of the politician, not the individual.

The consequences of this false step were almost as injurious as those which resulted from the unprincipled invasion of Spain. To place that kingdom under his more immediate control, Napoleon converted a whole nation of docile allies into irreconcilable enemies; and, for the vanity of adding to the empire of France the ancient capital of the world, he created a revolt in the opinion of the Catholics, which was in the long-run of the utmost prejudice to his authority. The bulls of the Pope, in spite of the attention of the police, obtained a general circulation; and, by affording a religious motive, enhanced and extended the disaffection to Napoleon, which, unavowed and obscure, began generally to arise against his person and government even in France, from the repeated draughts upon the conscription, the annihilation of commerce, and the other distressing consequences arising out of the measures of a government which seemed only to exist in war.

The crisis, however, approached, which was to determine the fate of Austria. The definitive treaty of peace, when at length published, was found to contain the following articles: 1. Austria ceded, in favour of the Princes of the Confederation of the Rhine, Saltzburg, Berchtolsgaden, and a part of Upper Austria; II. To France directly, she ceded her only seaport of Trieste, the districts of Carniola, Friuli, the circle of Villach, and some parts of Croatia and Dalmatia; III. To the King of Saxony, in that character, Austria ceded some small part of Bohemia, and in the capacity of Duke of Warsaw, she gave up to him the city of Cracow, and the whole of Western Galicia; IV. Russia was to receive, in reward of her aid, though tardily and unwillingly tendered, a portion of Eastern Galicia, containing a population of 400,000 souls.

Europe in general was surprised at the moderation of the terms; for though Austria yielded up a surface of 45,000 square miles, and a population of between three and four million, yet the extremity in which she was placed seemed to render this a cheap ransom, as she still retained 180,000 square miles, and upwards, of territory, which, with a population of 21 million, rendered her, after France and Russia, even yet the most formidable power on the continent. But her good angel had not slept. The house of Rodolph of Hapsburg had arisen, from small beginnings, to its immense power, chiefly by matrimonial alliances, and it was determined that, by another intermarriage, with the most successful conqueror whom the world had ever seen, she should escape with comparative ease from the greatest extremity in which she had ever been placed.

*C*HAPTER L

There is perhaps no part of the varied life of the wonderful person of whom we treat, more deeply interesting than the change which took place in his domestic establishment shortly after the peace of Vienna.

The sterility of the Empress Josephine was now rendered, by the course of nature, an irremediable evil, over which she mourned in hopeless distress. She exerted her influence over her husband to induce him to declare someone his successor, according to the unlimited powers vested in him. In the selection, she naturally endeavoured to direct his choice towards her step-son, Eugene Beauharnois, her own son by her first marriage; but this did not meet Buonaparte's approbation. A child, the son of his brother Louis, by Hortense Beauharnois, appeared, during its brief existence, more likely to become the destined heir. Napoleon seemed attached to the boy; and when he manifested any spark of childish spirit, rejoiced in the sound of the drum, or showed pleasure in looking upon arms and the image of war, he is said to have exclaimed – "*There* is a child fit to succeed, perhaps to surpass me."

The fixing his choice on an heir so intimately connected with herself, would have secured the influence of Josephine, as much as it could receive assurance from any thing save bearing her husband issue herself; but she was not long permitted to enjoy this prospect. The son of Louis and Hortense died. Napoleon showed the deepest grief, but Josephine sorrowed as one who had no hope.

Yet, setting aside her having the misfortune to bear him no issue, the claims of Josephine on her husband's affections were as numerous as could be possessed by a wife. She had shared his more lowly fortunes, and, by her management and address during his absence in Egypt, had paved the way for the splendid success which he had attained on his return. She had also done much to render his government popular, by softening the sudden and fierce bursts of passion to which his temperament induced him. No one could understand, like Josephine, the peculiarities of her husband's temper – no one dared, like her, to encounter his displeasure, rather than not advise him for his better interest – no one could possess such opportunities of watching the fit season for intercession – and no one, it is allowed on all hands, made a more prudent, or a more beneficent use of the opportunities she enjoyed. The character of Buonaparte required peculiarly the moderating influence of such a mind, which could interfere without intrusion, and remonstrate without offence.

It was evident to the politicians of the Tuileries that whatever attachment and veneration for the Empress Napoleon might profess and feel, it was likely, in the long-run, to give way to the eager desire of a lineal succession. As age advanced, every year weakened, though in an imperceptible degree, the influence of the Empress, and must have rendered more eager the desire of her husband to form a new alliance, while he was yet at a period of life enabling him to hope he might live to train to maturity the expected heir. Fouché discovered speedily to what point the Emperor must ultimately arrive. Having been able to conjecture the state of the Emperor's inclinations, the crafty counsellor determined to make Josephine herself the medium of suggesting to Buonaparte the measure of her own divorce, and his second marriage, as a sacrifice necessary to consolidate the empire, and complete the happiness of the Emperor.

One evening at Fontainebleau, as the Empress was returning from mass, Fouché detained her in the embrasure of a window in the gallery, while, with an audacity almost incomprehensible, he explained, with all the alleviating qualifications his ingenuity could suggest, the necessity of a sacrifice, which he represented as equally sublime and inevitable. The tears gathered in Josephine's eyes – her colour came and went – her lips swelled – and the least which the counsellor had to fear was his advice having brought on a severe nervous affection. She commanded her emotions, however, sufficiently to ask Fouché with a faltering voice, whether he had any commission to hold such language to her, he replied in the negative, and said that he had only ventured on such an insinuation from his having predicted with certainty what must necessarily come to pass; and from his desire to turn her attention to what so nearly concerned her glory and happiness.

In consequence of this interview, an impassioned and interesting scene is said to have taken place betwixt Buonaparte and his consort, in which he naturally and truly disavowed the communication of Fouché and attempted, by every means in his power, to dispel her apprehensions. But he refused to dismiss Fouché when she demanded it; and this refusal alone might have convinced Josephine, that though ancient habitual affection might for a time maintain its influence in the nuptial chamber, it must at length give way before the suggestions of political interest, which were sure to predominate in the cabinet. In fact, when the idea had once been started, the chief objection was removed, and Buonaparte, being spared the pain of directly communicating the unkind and ungrateful proposal to Josephine, had now only to afford her time to familiarise herself with the idea of a divorce, which political combinations rendered inevitable.

The communication of Fouché was made before Napoleon undertook his operations in Spain; and by the time of the meeting at Erfurt, the divorce seems to have been a matter determined, since the subject of a match betwixt Buonaparte and one of the archduchesses, was resumed, seriously treated of, and if not received with cordiality by the Imperial family of Russia, was equally far from being finally rejected.

Whether the successor of Josephine were or were not already determined upon, the measures for separating this amiable and interesting woman from him whose fortunes she had assisted to raise, and to whose person she was so much attached, were in full and public operation soon after her husband's return from the campaign of Wagram.

On the 15th December, just ten days after the official communication of her fate had been given to the Empress, Napoleon and Josephine appeared in presence of the full Imperial Council. In this assembly, Napoleon stated the deep national interest which required that he should have successors of his own body, the heirs of his love for his people, to occupy the throne on which Providence had placed him. He informed them that he had for several years renounced the hope of having children by his well-beloved Empress Josephine; and that therefore he had resolved to subject the feelings of his heart to the good of the state, and desire the dissolution of their marriage. He was, he said, but forty years old and might well hope to live to train up such children as Providence might send him, in his own sentiments and arts of government. Again he dwelt on the truth and tenderness of his beloved spouse, his partner during fifteen years of happy union. Crowned as she had been by his own hand, he desired she should retain the rank of Empress during her life. Josephine arose, and with a faltering voice, and eyes suffused with tears, expressed in a few words sentiments similar to those of her husband. The Imperial pair then demanded from the Arch-Chancellor a written instrument in evidence of their mutual desire of separation; and it was granted accordingly.

The Senate were next assembled; and on the 16th December, pronounced a consultum, authorising the separation of the Emperor and Empress, and assuring to Josephine a dowry of two million francs, and the rank of Empress. Addresses were voted to both the Imperial parties, in which all possible changes were rung on the duty of subjecting our dearest affections to the public good; and the conduct of Buonaparte in exchanging his old consort for a young one, was proclaimed a sacrifice, for which the eternal love of the French people could alone console his heart.

The union of Napoleon and Josephine being thus abrogated by the supreme civil power, it only remained to procure the intervention of the spiritual authorities. The Arch-Chancellor presented a request for this purpose to the ecclesiastical court of Paris, who did not hesitate to declare the marriage dissolved, assigning, however, no reason for such their doom. When this sentence had finally dissolved their union, the Emperor retired to St. Cloud, where he lived in seclusion for some days. Josephine, on her part, took up residence in the beautiful villa of Malmaison, near St. Germain.

The Great Council was summoned on the 1st February to assist the Emperor in the selection of a new spouse. They were given to understand that a match with a Grand Duchess of Russia had been proposed, but was likely to be embarrassed by disputes concerning religion. A daughter of the King of Saxony was also mentioned, but it was easily indicated to the Council that their choice ought to fall upon a Princess of the House of Austria. At the conclusion of the meeting, Eugene, the son of the repudiated Josephine, was commissioned by the Council to propose to the Austrian ambassador a match between Napoleon and the Archduchess Maria Louisa. Prince Schwarzenberg had his instructions on the subject; so that the match was proposed, discussed, and decided in the Council, and afterwards adjusted between plenipotentiaries on either side, in the space of 24 hours. The espousals of Napoleon and Maria Louisa were celebrated in Vienna on the 11th March, 1810. The person of Buonaparte was represented by his favourite Berthier, while the Archduke Charles assisted at the ceremony, in the name of the Emperor Francis. A few days afterwards, the youthful bride proceeded towards France.

With good taste, Napoleon dispensed with the ceremonies used in the reception of Marie Antoinette, whose marriage with Louis XVI, though never named or alluded to, was in other respects the model of the present solemnity. Near Soissons, a single horseman, no way distinguished by dress, rode past the carriage in which the young Empress was seated, and had the boldness to return, as if to reconnoitre more closely. The carriage stopped, the door was opened, and Napoleon, breaking through all the tediousness of ceremony, introduced himself to his bride, and came with her to Soissons. The marriage ceremony was performed at St. Cloud by Buonaparte's uncle, the Cardinal Fesch. The most splendid rejoicings, illuminations, concerts and festivals took place upon this important occasion.

As a domestic occurrence, nothing could more contribute to Buonaparte's happiness than his union with Maria Louisa. He was wont to compare her with Josephine, by giving the latter all the advantages of art and grace; the former the charms of simple modesty and innocence. His former Empress used every art to support or enhance her personal charms; but with so much prudence and mystery, that the secret cares of her toilette could never be traced – her successor trusted for the power of pleasing, to youth and nature. Josephine mismanaged her revenue, and incurred debt without scruple. Maria Louisa lived within her income, or if she desired any indulgence beyond it, which was rarely the case, she asked it as a favour of Napoleon. Josephine, accustomed to political intrigue, loved to manage, to influence, and to guide her husband; Maria Louisa desired only to please and to obey him. Both were excellent women, of great sweetness of temper, and fondly attached to Napoleon.

Buonaparte behaved with the utmost kindness to his princely bride. He observed, however, the strictest etiquette, and required it from the Empress. If it happened, for example, as was often the case, that he was prevented from attending at the hour when dinner was placed on the table, he was displeased if, in his absence, which was often prolonged, she either took a book, or had recourse to any female occupation – if, in short, he did not find her in the attitude of waiting for the signal to take her place at table. Perhaps a sense of his inferior birth made Napoleon more tenacious of this species of form, as what he could not afford to relinquish.

As it influenced his political fate, Buonaparte had registered his complaint, that the Austrian match was a precipice covered with flowers, which he was rashly induced to approach by the hopes of domestic happiness. But if this proved so, it was the fault of Napoleon himself; his subjects and his allies augured very differently of its consequences. It was to have been expected that a connection formed with the most ancient imperial family in Christendom might have induced Buonaparte to adopt some sentiments of moderation. It constituted a point at which he might pause. It might have been thought that, satiated with success, and wearied with enterprise, he would have busied himself more in consolidating the power which he desired to transmit to his expected posterity, than in aiming at rendering his grandeur more invidious and more precarious. Even the charms which this union added to his domestic life, might, it was hoped, bring on a taste for repose, which, could it have influenced that fiery imagination and frame of iron, might have been of essential advantage to Europe.

Napoleon knew what was expected, and endeavoured to vindicate himself beforehand for the disappointment which he foresaw. "The good citizens rejoice sincerely at my marriage, monsieur?" he said to Decrés, his minister. "Very much, Sire." – "I understand they think the Lion will go to slumber, ha?" – "To speak the truth, Sire, they entertain some hopes of that nature." Napoleon paused an instant and then replied, "They are mistaken; yet it is not the fault of the Lion; slumber would be as agreeable to him as to others. But see you not that while I have the air of being constantly the attacking party, I am, in fact, acting only on the defensive?"

In the meantime, the Emperor Alexander judged most accurately of the consequences of the Austrian match when he said, on receiving the news, "Then the next task will be, to drive me back to my forests." He was certain that Napoleon would make his intimate alliance with the Emperor Francis the means of an attack upon Russia; and saw the germs of future and more desperate wars in a union from which more short-sighted politicians were looking for the blessings of peace.

*C*HAPTERS LI, LII, LIII, LIV

Scott describes Wellington's first campaign from Portugal, his victory at Talavera and the guerrilla war that pinned down so many French troops. Fouché is dismissed, ostensibly because he had undertaken private peace negotiations with Britain, but also because of Napoleon's increasingly regal desire to distance himself from revolutionary figures he never really trusted. The failings of the Continental System, notably the French government's corrupt exploitation of licenses to trade with Britain despite the embargo, are then addressed, notably with regard to the plight of Holland, forced into the system against her commercial interests. Louis Bonaparte sided with his adoptive kingdom, was removed, and Holland was peremptorily incorporated into France. The action shifts northward to Sweden's decision to invite Bernadotte to become heir to the throne and Napoleon's reluctant acceptance. Sweden was forced into the Continental System, while, to counter widespread smuggling, Napoleon ordered the annexation, to France, of the coast along the 'German Ocean', thus irritating the Tsar, who had previously insisted on the independence of the Duchy of Oldenburg. Tensions between the two Emperors were also increasing because of Russia continuing to conduct a limited trade with Britain.

The natural consequences of an overgrown empire were already sapping that of Napoleon; for extent of territory does not constitute power any more than corpulence in the human frame constitutes strength or health; and Napoleon's real authority was in truth greater some years before than now when his dominion was so much enlarged. The war in Spain, maintained at such an expense of blood and treasure, was a wasting and consuming sore. The kingdom of Holland had afforded him supplies more readily, and had more the means of doing so when under the dominion of his brother Louis, than when ranked as a part of the French empire. The same might be said of the states and free towns in the north of Germany; where, in many instances, strong bands of smugglers maintained a desultory war with the officers of the French customs. Yet, though such cankerworms gnawed the root of the tree, the branches and foliage extended a broader shade than ever. It was especially when a formal annunciation, in France and Austria, called the good subjects of both realms to rejoice in the prospect that Maria Louisa would soon give an heir to Napoleon, that men who opened the map of Europe saw with fear and wonder the tremendous inheritance to which the expected infant was likely to succeed.

The actual dominions of France, governed by Napoleon in his own right as Emperor of the French, extended, from north-east to south-west, from Travemunde, on the Baltic, to the foot of the Pyrenées; and, from north-west to south-east, from the port of Brest to Terracina, on the confines of the Neapolitan territories. A population of forty-two million people, inhabiting by far the finest portion of the civilised earth, formed the immediate liege subjects of this magnificent empire. Yet to stop here were greatly to undervalue the extent of Napoleon's power. We have to add to his personal empire Carniola and the Illyrian provinces and also the fine kingdom of Italy. Then, in his character of Mediator of the Helvetian Republic, the Emperor exercised an almost absolute authority in Switzerland, which furnished him, though unwillingly, with several fine regiments. The Confederation of the Rhine, though numbering kings, were at the slightest hint bound to supply him each with his prescribed quota of forces, with a readiness and an affectation of zeal very different from the slack and reluctant manner in which they formerly supplied their paltry contingents to the Emperor of Germany. Murat, with his kingdom of Naples, was at his brother-in-law's disposal; and if, as Buonaparte's hopes whispered, the Peninsula should ultimately prove unable to resist, then Spain and Portugal would be added to his immense empire. Thus 800,000 square miles, containing a population of 85 million, in territory one-fifth part, and in the number of inhabitants one-half, of united Europe, was either in quiet subjection to Napoleon's sceptre, or on the point, as was supposed, of becoming so.

The people in Prussia, and many other parts of Germany, waited as for the day dawning, for the hope of winning back their freedom; but outward appearances indicated nothing of these smothered hopes, wishes, and preparations.

Within a year after her marriage, the young Empress was announced to have been taken with the pains of labour. The case was a difficult and distressing one; and the professional person employed lost courage, and was afraid to do what was necessary. Napoleon appeared in the apartment, and commanded him to proceed as if the patient were the wife of an ordinary burgess. She was at length successfully and safely delivered of a fine boy, which Buonaparte, with feelings, doubtless, as highly strung as after a battle gained, carried into the next apartment and exhibited in triumph to the great officers and courtiers, by whom he was unanimously hailed King of Rome, the dignity which had been destined to the heir of the French Republic.

*C*HAPTER LV

We are now approaching the verge of that fated year, when Fortune, hitherto unwearied in her partiality towards Napoleon, turned first upon himself, personally, a clouded and stormy aspect. Losses he had sustained both by land and sea, but he could still remark, as when he first heard of the defeat at Trafalgar – "I was not there – I could not be everywhere at once." But he was soon to experience misfortunes to the narrative of which he could not apply this proud commentary. The reade must be first put in remembrance of the causes of the insipient quarrel betwixt the empire of France and that of Russia.

Notwithstanding the subsequent personal intimacy which took place betwixt the two sovereigns, and which for five years prevented the springing of any enmity betwixt Alexander and Napoleon, the seeds of that quarrel were, nevertheless, to be found in the treaty Tilsit itself. Russia, lying remote from aggression in every other part of her immense territory, is open to injury on that important western frontier by which she is united with Europe, and in those possessions by virtue of which she claims to be a member of the European republic. The partition of Poland, unjust as it was in every point of view, was a measure of far greater importance to Russia than either to Austria or Prussia; for, while that state possessed its former semi-barbarous and stormy independence, it lay interposed in a great measure betwixt Russia and the rest of Europe, or, in other words, betwixt her and the civilised world. Any revolution which might restore Poland to independence, would have effectually thrust the Czar back upon his forests, destroyed his interest and influence in European affairs, and reduced him comparatively to the rank of an Asiatic sovereign. This liberation of their country was what the Poles expected from Buonaparte. For this, they crowded to his standard after the battle of Jena; and although he was too cautious to promise any thing explicitly concerning the restoration of Poland, yet most of his measures indicated a future purpose of accomplishing that work. Thus, when those Polish provinces which had fallen to the portion of Prussia, were formed into the Grand Duchy of Warsaw, as an independent principality, and the sovereignty was conferred, not without a secret meaning, on the King of Saxony, a descendant of the ancient monarchs of Poland, what could this be supposed to indicate, save the commencement of an independent state, to which might be added, as opportunity occurred, the remaining districts of Poland which had been seized upon by Austria and Russia?

These suspicions were considerably increased by the articles of peace concluded with Austria at Schönbrunn. By that treaty all Western Galicia, together with the city of Cracow, and other territories, were added to the dukedom of Warsaw, marking, it was supposed, still further, the intention of Napoleon, at one time or another, to restore in its integrity the kingdom of Poland, of which Russia alone now held the full share allotted to her by the partition treaties.

Other causes led to the same conclusion. The old Russians, a numerous and strong party in the empire, which comprehended the greater part of the large landholders, felt, as they had done under the Emperor Paul, much distress, from the interruption of the British trade by Buonaparte's Continental System. Their timber, pitch, potash, hemp, and other commodities, the chief produce of their estates, for which the British had been ready customers, remained on their hands, while they were deprived of the colonial produce and manufactures of Britain.

The alliance with Austria was of a character calculated to alarm Alexander. Russia and Austria, though they had a common interest to withstand the overpowering strength of Buonaparte, had been in ordinary times always rivals, and sometimes enemies. It was the interference of Austria, which, on several occasions, checked the progress of the Russians in Turkey, and it was Austria also which formed a barrier against the increase of their power in the south of Europe. The family connection, therefore, formed by Buonaparte with the House of Habsburg, made him still more formidable to Russia, as likely to embrace the quarrels and forward the pretensions of that power against the Czar, even if France herself should have none to discuss with him.

To remain the ally of Buonaparte, Alexander must have become his vassal; to attempt to be independent of him, was to make him his enemy; and it can be no wonder that a sovereign so proud and powerful as the Czar, chose rather the hazard of battle than diminish the lustre, or compromise the independence, of his ancient crown.

The time, too, for resistance, seemed as favourable as Russia could ever expect. The war of Spain, though chequered in its fortune, was in no respect near a sudden end. It occupied 250,000 of the best French troops; demanded also an immense expenditure, and diminished, of course, the power of the French Emperor to carry on the war on the frontiers of Russia.

The same arguments which recommended to Russia to choose the immediate moment for resisting the pretensions of France, ought, in point of prudence, to have induced Napoleon to desist from urging such pretensions, and to avoid the voluntarily engaging in two wars at the same time, both of a character decidedly national, and to only one of which he could give the influence of his own talents. His best and wisest generals, whom he consulted, or to whom he opened his purpose, used various arguments to induce him to alter, or at least defer his resolution. He himself hesitated for more than a year, and was repeatedly upon the point of settling with Russia the grounds of disagreement.

*C*HAPTER LVI

In his struggle with Russia, Napoleon might have counted on Denmark – but she barely had an army – and Saxony. Prussia hawked her services to both sides. They were rejected by Russia, her ideological friend, on tactical grounds – an alliance with the weak Prussian army would have obliged her to fight beyond her borders – and reluctantly accepted by Napoleon, her tactical bedmate, who probably entertained notions of dissolving the Kingdom. Austria was allied to France, and supported her Russian campaign to a limited extent, but this prevented Napoleon from re-establishing an independent Poland, thus depriving him of the far greater potential support of a 'nation on horseback'. Sweden, France's traditional ally in Northern Europe, could not be tempted into an alliance, despite the offer of recuperating Finland. Napoleon reacted by annexing Swedish Pomerania, thus driving the Swedes into an alliance with the Russians [24th March 1812], who promised them Norway, then a Danish possession. Equally damagingly, France was unable to induce her other traditional anti-Russian ally, Turkey, into the fray. Under pressure from Britain, she preferred making peace with Russia to trusting Napoleon.

Thus was France, on the approaching struggle, deprived of her two ancient allies, Sweden and Turkey. Prussia she brought to the field like a slave at her chariot-wheels; Denmark and Saxony in the character of allies, who were favoured so long as they were sufficiently subservient; and Austria, as a more equal confederate, but who had contrived to stipulate, that, in requital of an aid coldly granted, the French Emperor should tie himself down by engagements respecting Poland, which interfered with his using his influence over that country in the manner which would best have served his purposes. The result must lead to one of two conclusions. Either that Napoleon, confident in the immense preparations of his military force, disdained to enter into negotiations to obtain that assistance which he could not directly command, or else that his talents in politics were inferior to those which he displayed in military affairs.

It is true that if the numbers, and the quality, of the army which France brought into the field, were alone to be considered, Napoleon might be excused for holding cheap the assistance which he might have derived from Sweden or the Porte. He had anticipated the conscription of 1811, and he now called out that of 1812. To these were to be added the contingents of household kings, vassal princes, subjected republics – of two-thirds of Europe, in short. No such army had taken the field since the reign of Xerxes, supposing the exaggerated accounts of the Persian invasion to be admitted as historical. The head almost turns dizzy as we read the amount of their numbers.

The gross amount of the whole forces of the empire of France, and its dependencies and allies, is thus given by Boutourlin:

Total amount of the French army,	850,000
The army of Italy, under the Viceroy Eugene,	50,000
of the Grand Duchy of Warsaw, with other Poles,	60,000
of Bavaria,	40,000
of Saxony,	30,000
of Westphalia,	30,000
of Wurtemberg,	15,000
of Baden,	9,000
of the Princes of the Confederacy of the Rhine,	23,000
The corps of Prussian auxiliaries,	20,000
of Austrian auxiliaries,	30,000
The army of Naples,	30,000
Total number of men	1,187,000

But to approximate the actual force, we must deduce from this total of 1,187,000, about 387,000 men, for those in the hospital, absent upon furlough, and for incomplete regiments. Still there remains the appalling balance of 800,000 men; so that Buonaparte was enabled to detach an army to Russia greatly superior to what the Emperor Alexander could, without immense exertions, get under arms, and this without withdrawing any part of his forces from Spain.

The most active preparations for war were taking place on both sides. Those of Russia were defensive; but she mustered great armies on the Niemen; while France was rapidly pouring troops into Prussia, and into the grand duchy of Warsaw, and assuming those positions most favourable for invading the Russian frontier. Yet there seemed to be a lingering wish on the part of both Sovereigns, even at this late hour, to avoid the conflict. This indeed might have been easily done, had there been on the part of Napoleon a hearty desire to make peace, instead of what could only be termed a degree of hesitation to commence hostilities. In fact, the original causes of quarrel were already settled, or, what is the same thing, principles had been fixed on which their arrangement might be easily adjusted. Yet still the preparations for invading Russia became more and more evident. The anxiety of Alexander was therefore diverted from the source of the dispute to its important consequences; and he became naturally more solicitous about having the French troops withdrawn from the frontiers of Poland, than about the cause that originally brought them there.

Accordingly, Prince Kourakin, the Russian plenipotentiary, had orders to communicate to the Duke of Bassano his master's ultimatum. The grounds of arrangement proposed by the Czar were the evacuation of Prussia and Pomerania by the French troops; a diminution of the garrison of Dantzic; and an amicable arrangement of the dispute between Napoleon and Alexander. On these conditions, which, in fact, were no more than necessary to assure Russia of France's peaceable intentions, the Czar agreed to place his commerce upon a system of licenses as conducted in France; to introduce the clauses necessary to protect the French trade; and further, to use his influence with the Duke of Oldenburg, to obtain his consent to accept some reasonable indemnification for the territory which had been so summarily annexed to France.

In looking back at this document, it appears to possess as much the character of moderation, and even of deference, as could be expected from the chief of a great empire. His demand that France should withdraw the armies which threatened the Russian frontier seems no more than common sense would commend. Yet this condition was made by Napoleon, however unreasonably, the direct cause of hostilities. The demand, he said, was insolent; he was not accustomed to being addressed in that style, nor to regulate his movements by the commands of a foreign sovereign. The Russian ambassador received his passports; and the unreasonable caprice of Napoleon, which considered an overture towards an amicable treaty as a gross offence, because it summoned him to desist from his menacing attitude, led to the death of millions, and the irretrievable downfall of the most extraordinary empire which the world had ever seen. On the 9th May, 1812, Buonaparte left Paris.

Upon his former military expeditions, it had been usual for Napoleon to join his army suddenly, and with a slender attendance; but on the present occasion he assumed a style of splendour and dignity becoming one, who might, if any earthly sovereign ever could, have assumed the title of King of Kings. Dresden was appointed as a mutual rendezvous for all the

Kings, Dominations, Princes, Dukes, and dependent royalties of every description, who were subordinate to Napoleon, or hoped for good or evil at his hands. The Emperor of Austria, with his Empress, met his mighty son-in-law upon this occasion, and the city was crowded with princes of the most ancient birth, as well as with others who claimed still higher rank, as belonging to the family of Napoleon. The King of Prussia also was present, neither a willing nor a welcome guest, unless so far as his attendance was necessary to swell the victor's triumph.

Buonaparte made a last attempt to discover what was the state of the Emperor Alexander's mind, who, while he was himself surrounded by sovereigns, as the sun by planets, remained lonely in his own orbit, collecting around him means of defence, which, immense as they were, seemed scarcely adequate to the awful crisis in which he stood. General Lauriston had been despatched to Wilna, to communicate definitively with Alexander. Count de Narbonne, the most adroit courtier of the Tuileries was sent to invite the Czar to meet Napoleon at Dresden, in hopes that, in a personal treaty, the two sovereigns might settle between themselves what they had been unable to arrange through their ambassadors. But Lauriston could obtain no audience of the Emperor, and the report of Narbonne was decidedly warlike. He found the Russians neither depressed nor elated, but arrived at the general conclusion, that war was become inevitable, and therefore determined to submit to its evils, rather than avoid them by a dishonourable peace.

CHAPTER LVII

In ancient history, we often read of the inhabitants of the northern regions, impelled by want and by the desire of exchanging their frozen deserts for the bounties of a more genial climate, breaking forth from their own bleak regions, and, with all the terrors of an avalanche, bursting down upon those of the south. But it was reserved for our generation to behold the invasion reversed, and to see immense hosts of French, Germans, and Italians, leaving their own fruitful, rich, and delightful regions, to carry at once conquest and desolation through the dreary pine forests, swamps, and barren wildernesses of Scythia.

The sovereigns had their different plans. Buonaparte's was formed on his usual system of warfare. It was his primary object to accumulate a great force on the centre of the Russian line, to break it asunder, and cut off as many divisions, as activity could surprise and over-master in such a struggle. To secure the possession of large towns, if possible one of the two capitals; and to grant that which he doubted not would by that time be humbly craved, the terms of a peace which should strip Russia of her European influence, and establish a Polish nation in her bosom.

The tactics of Napoleon had, by long practice been pretty well understood. Barclay de Tolly, whom Alexander made his generalissimo, had laid down and recommended to the Czar, with whom he was in great favour, a plan of fighting Buonaparte upon his own system. He proposed that the Russians should first show only so much opposition on the frontier of their country as should lay the invaders under the necessity of marching with precaution; that they should omit no means of annoying their communications, and disturbing the base on which they rested, but should carefully avoid a general action. On this principle it was proposed to fall back before the invaders, refusing to engage in any other action than skirmishes, and those upon advantage, until the French lines of communication should become liable to be cut off even by the insurgent peasantry. In the meanwhile, as the French became straitened in provisions, and deprived of recruits, the Russians were to be reinforcing their army, and at the same time refreshing it. Thus, it was the object of this plan of the campaign not to fight the French, until the bad roads, want of provisions, toilsome marches, diseases, and loss in skirmishes, should have deprived the invading army of all its original advantages. This procrastinating system of tactics suited Russia the better, that her preparations for war were very far from being completed, and that it was important to gain time to receive arms and other supplies from England, as well as, by making peace with the Turks, to obtain the disposal of the large army now engaged upon the Danube.

The grand imperial army marched upon the river Niemen in its three masses; the King of Westphalia upon Grodno, the Viceroy of Italy on Pilony, and the Emperor himself on Nagaraiski, three leagues beyond Kowno. When the head of Napoleon's column reached the river which rolled silently along under cover of immense forests on the Russian side, he advanced in person to reconnoitre the banks, when his horse stumbled and threw him. "A bad omen," said a voice, but whether that of the Emperor or one of his suite, could not be distinguished; "a Roman would return." On the Russian bank appeared only a single Cossack, who challenged the first party of French that crossed the river, and demanded their purpose in the territories of Russia. "To beat you, and to take Wilna," was the reply. The patrol withdrew, nor was another soldier seen.

A dreadful thunder-storm was the welcome which they received in this wild land; and shortly after the Emperor received intelligence that the Russians were falling back on every side, and manifested an evident intention to evacuate Lithuania without a battle. The Emperor urged forward his columns with even more than his usual promptitude, eager to strike one of those formidable blows by which he was wont to annihilate his enemy at the very commencement of the campaign. This gave rise to an event more ominous than the fall of his horse, or the tempest which received him. The river Wilna being swollen with rain, and the bridges destroyed, the Emperor commanded a body of Polish cavalry to cross by swimming. They did not hesitate to dash into the river. But ere they reached the middle of the stream, the irresistible torrent broke their ranks, and they were swept down and lost almost to a man, before the eyes of Napoleon, to whom some of them in the last struggle turned their faces, exclaiming, "*Vive l'Empereur!*" The spectators were struck with horror. But much greater would that feeling have been, could they have known that the fate of this handful of brave men was but an anticipation of that which impended over the hundreds of thousands.

While his immense masses were traversing Lithuania, Napoleon fixed his headquarters at Wilna, where he began to experience the first pressure of those difficulties which attended his gigantic undertaking.

Only 6000 patients could be accommodated in the hospitals at Wilna, which is too small a proportion for 400,000 men, even if lying in quarters in a healthy and peaceful country, where one invalid in fifty is a most restricted allowance; but totally inadequate to the numbers which actually required assistance, as well from the maladies introduced by fatigue and bad diet, as by the casualties of war. Although scarce a skirmish had been fought, 25,000 patients encumbered the hospitals of Wilna; and the villages were filled with soldiers who were dying for want of medical assistance.

Upon arriving at Wilna, Napoleon had the mortification to find, that although the Emperor Alexander had not left the place until two days after he had himself crossed the Niemen, yet the Russian retreat had been made with the utmost regularity; all magazines and provisions, which could yield any advantage to the invaders, having been destroyed.

Chapter LVIII

Napoleon continued to occupy his headquarters at Wilna, from 28th June to 16th July, the space of eighteen days. It was not usual with him to make such long halts; but Wilna was his last point of communication with Europe, and he had probably much to arrange ere he could plunge into the forests and deserts of Russia. It must not be supposed, however, that these eighteen days passed without military movements of high importance. When Napoleon arrived at Wilna, the danger of the Russian Prince Bagration's army became imminent; for the entrenched camp at Drissa was the rendezvous of all the Russian corps, and Napoleon being seven days' march nearer to Drissa than Bagration, neither Napoleon nor any other general had ever so fair an opportunity for carrying into execution the French Emperor's favourite plan of dividing into two the line of his enemy.

Buonaparte formed a plan for the campaign on the 10th of July, we are assured by Segur; but it was then too late – yet another week was lost at Wilna. All seem to have been sensible of an unusual slowness in Napoleon's motions on this important occasion; and Ségur attributes it to a premature decay of constitution, of which, however, we see no traces in the campaigns of 1813 and 1814. But the terrible disorder of an army, and that army one of such immense size, required considerable time to remodel and new-organise it; and this of itself, a misfortune inherent in the enterprise, is sufficient to account for the halt at Wilna.

At this period Napoleon was directing his whole reserve forces upon Witepsk, to prevent the junction of the two Russian armies. The Emperor found himself in front of the grand army of Russia, in a situation where they could not easily be brought to action.

The Russians retreated to a point where their armies could be reunited without material loss and attempted to surprise the French centre, only to discover that they had been out-manœuvred and that Smolensk, where they had joined forces, was threatened.

Ney arrived first under the walls of the city, and instantly rushed forward to attack the citadel. He failed entirely, being himself wounded, and two-thirds of the storming party cut off. A second attempt was made to as little purpose, and at length he was forced to confine his efforts to a cannonade, which was returned from the place with equal spirit. Later in the day, the troops of Napoleon appeared advancing from the eastward on one side of the Dnieper, while almost at the same moment there were seen upon the opposite bank clouds of dust enveloping long columns of men, moving from different points with uncommon celerity. This was the grand army of Russia under Barclay, and the troops of Bagration, who, breathless with haste and anxiety, were pressing forward to the relief of Smolensk.

But the cautious Barclay de Tolly was determined that not even for the protection of the sacred city would he endanger the safety of his army, so indispensably necessary to the defence of the empire. He dismissed to Ellnia his more impatient coadjutor, Prince Bagration, who would willingly have fought a battle. Barclay in the meanwhile occupied Smolensk, but only for the purpose of covering the flight of the inhabitants, and emptying the magazines.

Buonaparte's last look that evening was on the still empty fields betwixt his army and Smolensk. There was no sign of any advance from its gates, and Murat prophesied that the Russians had no purpose of fighting. Davoust entertained a different opinion; and Napoleon, continuing to believe what he most wished, expected with the peep of day to see the whole Russian army drawn up betwixt his own front and the walls of Smolensk. Morning came, however, and the space in which he expected to see the enemy was vacant as before. On the other hand, the high-road on the opposite side of the Dnieper was filled with troops and artillery, which showed that the grand army of the Russians was in full retreat. Meantime, the attack commenced on Smolensk, but the place was defended with the same vigour as on the day before. The field-guns were found unable to penetrate the walls; and the French lost 4000 or 5000 men in returning repeatedly to the attack. But this successful defence did not alter Barclay's resolution of evacuating the place. It might no doubt have been defended for several days more, but the Russian general feared that a pro-tracted resistance on this advanced point might give Napoleon time to secure the road to Moscow, and drive the Russian armies back upon the barren and exhausted provinces of the northwest, besides getting betwixt them and the ancient capital. In the middle of the night, then, while the French were throwing some shells into the place, they saw fires beginning to kindle, far faster and more generally than their bombardment could have occasioned. They were the work of the Russian troops, who, having completed their task of carrying off or destroying the magazines, and having covered the flight of the inhabitants, had now set the dreadful example of destroying their own town, rather than that its houses or walls should afford assistance to the enemy.

When the Frenchmen entered Smolensk, which they did the next morning, 18th August, most of the town, which consisted chiefly of wooden houses, was yet blazing – elsewhere they found nothing but blood and ashes. The French were struck with horror at the inveterate animosi-ty of the Russians, and the desperation of the resistance which they met with. There was nothing to be gained from the retreating enemy except a long vista of advance through an inhospitable wilderness; without provi-sions; without shelter; without hospitals for the sick; and without even a shed where the weary might repose or the wounded might die.

Buonaparte himself hesitated, and is reported to have then spoken of concluding the campaign at Smolensk, which would, he said, be an admirable head of cantonments. "Here," he said, "the troops might rest and receive reinforcements. Enough was done for the campaign. Poland was conquered. The next year they would have peace, or they would seek it at Moscow." But in the interior of his councils, he held a different lan-guage, and endeavoured to cover, with the language of prudence, the pride and pertinacity of character which forbade him to stop short in an enterprise which had yet produced no harvest of renown. He stated to his generals the exhausted state of the country, in which his soldiers were liv-ing from hand to mouth; and the difficulty of drawing his supplies from Dantzic or Poland, through Russian roads, and in the winter season. He alleged the disorganised state of the army, which might move on, though it was incapable of stopping. "Motion," he said, "might keep it together; a halt or a retreat would be at once to dissolve it. It was an army of attack, not of defence; an army of operation, not of position. The result was, they must advance on Moscow, possess themselves of the capital, and there dictate a peace."

The language which Ségur has placed in the mouth of the Emperor, by no means exaggerates the dreadful condition of the French army. When Napoleon entered the country, only six weeks before, the corps which formed his operating army amounted to 297,000 men; by the 5th August, when preparing to break up from Witepsk, that number was diminished to 185,000, and a great additional loss had been sustained in the movements and encounters on the Dnieper. The wounded of the army were in the most miserable state, and it was in vain that the surgeons tore up their own linen for dressings; they were obliged to use parchment, and the down that grows on the birch-trees; it is no wonder that few recovered.

While the French army was thus suffering a hasty decay, that of the Russians was receiving rapid reinforcements. For Napoleon to await at Smolensk, in a wasted country, the consequences of these junctions, would have been a desperate resolution. It seemed waiting for the fate which he had been wont to command. If Napoleon could yet strike a gallant blow at the Russian grand army, if he could yet obtain possession of Moscow the Holy, he reckoned on sending dismay into the heart of Alexander, and dictating to the Czar, as he had done to many other princes, the conditions of peace from within the walls of his own palace. Buonaparte, therefore, resolved to advance upon Moscow. And perhaps, circumstanced as he was, he had no safer course, unless he had abandoned his whole undertaking, and fallen back upon Poland, which would have been an acknowledgment of defeat that we can hardly conceive his stooping to while he was yet at the head of an army.

*C*HAPTER LIX

The plan of Barclay de Tolly had hitherto been scrupulously adhered to.

All general actions had been cautiously avoided; and while no means were left unemployed to weaken the enemy in partial actions, the end had been in a great measure attained, of undermining the force and breaking the moral courage of the invading army. But they were now approaching Moscow the Grand, the Sanctified – and the military councils of Russia were about to change their character.

The spirit of the Russians, especially of the new levies, was more and more exasperated at the retreat, which seemed to have no end; and at the style of defence, which seemed only to consist in inflicting on the country, by the hands of Cossacks or Tartars, the very desolation which was perhaps the worst evil they could experience from the French. The natural zeal of the new levies eagerly declared against further retreat; and demanded a halt and a battle under a Russian general, more interested, as they supposed such must be, in the defence of the country than a German stranger. The Emperor almost alone continued to adhere to the opinion of Barclay de Tolly. But he could not bid defiance to the united voice of his people and his military council. The political causes which demanded a great battle in defence of Moscow were strong and numerous, and overcame the military reasons which certainly recommended that a risk so tremendous should not be incurred. The Emperor sacrificed his own opinion. General Koutousoff was sent for to take the chief command of the grand army; and it was to Barclay's great honour that, thus superseded, he continued to serve with the utmost zeal in a subordinate situation.

The French were not long of learning that their enemy's system of war was to be changed, and that the new Russian general was to give them battle, the object which they had so long panted for. Buonaparte, who had halted six days at Smolensk, moved from thence on the 24th August. He arrived at the destined field of battle, an elevated plain, called Borodino, which the Russians had secured with lines and batteries. The French army were opposed to them on the 5th September, having consumed seventeen days in marching 280 wersts. Their first operation was a successful attack upon a redoubt in the Russian front. The French gained it and kept it. The armies lay in presence of each other all the next day, preparing for the approaching contest. In strong position was stationed the Russian army, equal now in numbers to the French, as each army might be about 120,000 men. They were commanded by a veteran, slow, cautious, tenacious, wily, too, as Napoleon afterwards found to his cost, but perhaps not otherwise eminent as a military leader. The army he led were of one nation, all conscious that this battle had been granted to their own ardent wishes. The French army consisted of various nations; but they were the *elite*, seasoned soldiers who had survived the distresses of a most calamitous march; they were the veterans of the victors of Europe; they were headed by Napoleon in person, and under his immediate command by those marshals, whose names in arms were only inferior to his own. Besides a consciousness of their superiority in action, of which, from the manner in which they had covered themselves in entrenchments, the enemy seemed aware, the French had before them the prospect of utter destruction if they should sustain a defeat. Buonaparte's address to his troops had less of the tinsel of oratory than he generally used on such occasions. "Soldiers," he said, "here is the battle you have longed for; it is necessary, for it brings us plenty, good winter-quarters, and a safe return to France. Behave yourselves so that posterity may say of each of you, 'He was in that great battle under the walls of Moscow.'"

In the Russian camp was a scene of a different kind, calculated to awaken feelings to which France had long ceased to appeal. The Greek clergy showed themselves to the troops, arrayed in their rich vestments, and displaying for general worship the images of their holiest saints. They told their countrymen of the wrongs which had been offered by the invaders to earth as well as Heaven, and exhorted them to merit a place in paradise by their behaviour in that day's battle.

The battle began about seven o'clock by Ney's attacking the bastioned redoubt on the Russian centre with the greatest violence, while Prince Eugene made equal efforts to dislodge the enemy from the village of Semoneskoie, and the adjoining fortifications. No action was ever more keenly debated nor at such a wasteful expenditure of human life. The fury of the French onset at length carried the redoubts, but the Russians rallied under the very line of their enemy's fire, and advanced again to the combat, to recover their entrenchments. Regiments of peasants, who till that day had never seen war and who still had no other uniform than their grey jackets, formed with the steadiness of veterans,

crossed their brows, and having uttered their national exclamation –
"*Gospodee pomiloui nas!* – God have mercy upon us!" – rushed into the
thickest of the battle, where the survivors, without feeling fear or
astonishment, closed their ranks over their comrade as they fell, while,
supported at once by enthusiasm for their cause, and by a religious sense
of predestination, life and death seemed alike indifferent to them.

The fate of the day seemed more than once so critical that Napoleon
was strongly urged on more than one occasion to bring up the Young
Guard, whom he had in reserve, as the last means of deciding the
contest. He was censured by some of those around him for not having
done so; and it has been imputed to illness, as he had passed a bad night,
and seemed unusually languid during the whole of the day. But the
secret of his refusal seems to be contained in his reply to Berthier, when
he urged him on the subject – "And if there is another battle to-morrow,
where is my army?" The fact is, that this body of 10,000 household
troops were his last reserve. They had been spared as far as possible in
the march, and had, of course, retained their discipline in a proportional
degree; and had they sustained any considerable loss, which, from the
obstinate resistance and repeated efforts of the Russians, was to be
apprehended, Buonaparte, whom even victory must leave in a perilous
condition, would in that case have lost the only corps upon whom, in
the general disorganisation of his army, he could depend.

The Russians, whose desperate efforts to recover their line of
redoubts had exposed them to so much loss, were at length commanded
to retreat; and although the victory was certainly with the French, yet
their enemies might be said rather to desist from fighting, than to have
suffered a defeat. Indeed, it was the French who, after the battle, drew
off to their original ground, and left the Russians in possession of the
bloody field of battle, where they buried their dead, and carried off their
wounded, at their leisure. Their cavalry even alarmed the French camp
on the very night of their victory.

Both parties sustained a dreadful loss in this sanguinary battle.
Among that of the Russians, the death of the gallant Prince Bagration
was generally lamented. Their loss amounted to the awful sum total of
15,000 men killed and more than 30,000 wounded. The French were
supposed to have at least 10,000 men killed, and double the number

wounded. Of these last few recovered, for the great convent of Kolotskoi, which served them as a hospital, was very ill provided with any thing for their relief; and the medical attendants could not procure a party to scout the neighbouring villages, to obtain lint and other necessaries – for it seems even the necessities of a hospital could, in this ill-fated army, only be collected by marauding. Eight French generals were slain. About thirty other generals were wounded. Neither party could make any boast of military trophies, for the Russians made 1000 prisoners and the French scarce twice the number; and Koutousoff carried away 10 pieces of cannon belonging to the French, leaving in their hands 13 guns of his own.

According to Russian accounts, Koutousoff entertained thoughts of giving battle again the next day; but the reports from various corps having made him acquainted with the very large loss they had sustained, he deemed the army too exhausted to incur such a risk. A council of war, of the Russian generals, had been called to deliberate on the awful question, whether they should expose the only army which they had in the centre, to the consequences of a too probable defeat, or whether they should abandon without a struggle the holy Moscow – the Jerusalem of Russia – the city beloved of God and dear to man, with the name and existence of which so many historical, patriotic, national, and individual feelings were now involved. Reason spoke one language, pride and affection held another. To hazard a second battle, was too perilous an adventure, even for the protection of the capital. The consideration seems to have prevailed, that Napoleon being now in the centre of Russia, with an army daily diminishing, and the hard season coming on, every hour during which a decisive action could be delayed was a loss to France, and an advantage to Russia. Besides, the Russian generals reflected, that by evacuating Moscow, a measure which the inhabitants could more easily accomplish than those of any other city in the civilised world, they would leave him nothing to triumph over save the senseless buildings. On the 14th of September, the troops marched with downcast looks, furled banners, and silent drums, through the streets of the metropolis, and went out at the Kolomna gate. Their long columns were followed by the greater part of the remaining population.

CHAPTER LX

On the 14th September, 1812, while the rear-guard of the Russians were in the act of evacuating Moscow, Napoleon reached the hill called the Mount of Salvation, because it is there where the natives kneel and cross themselves at first sight of the Holy City. Moscow seemed lordly and striking as ever, with the steeples of its thirty churches, and its copper domes glittering in the sun; its palaces of Eastern architecture mingled with trees, and surrounded with gardens; and its Kremlin, which rose like a citadel out of the general mass of groves and buildings. But not a chimney sent up smoke, not a man appeared on the battlements, or at the gates. Napoleon gazed, every moment expecting to see a train of bearded boyards arriving to fling themselves at his feet, and place their wealth at his disposal. His first exclamation was, "Behold at last that celebrated city!" His next, "It was full time." His army, less regardful of the past or the future, fixed their eyes on the goal of their wishes, and a shout of "Moscow Moscow!" – passed from rank to rank.

After waiting two hours, he received from some French inhabitants, who had hidden themselves during the evacuation, the strange intelligence that Moscow was deserted. The tidings that a population of 250,000 persons had left their native city was incredible, and Napoleon still commanded the boyards, the public functionaries, to be brought before him; nor could he be convinced of what had actually happened, till they led to his presence the only live creatures they could find in the city, but they were wretches of the lowest rank. When he was at last convinced, he smiled bitterly, and said, "The Russians will soon learn better the value of their capital."

Buonaparte, as if unwilling to encounter the sight of the empty streets, stopped immediately on entering the first suburb. His troops were quartered in the desolate city. During the first few hours after their arrival, an obscure rumour, which could not be traced, announced that the city would be endangered by fire in the course of the night. The report seemed to arise from those evident circumstances which rendered the event probable, but no one took any notice of it, until midnight, when the soldiers were startled from their quarters by the report that the town was in flames. The memorable conflagration began amongst the coachmakers' warehouses and workshops in the Bazaar, which was the most rich district of the city. It was imputed to accident, and the progress of the flames was subdued by the exertions of the French soldiers. Napoleon, who had been roused by the tumult, hurried to the spot, and when the alarm seemed at an end, he retired, not to his former quarters in the suburbs, but to the Kremlin, the hereditary palace of the only sovereign whom he had ever treated as an equal, and over whom his successful arms had now attained such an apparently immense superiority. Yet he did not suffer himself to be dazzled by the advantage he had obtained, but availed himself of the light of the blazing Bazaar, to write to the Emperor proposals of peace with his own hand. They were despatched by a Russian officer of rank, who had been disabled by indisposition from following the army. But no answer was ever returned.

Next day the flames had disappeared, and the French officers luxuriously employed themselves in selecting out of the deserted palaces, that which best pleased the fancy of each for his residence. At night the flames again arose in the north and west quarter of the city. As far the greater part of the houses were built of wood, the conflagration spread with the most dreadful rapidity. This was at first imputed to the blazing brands and sparkles carried by the wind; but at length it was observed, that, as often as the wind changed, and it changed three times in that terrible night, new flames broke always forth in that direction, where the existing gale was calculated to direct them on the Kremlin. Morning came, and with it a dreadful scene. During the whole night, the metropolis had glared with an untimely and unnatural light. It was now covered with a thick and suffocating atmosphere, of almost palpable smoke. The flames defied the efforts of the soldiery, and it is said that the fountains of the city had been rendered inaccessible, the water-pipes cut, and the fire-engines destroyed or carried off.

Then came the reports of fire-balls having been found burning in deserted houses; of men and women, that, like demons, had been seen openly spreading the flames, and who were said to be furnished with combustibles. Several wretches were seized upon, and, probably without much inquiry, shot on the spot. While it was almost impossible to keep the roof of the Kremlin clear of the burning brands which showered down, Napoleon watched from the windows the course of the fire which devoured his fair conquest, and the exclamation burst from him, "These are indeed Scythians!"

The equinoctial gales rose higher and higher upon the third night, and extended the flames, with which there was no longer any human power of contending. At the dead hour of midnight, the Kremlin itself was found to be on fire. Buonaparte was then, at length, persuaded to relinquish his quarters, to which, as the visible mark of his conquest, he had seemed to cling with the tenacity of a lion holding a fragment of his prey. He encountered both difficulty and danger in retiring from the palace, and before he could gain the city-gate, he had to traverse with his suite streets arched with fire, and in which the very air they breathed was suffocating. At length, he gained the open country, and took up his abode in a palace of the Czar's called Petrowsky, about a French league from the city. As he looked back on the fire, which, under the influence of the autumnal wind, swelled and surged around the Kremlin, like an infernal ocean around a sable Pandemonium, he could not suppress the ominous expression, "This bodes us great misfortune."

The fire raged till the 19th with unabated violence, and then began to slacken for want of fuel. It is said, four-fifths of this great city were laid in ruins. On the 20th, Buonaparte returned to the Kremlin; and, as if in defiance of the terrible scene which he had witnessed, took measures as if he were disposed to make Moscow his residence for some time. He even caused a theatre to be fitted up, and plays to be acted by performers sent from Paris.

The conflagration of Moscow was so complete in its devastation; so important in its consequences; so critical in the moment of its commencement, that almost all the eye-witnesses have imputed it to a sublime, yet almost horrible exertion of patriotic decision on the part of the Russians, their government, and, in particular, of the governor, Count Rostopchin. Nor has the positive denial of Count Rostopchin himself diminished the general conviction, that the fire was directed by him. All the French officers continue to this day to ascribe the conflagration to persons whom he had employed. On the other hand, there are many, and those good judges of the probabilities in such an event, who have shown strong reasons for believing that Moscow shared but the fate of a deserted city, which is almost always burnt as well as pillaged. We shall only observe, that should the scale of evidence incline to the side of accident, History will lose one of the grandest, as well as most terrible incidents which she has on record. Considered as a voluntary Russian act, the burning of their capital is an incident of gigantic character, which we consider with awe and terror; our faculties so confused by the immensity of the object, considered in its different bearings, that we hardly know whether to term it vice or virtue, patriotism or vengeance.

Whether the conflagration of Moscow was or was not the work of Russian will, the effects which it was to produce on the campaign were likely to be of the most important character. Buonaparte's object in pressing on to the capital at every risk, was to grasp a pledge, for the redemption of which he had no doubt Alexander would be glad to make peace on his own terms. But the prize, however fair to the sight, had, like that fabled fruit, said to grow on the banks of the Dead Sea, proved in the end but soot and ashes. Far from being able to work upon Alexander's fears for its safety, it was reasonable to think that its total destruction had produced the most vehement resentment on the part of the Russian, since Napoleon received not even the civility of an answer to his conciliatory letter. Neither was it a trifling consideration, that Napoleon had lost by this dreadful fire a great part of the supplies which he expected the capture of the metropolis would have contributed for the support of his famished army.

Meanwhile, the remnant which was left standing afforded the common soldiers an abundance of booty during their short day of rest; and, as is their nature, they enjoyed the present moment without thinking of futurity. The army was dispersed over the city, plundering at pleasure whatever they could find; sometimes discovering quantities of melted gold and silver, sometimes rich merchandise and precious articles, of which they knew not the value; sometimes articles of luxury, which contrasted strangely with their general want of comforts, and even necessaries. It was not uncommon to see the most tattered, shoeless wretches, sitting among bales of rich merchandise, or displaying costly shawls, precious furs, and vestments rich with barbaric pearl and gold. In another place, there were to be seen soldiers possessed of tea, sugar, coffee, and similar luxuries, while the same individuals could scarce procure carrion to eat, or muddy water to drink. Of sugar, in particular, they had such quantities, that they mixed it with their horse-flesh soup. *They* esteemed themselves happiest of all, who could procure intoxicating liquors, and escape by some hours of insensibility the scene of confusion around them.

The utmost exertion could not render Moscow a place of rest for many days; and the difficulty of choosing the route by which to leave it became now an embarrassing consideration. It was in vain that Napoleon expected that Alexander would open some communication on the subject of the letter which he had sent. He grew impatient at length, and resolved himself to make further advances. But not even to his confidential advisers would he own that he sought peace on his own score; he affected to be anxious only on account of Alexander. "He is my friend," he said; "a prince of excellent qualities; and should he yield to his inclinations, and propose peace, the barbarians in their rage will dethrone and put him to death, and fill the throne with someone less tractable. We will send Caulaincourt to break the way for negotiation, and prevent the odium which Alexander might incur, by being the first to propose a treaty." The Emperor was persuaded with some difficulty to despatch General Count Lauriston, his aide-de-camp; lest Caulaincourt's superior rank of Master of the Horse, might indicate that his master sought a treaty, less for Alexander's security than his own. Lauriston, who was well acquainted with the Russian character, urged several doubts against the mission, as betraying their necessity to the enemy; and recommended that the army should, without losing a day, commence its retreat by Kalouga and the more southern route. Buonaparte, however, retained his determination, and Lauriston was dismissed with a letter to the Emperor Alexander, and the parting instruction – "I must have peace, and will sacrifice, to obtain it, all except my honour."

CHAPTER LXI

On leaving Moscow, the Russians had feinted a march to the southeast before taking up position to the southwest, whence they could protect the stores held in Kalouga and Toula, harass Napoleon's communications with Smolensk and Poland, and be resupplied. Murat was sent to dislodge them, but managed little more than a few skirmishes and an armistice. The Russians broke the armistice and successfully attacked Murat who, but for Poniatowski's Poles, would have been annihilated. As it is, the 'beau sabreur' lost all his artillery and most of his cavalry.

It was the 18th of October when first the noise of the cannon, and soon after, the arrival of an officer, brought intelligence of this mishap to Buonaparte. His energy, which had appeared to slumber during the days he had spent in a species of irresolution, seemed at once restored. He poured forth, without hesitation, a torrent of orders, directing the march of the troops to support Murat.

On the 19th October, before day-break, the Emperor in person left Moscow, after an abode of thirty-four days. "Let us march," he said, "on Kalouga, and woe to those who shall oppose us." In this brief sentence he announced the whole plan, which was to defeat the army of Koutousoff, or compel him to retire, and then himself to return to the frontiers of Poland, by the unwasted route of Kalouga, Medyn, Ynkowo, Elnia, and Smolensk.

The army was intercepted by the Russians en route from Moscow and the terrifying Cossacks pursued them on their journey to Smolensk.

On the 6th November commenced that terrible Russian winter, of which the French had not yet experienced the horrors, although the weather had been cold, frosty, and threatening. No sun was visible, and the dense and murky fog which hung on the marching column, was changed into a heavy fall of snow in large broad flakes, which at once chilled and blinded the soldiers. The march, however, stumbled forward, the men struggling, and at last sinking, in the holes and ravines which were concealed from them by the new and disguised appearance of nature. A stormy wind also began to arise, and whirl the snow from the earth, as well as that from the heavens, into dizzy eddies around the soldiers' heads. There were many hurled to the earth in this manner, where the same snows furnished them with an instant grave, under which they were concealed until the next summer came, and displayed their ghastly remains in the open air. A great number of slight hillocks on each side of the road, intimated, in the meanwhile, the fate of these unfortunate men.

At length Smolensk was visible. At the sight of its strong walls and lofty towers, the stragglers of the army, who now included treble the number of those who kept their ranks, rushed headlong to the place. But instead of giving them ready admission, their countrymen in the town shut the gates against them with horror; for their confused and irregular state, their wild, dirty, and unshaved appearance, their impatient cries for entrance – above all, their emaciated forms, and starved, yet ferocious aspects – made them to be regarded rather as banditti than soldiers. At length, the Imperial Guards arrived and were admitted; the miscellaneous crowd rushed in after them. To the guards, and some few others who had kept order, rations were regularly delivered; but the mass of stragglers, being unable to give any account of themselves or their regiments, or to bring with them a responsible officer, died, many of them, while they besieged in vain the doors of the magazines. Such was the promised distribution of food – the promised quarters were nowhere to be found. Smolensk had been burnt by the Russians, and no other covering was to be had than was afforded by miserable sheds, reared against such blackened walls as remained yet standing. But even this was shelter and repose, compared to the exposed bivouac on wreaths of snow; and as the straggling soldiers were compelled by hunger to unite themselves once more with their regiments, they at length obtained their share in the regular distribution of rations, and an approach towards order and discipline began to prevail in the headmost division of the Grand Army of France.

CHAPTER LXII

Cooped up in the ruins of Smolensk, and the slender provision of food and supplies which that place offered almost entirely exhausted, Napoleon had to consider in what direction he should make an effort to escape. As he had heard of the loss of Witepsk, by which town he had advanced, and understood that Witgenstein was in possession of the line of the Dwina, he naturally determined to take the road to Wilna, by Krasnoi, Borizoff, and Minsk.

For this effort he proceeded as well as circumstances would admit, to re-organise his army. It was reduced to about 40,000 men, with a dispro-portioned train of baggage and of artillery, although much of the former, and 350 cannon, had already been left behind. This force the Emperor divided into four corps, which were to leave Smolensk, placing a day's interval betwixt the march of each. He himself led the van, with 6000 of his Guard and about as many soldiers, the relics of different corps, amal-gamated into battalions as well as circumstances would permit. The Emperor's division left Smolensk on the evening of the 13th and morn-ing of the 14th November.

Ney remained. As he had once more the perilous task of covering the retreat, which duty he had performed admirably betwixt Wiazma and Smolensk, his division was fortified with about 4000 of the Imperial Guard, to whom, as better fed than the other troops, besides their high character as veterans, more could be trusted even in the most desperate circumstances. Ere the French left the town, they obeyed the strict com-mands of the Emperor, in blowing up the towers with which Smolensk was surrounded, that it might not again, as Napoleon expressed himself, form an obstacle to a French army. Such was the language of this extraor-dinary man, as if affecting to provide for re-entering into Russia, at a time when it was the only question whether he himself, or any individual of his army, should ever be able to leave the fatal country.

The Russians attacked the retreating army with ferocity at Krasnoi and Napoleon resolved to escape to Liady as quickly as possible.

On the 17th of November, Ney, last of the invading army, left Smolensk at the head of 7 or 8000 fighting men, leaving behind 5000 sick and wounded, and dragging along with them the remaining stragglers whom the cannon of Platow, who entered the town immediately on Ney's depar-ture, had compelled to resume their march. They advanced without much interruption till they reached the field of battle of Krasnoi, where they saw all the relics of a bloody action, and heaps of dead, from whose dress and appearance they could recognise the different corps in which they had served in Napoleon's army, though there was no one to tell the fate of the survivors. They had not proceeded much further beyond this fatal spot, when they approached the banks of the Losmina, where all had been prepared at leisure for their reception. Miloradowitch lay here at the head of a great force; and a thick mist, which covered the ground, occasioned Ney's column to advance under the Russian batteries before being aware of the danger.

Ney was invited to capitulate but declined and was forced to fight and then retreat under the shelter of night to follow the banks of the river Dneiper to safety. Eventually he and his men were reunited with the rest of the French troops.

All Napoleon's grand army was now united. But the whole, which had at Smolensk amounted to 40,000, consisted now of scarcely 12,000 who retained the name and discipline of soldiers. There were, besides, perhaps 30,000 stragglers of every description, but these added little or nothing to the strength of the army. At this dreadful crisis, too, Napoleon had the mortification to learn the fall of Minsk, and the retreat of Schwartzenberg to cover Warsaw, which, of course, left him no hopes of receiving succour from the Austrians.

Minsk being out of the question, Napoleon's next point of direction was Borizoff. They were moving towards Borizoff, when loud shouts from the forest at first spread confusion among their ranks, under the idea of an unexpected attack; but this fear was soon changed into joy, when they found themselves on the point of uniting with the army of Victor and Oudinot, amounting to 50,000 men provided with everything. When the French arrived at Studzianka, their first business was to prepare two bridges, a work which was attended with much danger and difficulty. They laboured by night, expecting in the morning to be saluted with a cannonade from the Russian detachment under Tschaplitz. The French generals, and particularly Murat, considered the peril as so eminent, that they wished Buonaparte to commit himself to the faith of some Poles who knew the country and leave the army to their fate; but Napoleon rejected the proposal as unworthy of him. All night the French laboured at the bridges, which were yet but little advanced, and might have been easily demolished by the artillery of the Russians. But what was the joy and surprise of the French to see, with the earliest beams of the morning, that artillery, and those Russians in full march, retreating front their position! Availing himself of their disappearance, Buonaparte threw across a body of men who swam their horses over the river, with each a voltigeur behind him. Thus a footing was gained on the other bank of this perilous stream.

During the 26th and 27th, Napoleon pushed troops across the river; and was soon so secure, that Tschaplitz, discovering his error, and moving back to regain his important position at Studzianka, found the French too strongly posted on the left bank for his regaining the opportunity which he had lost. He halted, therefore, at Stakhowa, and waited for reinforcements and orders.

The indefatigable Witgenstein was in motion on the left bank, pressing forward as Victor closed up towards Napoleon; and, throwing himself betwixt Studzianka and Borizoff, on a plain called Staroi-Borizoff, he cut off Partouneaux's division from the rest of the French army. That general made a gallant resistance, and attempted to force his way at the sword's point through the troops opposed to him. Three generals, with artillery, and according to the Russian accounts, about 7000 men, fell into the hands of the Russians – a prize the more valuable, as the prisoners belonged chiefly to the unbroken and unexhausted division of Victor, and comprehended 800 fine cavalry in good order.

Witgenstein marched down the left bank of the Beresina, engaged in a fierce combat with the rear-guard; and the balls of the Russians began to fall among the mingled and disordered mass. It was then that the whole body of stragglers and fugitives rushed like distracted beings towards the bridges, every feeling of prudence or humanity swallowed up by the animal instinct of self-preservation. The horrible scene of disorder was augmented by the desperate violence of those who, determined to make their own way at all risks, threw down and trampled upon whatever came in their road. The weak and helpless either shrunk back from the fray, and sat down to wait their fate at a distance, or, mixing in it, were thrust over the bridges, crushed under carriages, cut down perhaps with sabres, or trampled to death under the feet of their countrymen. All this while the action continued with fury, and, as if the Heavens meant to match their wrath with that of man, a hurricane arose, and added terrors to a scene which was already of a character so dreadful.

About mid-day the French, still bravely resisting, began to lose ground. The Russians, coming gradually up in strength, succeeded in forcing the ravine, and compelling them to assume a position nearer the bridges. About the same time, the larger bridge, that constructed for artillery and heavy carriages, broke down, and multitudes were forced into the water. The scream of mortal agony, which arose from the despairing multitude, became at this crisis for a moment so universal, that it rose shrilly audible over the noise of the elements and the thunders of war, above the wild whistling of the tempest, and the sustained and redoubled hourras of the Cossacks. This dreadful scene continued till dark, many being forced into the icy river, some throwing themselves in, betwixt absolute despair and the faint hope of gaining the opposite bank by swimming, some getting across only to die of cold and exhaustion. As the obscurity came on, Victor, with the remainder of his troops, which was much reduced, quitted the station he had defended so bravely, and led them in their turn across. All night the miscellaneous multitude continued to throng along the bridge, under the fire of the Russian artillery. At daybreak, General Eblé, finally set fire to the bridge. All that remained on the other side, including many prisoners, and a great quantity of guns and baggage, became the prisoners and the prey of the Russians. The amount of the French loss was never exactly known; but the Russian report concerning the bodies of the invaders which were collected and burnt as soon as the thaw permitted, states that upwards of 36,000 were found in the Beresina.

CHAPTER LXIII

On the 29th November, the Emperor left the fatal banks of the Beresina at the head of an army more disorganised than ever; for few of Oudinot's corps, and Victor's, who were yet remaining, were able to resist the general contagion of disorder. They pushed on without any regular disposition, having no more vanguard, centre, or rear, than can be ascribed to a flock of sheep. To outstrip the Russians was their only desire, and yet numbers were daily surprised by the partisans and Cossacks. Most fortunately for Napoleon, the precaution of the Duke of Bassano had despatched to the banks of the Beresina a division of French, who were sufficient to form a rear-guard, and to protect this disorderly and defence-less mass of fugitives. Thus they reached Malodeczno on the 3rd December.

Here Buonaparte opened to his confidants his resolution to leave the army, and push forward to Paris. The late conspiracy of Mallet had con-vinced him of the necessity of his presence there. His remaining with an army which scarce had existence in a military sense, could be of no use. On the 5th December, Buonaparte was at Smorgoni, where he again received a welcome reinforcement being joined by Loison, advancing at the head of the garrison of Wilna, to protect his retreat to that place. The order of march thus arranged, Napoleon determined on his own depar-ture. Three sledges were provided; one of which was prepared to carry him and Caulaincourt, whose title the Emperor proposed to assume while travelling incognito, although their figures were strikingly dissimilar. In a general audience, at which were present the King of Naples, the viceroy, Berthier, and the maréchals, Napoleon announced that he had left Murat to command the army. He talked to them in terms of hope and confi-dence. He promised to check the Austrians and Prussians in their disposition for war, by presenting himself at the head of the French nation, and 1,200,000 men; he said he had ordered Ney to Wilna to reorganise the army and to strike such a blow as should discourage the advance of the Russians; lastly, he assured them of winter-quarters beyond the Niemen. He then took an affectionate and individual farewell of each of his generals, and, stepping into his traineau, a lively emblem of the fishing-boat of Xerxes, he departed at ten at night.

With what feelings this extraordinary man left the remains of the army, we have no means even of guessing. His outward bearing, during his extreme distresses, had been in general that of the utmost firmness; so that such expressions of grief or irritation as at times broke from him, were picked up and registered, as curious instances of departure from his usual state of composure. To preserve his tranquillity, he permitted no details to be given him of the want and misery with which he was sur-rounded. Thus, when Colonel d'Albignac brought news of Ney's distress-es, after the battle of Wiazma, he stopped his mouth by saying sharply, "He desired to know no particulars." It was of a piece with this resolution, that he always gave out orders as if the whole Imperial army had existed in its various divisions, after two-thirds had been destroyed, and the remainder reduced to an undisciplined mob. "Would you deprive me of my tranquillity?" he said angrily to an officer, who thought it necessary to dwell on the actual circumstances of the army, when some orders, expressed in this manner, had been issued. And when the persevering functionary persisted to explain – thinking, perhaps, in his simplicity, that Napoleon did not know that which in fact he only was reluctant to dwell upon – he reiterated angrily, "I ask you, sir, why you would deprive me of my tranquillity?"

It is evident that Napoleon must have known the condition of his army as well as anyone around him; but, to admit that he was acquainted with that which he could not remedy would have been acknowledging a want of power inconsistent with the character of one, who would willingly be thought rather the controller than the subject of Fate.

After narrowly escaping being taken by the Russian partisan Seslawin, Napoleon reached Warsaw upon the 10th December. He continued his journey in secrecy and with rapidity. On the 14th December he was at Dresden and on the 18th, in the evening, he arrived at Paris, where the city had been for two days agitated by the circulation of the 29th Bulletin, in which the veil, though with a reluctant hand, was raised up to show the disasters of the Russian war.

Thus ended the Russian expedition, the first of Napoleon's undertakings in which he was utterly defeated, and of which we scarce know whether most to wonder at the daring audacity of the attempt, or the terrific catastrophe. The loss of the grand army was total, and the results are probably correctly stated by Boutourlin as follows:

Slain in battle	125,000
Died from fatigue, hunger, and the severity of the climate	132,000
Prisoners, comprehending 48 generals, 3000 officers, and upwards of 190,000 men	193,000
Total	450,000

The relics of the troops which escaped from that overwhelming disaster, independent of the two auxiliary armies of Austrians and Prussians, who were never much engaged in its terrors, might be about 40,000 men, of whom scarcely 10,000 were Frenchmen.

The causes of this total and calamitous failure lay in miscalculations, both moral and physical, which were involved in the first concoction of the enterprise, and began to operate from its very commencement. We are aware that this is, with the idolaters of Napoleon, an unpalatable view of the case. They believe, according to the doctrine which he himself promulgated, that he could be conquered by the elements alone. This was what he averred in the 29th bulletin. Till the 6th November, he stated that he had been uniformly successful. The snow then fell, and in six days destroyed the character of the army, depressed their courage, elated that of the "despicable" Cossacks, deprived the French of artillery, baggage, and cavalry, and reduced them, with little aid from the Russians, to the melancholy state in which they returned to Poland.

The fact is that Napoleon, whose judgment was seldom misled save by the ardour of his wishes, had foreseen, in October, the coming of the frost, as he had been aware, in July, of the necessity of collecting sufficient supplies for his army, yet without making adequate provision against what he knew was to happen, in either case. It is impossible that he could have been surprised by the arrival of snow on the 6th November. Even the most ordinary precaution, that of rough-shoeing the horses of the cavalry and the draught-horses, was totally neglected. This is saying, in other words, that the animals had not been new-shod at all; for French horses may be termed always rough-shod, until the shoes are grown old and worn smooth through use. If, therefore, frost and snow be so very dangerous to armies, Napoleon wilfully braved their rigour, and by his want of due preparations, brought upon himself the very disaster of which he complained so heavily.

Though unquestionably the severity of the frost did greatly increase the distress and loss of an army suffering under famine, nakedness, and privations of every kind, yet it was neither the first, nor, in any respect, the principal, cause of their disasters. When the severe frost came, it aggravated greatly the misery, and increased the loss, of the French army. But winter was only the ally of the Russians; not, as has been contended, their sole protectress. She rendered the retreat of the grand army more calamitous, but it had already been an indispensable measure; and was in the act of being executed at the lance-point of the Cossacks, before the storms of the north contributed to overwhelm the invaders.

What, then, occasioned this most calamitous catastrophe? We venture to reply, that a moral error, or rather a crime, converted Napoleon's wisdom into folly; and that he was misled, by the injustice of his views into the great political, nay, military errors, which he acted upon in his attempt to realise them.

CHAPTER LXIV

Upon the morning succeeding his return, which was like the sudden appearance of one dropped from the heavens, Paris resounded with the news; which had, such was the force of Napoleon's character, and the habits of subjection to which the Parisians were inured, the effect of giving a new impulse to the whole capital. The safe return of Napoleon was a sufficient cure for the loss of 500,000 men, and served to assuage the sorrows of as many widows and orphans. The Emperor convoked the Council of State. He spoke with apparent frankness of the misfortunes which had befallen his army, and imputed them all to the snow.

The *Moniteur* was at first silent on the news from Russia, and announced the advent of the Emperor as if he had returned from Fontainebleau; but after an interval of this apparent coldness, like the waters of a river in the thaw, accumulating behind, and at length precipitating themselves over, a barrier of ice, arose the general gratulation of the public functionaries, whose power and profit must stand or fall with the dominion of the Emperor, and whose voices alone were admitted to represent those of the people. The cities of Rome, Florence, Milan, Turin, Hamburg, Amsterdam, Mayence, and whatever others there were of consequence in the empire, joined in the general asseveration, that the presence of the Emperor alone was all that was necessary to convert disquietude into happiness and tranquillity.

Buonaparte proceeded, while straining every effort, for supporting foreign war, to take such means as were in his power for closing domestic wounds, which were the more dangerous that they bled inwardly, without any external effusion to indicate their existence. The chief of these was the dispute with the Pope, which continued to foster so much scandal in the Gallican Church. We have mentioned already that the Pope, refusing to consent to any alienation of his secular dominions, had been forcibly carried off from Rome, removed to Grenoble, then brought back over the Alps to Savona, in Italy. Napoleon denied that he had authorised this usage towards the father of the Church, yet continued to detain him at Savona. He was confined there until June, 1812. In the meantime, a deputation of the French bishops were sent with a decree by Napoleon, determining that if his holiness should continue to refuse canonical institution to the French clergy, as he had done ever since the seizure of the city of Rome and the patrimony of Saint Peter's, a council of prelates should be held for the purpose of pronouncing his deposition. On 4th September, 1811, the holy father admitted the deputation, listened to their arguments with patience, then knelt down before them, and repeated the psalm, *Judica me, Domine.* When the prelates attempted to vindicate themselves, Pius VII, in an animated tone, threatened to fulminate an excommunication against anyone who should attempt to justify his conduct.

His Holiness was transported to Fontainebleau, where he arrived 19th June, 1812. The French historians boast that the old man was not thrown into a dungeon, but, on the contrary, was well lodged in the palace, and was permitted to attend mass – a wonderful condescension towards the head of the Catholic religion. But still he was a captive. He abode at Fontainebleau till Napoleon's return from Russia; and it was on the 19th January, 1813 that the Emperor, having left Saint Cloud under pretext of a hunting-party, suddenly presented himself before his venerable prisoner. He exerted all the powers he possessed to induce the Pontiff to close with his propositions; and we readily believe that the accounts, which charge him with having maltreated his person, are not only unauthenticated, but positively false. He rendered the submission which he required more easy to the conscience of Pius VII by not demanding from him any express cession of his temporal rights, and by granting a delay of six months on the subject of canonical instalment. Eleven articles were agreed on, and subscribed by the Emperor and the Pope.

But hardly was this done ere the feud broke out afresh. It was of importance to Napoleon to have the schism soldered up as soon as possible, since the Pope refused to acknowledge the validity of his second marriage, and, of course, to ratify the legitimacy of his son. He, therefore, published the articles of treaty in the *Moniteur*, as containing a new concordat. The Pope complained, stating that the articles were not a concordat, but only the preliminaries on which such a treaty might have been formed. He was indignant at what he considered as circumvention on the part of the Emperor, and refused to abide by the alleged concordat. Thus failed Napoleon's attempt to close the schism of the Church, and the ecclesiastical feuds recommenced with more acrimony than ever.

CHAPTERS LXV, LXVI, LXVII

Prussia joined Sweden and Russia in declaring war on France. The Austrians, meanwhile, pondered their options, less because of the matrimonial alliance than the belief that they might wring concessions out of Napoleon without having to fight.

Having expelled the French, the Russians might have stopped on the German borders to regroup. In 1813, however, they advanced all the way to the Elbe in order to capitalise on German resentment of the French and to link up, in the north, with a Swedish expeditionary force. This bold advance, before the allies had completed their military preparations, left them dangerously exposed when Napoleon led his new levies into Germany. Finding the allies in his way at Lutzen, Napoleon defeated them on 2nd May, and reached Dresden on the 12th. The allies retreated from the Elbe to Bautzen, on the Spree, where they were again defeated on the 20th. Napoleon had won two battles but neither had been tactically decisive. An armistice, beginning on 4th June, was agreed upon in order to allow negotiations to take place in Prague.

The armistice afforded an apt occasion for arranging a general peace, or rather (for that was the real purpose) for giving Austria an opportunity of declaring her real intentions in this unexpected crisis, which had rendered her to a great degree arbitress of the fate of Europe. Napoleon, from his arrival in Saxony, had adopted a belief that, although Austria was likely to use the crisis as an opportunity of compelling him to restore the Illyrian provinces, and perhaps other territories, yet that in the end, the family connection, with the awe entertained for his talents, would hinder her cabinet from uniting their cause to that of the allies. An expression had dropped from the Austrian minister Metternich, which would have altered this belief, had it been reported to him. Marat, Duke of Bassano, had pressed the Austrian hard on the ties arising from the marriage, when the Austrian answered emphatically, "The marriage – yes, the marriage – it was a match founded on political considerations; *but*."

This single brief word disclosed as much as the least key when it opens the strongest cabinet – it made it clear that the connection formed by the marriage would not prevent Austria from taking the line which policy demanded. And this was soon seen when Count Metternich came to Dresden to have an audience of Napoleon. This celebrated statesman and accomplished courtier had been very acceptable at the Tuileries, and Napoleon seems to have imagined him one of those persons whose gaiety and good-humour were combined with a flexible character, liable to be mastered and guided by one of power and energy like his own. This was a great mistake. Metternich, a man of liveliness and address when in society, was firm and decisive in business. He saw that the opportunity of controlling the absolute power of France had at length arrived, and was determined, so far as Austria was concerned, that no partial views should prevent its being effectually employed.

Napoleon upbraided Metternich with having favoured his adversaries, by being so tardy in opening the negotiation. In claiming to be a negotiator, Austria, he said, was neither his friend nor his impartial judge – she was his enemy. "You were about to declare yourself," he said, "when the victory at Lutzen rendered it prudent in the first place to collect more forces. Now you have assembled behind the screen of the Bohemian mountains 200,000 men under Schwartzenberg's command. Ah, Metternich! I guess the purpose of your Cabinet. You wish to profit by my embarrassments, and seize on the favourable moment to regain as much as you can of what I have taken from you. The only question with you is, whether you will make most by allowing me to ransom myself, or by going to war with me? – You are uncertain on that point; and perhaps you only come here to ascertain which is your best course. Well, let us drive a bargain – how much is it you want?"

To this insulting commencement Metternich replied, that "the only advantage desired by his master, was to see that moderation and respect for the rights of nations which filled his own bosom, restored to the general councils of Europe, and such a well-balanced system introduced as should place the universal tranquillity under the guarantee of an association of independent states."

It was easy to see which way this pointed, and to anticipate the conclusion. Napoleon affected to treat it as a figure of speech, which was to cloak the private views of Austria. "I speak clearly," he said, "and come to the point. Will it suit you to accept of Illyria, and to remain neuter? Your neutrality is all I require. I can deal with the Russians and Prussians with my own army." "Ah, Sire," replied Metternich, "it depends solely on your Majesty to unite all our forces with yours. But the truth must be told. Matters are come to that extremity that Austria cannot remain neutral — We must be with you, or against you."

After this explicit declaration, from which it was to be inferred that Austria would not lay aside her arms, unless Buonaparte would comply with the terms which she had fixed upon as the conditions of a general pacification, and that she was determined to refuse all that might be offered as a bribe for her neutrality, the Emperor of France and the Austrian statesman retired into a cabinet, apart from the secretaries, where it is to be presumed Metternich communicated more specifically the conditions which Austria had to propose. Napoleon's voice was presently heard exclaiming aloud, "What! not only Illyria, but half of Italy, the restoration of the Pope, and the abandoning of Poland, and the resignation of Spain, and Holland, and the confederation of the Rhine, and Switzerland! Is this your moderation? You hawk about your alliance from the one camp to the other, where the greatest partition of territory is to be obtained, and then you talk of the independence of nations! In plain truth, you would have Italy; Sweden demands Norway; Prussia requires Saxony; England would have Holland and Belgium — You would dismember the French empire; and all these changes to be operated by Austria's mere threat of going to war. Can you pretend to win, by a single stroke of the pen, so many of the strongest fortresses in Europe, the keys of which I have gained by battles and victories?"

Napoleon insisted that the congress should be assembled, and that, even if hostilities should recommence, negotiations for peace should not be discontinued. And, like a wary trader, when driving a bargain, he whispered to Metternich, that his offer of Illyria was *not his last word.*

At length, so late as the 7th August, Austria produced her plan of pacification, of which the basis were the following: I. The dissolution of the grand duchy of Warsaw, which was to be divided between Russia, Prussia, and Austria; II. The re-establishment of the Hanseatic towns in their independence; III. The reconstruction of Prussia, assigning to that kingdom a frontier on the Elbe; IV. The cession to Austria of the maritime town of Trieste, with the Illyrian provinces. The emancipation of Spain and Holland, as matters in which England took chief interest, was not stirred for the present, but reserved for consideration at the general peace.

Buonaparte in return offered much, but most of his cession were clogged with conditions, which at once showed how unwillingly they were made, and seemed in most cases, to provide the means of annulling them when times should be favourable: I. The grand duchy of Warsaw Napoleon agreed to yield up, but stipulated that Dantzic with its fortifications demolished, should remain a free town, and that Saxony should be indemnified for the cession of the duchy, at the expense of Prussia and Austria; II. The cession of the Illyrian provinces was agreed to, but the seaport of Trieste was reserved; III. Contained a stipulation that the German confederation should extend to the Oder. Lastly, the territory of Denmark was to be guaranteed.

Before this tardy agreement to grant some of the terms could arrive at Prague, the 10th of August had expired and Austria had passed into the federation of the allies. On the night betwixt the 10th and 11th, rockets flickered in the air from height to height, betwixt Prague and Trachenberg, the Headquarters of the Emperor of Russia and King of Prussia, to announce that the armistice was broken off. Metternich and Caulaincourt continued their negotiations; and Napoleon seemed on a sudden sincerely desirous of the peace. Metternich persisted in his demand of Trieste and the Hanse towns. He rejected the extension of the Confederation of the Rhine, as a demand made at a time so ill-chosen as to be nearly ridiculous; and he required that the independence of Germany should be declared free, as well as that of Switzerland. Buonaparte at length consented to all these demands, which, if they had been admitted during his interview with Metternich, or declared to the Congress before the 10th August, must have availed to secure peace. It is probable, either that

Napoleon was unwilling to make his mind up to consent to terms which he thought humiliating, or that he made the concessions at a time when they would not be accepted, in order that he might obtain the chance of war, yet preserve with his subjects the credit of having been willing to make peace.

It has been said, with much plausibility, that the allies, on their part, were confirmed in their resolution to demand high terms, by the news of the decisive battle of Vittoria, and the probability that the Duke of Wellington's army might be soon employed in the invasion of France.

CHAPTER LXVIII

By the beginning of August, Napoleon had assembled about 250,000 men in Saxony and Silesia. At Leipzig, there were 60,000 men and at Loewenberg, Goldberg, Bantzlau, and other towns on the borders of Silesia, were 100,000 men. Another army of 50,000 were quartered in Lusatia, near Zittau. St. Cyr, with 20,000, was stationed near Pirna. In Dresden the Emperor himself lay with his guard, amounting to 25,000 men, the flower of his army. Almost all his old lieutenants, who had fought and won so often in his cause, were summoned; and even Murat, who had been on indifferent terms with his relative, came anew from Naples, to enjoy the pleasure of wielding his sabre against his old friends the Cossacks.

The allies had agreed upon a plan of operations equally cautious and effective. They saw that [Napoleon] intended to join his strong reserve of the Guard to any of the armies placed on the frontier of Saxony and thus advance upon, overpower, and destroy the enemy whom he should find in front. To meet this mode of attack, which might otherwise have been the means of the allied armies being defeated in detail, it was resolved that the general against whom Buonaparte's first effort should be directed, should on no account accept battle, but, withdrawing his troops, should decoy him as far as possible in pursuit, while at the same time the other armies of the allies should advance upon his rear, destroy his communications, and finally effect their purpose of closing round him in every direction.

Blücher was the first who, advancing from Silesia and menacing the armies of Macdonald and Ney, induced Buonaparte to join them with his Guard, and with a great body of cavalry. He left Dresden on the 15th August; he threw bridges over the Bober, and advanced with rapidity. But the Prussian general was faithful to the plan. He made an admirable retreat across the Katzbach, admitting the French to nothing but skirmishes, in which the allies had some advantage. Finally, he established himself in a position on the river Niesse, near Jauer, so as to cover Silesia and its capital.

On the 21st August, Napoleon learned that while he was pressing the retreating Prussians, Dresden was in the utmost danger of being taken. His guards had instant orders to return to Saxony. He himself set out early on the 23rd. It was full time; for Schwartzenberg, with the Sovereigns of Russia and Prussia, had descended from Bohemia, and, concentrating their grand army on the left bank of the Elbe, were already approaching the walls of Dresden, Napoleon's point of support and pivot. Leaving to Macdonald the task of controlling Blücher, the Emperor set out with the *élite* of his army; yet, with all the speed he could exert, very nearly came too late to save the object of his solicitude.

General St. Cyr, who had been left with about 20,000 men to observe the Bohemian passes, was in no condition to make a stand, when they poured out upon him six or seven times his own number. He threw himself into Dresden in hopes to defend it until the arrival of Napoleon. The allies, having found little resistance on their march, displayed their huge army before the city, divided into four columns, about four o'clock on the 25th August. If they should take Dresden before it could be relieved by Buonaparte, the war might be considered as nearly ended, since they would command his line of communication with France. The scheme was excellently laid, but the allied generals did not pursue it with the necessary activity. The signal for onset should have been given instantly, yet they paused for the arrival of Klenau, with an additional *corps d'armée*, and the assault was postponed until next morning.

On the 26th, at break of day, the allies advanced in six columns under tremendous fire. They carried a great redoubt near the city-gate of Dippoldiswalde, and soon after another; they closed on the French on every point; the bombs and balls began to fall thick on the streets and houses of the terrified city; and in engaging all his reserves, St. Cyr, whose conduct was heroic, felt he had yet too few men to defend works of such extent. It was at this crisis, while all thought a surrender was inevitable, that columns, rushing forward with the rapidity of a torrent, were seen advancing on Dresden from the right side of the Elbe, sweeping over its magnificent bridges and pressing through the streets. The Child of Destiny himself was beheld amidst his soldiers, who, notwithstanding a severe forced march from the frontiers of Silesia, demanded, with loud cries, to be led into immediate battle. Napoleon halted to reassure the King of Saxony, who was apprehensive of the destruction of his capital, while his troops, marching through the city, halted on the western side, at those avenues, from which it was designed they should debouche upon the enemy.

Two sallies were then made under Napoleon's eye, by Ney and Mortier. The one column, pouring from the gate of Plauen, attacked the allies on the left flank; the other, issuing from that of Pirna, assailed their right. The Prussians were dislodged and the war began already to change its face; the allies drawing off from the points they had attacked so fiercely. They remained, however, in front of each other, the sentinels on each side being in close vicinity.

On the 27th of August, the battle was renewed under torrents of rain, and amid a tempest of wind. Napoleon, manoeuvring with excellence altogether his own, caused his troops, now increased by concentration to nearly 200,000 men, to file out from the city upon different points, the several columns diverging from each other like the sticks of a fan when it is expanded; and thus directed them upon such points as seemed most assailable along the allies' whole position, which occupied the heights from Plauen to Strehlen. In this manner, assisted by the stormy weather, which served to conceal his movements, he commenced an attack upon both flanks of the enemy. On the left he obtained an advantage, from a large interval left in the allied line, to receive the division of Klenau.

But besides this, the allies had calculated upon Buonaparte's absence, and upon the place being slightly defended. They were disappointed in both respects; and his sudden arrival had entirely changed the nature of the combat. They had become defenders at the very time when they reckoned on being assailants; and their troops, particularly the Austrians, were discouraged. Even if they repelled the French into Dresden, they had provided no magazines of support in front of it, should the allied army be designed to remain there. A retreat was, therefore, resolved upon, and, owing to the weather, the state of the roads, and the close pursuit of the French, it was a disastrous one. The successful operations of the French had established the King of Naples on the western road to Bohemia; and Vandamme, with a strong division, blocked up that which led directly southward up the Elbe, by Pirna. The two principal roads being thus closed against Schwartzenberg and his army, nothing remained for them but to retreat through the interval between these highways by such country paths as they could find, which had been rendered almost impassable by the weather. They were pursued by the French in every direction, and lost, what had of late been unusual, a great number of prisoners. 7000 or 8000 of the French were killed and wounded; but the loss of the allies was as great, while their prisoners, almost all Austrians, amounted to 13,000 to 15,000.

On the 29th of August, the French continued to push their advantages. A *corps d'armée* of about 30,000 men, had been entrusted to the conduct of Vandamme, whose character as a general, for skill, determined bravery, and activity, was respected, while he was detested by the Germans on account of his rudeness and rapacity, and disliked by his comrades because of the ferocious obstinacy of his disposition.[iii] With this man, who, not without some of the good qualities which distinguished Buonaparte's officers, presented even a caricature of the vices ascribed to them, the misfortunes of his master in this campaign were destined to commence.

Vandamme had advanced as far as Peterswald, a small town in the Bohemian mountains, forcing before him a column of Russians, feeble in number, but excellent in point of character and discipline, commanded by Count Ostermann, who were retreating upon Toplitz. This town was the point on which all the retiring divisions of the allies were directing their course. If Vandamme could have defeated Ostermann, and carried this place, he might have established himself on the only road practical for artillery, by which the allies could march to Prague; so that they must either have remained enclosed between his corps, and those of the other French generals who pressed on their rear, or else they must have abandoned their guns and baggage, and endeavoured to cross the mountains by wild tracks.

It was on the 29th, in the morning, that, acting under so strong a temptation as we have mentioned, Vandamme had the temerity to descend the hill from Peterswald to the village of Culm, which is situated in a very deep valley betwixt that town and Toplitz. As he advanced towards Toplitz, it appeared that his plan was about to be crowned with success. The persons of the Emperor of Russia and the King of Prussia, the members of their Cabinet, and the whole depot of the headquarters of the allies, seemed now within his clutch, and, already alarmed, his expected prey were beginning to attempt their escape in different directions. Vandamme seemed within a hand's grasp of the prize; for his operation, if complete, must have totally disorganised the allied army, and the French might perhaps have pursued them to the very gates of Prague, nay, of Vienna. The French advanced-guard was within half a league of Toplitz, when all of a sudden Count Ostermann, who had hitherto retreated slowly, halted, and commenced the most obstinate resistance. His troops were few, but, as already said, of excellent quality, being a part of the Imperial Russian Guard, whom their commander gave to understand, that the safety of their father (as the Russians affectionately term the Emperor) depended upon their maintaining their ground. They stood firm as a grove of pines opposed to the tempest, while Vandamme led down corps after corps, to support his furious and repeated attacks, until at length he had brought his very last reserves, and accumulated them in the deep valley between Culm and Toplitz. The brave Ostermann had lost an arm in the action, and his grenadiers had suffered severely; but they had gained the time necessary. Barclay de Tolly, who now approached, brought up the first columns of the Russians to their support; Schwartzenberg sent other succours; and Vandamme, in his turn, overpowered by numbers, retreated to Culm as night closed.

Prudence would have recommended to the French to have continued their retreat to the heights of Peterswald; but, expecting probably the appearance of some of the French columns of pursuit, morning found Vandamme in the valley of Culm. In the meantime, still greater numbers of the allied corps, which were wandering through these mountain regions, repaired to the banners of Schwartzenberg and Barclay, and the attack was renewed upon the French column at break of day on the 30th, with a superiority of force with which it was fruitless to contend. Vandamme therefore disposed himself to retreat towards Peterswald. But at this moment took place one of the most singular accidents which distinguished this eventful war.

Among other *corps d'armée* of the allies, which were making their way through the mountains, was that of the Prussian General Kleist, who had evaded the pursuit of St. Cyr by throwing himself into the wood of Schoenwald, out of which he debouched on Peterswald, towards which Vandamme was making his retreat. While, therefore, Vandamme's retreating columns were ascending, the ridge which they proposed to gain was suddenly occupied by the troops of Kleist, in such a state of disorder as announced they were escaped from some pressing scene of danger, or hurrying on to some hasty attack.

When the Prussians came in sight of the French, they conceived that the latter were there for the purpose of cutting them off; and, instead of taking a position on the heights to intercept Vandamme, they determined to precipitate themselves down, break their way through his troops, and force themselves on to Toplitz. The French, seeing their way interrupted, formed the same conclusion with regard to Kleist's corps; and each army being bent on making its way through that opposed to them, the Prussians rushed down the hill, while the French ascended it with a bravery of despair, that supplied the advantage of ground.

The two armies were thus hurled on each other like conflicting mobs, enclosed in a deep and narrow road, forming the descent along the side of a mountain. The onset of the French horse, under Corbineau, was so desperate, that many or most of them broke through, although the acclivity against which they advanced would not, in other circumstances, have permitted them to ascend at a trot and the guns of the Prussians were for a moment in the hands of the French. The Prussians, however, soon rallied, and the two struggling bodies again mixing together, fought less for the purpose of victory or slaughter, than to force their way through each other's ranks. All became for a time a mass of confusion, the Prussian generals finding themselves in the middle of the French – the French officers in the centre of the Prussians. But the army of the Russians, who were in pursuit of Vandamme, appearing in his rear, put an end to this singular conflict. Generals Vandamme, Haxo, and Guyot, were made prisoners, with two eagles and 7000 prisoners, besides a great loss in killed and wounded, and the total dispersion of the army, many of whom, however, afterwards rejoined their eagles.

The victory of Culm, an event so unexpected and important in a military view, was beyond appreciation in the consequences which it produced upon the moral feelings of the allied troops. The spirits of all were reconciled to the eager prosecution of the war, and the hopes of liberation spread wider and wider through Germany.

Napoleon received the news of this calamity, however unexpected, with the imperturbable calmness which was one of his distinguishing qualities. General Corbineau presented himself before the Emperor in the condition in which he escaped from the field, covered with his own blood and that of the enemy, and holding in his hand a Prussian sabre, which, in the thick of the mêlée he had exchanged for his own. Napoleon listened composedly to the details he had to give. "One should make a bridge of gold for a flying enemy," he said, "where it is impossible, as in Vandamme's case, to oppose to him a bulwark of steel." He then anxiously examined the instructions to Vandamme, to discover if any thing had inadvertently slipped into them, to encourage the false step which that general had taken. But nothing was found which could authorise his advancing beyond Peterswald, although the chance of possessing himself of Toplitz must have been acknowledged as a strong temptation.

CHAPTERS LXIX, LXX

Vandamme was not the only French general to suffer defeat in August 1813. Oudinot and Ney, sent to threaten Berlin, failed for want of troops, and were compelled to retreat onto the Elbe before Bernadotte. Macdonald, operating in Silesia, was defeated by Blücher and obliged to retreat upon Dresden. Napoleon himself made several sorties, in September, to tempt Schwarzenberg into battle. The allies, now vastly superior in numbers, concentrated their forces on the left bank of the Elbe early in October. Napoleon yet again moved against Blücher at

Duben, but the latter, joined by the Bernadotte, retreated on the line of the Saale, beyond the Emperor's reach yet placed upon his communications. Napoleon had little option but to retreat upon Leipzig, hoping for the 'thunderbolt' that would place him securely back on the line of the Elbe.

The columns of the grand army of the allies advanced on Leipzig *on 15th October 1813, while Napoleon made arrangements for its defence.*

At break of day, on the 16th October, the battle began. The French position was attacked along all the southern front with the greatest fury.

The battle continued to rage till nightfall, when the bloody work ceased as if by mutual consent. Three cannon-shot, fired as a signal to the more distant points, intimated that the conflict was ended for the time, and the armies on the southern line retired to rest, in the very positions which they had occupied the night before. The French had lost the ground which they had gained, but they had not relinquished one foot of their original position, though so fiercely attacked during the whole day by greatly superior numbers. On the north their defence had been less successful. Marmont had been forced back, and the whole line of defence was crowded nearer to the walls of Leipzig.

Napoleon had the melancholy task of arranging his soldiers for a defence, sure to be honourable, and yet at length to be unavailing. Retreat became inevitable; yet, how to accomplish it through the narrow streets of a crowded city; how to pass more than 100,000 men over a single bridge, while double that number were pressing on their rear, was a problem which even Buonaparte could not solve.

He was now willing to adopt the terms proposed at Prague. He offered to renounce Poland and Illyria. He would consent to the independence of Holland, the Hanse towns, and Spain. Italy, he proposed, should be considered as independent, and preserved in its integrity. Lastly, as the price of the armistice to be immediately concluded, he was willing to evacuate Germany and retreat towards the Rhine.

These terms contained what, at an early part of the campaign, would have been gladly accepted by the allies. But Buonaparte's ability and pertinacity; the general impression, that, if he relinquished his views for a time, it was only to recur to them in a more favourable season; and his terrible power of making successful exertions for that purpose, hardened the hearts of the allied sovereigns against what, from another would have been favourably received. "Adieu, General Mehrfeldt," said Napoleon, dismissing his prisoner; "when, on my part, you name the word armistice to the two Emperors, I doubt not that the voice which then strikes their ears will awaken many recollections." Words affecting by their simplicity, and which, coming from so proud a heart, and one who was reduced to ask the generosity which he had formerly extended, cannot be recorded without strong sympathy.

General Mehrfeldt went out, like the messenger from the ark, and long and anxiously did Buonaparte expect his return. But he was the raven envoy, and brought back no olive branch. Napoleon did not receive an answer until his troops had recrossed the Rhine. The allies had engaged themselves solemnly to each other that they would enter into no treaty with him while an individual of the French army remained in Germany.

At eight o'clock on the 18th of October, the battle was renewed with tenfold fury. Napoleon had considerably contracted his circuit of defence, so the French had the advantage of situation and cover, and the allies that of greatly superior numbers.

The allies, notwithstanding their gallantry and their numbers, felt themselves obliged to desist from the murderous attacks upon the villages which cost them such immense loss; and contented themselves with maintaining a dreadful fire on the French masses as they showed themselves, and throwing shells into the villages. The French replied with great spirit; but they had fewer guns in position, and, besides, their ammunition was falling short. Still, Napoleon completely maintained the day on the south of Leipzig.

On the north, the superiority of numbers, still greater than that on the south, placed Ney in a precarious situation. He was pressed at once by the army of Blücher and by that of the Crown Prince, and was obliged to contract his line of defence. Even the valour and exertions of that distinguished general could not defend Schoenfeld. It was in vain that Buonaparte despatched his reserves of cavalry to check the advance of the Crown Prince. He defeated all opposition, and pressed Ney into a position close under the walls of Leipzig. The battle once more ceased on all points; and after the solemn signal of three cannon-shot, the field was left to the slain and the wounded.

Although the French army kept its ground most valiantly during the whole of this tremendous day, there was no prospect of their being able to sustain themselves any longer. The allies had approached so close to them, that their attacks might, on the third day, be expected to be more combined and simultaneous than before. The superiority of numbers became more efficient after the great carnage. It is said also that 250,000 cannon-bullets had been expended by the French during the last four days, and that there only remained to serve their guns about 16,000 cartridges, which could scarce support a hot fire for two hours.

The retreat was commenced in the night time; and Buonaparte, retiring in person to Leipzig, spent a third exhausting night dictating the orders for drawing the corps of his army successively within the town, and transferring them to the western bank of the two rivers. The French troops came into Leipzig from all sides, filling the town with the ineffable confusion which must attend the retreat of so large a body in the presence of a victorious enemy. Macdonald and Poniatowski, with their corps, were appointed to the perilous honour of protecting the rear.

The arrival of daylight had no sooner shown to the allies the commencement of the French retreat, than their columns began to advance in pursuit on every point, pushing forward, with all the animation of victory, to overtake the enemy in the suburbs and streets of Leipzig. The King of Saxony, the magistrates and some of the French generals, endeavoured to secure the city from the dangers which were to be expected from a battle. They sent proposals that the French should be permitted to effect their retreat unmolested, in mercy to the unfortunate town. But when were victorious generals prevented from prosecuting military advantages, by the mere consideration of humanity?

At nine o'clock Napoleon had a farewell interview with Frederick Augustus, releasing him formally from all the ties which had hitherto combined them and leaving him at liberty to form such other alliances as the safety of his states might require. Their parting scene was hurried to a conclusion by the heavy discharge of musketry from several points, which intimated that the allies, forcing their way into the suburbs, were fighting hand to hand, and house to house.

The furious defence which was maintained in the suburbs continued to check the advance of the allies, otherwise the greater part of the French army must inevitably have been destroyed. But the defenders themselves, with their brave commanders, were at length, after exhibiting prodigies of valour, compelled to retreat; and ere they could reach the banks of the river, a dreadful accident had taken place. The bridge, so necessary to the escape of the army, had been mined by Buonaparte's orders, and an officer of engineers was left to execute the necessary measure of destroying it as soon as the allies should approach in force. Whether the officer to whom this duty was entrusted had fled, or had fallen, or had been absent from his post by accident, no one seems to have known; but at this critical period a sergeant commanded in his stead. A body of Swedish sharp-shooters pushed up the side of the river at about eleven o'clock, with loud cries and huzzas, firing upon the crowds who were winning their way slowly along the bridge. Meanwhile, Cossacks and Hulans were seen on the southern side, rushing towards the same spot; and the troops of Saxony and Baden, who had now entirely changed sides, were firing on the French from the wall of the suburbs. The non-commissioned officer of engineers imagined that the retreat of the French was cut off and set fire to the mine. The bridge exploded with a horrible noise.

The remainder of the French army, after many had been killed and drowned in an attempt to cross these relentless rivers, received quarter from the enemy. About 25,000 men were made prisoners, and as Napoleon seems only to have had about 200 guns at the battle of Hannau, many must have been abandoned in Leipzig and its neighbourhood. The quantity of baggage taken was immense. The triumph of the allied monarchs was complete. Advancing at the head of their victorious forces, each upon his own side, the Emperor of Russia, the King of Prussia, and the Crown Prince of Sweden, met and greeted each other in the great square of the city, where they were soon joined by the Emperor of Austria. General Bertrand, the French commandant of the city, surrendered his sword to these illustrious personages. No interview took place between the allied monarchs and the King of Saxony. He was sent under guard to Berlin, nor was he afterwards restored to his throne until he had paid a severe fine for his adherence to France.

When reflecting upon these scenes, the rank and dignity of the actors naturally attract our observation. It seems as if the example of Buonaparte, in placing himself at the head of his armies, had in some respects changed the condition of sovereigns from the reserved and retired dignity in which most had remained, estranged from the actual toils of government and dangers of war, into the less abstracted condition of sharing the risk of battle and the labours of negotiation. Such scenes as those which passed at Leipzig on this memorable day, whether we look at the parting of Napoleon from Frederick Augustus, amid the fire and shouting of hostile armies, or the triumphant meeting of the allied sovereigns in the great square of Leipzig, had been for centuries only to be paralleled in romance. But considering how important it is to the people that sovereigns should not be prompt to foster a love of war, there is great room for question whether the encouragement of this warlike propensity be, upon the whole, a subject for Europe to congratulate itself upon.

*C*HAPTERS LXXI, LXXII, LXXIII

The Empire collapsed in Germany. Napoleon retreated behind the Rhine; the allies accepted the surrender of the last French garrisons in Germany; the Austrians invaded Italy, and Wellington crossed the Pyrenées. Despite their overwhelming advantage, remembering 1792, the allies were wary of invading France, and so favoured negotiations. Napoleon was offered France's natural boundaries – the Rhine, Alps, and Pyrenées – an offer that generously included Belgium. Napoleon accepted this basis for negotiation, though with enough provisos to bring his good faith into question. Meanwhile, preparations were made for war. As the allies massed on the borders, 280,000 conscripts were drafted in France.

Upon the 21st December, Maréchal Prince Schwartzenberg crossed the Rhine with the Austrian army at four points and advanced upon Langres. Moving with extreme slowness and precision, the Austrians did not arrive till the 17th January, 1814. The army of Silesia made equal progress, though against greater resistance and more difficulties.

Blücher and Schwartzenberg "formed an almost complete military line from Langres to Châlons". A third allied army, commanded by Bernadotte, concentrated on clearing Northern Germany, defeating Denmark, and liberating Holland and Belgium. Elements of this force, under Winzengerode and Thielman, were ordered to march into Northern France in support the army of Silesia. Despite their preponderance, the allies were unsure how to proceed, fearing the consequences of a defeat so far from their own supplies.

This spirit predominating in the councils of the allies led to a degree of uncertainty in their movements, which, as is usual, endeavoured to disguise itself under the guise of prudence. They resolved that the grand army should halt a short space at Langres, in hopes either that Napoleon, renewing the negotiation, would avert his present danger by acquiescing to the terms of the allies; or that the French nation, an event still likely to happen, would become tired of the military monarch, whose ambition had brought such distress upon the country. But Napoleon, as firmly determined in his purpose as the allies were doubtful, knowing himself to be the soul of his army, and absolute lord of his own actions, felt all the advantage which a bold, active, and able swordsman has in encountering an opponent whose skill is less distinguished, and whose determination is more flexible. The allies had presented in the grand army a front of 97,000 men, Maréchal Blücher one of 40,000. To oppose this, the French Emperor had only, of old troops, independent of those under Suchet in Catalonia, under Soult near Bayonne, and also of garrisons, about 50,000 men; nor could he hope to add to them more than 70,000 conscripts. Nay, his levies, so far as they could be brought into the field, fell greatly short of this number; for the allies were in possession of a considerable part of the kingdom, and, in this moment of general confusion, it was impossible to enforce the law of conscription.

The defensive war had no doubt considerable advantages to one who knew so well how to use them. The highways by which the allies must advance formed a half or quarter circle of rays, converging on Paris. A much smaller army might, therefore, oppose a large one, because, lying between Paris and the enemy, they must occupy the same roads by a much shorter line of communication. With this advantage, Buonaparte advanced to play for the most momentous stake ever disputed, with a degree of military skill which has never been matched. Arriving at

Châlons on the 26th January, Buonaparte took the command of such an army as he had been able to assemble.

Blücher was, as usual, the foremost in advance, and Napoleon resolved to bestow on this active and inveterate enemy the terrible honour of his first attack, hoping to surprise the Silesian *corps d'armée* before it could receive succour from Schwartzenberg. The maréchal was apprised of the Emperor's purpose and lost no time in concentrating his forces at Brienne. It was at the military school of Brienne that Napoleon acquired the rudiments of that skill in the art with which he had almost prostrated the world, and had ended by placing it in array against him; and it was here he came to commence what seemed his last series of efforts for victory; like some animals of the chase, who, when hard pressed by the hunters, are said to direct their final attempts at escape upon the point from which they have first started.

The alert movements of Napoleon surpassed the anticipation of Blücher. He was at table with his staff in the Chateau. At once a horrible tumult was heard. The Russian cavalry, 2000 in number, were completely driven in by those of Napoleon, and at the same moment Ney attacked the town; while a body of French grenadiers threatened to make prisoners all who were in the Chateau. Blücher, with his officers, had barely time to reach a postern, where they were under the necessity of leading their horses down a stair, and in that way made their escape. The bold resistance of Alsusiev defended the town against Ney, and Sacken advanced to Alsusiev's assistance. The Cossacks also fell on the rear of the French in the park, and Buonaparte's own safety was compromised in the mêlée. Men were killed by his side, and he was obliged to draw his sword in his own defence. At the very moment of attack, his attention was engaged by the sight of a tree, which he recollected to be the same under which, during the hours of recreation at Brienne, he used to peruse the Jerusalem Delivered of Tasso. If the curtain of fate had risen before the obscure youth, and discovered to him in the same spot, his own image as Emperor of France, contending against the Scythians of the desert for life and power, how wonderful would have seemed the presage, when the mere concurrence of circumstances strikes the mind of those who look back upon it with awful veneration for the hidden ways of Providence! The town caught fire, and was burned to the ground; but it was not until eleven at night that the Silesian army ceased to make efforts for recovering the place, and that Blücher, retreating from Brienne, took up a position upon La Rothière.

The result of the battle was indecisive, and the more unsatisfactory to Buonaparte, as the part of Blücher's force engaged did not amount to 20,000 men, and the sole advantage gained over them was that of keeping the field of battle. Napoleon's principal object, which was to divide Blücher from the grand army, had altogether failed. It was necessary, however, to proclaim the engagement as a victory, and much pain was taken to represent it as such.

On the 1st February, Blücher, strongly reinforced from the grand army, prepared in his turn to assume the offensive. It would have been Napoleon's wish to have avoided an engagement; but a retreat across the Aube, by the bridge of Lesmont, which was the only mode of passing that river, would have exposed his rear to destruction. He therefore risked a general action. Blücher attacked the line of the French on three points, assaulting at once the villages of La Rothière, Dienville, and Chaumont. The conflict was hard fought during the whole day, but in the evening, the French were repulsed on all points, and Buonaparte was compelled to retreat across the Aube after losing 4000 prisoners and no less than 73 guns. Ney, by the Emperor's orders, destroyed the bridge at Lesmont. The allies were not aware of the amount of their advantage, and suffered the French to retire unmolested.

A general council of war, held at the castle of Brienne [February 2nd,] resolved that the two armies should separate from each other and that Blücher, detaching himself to the northward, and uniting under his command the division of d'Yorck and Kleist, should approach Paris by the Marne; while Prince Schwartzenberg and the grand army should descend on the capital by the course of the Seine. The difficulty of finding provisions for such immense armies was doubtless in part the cause of this resolution. But it was likewise recommended by the success of a similar plan of operations at Dresden, and afterwards at Leipzig.

Buonaparte resolved, taking advantage of the division of the two armies of the allies, to march upon that of Blücher. But, in order to disguise his purpose, he first sent a small division upon Bar-sur-Seine, to alarm the Austrians with an attack upon their right wing. Schwartzenberg immediately apprehended that Buonaparte was about to move with his whole force in that direction. Terrified by the idea that his left flank might be turned or forced, the Austrian general moved his chief strength in that direction; thus at once suspending his meditated march on the Seine, and increasing the distance betwixt the grand army and that of Silesia. Buonaparte, having deceived Schwartzenberg, evacuated Troyes, leaving Victor and Oudinot to oppose the Austrians with very inadequate means, while he directed his own march against Blücher.

Buonaparte fell upon the central division of Alsusiev, at Champ-Aubert, surrounded, defeated, and totally dispersed them, taking their artillery, and 2000 prisoners, while the remainder fled into the woods, and attempted to escape individually. War began now to show itself in its most hideous forms. The stragglers and fugitives, who could not cross the bridge before its destruction, were murdered by the peasantry, while the allied soldiers, in revenge, plundered the village of Chateau-Thierry, and practised every excess of violence. The defeat of Sacken took place on the 12th of February.[20]

Blücher, ignorant of the extent of the force by which his vanguard had been attacked, pressed forward to their support, and, in a wide and unenclosed country, suddenly found himself in the front of the whole army of Napoleon, flushed with the double victory which they had already gained, and so numerous as to make a retreat indispensable on the part of the Prussians. Blücher, if surprised, remained undismayed. Having only three regiments of cavalry, he had to trust for safety to the steadiness of his infantry. He formed them into squares, protected by artillery, and thus commenced his retreat by alternate divisions; those battalions which were in motion to the rear, being protected by the fire of the others. The French cavalry, though so strong as to operate at once on the flanks and rear, failed to break a single square. After the Prussians had retired several leagues in this manner, fighting every foot of their way, they were nearly intercepted by a huge column of French horses, which, having made a circuit, had drawn up on the causeway to intercept their retreat. Without a moment's hesitation, Blücher instantly attacked them with such a murderous fire of infantry and artillery, as forced them from the high-road, and left the passage free. The Prussians found the village of Etoges, through which they were obliged to pass, also occupied by the enemy; but here also they cleared their way by dint of fighting. This expedition of the Marne, as it is called, is always accounted one of Napoleon's military *chefs-d'œuvres* for a flank march undertaken through such a difficult country, and so completely successful, is not perhaps recorded in history. On the other hand, if Blücher lost any credit by the too great security of his march, he regained it by the masterly manner in which he executed his retreat. Had the army which he commanded shared the fate of his vanguard, it is probable there would have been no campaign of Paris.

The Parisians, in the meantime, saw at length actual proofs that Napoleon had been victorious. Long columns of prisoners moved through their streets, banners were displayed, the cannon thundered, the press replied, and the pulpit joined in extolling and magnifying the dangers which the citizens had escaped, and the merits of their preserver.

In the midst of the joy, the Parisians suddenly learned that the town of Fontainebleau was occupied by Hungarian hussars, and that not Cossacks only, but Tartars, Baskirs, and Kalmouks, tribes of a wild and savage aspect, a kind of Asiatic Ogres, to whom popular credulity imputed a taste for the flesh of children, had appeared in the neighbourhood of Nangis. This alarm to Paris was accompanied by another. Schwartzenberg, learning the disasters on the Marne, not only pushed forward from three directions on the capital, but despatched forces from his right towards Provins, to threaten Napoleon's rear and communications. Leaving the pursuit of Blücher, the Emperor countermarched on Meaux, and joined the army of Oudinot and Victor, who were retreating before Schwartzenberg. He here found the reinforcements which he had drawn from Spain, about 20,000 in number, tried and excellent troops. With this army he now fronted that of Schwartzenberg, and upon the 17th February, commenced the offensive at all points, possessing himself of Nangis, and nearly destroying the corps under Count Pahlen at Mormant. The Prince Royal of Wirtemberg was forced to retreat to Montereau.

So alarmed were the allies at the near approach of their terrible enemy that a message was sent to Napoleon from the allied sovereigns, stating their surprise at his offensive movement, since they had given orders to their plenipotentiaries at Châtillon to sign the preliminaries of peace, on the terms which had been assented to by the French envoy, Caulaincourt.

This letter, of which we shall hereafter give a full explanation, remained for some days unanswered, during which Napoleon endeavoured to push his advantages. He recovered the bridge at Montereau, after a desperate attack, in which Napoleon returned to his old profession of an artilleryman, and pointed several guns himself, to the great delight of the soldiers. They trembled, however, when the fire attracted the attention of the enemy, whose balls began to be aimed at the French battery. "Go, my children," said Buonaparte, ridiculing their apprehensions; "the ball is not cast that is to kill me."

On the evening of the 22nd February, an answer to the letter of Schwartzenberg was received, but it was addressed exclusively to the Emperor of Austria; and while its expressions of respect are bestowed liberally on that power, the manner in which the other members of the coalition are treated, shows unabated enmity, ill-concealed under an affectation of contempt. The Emperor of France expressed himself willing to treat upon the basis of the Frankfurt declaration, but exclaimed against the terms which his own envoy, Caulaincourt, had proposed. In short, the whole letter indicated not that Napoleon desired a general peace with the allies, but that it was his anxious wish to break up the coalition, by making a separate peace with Austria.

The Emperor Francis and his ministers were resolved not to listen to any proposals which went to separate the Austrian cause from that of their allies. It was therefore at first resolved that no answer should be sent to the letter; but the desire of gaining time for bringing up the reserves determined them to accept the offer of a suspension of hostilities. Under these considerations, Prince Wenceslaus of Lichtenstein was sent to the headquarters of Napoleon, to treat concerning an armistice. The Emperor seemed to be in a state of high hope, and called upon the Austrians not to sacrifice themselves to the selfish views of Russia, and the miserable policy of England. He appointed Count Flahault his commissioner to negotiate for a line of demarcation, and directed him to meet with the envoy from the allies at Lusigny, on 24th February.

On the night of the 23rd, the French bombarded Troyes, which the allied troops evacuated according to their latest plan of the campaign. The French entered the town on the 24th, when the sick and wounded, left behind by the allies, were dragged out to grace Napoleon's triumph.

The villages were everywhere burnt, the farms wasted and pillaged, the abodes of man, and all that belongs to peaceful industry and domestic comfort, desolated and destroyed. Wolves, and other savage animals, increased fearfully in the districts which had been laid waste by human hands, with ferocity congenial to their own. Thus were the evils which France had unsparingly inflicted upon Spain, Prussia, Russia, and almost every European nation, terribly retaliated within a few leagues of her own metropolis; and such were the consequences of a system which, assuming military force for its sole principle and law, taught the united nations of Europe to repel its aggressions by means yet more formidable in extent than those which had been used in supporting them.

CHAPTERS LXXIV, LXXV

Various negotiations took place between the allies and the French, in which Napoleon was represented by the diplomatic Caulaincourt. Napoleon, however, stubbornly refused to accept the treaty terms proposed by the allies until the deadline for accepting them had already passed.

A new treaty, that of Chaumont, was entered into upon the 1st of March between Austria, Russia, Prussia, and England, by which the high contracting parties bound themselves each to keep up an army of 150,000 men, with an agreement on the part of Great Britain to advance four million to carry on the war, which was to be prosecuted without relaxation, until France should be reduced within her ancient limits.

As Caulaincourt left Châtillon, he met the secretary of Buonaparte posting towards him with the full and explicit powers of treating which he had so long vainly solicited. Had Napoleon adopted this final decision of submitting himself to circumstances but one day earlier, the treaty of Châtillon might have proceeded, and he would have continued in possession of the throne of France. But it was too late.

The sword was now again brandished, not to be sheathed, until one party or the other should be irretrievably defeated. The situation of Buonaparte, even after the victory of Montereau, and capture of Troyes, was most discouraging. If he advanced on the grand army which he had in front, there was every likelihood that they would retire before him, wasting his force in skirmishes, without a possibility of his being able to force them to a general action; while it might be reckoned for certain that Blücher, master of the Marne, would march upon Paris. On the contrary, if Napoleon moved with his chief force against Blücher, he had, in like manner, to apprehend that Schwartzenberg would resume the route upon Paris by way of the Seine.

After weighing all the disadvantages on either side, Napoleon determined to turn his arms against Blücher, as most hostile to his person, most rapid in his movements, and most persevering in his purposes. At eleven in the morning of the 7th March, the French began their attack with the utmost bravery. But the assault was met by a defence equally obstinate, and the contest became one of the most bloody and best-sustained during the war. It was four in the afternoon and the French had not yet been able to dislodge the Russians on any point, when the latter received orders from Blücher to withdraw from the disputed ground and unite with the Prussian army on the splendid position of Laon. The Russians, despite a general charge of the French cavalry, retreated as on the parade. As the armies were nearly equal, the indecisive event of the battle was the more ominous. The slain and wounded were about the same number on both sides, and the French only retained as a mark of victory the possession of the field of battle.

Napoleon himself followed the retreat of the Russians as far as an inn between Craonne and Laon, called L'Ange Gardien. He, indeed, never more needed the assistance of a guardian angel, and his own appears to have deserted his charge. At this cabaret, he regulated his plan for attacking Blücher on the next morning; and thus ridding himself finally of that Silesian army, which had been his object of disquietude for forty-two days. When his plan for the attack was finished, he is said to have exclaimed, "I see this war is an abyss without a bottom, but I am resolved to be the last whom it shall devour."

Only one day elapsed between the bloody battle of Craonne and that of Laon. On the 9th, availing himself of a thick mist, Napoleon pushed his columns of attack to the very foot of the eminence on which Laon is situated, possessed himself of two of the villages, Semilly and Ardon, and prepared to force his way up the hill towards the town. The weather cleared, the French attack was repelled by a tremendous fire from terraces, vineyards, windmills, and every point of advantage. Two battalions of Yagers, the impetus of their attack increased by the rapidity of the descent, recovered the villages, and the attack of Laon in front seemed to be abandoned. The French, however, continued to retain possession, in that quarter, of a part of the village of Clacy. Thus stood the action on the right and centre. On the left Maréchal Marmont had advanced upon the village of Athies, which was the key of Blücher's position in that point. Marmont made some progress, and night found him bivouacking in front of the enemy, and in possession of part of the disputed village. But he was not destined to remain there till daybreak. Upon the 10th, at four in the morning, just as Buonaparte, arising before daybreak, was calling for his horse, two dismounted dragoons were brought before him, with the unpleasing intelligence that the enemy had made a *hourra* upon Marmont, surprised him in his bivouac, and cut to pieces, taken, or dispersed his whole division, and they alone had escaped to bring the tidings. All the maréchal's guns were lost, and they believed he was either killed or prisoner. Officers sent to reconnoitre, brought back confirmation of this intelligence, excepting as to the situation of the maréchal. He was on the road to Rheims, endeavouring to rally the fugitives. Notwithstanding this great loss, and as if in defiance of bad fortune, Napoleon renewed the attack upon Clacy and Semilly; but all his attempts being fruitless, he was induced to relinquish the undertaking. On the 11th, he withdrew, having been foiled in all his attempts, and having lost thirty guns and nearly 10,000 men. The allies suffered comparatively little, as they fought under cover.

Despite the victory, Schwartzenberg was yet again alarmed, this time by Napoleon's possession of Rheims, and wished to retreat. The British envoy and the Tsar overruled him.

Napoleon broke up from Rheims on the 17th, and sending Ney to take possession of Châlons, marched to Épernay, with the purpose of placing himself on the right flank and in the rear of Schwartzenberg, in case he should advance to Paris. At Épernay, he learned that the allies, alarmed by his movements, had retired to Troyes, and that they were about to retreat upon the Aube, and probably to Langres. He also learned that Macdonald and Oudinot had resumed their advance so soon as their adversaries began to retreat. He hastened to form a junction with these persevering leaders, and proceeded to ascend the Aube as high as Bar, where he expected to throw himself into Schwartzenberg's rear, having no doubt that his army was retiring from the banks of the Aube.

In these calculations, accurate as far as the information permitted, Buonaparte was greatly misled. He conceived himself to be acting upon the retreat of the allies, and expected only to find a rear-guard at Arcis; he was even talking jocularly, of making his father-in-law prisoner during his retreat. If, contrary to his expectation, he should find the enemy, or any considerable part of them, still upon the Aube, it was, from all he had heard, to be supposed his appearance would precipitate their retreat towards the frontier.

The town of Arcis had been evacuated by the allies upon his approach, and was occupied by the French on the morning of the 20th March. That town forms the outlet of a sort of defile, where a succession of narrow bridges cross a number of feeders of the river Aube, and a bridge in the town crosses the river itself. On the other side of Arcis is a plain, in which some few squadrons of cavalry, resembling a reconnoitring party, were observed manoeuvring.

Behind these horse, at a place called Clermont, the Prince Royal of Wirtemberg, was posted with his division, while the elite of the allied army was drawn up on a chain of heights still further in the rear. But these forces were not apparent to the vanguard of Napoleon's army. The French cavalry had orders to attack the light troops of the allies; but these were instantly supported by whole regiments and by cannon, so that the attack was unsuccessful; and the squadrons of the French were driven back on Arcis at a moment when the infantry could with difficulty debouche from the town to support them. Napoleon showed, as he always did in extremity, the same heroic courage which he had exhibited at Lodi and Brienne. He drew his sword, threw himself among the broken cavalry, called on them to remember their former victories, and checked the enemy by an impetuous charge, in which he and his staff-officers fought hand to hand with their opponents, so that he was in personal danger from the lance of a Cossack, the thrust of which was averted by his aide-de camp. His Mameluke Rustan fought stoutly by his side, and received a gratuity for his bravery. The superior number of the allies rendered them the assailants on all points, and night alone separated the combatants, by inducing the allies to desist from the attack.

In the course of the night, Buonaparte was joined by Macdonald, Oudinot, and Gerard, with the forces with which they had lately held the defensive upon the Seine; and the anxious question remained, whether he should venture an action with the grand army, to which he was still much inferior in numbers. Schwartzenberg drew up on the heights of Mesnil La Comtesse, prepared to receive battle. On consideration of the superior strength of the enemy, and of the absence of some troops not yet come up, Napoleon finally determined not to accept battle. He therefore commenced a retreat, the direction of which was doomed to prove the crisis of his fate.

CHAPTER LXXVI

Two courses remained; either to draw back within the closing circle which his enemies were about to form around him, and, retreating until he had collected his whole forces, make a stand under the walls of Paris, aided by whatever strength that capital possessed; or, on the contrary, to march eastward, and, breaking through the same circle, to operate on the rear of the allies. Before Lyons, Napoleon might reckon on being reinforced by the veteran army of Suchet, arrived from Catalonia; and he would be within reach of the numerous chain of fortresses which had garrisons strong enough to form an army.

The preparations for arranging such a force, and for arming the peasantry, had been in progress for some time. Trusty agents, bearing orders concealed in the sheaths of their knives, the collars of their dogs, or about their persons, had been detached to warn the various commandants of the Emperor's pleasure. Several were taken by the blockading troops of the allies, and hanged as spies, but others made their way. While at Rheims, Buonaparte had issued an order for rousing the peasantry, in which he not only declared their arising in arms was an act of patriotic duty, but denounced as traitors the mayors of the districts who should throw obstructions in the way of a general levy. The allies threatened military execution on all the peasantry who should obey Napoleon's call to arms.

But there were two especial considerations which must have made Napoleon hesitate in adopting this species of back-game. The one was the military question, whether Paris could be defended, if Napoleon was to move to the rear of the allied army. The other was of yet deeper import, and of a political nature. The means of the capital for defence being supposed adequate, was it likely that Paris, a town of 700,000 inhabitants, divided into factions unaccustomed to the near voice of war, would submit to the sacrifices which a successful defence must have required? Was, in short, their love and fear of Buonaparte so great, that without his personal presence and that of his army, to encourage and at the same time overawe them, they would willingly incur the risk of seeing their beautiful metropolis destroyed, and all the horrors of a sack inflicted by the mass of nations who proclaimed themselves the enemies, not of France, but of Buonaparte?

Neither of these questions could be answered with confidence. Napoleon, although he had embodied 30,000 national guards, had not provided arms for a third part of the number. This is hinted at by some as if the want of these arms ought to be imputed to some secret treason. But this accusation has never been put in any tangible shape. The arms never existed and never were ordered: Napoleon never thought of arming the Parisians in general. Perhaps he doubted their fidelity to his cause. He ordered, it is said, 200 cannon to be provided for the defence of the northern and eastern line of the city, but neither were these obtained in sufficient quantity. The number of individuals who could be safely entrusted with arms was also much limited. Whether, therefore, Paris was capable of defence or not, must have depended on the strength of the military force left to protect it. This Napoleon knew must be very moderate. His hopes were therefore necessarily limited by circumstances, to the belief that Paris, though incapable of a protracted defence, might yet hold out for such a space as might enable him to move to its relief.

It must be candidly admitted that this reasoning, being subsequent to the fact, has a much more decisive appearance than it could have had when subjected to the consideration of Napoleon. He was entitled, from the feverish anxiety hitherto shown by the Austrians, upon any approach to flank movements, and by the caution of their proceedings, to think, that they would be greatly too timorous to adopt the bold step of pressing to Paris. It was more likely that they would follow him to the frontier with the purpose of preserving their communications. Besides, Napoleon at this crisis had but a very slender choice of measures. To remain where he was was not possible; and, in advancing to either flank, he must have fought with a superior enemy. To retreat upon Paris was sure to induce the allies to pursue; and the encouragement which such a retreat must have given to his opponents might have had the most fatal consequences.

Buonaparte seems, as much from a sort of necessity as from choice, to have preferred breaking through the circle of hunters, trusting to strengthen his army with the garrisons drawn from the frontier fortresses, and, with the warlike peasantry of Alsace and Franche Comté, to advance with rapidity on the rear of his enemies, ere they had time to execute offensive operations. Napoleon could not disguise from himself what indeed he had told the French, that a *hourra* upon Paris was the principal purpose of the allies. Every movement made in advance, whether by Blücher or Schwartenberg, had this for its object. But they had uniformly relinquished the undertaking, upon his making any demonstration to prevent it; and therefore he did not suspect them of a resolution so venturous as to move upon Paris, leaving the French army unbroken in their rear. Napoleon had been so much accustomed to see his antagonists bend their attention rather to parry blows than to aim them, and was so confident in the dread impressed by his rapidity of movement, that he seems to have entertained little apprehension of the allies adopting a plan of operations which had no reference to his own. There were other considerations: the ground to the north of Paris is very strong; the national guard was numerous; the lower part of the population of a military character, and favourable to his cause. A defence, if resolute, however brief, would have the double effect of dampening the ardour of the assailants and of detaining them before the walls of the capital, until Buonaparte should advance to its relief. It was not to be supposed that the surrender of Paris would be the work of a single day. The unanimous voice of the journals, of the ministers of the police and of the thousands whose interest deeply entwisted with that of Buonaparte, assured their master on that point.

The movement to the rear, therefore, though removing him from Paris, might not seriously compromise the security of the capital. Though the Emperor's movement was out of the rules of ordinary war, and though it enabled the allies to execute the daring scheme which put an end to the campaign, yet it was by no means hopeless in its outset; or, we would rather say, was one of the few alternatives which the crisis of his affairs left to Buonaparte.

The allies, who had in their latest councils wound up their resolution to the decisive experiment of marching on Paris, were at first at a loss to account for Napoleon's disappearance, or to guess whither he had gone. This occasioned some hesitation and loss of time. At length, by the interception of a French courier, they found despatches addressed by Buonaparte to his government at Paris, from which they were enabled to conjecture the real purpose and direction of his march.

The allies continued to advance upon Paris. The military sovereigns and their victorious armies were now in sight of that metropolis, whose rules and his soldiers had so often and so long lorded it in theirs; of that Paris, which, unsatisfied with her high rank among the cities of Europe, had fomented constant war until all should be subjugated to her empire; of that proud city, who boasted herself the first in arms and in science, the mistress and example of the civilised world, the depository of all that is wonderful in the fine arts, and the dictatress as well of taste as of law to continental Europe.

Preparations were made by the government to remove beyond the Loire, or at least in that direction. Maria Louisa had none of the spirit of an Amazon, though graced with all the domestic virtues. She was also placed painfully in the course of a war betwixt her husband and father. Besides, she obeyed, and probably with no lack of will, Napoleon's injunctions to leave the capital, if danger should approach. She left Paris, therefore, with her son. Almost all the civil authorities of Buonaparte's government left the city at the same time, after destroying the private records of the high police, and carrying with them the crown jewels, and much of the public treasure.

The attack began along the whole north-north-eastern line on the morning of 30th March. After a brief but bloody fight, the allies secured control of all the heights save

Montmartre. Joseph Bonaparte, who had vowed to remain with the city's defenders, fled, though not before giving Marmont powers to negotiate a surrender.

Marshal Marmont despatched a flag of truce to General Barclay de Tolly, requesting a suspension of hostilities to arrange the terms on which Paris was to be surrendered. The armistice was granted, on condition that Montmartre, the only defensible part of the line which the French still continued to occupy, should be delivered up to the allies. The French regular troops were permitted to retire from Paris unmolested, and the metropolis was next day to be delivered up to the allied sovereigns, to whose generosity it was recommended.

Thus ended the assault of Paris, after a bloody action, in which the defenders lost upwards of 4000 in killed and wounded, and the allies, who had to storm well-defended batteries, redoubts, and entrenchments, perhaps about twice the number. They remained masters of the line at all points, and took nearly 100 pieces of cannon. When night fell, the multiplied and crowded watch-fires that occupied the whole chain of heights on which the victors now bivouacked, indicated to the astonished inhabitants of the French metropolis, how numerous and how powerful were the armies into whose hands the fate of war had surrendered them.

CHAPTER LXXVII

The royalists were in the highest state of activity, and prepared to use their utmost exertions to obtain the mastery of the public spirit. At this most critical moment all was done by Monsieur de Châteaubriand, which eloquence could effect, to appeal to the affections, perhaps even the prejudices of the people, in his celebrated pamphlet, entitled, *Buonaparte and the Bourbons*. This vigorous and affecting comparison between the days when France was in peace and honour under her own monarchs, contrasted with those in which Europe appeared in arms under her walls, had been written above a month, and the manuscript was concealed by Madame de Châteaubriand in her bosom. It was now privately printed. So was a proclamation by Monsieur, made in the name of his brother, the late King of France.

Finally, in a private assembly of the principal royalists, it was resolved to send a deputation to the allied sovereigns, to learn, if possible, their intention. Monsieur Douhet, the gentleman entrusted with this communication, returned into Paris with the answer that the allies had determined to avoid all appearance of dictating to France respecting any family or mode of government, and that although they would most joyfully and willingly acknowledge the Bourbons, yet it could only be in consequence of a public declaration in their favour. It belonged to the city of Paris to pronounce their opinion, and accelerate the peace of the world.

Nevertheless, the state of the capital continued very alarming, the lower classes exhibiting alternately the symptoms of panicked terror, of fury, and of despair. They demanded arms, of which a few were distributed to them; and there is no doubt, that had Napoleon arrived among them in the struggle, there would have been a dreadful battle, in which Paris, in all probability, would have shared the fate of Moscow. But when the cannonade ceased, when the flight of Joseph, and the capitulation of the city became publicly known, this conflict of jarring passions died away into silence, and the imperturbable and impassive composure of the national guard maintained the absolute tranquillity of the metropolis.

Chapter LXXVIII

When the enthusiasm attending the entrance of the allies began to subside, the perilous question occurred to those who found themselves suddenly embarked on a new revolution, where were Napoleon and his army, and what means did his active and enterprising genius possess of still re-establishing his affairs, and taking vengeance on his revolted capital?

On the 27th March, pushing a reconnoitring party as far west as Vitry, Napoleon learned the state of the case; that both allied armies had marched upon Paris; and that the cavalry with which he had skirmished were 10,000 men left behind as a curtain to screen their motions. Every word in this news had a sting in it. To hasten after the allies, to surprise them, if possible, ere the cannon on Montmartre were yet silenced, was the most urgent thought that ever actuated the mind even of Napoleon. But the direct route on Paris had been totally exhausted of provision, by the march and counter march of such large armies. It was necessary to go round by Troyes, and, for that purpose, to retrograde as far as Doulevent. At the bridge of Doulancourt, on the banks of the Aube, the Emperor received despatches, informing him that an assault on Paris was hourly to be expected. He advanced to Troyes, which he reached on that same night [29th March]. On the 30th, Napoleon left Troyes, threw himself into a post-carriage, and travelled at full speed with a very slight attendance. Having in this way reached Villeneuve L'Archevêque, he rode to Fontainebleau on horseback, and, though it was then night, took a carriage for Paris. On reaching an inn, called La Cour de France, at a few miles' distance from Paris, he at length met ample proof of his misfortune in the person of General Belliard, with his cavalry.

Leaping from his carriage, Napoleon turned back with Belliard, exclaiming – "What means this? Why here with your cavalry, Belliard? And where are the enemy?" – "At the gates of Paris." – "And the army?" – "It is following me." – "Where are my wife and son? – Where Marmont? – Where Mortier?" – "The Empress set out for Rambouillet, and thence for Orléans. The maréchals are busy completing their arrangements at Paris." He then gave an account of the battle; and Napoleon instantly ordered his carriage for Paris.

General Belliard reminded him there were no longer any troops in Paris. "It matters not," said Napoleon; "I will find the national guard there. The army will join me to-morrow, or the day after, and I will put things on a proper footing. Come, we must to Paris – nothing goes right when I am absent – they do nothing but make blunders."

Berthier and Caulaincourt tried to divert the Emperor from his purpose. They had advanced a mile further from the Cour de France, when they met a body of infantry under General Curial. Napoleon inquired after the Duke of Treviso, and was informed he was still at Paris.

It was then, that on the pressing remonstrances of his officers, that Napoleon at length turned back. He returned to the Cour de France, and gave orders for disposing the forces, as they should come up, on the heights of Longjumeau, behind the little river of Essonne. Desirous at the same time of renewing the negotiation for peace, which he had broken off at Châtillon, Napoleon despatched Caulaincourt to Paris, no longer to negotiate, but to submit to such terms as the allied sovereigns might be inclined to impose. He returned to Fontainebleau the same night.

CHAPTER LXXIX

While Napoleon breathed nothing save the desire of recovering by war what war had taken from him, or at least that of making such a peace as should leave him at the head of the French government, political events were taking place in Paris which pointed directly at the overthrow of his power.

His great military talents, together with his extreme inflexibility of temper, had firmly impressed the allied monarchs with the belief that no lasting peace could be made in Europe while he remained at the head of the French nation. Every concession which he had seemed willing to make was yielded with such extreme reluctance as to infer the strongest suspicion that they would all be again resumed should the league of the allies be dissolved, or their means of opposing his purposes become weaker.

When the Emperor of Russia halted, after the progress of the allied sovereigns through the city, it was at the hotel of Talleyrand. He was scarcely arrived there ere the principal Royalists waited on him to crave an audience. Three points were discussed: 1st, The possibility of a peace with Napoleon, upon sufficient guarantees; 2nd, The plan of a regency; 3rd, The restoration of the Bourbons.

The first proposition seemed inadmissible. The second was carefully considered. It was particularly urged that the French were indifferent to the cause of the Bourbons – that the allied monarchs would observe no mark of recollection of them exhibited by the people of France – and that the army seemed particularly averse to them. The united testimony of the French gentlemen present was offered to repel these doubts; and it was at length agreed that the third proposition – the restoration of the ancient family, and the ancient limits – should be the terms adopted for the settlement of France. A proclamation was immediately dispersed, by which the sovereigns made known their determination not to treat with Buonaparte or any of his family.

But more formal evidence, in the shape of legal procedure, was necessary to establish the desire of the French people to coincide in the proposed change. The searching genius of Talleyrand sought an organ of opinion where few would have looked for it – in the Conservative Senate, whose members had been so long the tools of Buonaparte's wildest projects – that very body, of which he himself said that they were more eager to yield up national rights than he had been to demand the surrender, and that a sign from him had always been an order for the Senate. Yet when, on the summons of Talleyrand, who knew well with whom he was dealing, this Senate was convoked, in a meeting attended by sixty-six of their number, forming a majority of the body, they at once, and without hesitation, named a Provisional Government, consisting of Talleyrand, Bournonville, Jaucourt, Dalberg, and the Abbé de Montesquiou; men recommended by talents and moderation, and whose names, known in the Revolution, might, at the same time, be a guarantee to those who dreaded a renovation of the old despotic government with the restoration of the ancient race of kings.

On the 2nd and 3rd of April the axe was laid to the roots. A decree of the Senate sent forth the following statement: 1st, That Napoleon, after governing for some time with prudence and wisdom, had violated the constitution by raising taxes in an arbitrary and lawless manner, contrary to the tenor of his oath; 2nd, That he had adjourned without necessity the Legislative Body, and suppressed a report of that assembly, besides disowning its right to represent the people; 3rd, That he had published several unconstitutional decrees, particularly those of 5th March last, by which he endeavoured to render national a war, in which his own ambition alone was interested; 4th, That he had violated the constitution by his decrees respecting state prisons; 5th, That he had abolished the responsibility of ministers, confounded together the different powers of the state, and destroyed the independence of judicial authorities; 6th, That the liberty of the press, constituting one of the rights of the nation, had been uniformly subjected to the arbitrary censure of his police; while, at the same time, he himself had made use of the same engine to fill the public ear with invented fictions, doctrines favourable to despotism, and insults upon foreign governments; 7th, That he had caused acts and reports, adopted by the Senate, to be altered by his own authority, before publication; 8th, That instead of reigning according to his oath for the honour, happiness, and glory of the French nation, he had put the finishing stroke to the distresses of the country, by a refusal to treat on honourable conditions – by the abuse which he had made of the means entrusted to him, in men and money – by abandoning the wounded, without dressing or sustenance – and by pursuing measures of which the consequences have been the ruin of towns, the depopulation of the country, famine and pestilence. From all these inductive causes, the Senate, considering that the Imperial government, established by the decree of 28th Floreal, in the year XII, had ceased to exist, and that the manifest desire of all Frenchmen was to obtain an order of things, of which the first result should be peace and concord among the great members of the European family: Therefore, the Senate declared and decreed, 1st, That Napoleon Buonaparte had forfeited the throne, and the right of inheritance established in his family; 2nd, That the people and army of France were disengaged and freed from the oath which they had taken to Napoleon and his constitution.

About eighty members of the Legislative Body, at the summons of the Provisional Government, assembled on the 3rd April, and formally adhered to the decree. The consequences of these bold measures showed either that Napoleon had, in reality, never had more than a slight hold on the affections of the people of France, or that the interest they took in his fortunes had been in a great degree destroyed by the immediate crisis. The decree was followed by declarations from all the public bodies in and around Paris that they adhered to the Provisional Government, and acquiesced in the decree of forfeiture. Numerous individuals who had been favoured and enriched by Buonaparte were among the first to join the tide when it set against him. But it had been always his policy to acquire adherents by addressing himself rather to men's interests; and many of his friends so gained, naturally became examples of the politic observation, "that if a prince places men in wealthy circumstances, the first thing they think of, in danger, is how to preserve the advantages they have obtained, without regard to his fate to whom they owe them."

In the night betwixt the 2nd and 3rd of April, Caulaincourt returned from his mission to Paris. He reported that the allies persisted in their determination to entertain no treaty with Buonaparte; but he was of opinion that a regency by the Empress, as the guardian of their son, might yet be granted. Austria, he stated, was favourable to such an arrangement, and Russia seemed not irreconcilably averse to it. But the abdication of Buonaparte was a preliminary condition. As this news circulated among the maréchals it fixed them in their resolution not to march against Paris, as, in their opinion, the war ought to be ended by this personal sacrifice on the part of Napoleon.

Buonaparte had not, probably, expected this separation between the duties of a soldier and of a citizen. With considerable reluctance, and after long debate, Napoleon assumed the pen, and acquiescing in the reasoning, wrote the following words, which we translate as literally as possible, as showing Napoleon's power of dignity of expression, when deep feeling predominated over his affectation of antithesis and Orientalism of composition:

The allied powers having proclaimed that the Emperor Napoleon is the sole obstacle to the re-establishment of peace in Europe, the Emperor Napoleon, faithful to his oath, declares that he is ready to descend from the throne, to quit France, and even to relinquish life, for the good of the country, which is inseparable from the rights of his son, from those of the Regency in the person of the Empress, and from the maintenance of the laws of the empire. Done at our Palace of Fontainebleau, 4th April, 1814.

Caulaincourt and Ney were appointed to be bearers of this document, and commissioners to negotiate with the allies concerning the terms of accommodation. Caulaincourt was the personal representative of Napoleon; and Ney, who had all along been zealous for the abdication, was a plenipotentiary proposed by the maréchals. Macdonald was suggested as the third plenipotentiary, to represent the army.

When the terms were being adjusted, the maréchals desired to know upon what stipulations they were to insist on Napoleon's behalf. "Upon none," – said Buonaparte. "Do what you can to obtain the best terms for France: for myself, I ask nothing." They were instructed particularly to obtain an armistice until the treaty should be adjusted. Through the whole scene Buonaparte conducted himself with firmness, but he gave way to a natural emotion when he had finally signed. He threw himself on a sofa, hid his face for a few minutes, and then looking up, with that smile of persuasion which he had so often found irresistible, implored his brethren of the field to annul the resolutions they had adopted, to destroy the papers, and follow him yet again to the contest. "Let us march," he said; "let us take the field once more! We are sure to beat them, and to have peace on our own terms." The maréchals were deeply affected, but could not give way. They renewed their arguments on the wretched state of the army – on the reluctance with which the soldiers would move against the Senate – on the certainty of a destructive civil war – and on the probability that Paris would be destroyed. He acquiesced, and permitted them to depart on their embassy.

Chapter LXXX

When the maréchals arrived in Paris, they found the popular tide had set strongly in favour of the Bourbons. The populace seemed as enthusiastic in their favour as they had been indifferent a few days before. All boded an unfavourable termination for their mission, so far as respected the proposed regency.

The names of the commissioners instantly obtained their introduction to Alexander, who received them with his natural courtesy. "On the general subject of their mission," he said, "he could not treat but in concert with his allies." But he enlarged on the subject of Napoleon personally. "He was my friend," he said, "I loved and honoured him. His ambition forced me into a dreadful war, in which my capital was burnt, and the greatest evils inflicted on my dominions. But he is unfortunate, and these wrongs are forgotten. Have you nothing to propose on his personal account? I will be his willing advocate." The maréchals replied that Napoleon had made no conditions for himself whatever. The Emperor would hardly believe this until they showed him their instructions, which entirely related to public affairs. The Emperor then asked if they would hear a proposal from him. They replied with suitable respect and gratitude. He then mentioned the plan that Buonaparte should retain the imperial title over a small territory, with an ample revenue, guards, and other emblems of dignity. "The place," continued the Emperor of Russia, "may be Elba, or some other island." With this annunciation the commissioners of Buonaparte were dismissed for the evening.

Maréchal Marmont had done all in his power to stop the military movement which he had undertaken to execute, thinking it better to move hand in hand with his brethren in a matter of such responsibility; but accident precipitated what he desired to delay. Napoleon summoned Count Souham, who commanded the division at Essonne in Marmont's absence. No reason was given for this command. Souham was therefore induced to suspect that Napoleon had gained intelligence of the Convention of Chevilly. Under this apprehension, he called the other generals who were in the secret to a council, in which it was determined to execute the convention instantly, by passing the troops within the lines of the allies, without awaiting any further orders from Marmont.

Meanwhile, the commissioners were admitted to a conference with the allied sovereigns and ministers, but which, it may be conjectured, was indulged to them more as a form, that the allies might treat with due respect the representatives of the French army, than with any purpose on the part of the sovereigns of altering the plan to which they had pledged themselves. However, the question, whether to adopt the projected regency, or the restoration of the Bourbons, was announced as a subject of consideration to the meeting. The maréchals pleaded the cause of the Regency. Ere the debate had terminated, news arrived of the march of Marmont's division to Versailles. The commissioners were astounded with this intelligence; and the Emperor took the opportunity to determine that the allies would not treat with Buonaparte save on the footing of unconditional abdication. With this answer, mitigated with the offer of an independent principality, the maréchals returned to Fontainebleau, while the Senate busied themselves to arrange the plan of a free constitution, under which the Bourbons were to be called to the throne.

Napoleon, in Fontainebleau, mused on the future with little hope of advantage from the mission of the maréchals. He judged that the sovereigns, if they listened to the proposal of a regency, would exact the most formidable guarantees against his own interference; and that under his wife, Maria Louisa, who had no talent for public business, France would probably be managed by an Austrian committee.

When the maréchals returned, he listened to the news of the failure of their negotiation, as a termination which he had expected. But to their surprise, recollecting his disinterested behaviour, he almost instantly demanded what provision had been made for him? They informed him that it was proposed he should reside as an independent sovereign, "in Elba, or somewhere else." Napoleon paused for a moment. "Somewhere else!" he exclaimed. "That must be Corsica. No, no. I will have nothing to do with Corsica. Who knows any thing of Elba? Seek out some officer who is acquainted with Elba. Look out what books or charts can inform us about Elba." In a moment he was as deeply interested in this islet, as if he had never been Emperor of France, nay, almost of the world. But Buonaparte's nature was egotistical. He well knew how little it would become an Emperor resigning his crown, to be stipulating for his future course of life; and had reason to conclude, that by playing his part with magnanimity he might best excite a corresponding liberality. But when the die was cast, when his fate seemed fixed, he examined with minuteness what he must consider as his sole fortune. To turn his thoughts from France to Elba was like the elephant, which can transport artillery, applying his trunk to gather pins. But Napoleon could do both easily, because he regarded these two objects not as they differed from each other, but as they belonged, or did not belong, to himself.

Buonaparte was to be recognised as one of the crowned heads of Europe – was to be allowed body-guards, and a navy on a scale suitable; and, to maintain this state, a revenue of six million francs, over and above the revenues of the isle of Elba, were settled on him. Two million and a half were also assigned in pensions to his brothers, Josephine, and the other members of his family – a revenue more splendid than even the King of England had at his personal disposal. It was well argued that if Buonaparte deserved such advantageous terms, it was injustice to dethrone him. In other points the terms of this treaty seemed as irreconcilable with sound policy as they are with all former precedents. The name, dignity, military authority, and absolute power of an Emperor, conferred on the potentate of such Lilliputian domains, were ludicrous, if it was supposed that Napoleon would remain quiet in his retreat, and hazardous if he should seek the means of again agitating Europe.

Napoleon belonged to the Roman school of philosophy; and it is confidently reported, though it has not been universally believed, that he designed to escape from life by an act of suicide. The Emperor had carried with him, ever since the retreat from Moscow, a packet containing a preparation of opium, made up in the same manner with that used by Condorcet for self-destruction. His valet-de-chambre, in the night betwixt the 12th and 13th of April, heard him arise and pour something into a glass of water, drink, and return to bed. In a short time, the man's attention was called by sobs and stifled groans – an alarm took place in the chateau – some of the principal persons were roused, and repaired to Napoleon's chamber. Yvan, the surgeon, who had procured him the poison, was also summoned; but hearing the Emperor complain that the operation of the potion was not quick enough, he was seized with a panic terror, and fled from the palace at full gallop. Napoleon took the remedies recommended, and a long fit of stupor ensued, with profuse perspiration. He awakened much exhausted, and surprised at finding himself still alive; he said aloud, after a few moments reflection, "Fate will not have it so," and afterwards appeared reconciled to his destiny.

There is, as we have already hinted, a difference of opinion concerning the cause of Napoleon's illness, some imputing it to indigestion. The fact of his having been very much indisposed is, however, indisputable. After this crisis, and having ratified the treaty, Napoleon appeared more at his ease than he had been for some time, and conversed frankly with his attendants upon the affairs of France.

He owned that, after all, the government of the Bourbons would best suit France, as tending to reconcile all parties. "Louis," he said, "has talents and means; he is old and infirm; he will not, I think, choose to give his name to a bad reign. If he is wise, he will occupy my bed, and content himself with changing the sheets. But," he continued, "he must treat the army well, and take care not to look back on the past, otherwise his reign will be of brief endurance." He also mentioned the inviolability of the sale of the national domains, as the woof upon which the whole web depended; cut one thread of it, and the whole will be unravelled. Of the ancient noblesse and people of fashion, he spoke in embittered language, saying they were an English colony in the midst of France, who desired only their own privileges, and would act as readily for as against him.

After these remarkable observations, Napoleon looked round upon his officers, and made them the following exhortation: "Gentlemen, when I remain no longer with you, and when you have another government, it will become you to attach yourselves to it frankly, and serve it as faithfully as you have served me. I request, and even command you to do this; therefore, all who desire leave to go to Paris have my permission, and those who remain here will do well to send in their adhesion to the government of the Bourbons."

Napoleon having now resigned himself entirely to his fate, prepared, on the 20th April, to depart. But first he had the painful task of bidding farewell to the body in the universe most attached to him, and to which he was probably most attached – his celebrated Imperial Guard. Such of them as could be collected were drawn out before him in review. Some natural tears dropped from his eyes, and his features had the marks of strong emotion, while reviewing for the last time, as he must then have thought likely, the companions of so many victories. He advanced to them on horseback, dismounted, and took solemn leave. "All Europe," he said, "had armed against him; France herself had deserted him, and chosen another dynasty. He might," he said, "have maintained with his soldiers a civil war of years, but it would have rendered France unhappy. Be faithful," he continued (and the words were remarkable,) "to the new sovereign whom France has chosen. Do not lament my fate; I will always be happy while I know you are so. I could have died – nothing was easier – but I will always follow the road of honour. I will record with my pen the deeds we have done together. I cannot embrace you all, but I embrace your general," (he pressed the general to his bosom.) "Bring hither the eagle," (he embraced the standard, and concluded,) "Beloved eagle, may the kisses I bestow on you long resound in the hearts of the brave! – Adieu, my children – Adieu, my brave companions – Surround me once more – Adieu." Drowned in grief, the veteran soldiers heard the farewell of their dethroned leader; sighs and murmurs broke from their ranks. They appeared resigned to the loss of their general, and to yield, like him, to necessity.

CHAPTER LXXXI

Upon his unpleasant journey, Napoleon was attended by Bertrand and Drouet. Four delegates from the allied powers accompanied him. Napoleon seemed to resent the presence of the representative of Prussia, a country which had been at one time the subject of his scorn, and always of his hatred. It galled him that she should assume an immediate share in deciding upon his fate. He received the English commissioner with particular expressions of esteem, saying he desired to pass to Elba in an English vessel, and was pleased to have the escort of an English officer. "Your nation," he said, "has an elevated character, for which I have the highest esteem. I desired to raise the French people to such a pitch of sentiment, but..." He stopped, and seemed affected.

At Montélimar, the exiled Emperor heard the last expressions of regard and sympathy. He was now approaching Provence, a region of which he had never possessed the affections, and was greeted with execrations and cries of "Perish the Tyrant!" – "Down with the butcher of our children!" At Orgon, the mob brought before him his own effigy dabbled with blood, and stopped his carriage till they displayed it before his eyes; and, in short, from Avignon to La Calade, he was grossly insulted in every town and village, and, but for the anxious interference of the commissioners, would probably have been torn to pieces. The unkindness of the people seemed to make much impression on him. He even shed tears. He showed, also, more fear of assassination than seemed consistent with his approved courage; but it must be recollected that the danger was of a new and peculiarly horrible description, and calculated to appal many to whom the terrors of a field of battle were familiar.

At length he arrived at Fréjus. He shut himself up in a solitary apartment, which he traversed with impatient steps, sometimes pausing to watch from the window the arrival of the vessels, one of which was to transport him from France, as it then seemed, forever. It was eleven at night on the 28th ere he embarked, under a salute of 21 guns. "Adieu, Caesar, and his fortune," said the Russian envoy. The Austrian and British commissioners accompanied him on his voyage.

Upon the 4th of May, when they arrived within sight of Porto Ferrajo, the principal town of Elba, they found the island in some confusion. The inhabitants had been recently in a state of insurrection against the French, which had been quieted by the governor and the troops giving in their adhesion to the Bourbon government. This state of things naturally increased Napoleon's apprehensions which had never entirely subsided since the dangers he underwent in Provence. Even on board the Undaunted, he had requested that a sergeant of marines might sleep each night on the outside of his cabin-door, a trusty domestic also mounting guard within. He now showed some unwillingness, when they made the island, to the ship running right under the batteries; and when he first landed in the morning, it was at an early hour, and in disguise, having obtained from Captain Usher, a party of marines to attend him.

Having returned on board to breakfast, after his incognito visit, the Emperor of Elba went on shore in form, about two o'clock, with the commissioners, receiving, at leaving the Undaunted, a royal salute. On the beach, he was received by the governor, prefect, and other official persons, with such means of honour as they possessed, who conducted him to the Hôtel-de-Ville in procession, preceded by a wretched band of fiddlers. The people welcomed him with many shouts. The name of Buonaparte had been unpopular among them as Emperor of France, but they anticipated considerable advantages from his residing among them as their own particular sovereign.

*C*HAPTER LXXXII

Elba, to the limits of which the mighty empire of Napoleon was now contracted, is about sixty miles in circumference. The air is healthy, excepting in the neighbourhood of the salt marshes. The country is mountainous, and, having all the florid vegetation of Italy, is, in general, of a romantic character. It produces little grain, but exports a considerable quantity of wines; and its iron ore has been famous since the days of Virgil, who describes Elba as, "Insula inexhaustis chalybum generosa metallis."[21]

The island boasts two good harbours, and is liberally productive of olives, fruits and maize. Perhaps, if an empire could be supposed to exist within such a brief space, Elba possesses so much both of beauty and variety, as might constitute the scene of a summer night's dream of sovereignty. Buonaparte seemed to lend himself to the illusion, as, accompanied by Sir Niel Campbell, he rode in his usual exploring mood around the shores of his little state. He did not fail to visit the iron mines, and, being informed the annual produce was 500,000 francs, "These, then," he said, "are mine." But being reminded that he had conferred that revenue on the Legion of Honour, he exclaimed, "Where was my head when I gave such a grant! But I have made many foolish decrees of that sort."

One or two of the poorer class of inhabitants, knelt, and even prostrated themselves when they met him. He seemed disgusted, and imputed this humiliating degree of abasement to the wretchedness of their education, under the auspices of the monks. On these excursions he showed the same apprehension of assassination which had marked his journey to Fréjus. Two couriers, well armed, rode before him, and examined every suspicious spot. But as he climbed a mountain above Ferrajo, and saw the ocean approach its feet in almost every direction, the expression broke from him, accompanied with a good-humoured smile, "It must be confessed my isle is very little." He professed, however, to be perfectly resigned to his fate; often spoke of himself as a man politically dead, and claimed credit for what he said upon public affairs, as having no remaining interest in them. His professed intentions were to devote himself exclusively to science and literature. At other times, he said he would live in his little island, like a justice of peace in a country town in England.

Napoleon, however, was little known to himself, if he seriously thought that his restless and powerful mind could be satisfied with the investigation of abstract truths, or amused by the leisure of literary research. The character of Buonaparte was singularly opposed to seclusion. His propensities continued to be exactly of the same description at Elba, which had so long terrified Europe. To change the external face of what was around him; to imagine extensive alterations, without accurately considering the means by which they were to be accomplished; to apply to Elba the system of policy which he had exercised so long in Europe, was the only mode in which he seems to have found amusement and exercise for the impatient energies of a temper, accustomed from his early youth to work upon others, but apt to become lethargic, sullen, and discontented, when it was compelled, for want of other exercise, to recoil upon itself.

In the course of two or three days' travelling with the same rapidity which characterised his movements in his frequent progresses through France, and showing the same impatience of rest or delay, Napoleon had visited every spot in his little island: mines, woods, salt-marshes, harbours, fortifications, and whatever was worthy of an instant's consideration, and had meditated improvements and innovations respecting everyone of them.

One of his first, and perhaps most characteristic proposals, was to aggrandise and extend his Liliputian dominions by occupation of an uninhabited island, called Rianosa, which had been left desolate on account of the frequent descents of the corsairs. He sent thirty of his guards, with ten of the independent company belonging to the island, upon this expedition (what a contrast to those which he had formerly directed!) sketched out a plan for fortifications, and remarked, with complacency, "Europe will say that I have already made a conquest."

In an incredibly short time Napoleon had planned several roads, had contrived means to convey water from the mountains to Porto Ferrajo, designed two palaces, one for the country, the other in the city, a separate mansion for his sister Pauline, stables for 150 horses, a lazaretto, buildings for accommodation of the tunny fishery, and salt-works on a new construction. The Emperor of Elba proposed, also, purchasing various domains, and had the price estimated; for the inclination of the proprietor was not reckoned essential to the transaction. He ended by establishing four places of residence in the different quarters of the island; and his amusement consisted in constant change and alteration. He travelled from one to another with the restlessness of a bird in a cage. It seemed as if the magnitude of the object was not so much the subject of his consideration, providing it afforded immediate scope for employing his constant desire of activity. He was like the thoroughbred gamester, who, deprived of the means of depositing large stakes, will rather play at small game than leave the table.

Napoleon placed his court also upon an ambitious scale, having more reference to what he had been, than to what he now had been reduced to, while, at the same time, the furniture and internal accommodations of the imperial palace were meaner by far than those of an English gentleman of ordinary rank. The interior of Napoleon's household, though reduced to thirty-five persons, still held the titles, and affected the rank, proper to an imperial court, of which it will be presently seen the petty sovereign made a political use. He displayed a national flag, having a red bend dexter in a white field, the bend bearing three bees. To dignify his capital, having discovered that the ancient name of Porto Ferrajo, was Comopoli, he commanded it to be called Cosmopoli, or the city of all nations.

About the middle of summer, Napoleon was visited by his mother, and his sister Princess Pauline. At this time he seems to have expected to be rejoined by his wife, who, it was said, was coming to take possession of her Italian dominions. Their separation was the only subject on which he appeared to lose temper. He said that interdicting intercourse with his wife and son excited universal reprobation at Vienna – that no such instance of inhumanity and injustice could be pointed out in modern times – that the Empress was a detained prisoner, an orderly officer constantly attending upon her – finally, that she had been given to understand that she was to obtain permission to join, though it was now denied her. The Austrian commissioner insisted that the separation took place by Maria Louisa's consent, and even at her request; and hinted that Napoleon's desire to have her society was dictated by other feelings than affection.

We have not thought it necessary to disturb the narrative by noticing details which belong rather to romance; but as we are now treating of Napoleon in his more private character, a mysterious circumstance may be mentioned. About the end of August 1814, a lady arrived from Leghorn, with a boy about five or six years old. She was received by Napoleon with great attention, but at the same time with an air of much secrecy, and was lodged in a villa in the most remote corner of the island; after remaining two days, she re-embarked for Naples. The Elbese naturally concluded that this must have been the Empress Maria Louisa and her son. But the individual was known by those near Napoleon's person to be a Polish lady from Warsaw, and the boy was the offspring of an intrigue betwixt her and Napoleon. The cause of her speedy departure might be delicacy towards Maria Louisa, and the fear of affording the Court of Vienna a pretext for continuing the separation.

As winter approached, a change was discernible in Napoleon's manners and habits. The alterations he had planned no longer gave him the same interest; he renounced, from time to time, the severe exercise in which he had at first indulged, used a carriage rather than his horse, and sunk occasionally into fits of deep contemplation, mingled with gloomy anxiety.

He became, also, subjected to uneasiness, to which he had hitherto been a stranger, being that arising from pecuniary inconveniences. He had plunged into expenses with imprudent eagerness. The ready money which he brought from France seems to have been soon exhausted, and to raise supplies, he commanded the inhabitants of his island to pay up, in the month of June, the contributions of the last year. This produced petitions, personal solicitations, and discontent. It was represented to him that so poor were the inhabitants, in consequence of want of sale for their wine for months past, that they would be driven to the most extreme straits if the requisition should be persisted in. In some of the villages, the tax-gatherers were resisted and insulted. Napoleon, on his side, sent part of his troops to quarter upon the insurgent peasantry, and to be supported by them, till the contributions should be paid up.

Thus we recognise, in his government of this miniature state, the same wisdom, and the same errors, by which Buonaparte won and lost the empire of the world. The plans of improvements and internal ameliorations which he forced were probably very good in themselves, but he proceeded to the execution of that which he had resolved with too much and too reckless precipitation; too much of a determination to work his own pleasure, and too little concern for the feelings of others.

The situation of Sir Niel Campbell was now very embarrassing. Napoleon, affecting to be more tenacious than ever of his dignity, not only excluded the British envoy from his own presence, but even threw obstacles in the way of his visiting his mother and sister. It was, therefore, only from interviews with Napoleon himself that he could hope to get any information, and to obtain these Sir Niel was obliged to absent himself from the island of Elba, which gave him an opportunity of desiring an audience, as he went away and returned. Symptoms of some approaching catastrophe could not, however, be concealed from the British resident. Napoleon had interviews with his mother, after which she appeared deeply distressed. She was heard also to talk of three deputations which he had received from France. It was besides accounted a circumstance of strong suspicion, that discharges and furloughs were granted to 200 or 300 of Napoleon's Old Guard, by whom, as was too late discovered, the allegiance of the military in France was corrupted, and their minds prepared for what was to ensue.

At length, the French consul at Leghorn, and the Tuscan governor of that town, informed Sir Niel Campbell that it was certainly determined at Elba that Buonaparte, with his guards, should embark for the continent. It was naturally concluded that Italy was the object of Napoleon, to join with his brother-in-law Murat, who was at that time, fatally for himself, raising his banner. The British envoy set sail in pursuit of the adventurer. But it was too late; the Partridge only obtained a distant sight of the flotilla, after Buonaparte and his forces had landed.

CHAPTERS LXXXIII, LXXXIV

As Napoleon made good his flight, Scott addresses the many weaknesses, notwithstanding the King's personal qualities, of the Bourbon restoration: the stigma – despite politic allied lenity – of having been reinstated in the wake of defeat; the absence, beyond the aristocracy, of any basis of support; the army's deep antipathy, exacerbated by peacetime cuts. Scott notes that Jacobinism and Bonapartism were equally devoid of mass support – the nation as a whole favoured moderation – but both parties were adept at exploiting Royalism's maladroitness.

In the absence of any credible alternative to Louis XVIII other than Napoleon, and despite their mutual dislike, the Jacobins, notably Fouché and Carnot, coalesced with the Bonapartists, intriguing and spreading disaffection, particularly in the army.

It was on 26th February that Napoleon embarked upon one of the most extraordinary and adventurous expeditions ever attempted. The force, with which he was once more to change the fortunes of France, amounted to about 1000 men. To keep the undertaking secret, his sister Pauline gave a ball on the night of his departure, and the officers were unexpectedly summoned, after leaving the entertainment, to go on board the little squadron.

In his passage Napoleon encountered two great risks. The first was from meeting a royal French frigate, who hailed the Inconstant. The guards were ordered to put off their caps, and go down below, or lie upon the deck, while the captain of the Inconstant exchanged some civilities with the commander of the frigate, with whom he chanced to be acquainted; and being well known in these seas, was permitted to pass. The second danger was caused by the pursuit of Sir Niel Campbell, who could but obtain a distant view of the vessels as they landed their passengers. This was on the 1st March, when Napoleon, causing his followers once more to assume the three-coloured cockade, disembarked at Cannes, a small seaport in the gulf of Saint Juan. A small party of his guard presented themselves before Antibes, but were made prisoners by General Corsin, the governor of the place.

Undismayed by a circumstance so unfavourable, Napoleon instantly began his march at the head of scarce 1000 men, towards the centre of a kingdom from which he had been expelled with execration. For some time the inhabitant gazed on them with doubtful and astonished eyes, as if uncertain whether to assist them, or to oppose them. A few peasants cried *Vive l'Empereur!* but the adventurers received neither countenance nor opposition from those of the higher ranks. As Napoleon approached Dauphiné, called the cradle of the Revolution, the peasants greeted him with more general welcome, but still no proprietors appeared, no clergy, no public functionaries. But they were now near to those by whom the success or ruin of the expedition must be decided. As Napoleon approached Grenoble, he came into contact with the outposts of the garrison, who drew out, but seemed irresolute. Buonaparte halted his own little party, and advanced almost alone, exposing his breast, as he exclaimed, "He who will kill his Emperor, let him now work his pleasure." The appeal was irresistible – the soldiers threw down their arm, crowded round the general who had so often led them to victory, and shouted *Vive l'Empereur!*

When news of Napoleon's arrival reached Paris, it excited surprise rather than alarm; but when he was found to traverse the country without opposition, some strange and combined treason began to be apprehended. Monsieur, with the Duke of Orléans, set out for Lyons, and the Duke d'Angoulême repaired to Nismes. The Legislative Bodies, and most of the better classes, declared for the royal cause. The residents of the various powers hastened to assure Louis of the support of their sovereigns. Corps of volunteers were raised both among the Royalists and the Constitutional or moderate party. The most animating proclamations called the people to arms.

Notwithstanding these demonstrations of zeal, the public mind had been much influenced by the causes of discontent which had been so artfully enlarged upon for months past. The decided Royalists were few, the Constitutionalists lukewarm. It became every moment more likely that not the voice of the people, but the sword of the army, must determine the controversy. A camp was established at Melun – troops were assembled there – and as much care as possible was used in selecting troops to whom the royal cause was to be entrusted.

The progress of Buonaparte, in the meantime, was uninterrupted. It was in vain that, at Lyons, Monsieur and the Duke of Orléans, with the assistance of Maréchal Macdonald, endeavoured to retain the troops in their duty, and the inhabitants in their allegiance. The latter, chiefly manufacturers, afraid of being undersold by those of England, shouted openly, *"Vive l'Empereur!"* The troops of the line remained silent and gloomy. "How will your soldiers behave?" said Monsieur to the colonel of the 13th Dragoons. The colonel referred him to the men themselves. They answered candidly, that they would fight for Napoleon alone. Monsieur dismounted, and addressed the soldiers individually. To one veteran, covered with scars, and decorated with medals, the prince said, "A brave soldier like you, at least, will cry, *"Vive le Roi!"* – "You deceive yourself," answered the soldier. "No one here will fight against his father – I will cry, *Vive Napoleon!"* The efforts of Macdonald were equally vain. He endeavoured to move two battalions to oppose the entry of Buonaparte's advanced guard. So soon as the troops came in presence of each other, they broke their ranks, and mingled together in the general cry of *Vive l'Empereur!* Monsieur was obliged to escape from Lyons, almost alone.

Buonaparte, now master of the ancient capital of the Gauls, and at the head of 7000 men, was acknowledged by Mâcon, Châlons, Dijon, and almost all Burgundy. Marseilles, and all Provence, declared against the invader, and the former city set a price upon his head.

Napoleon found it necessary to halt at Lyons for the refreshment of his forces; and, being joined by some civilians, he needed time also to organise his government. Hitherto, the addresses which he had published had been of a military character, abounding with the Oriental imagery which Buonaparte regarded as essential to eloquence, promising that victory should move at the charging step, and that the eagle should fly with the national colours from steeple to steeple, till she perched on the towers of Notre Dame. The present decrees were of a different character. Cambacérès was named minister of justice; Fouché that of police (a boon to the revolutionists;) Davoust was made minister of war. Decrees upon decrees issued forth, with a rapidity which showed how Buonaparte had employed those studious hours at Elba, which he was supposed to have dedicated to the composition of his Memoirs. The first of these abrogated all changes in the courts of justice and tribunals which had taken place during the absence of Napoleon. The second displaced all officers belonging to the class of emigrants, and introduced into the army by the King. The third suppressed the order of St. Louis, the white flag and cockade, and other royal emblems, and restored the three-coloured banner and the imperial symbols of Buonaparte's authority. The same decree abolished the Swiss Guard, and the household troops of the King. The 4th sequestered the effects of the Bourbons. A similar ordinance sequestered the restored property of emigrant families, and was so artfully worded as to represent great changes of property having taken place in this manner. The 5th decree suppressed the ancient nobility and feudal titles, and formally confirmed proprietors of national domains in their possessions. The 6th declared sentence of banishment against all emigrants not erased from the list previous to the accession of the Bourbons, to which was added confiscation of their property. The 7th restored the Legion of Honour, uniting to its funds the confiscated revenues of the order of St. Louis. The 8th and last decree was the most important of all. Under pretence that emigrants who had borne arms against France, had been introduced into the body of the Peers, and that the Chamber of Deputies had already sat for the legal time, it dissolved both Chambers, and convoked the Electoral Colleges of the empire, in order that they might hold, in the ensuing month of May, an extraordinary assembly of the *Champ-de-Mai*. This convocation, for which the inventor found a name in the history of the ancient Franks, was to have two objects: *First*, to make such alterations and reformations in the constitution of the empire as circumstances should render advisable; *secondly*, to assist at the coronation of the Empress and of the King of Rome.

We cannot pause to criticise these various enactments. In general, however, it may be remarked, that they were admirably calculated to serve Napoleon. They flattered the army, and at the same time heated their resentment against the emigrants, by insinuating that they had been sacrificed by Louis to the interest of these his followers. They held out to the Republicans a speedy prospect of confiscations, proscriptions, and revolutions of government; while the Imperialists were gratified with a view of ample funds for pensions, offices, and honorary decorations. To the proprietors of national domains was promised security; to the Parisians, the spectacle of the *Champ-de-Mai;* and to France, peace and tranquillity, since the arrival of the Empress and her son, so confidently asserted, must be considered as a pledge of the friendship of Austria. Russia was also said to be friendly to Napoleon. England, it was averred, befriended him, else how could he have escaped from an isle surrounded by her naval force? Prussia, therefore, alone, might be hostile and unappeased; but, unsupported, Prussia must remain passive, or would soon be reduced to reason. The very pleasure in mortifying one, at least, of the late victors of Paris, gave a zest and poignancy to the revolution, which the concurrence of the other great states would render easy and peaceful. Such news was carefully disseminated by Napoleon's adherents. They preceded his march, and prepared the minds of men to receive him as their destined master.

On the 13th, Buonaparte recommenced his journey. He travelled several hours in advance of his army, often without any guard, or, at most, attended only by a few Polish lancers. The country through which he journeyed was favourable to his pretensions. It had been severely treated by the allies during the last campaign, and the dislike of the suffering inhabitants extended itself to the family who had mounted the throne by the influence of these strangers. When, therefore, they saw the late

Emperor among them, without guards, inquiring, with his usual appearance of active interest, into the extent of their losses, and making liberal promises to repair them, it is no wonder that they should rather remember the battles he had fought on their behalf against the foreigners, than think on the probability that his presence might be the precursor of a second invasion.

Maréchal Ney was called to take command of an army destined to attack Napoleon in the flank and rear as he marched towards Paris, while the forces at Melun opposed him in front. He had an audience with the King on the 9th of March, when he accepted his appointment with expressions of the most devoted faith to the King, and declared his resolution to bring Buonaparte to Paris like a wild beast in an iron cage. The maréchal went to Besançon, where, on the 11th of March, he learned that Buonaparte was in possession of Lyons. But he continued to make preparations for resistance, and collected all the troops he could from the adjoining garrisons. To those who objected to the bad disposition of the soldiers, and remarked that he would have difficulty inducing them to fight, Ney answered determinedly, "They *shall* fight; I will take a musket from a grenadier and begin the action myself; I will run my sword to the hilt in the first who hesitates to follow my example." To the minister at war he wrote that all were dazzled by the activity and rapid progress of the invader; that Napoleon was favoured by the common people and the soldiers; but that the officers and civil authorities were loyal, and he still hoped "to see a fortunate close of this mad enterprise."

In these dispositions, Ney advanced to Lons le Saunier. Here, on the night betwixt the 13th and 14th March, he received a letter from Napoleon, summoning him to join his standard, as "bravest of the brave," a name which could not but awake a thousand remembrances. He had already sounded both his officers and soldiers, and discovered their unalterable determination to join Buonaparte. He therefore had it only in his choice to retain his command by passing over to the Emperor, or else to return to the King without executing any thing which might seem even an effort at realising his boast.

Maréchal Ney was a man of mean birth, who, by the most desperate valour, had risen to the highest ranks in the army. His early education had not endowed him with a delicate sense of honour or a high feeling of principle, and he had not learned either as he advanced in life. He appears to have been a weak man, with more vanity than pride, and who, therefore, was likely to feel the loss of power more than the loss of character. He accordingly resolved upon adhering to Napoleon. Sensible of the incongruity of changing his side so suddenly, he affected to be a deliberate knave, rather than content himself with being viewed in his real character, of a volatile, light-principled, and inconsiderate fool. He pretended that the expedition of Napoleon had been long arranged between himself and the other maréchals. But we are willing rather to suppose that this was a matter of mere invention, than to think that the protestations poured out at the Tuileries, only five days before, were, on the part of this unfortunate man, the effusions of premeditated treachery.

The maréchal now published an order of the day, declaring that the cause of the Bourbons was lost forever. It was received by the soldiers with rapture, and Buonaparte's standard and colours were instantly displayed. Many of the officers, however, remonstrated, and left their commands. Ney was received by Napoleon with open arms. His defection did incalculable damage to the King's cause, tending to show that the spirit of treason which possessed the common soldiers had ascended to and affected the officers of the highest rank in the army.

The King, notwithstanding these unpromising circumstances, used every exertion to induce his subjects to continue in their allegiance. He attended in person the sitting of the Chamber of Deputies, and was received with such enthusiastic marks of applause, that one would have thought the most active exertions must have followed. Louis next reviewed the national guards, about 25,000 men, who made a similar display of loyalty. He also inspected the troops of the line, 6000 in number, but his reception was equivocal. They placed their caps on their bayonets in token of respect, but they raised no shout. As a last resource, Louis convoked a general council at the Tuileries on the 18th March. The generals present declared there could be no effectual opposition to Buonaparte. The royalist nobles contradicted them, and, after some expressions of violence had been uttered, Louis was obliged to break up the meeting, and prepare to abandon a capital, which the prevalence of his enemies and the disunion of his friends left him no longer any chance of defending.

Meantime, the two armies approached each other at Melun; that of the

King was commanded by Macdonald. On the 20th, his troops were drawn up in three lines to receive the invaders, who were said to be advancing from Fontainebleau. There was a long pause of suspense, of a nature which seldom fails to render men more accessible to strong and sudden emotion. The glades of the forest, and the acclivity which ascends to it, were full in view of the royal army, but presented the appearance of a deep solitude. All was silence, except when the regimental bands of music, at the command of the officers, who remained generally faithful, played the airs of *Vive Henri Quatre – O, Richard – La Belle Gabrielle,* and other tunes connected with the Bourbons. The sounds excited no corresponding sentiments among the soldiers. At length, about noon, the galloping of horses was heard. An open carriage appeared, surrounded by a few hussars, and drawn by four horses. It came on at full speed; and Napoleon, jumping from the vehicle, was in the midst of the ranks which had been formed to oppose him. His escort threw themselves from their horses, mingled with their ancient comrades, and the effect of their exhortations was instantaneous on men, whose minds were already half made up. There was a general shout of *Vive Napoleon! –* The last army of the Bourbons passed from their side, and no further obstruction existed betwixt Napoleon and the capital, which he was once more – but for a brief space – to inhabit as a sovereign.

The King departed from Paris at one in the morning of the 20th March. Even at that untimely hour, the palace was surrounded by the national guards, and many citizens, who wept and entreated him to remain, offering to spend the last drop of their blood for him. But Louis wisely declined accepting of sacrifices, which could now have availed nothing. Escorted by his household troops, he departed to Ostend, and from thence to Ghent.

It was late in the evening ere Napoleon arrived in the open carriage he had used since his landing. There was a singular contrast betwixt his entry and the departure of the King. The latter was accompanied by the sobs, tears, and kind wishes of those citizens who desired peace and tranquillity, by the wailing of the defenceless, and the anxious fears of the wise and prudent. The former entered amid the shouts of armed columns, who, existing by war and desolation, welcomed with military acclamations the chief who was to restore them to their element. The inhabitants of the suburbs cheered in expectation of employment and gratuities, or by instigation of their ringleaders, who were chiefly under the management of the police, and well prepared. But among the immense crowds of citizens who turned out, few or none joined in the gratulation. The soldiers of the guard resented their silence, commanded the spectators to shout, struck with the flat of their swords, and pointed their pistols at the multitude, but could not extort the expected cry of Liberty and Napoleon, though making it plain by their demeanour that the last, if not the first, was returned. In the court of the Carousel, and before the Tuileries, all the adherents of the old government, and those who, having deserted Napoleon, were eager to expiate their fault, by now being first to acknowledge him, were assembled. They crowded around him so closely, that he was compelled to exclaim – "My friends, you stifle me!" and his adjutants were obliged to support him in their arms into the royal apartments, where he received the all-hail of the principal devisers and abettors of this singular undertaking.

CHAPTERS LXXXV, LXXXVI

Napoleon and France, with the possible exception of the army, hoped for peace. The Emperor even promised to abide by the Treaty of Paris. Assembled at the Congress of Vienna, however, the allied powers immediately declared Napoleon an outlaw, determined on war, and reaffirmed their unity of purpose with a new treaty.

For a little time after Buonaparte's return, crowds of the lowest order assembled under the windows of the Tuileries, and demanded to see the Emperor, whom, on his appearance, they greeted with shouts, as *le Grand Entrepreneur,* or general employer of the class of artisans, in language where the coarse phraseology of their rank was adorned with such flowers of rhetoric as the times of terror had coined. Latterly, the numbers of this assembly were maintained by a distribution of a few sous to the shouters. However disgusted with these degrading exhibitions, Buonaparte felt he could not dispense with this species of force, and was compelled to institute a day of procession, and a solemn festival, in favour of this description of persons, who were termed Federates.

On 14th May, the motley ranks which assembled, exhibited, in the eyes of disgusted and frightened spectators, all that is degraded by habitual vice and hardened by stupidity and profligacy. The portentous procession moved on along the Boulevards to the Tuileries, with shouts, in which the praises of the Emperor were mingled with imprecations, and with the Revolutionary songs – the Marseilloise, the Carmagnole, and the Day of Departure. The appearance of the men, the refuse of manufactories, of work-houses, of jails; their rags, their filth, their drunkenness; their ecstasies of blasphemous rage, and no less blasphemous joy, stamped them with the character of the willing perpetrators of the worst horrors of the Revolution. Buonaparte himself was judged, by close observers, to shrink with abhorrence from the assembly he himself had convoked. His guards were under arms, and the field artillery loaded, and turned on the Place de Carrousel, filled with the motley crowd, who, from the contrasted colour of the corn porters and charcoal-men, were facetiously called his Grey and Black Mousquetaires. He hasted to dismiss his hideous minions, with a sufficient distribution of praises and liquor. The haughty character of the French soldiers had kept them from fraternising with the rabble, even in the cause of Napoleon. In short, the disgraceful character of the alliance thus formed between Buonaparte and the lees of the people, was of a nature incapable of being glossed over even in the flattering pages of the *Moniteur*, which, amidst a flourishing description of this memorable procession, was compelled to admit, that, in some places, the name of the Emperor was incongruously mingled with expressions and songs, which recalled an era *unfortunately too famous*.

Fretted by external dangers and internal disturbances, and by the degrading necessity of appearing every night before a mob, who familiarly hailed him as *Père le Violette*,[22] Napoleon withdrew from the Tuileries to the more retired palace of the Elysée Bourbon. Here he took into his own hands, with the assistance of Benjamin Constant, and other statesmen, the construction of a new constitution. Their system included all those checks and regulations which are understood to form the essence of a free government, and greatly resembled that granted by the Royal Charter. Nevertheless, it was extremely ill received by all parties, but especially by those who expected from Napoleon a constitution more free than that which they had dissolved by driving Louis XVIII from the throne. There were other grave exceptions stated against the scheme.

First, the same objection was stated against this Imperial grant which had been urged with so much vehemence against the royal charter, namely, that it was not a compact between the people and the sovereign, in which the former called the latter to the throne under certain conditions, but a recognition by the sovereign of the liberties of the people. The meeting of the Champ de Mai had indeed been summoned, chiefly with the purpose of forming and adopting the new constitution; but, according to the present system, they were only to have the choice of adopting or rejecting that which Napoleon had prepared. The disappointment was great among those philosophers who desired "better bread than is made of wheat;" and could not enjoy liberty unless it emanated directly from the will of the people, and was sanctioned by popular discussion. But Napoleon was determined that the convention should have no other concern in the constitution, save to accept it when offered. He would not entrust such an assembly with the revision of the laws by which he was to govern. Secondly, this new constitution was published under the singular title of an "Additional Act to the Constitutions of the Emperor," and thereby constituted a sort of appendix to a huge mass of unrepealed organic laws, many of them inconsistent with the Additional Act in tenor and in spirit.

Those who had enjoyed the direct confidence of the Emperor while the treaty was framing, endeavoured to persuade themselves that Napoleon meant fairly, yet confessed they had found it difficult to enlighten his ideas on the subject of a limited monarchy. The more determined Republicans, besides their objections to an Upper House, which the Emperor could fill with his own minions so as to control the representatives of the people, found the proposed constitution utterly devoid of the salt which should savour it. There was no acknowledgment of abstract principles; no metaphysical discussions on the origin of laws; and they were as much mortified and disappointed as the zealot who hears a discourse on practical morality, when he expected a sermon on the doctrinal points of theology. The unfortunate Additional Act became the subject of attack and raillery on all sides, so that a bookseller being asked for a copy replied that he did not 'deal in periodical publications.'

On the whole, the Champ de Mai, was, in the language of Paris, *un piece tombée,*[23] a condemned farce, which was soon to be succeeded by a bloody tragedy.

The disputes of the Chamber of Representatives with the government commenced on June 4th. The Chamber promised their unanimous support in repelling the foreign enemy; but they announced their intention to take under their consideration the constitution, and to point out its defects, with the necessary remedies. They added a moderating hint. "The nation," they said, "nourishes no plans of aggrandisement. Not even the will of a victorious prince will lead them beyond the boundaries of self-defence."

Thus parted Buonaparte and his Chambers; he to try his fortune in battle, they to altering and modifying the laws, and inspiring a more popular spirit into the enactments he had made, in hopes that the dictatorship of the Jacobins might be once again substituted for the dictatorship of the Emperor. All men saw that the Imperialists and Republicans only waited till the field was won, that they might contend for the booty; and so little was the nation disposed to sympathise with the active, turbulent, demagogues by whom the contest was to be maintained against the Emperor, that almost all predicted with great unconcern their probable expulsion, either by Buonaparte or the Bourbons.

CHAPTER LXXXVII

The allies prepared for war, and up to one million men made their diverse way to the French borders. 150,000 Prussians under Blücher and 80,000 British and allied troops entered Flanders.

To meet this immense array, Napoleon, with his usual talent and celerity, had brought forward means of a surprising extent. The regular army had been, by calling out the retired officers and disbanded soldiers, increased from something rather under 100,000 men, to double that number of troops of the first quality. But this was dust in the balance; and the mode of conscription was so intimately connected with Napoleon's wars of conquest and disaster, that he dared not propose, nor would the Chamber of Representatives have agreed, to have recourse to the odious resource, which, however, Buonaparte trusted he might still find effectual in June, to the number of 300,000.

In the meantime, it was proposed to render moveable, for active service, 200 battalions of the national guard, choosing those most fit for duty, which would make a force of 112,000 men. It was also proposed to levy as many volunteers of the lower orders as could be brought together in the different departments. Thus prepared for action, no doubt was made that Buonaparte would open the campaign, by assuming offensive operations. To wait till the enemy had assembled their full force on his frontier would have suited neither the man nor the moment.

Buonaparte was desirous to aim a decisive blow at the most enterprising and venturous of the invading armies. He knew Blücher, and had heard of Wellington; he therefore resolved to move against those generals, while he opposed walls and fortified places to the more slow advance of Schwartzenberg, and trusted that distance might render ineffectual the progress of the Russians.

But although Napoleon's expressions were those of confidence and defiance, his internal feelings were of a different complexion. "I no longer felt," as he afterwards expressed himself, "that complete confidence in final success which accompanied me on former undertakings. Whether it was that I was getting beyond the period of life when men are usually favoured by fortune, or whether the impulse of my career seemed impeded in my own eyes, and to my own imagination, it is certain that I felt a depression of spirit. Fortune, which used to follow my steps to load me with her bounties, was now a severe deity, from whom I might snatch a few favours, but for which she exacted severe retribution. I had no sooner gained an advantage than it was followed by a reverse." With such feelings, not certainly unwarranted by the circumstances under which the campaign was undertaken, nor disproved by the event, Napoleon undertook his shortest and last campaign.

CHAPTER LXXXVIII

Wellington arrived in Flanders in April and set about garrisoning Ostend, Antwerp, and Nieuport, his line of communication with Britain, while receiving reinforcements.

Napoleon advanced to Vervins on 12th June, with his Guard, who had marched from Paris. The other divisions of his grand army had been assembled on the frontier, and the whole, consisting of five divisions of infantry, and four of cavalry, were combined at Beaumont with a degree of secrecy and expedition which showed the usual genius of their commander.

Upon the 15th June, the French army was in motion in every direction. Their advanced-guard swept the western bank of the Sambre of all the allied corps. They then advanced upon Charleroi, which was well defended by the Prussians under Ziethen, who was at length compelled to retire on the village of Gosselies. Here his retreat was cut off by the second division of the French army, and Ziethen was compelled to take the route of Fleurus, by which he united with the Prussian force, which lay about the villages of Ligny and St. Amand. The Prussian general had, however, obeyed his orders, by making such protracted resistance as gave time for the alarm being taken.

By this movement the plan of Napoleon was made manifest, it was at once most scientific and adventurous. His numbers were unequal to sustain a conflict with the armies of Blücher and Wellington united, but by forcing his way so as to separate the one from the other, he would gain the advantage of acting against either individually with the gross of his forces, while he could spare enough of detached troops to keep the other in check. To accomplish this masterly manœuvre it was necessary to push upon a part of the British advance, which occupied the position of Quatre-bras, and the yet more advanced post of Frasnes. But the extreme rapidity of Napoleon's forced marches had in some measure prevented the execution of his plan, by dispersing his forces so much, that at a time when every hour was of consequence, he was compelled to remain at Charleroi until his wearied army had collected. The manœuvre meditated by Napoleon thus failed, though it had nearly been successful. He continued, however, to entertain the same purpose of dividing, if possible, the British army from the Prussians.

The British general received intelligence of the advance of the French, but it was not of sufficient certainty to enable him to put his army in motion on an occasion when a false movement might have been irretrievable ruin. When certain accounts reached Brussels that the advance of the French was upon the line of the Sambre, reinforcements were hastily moved on Quatre-bras, and the Duke of Wellington arrived there in person. It appeared at this time that the whole French force was about to be directed against the Prussians.

Blücher was prepared to receive them. Three of his divisions, to the number of 80,000 men, had got into position on a chain of gentle heights, running from Brie to Sombref. The 4th Prussian division was at too great a distance to be brought up, though every effort was made for the purpose. Blücher undertook, however, to receive a battle in this position trusting to the support of the English army, who, by a flank movement to the left, were to march to his assistance.

Napoleon had, in the meantime, settled his own plan of battle. He determined to leave Ney with a division of 45,000 men, with instructions to drive the English from Quatre-bras, ere their army was concentrated and reinforced, and thus prevent their co-operating with Blücher, while he himself, with the main body of his army, attacked the Prussian position at Ligny.

That of Ligny was the principal action. After a continued attack of two hours, the French had only obtained possession of a part of St. Amand. Observing that Blücher drew his reserves together on St. Amand, he changed his point of attack, and directed all his force against Ligny, of which, after a desperate resistance, he at length obtained possession. The French Guards, supported by their heavy cavalry, ascended the heights, and attacked the Prussian position in the rear of Ligny. The reserves of the Prussian infantry having been despatched to St. Amand, Blücher had no means of repelling this attack, save by his cavalry. He placed himself at their head, and charged in the most determined manner, but without success. The cavalry were forced back in disorder.

The prince maréchal, as he directed the retreat, was involved in one of the charges, his horse struck down by a cannon-shot, and he himself prostrated on the ground. His aide-de-camp threw himself beside the veteran, determined to share his fate, and had the precaution to fling a cloak over him, to prevent his being recognised by the French. The enemy's cuirassiers passed over him, and it was not until they were repulsed, and in their turn pursued by the Prussian cavalry, that the gallant veteran was raised and remounted. Blücher's death, or captivity, at that moment, might have had most sinister effects on the event of the campaign, as it may be doubted whether any thing short of his personal influence and exertion could, after this hard-fought and unfortunate day, have again brought the Prussian army into action on the 18th of June. When again mounted, Blücher directed the retreat upon Tilly, and achieved it unmolested by the enemy, who did not continue their pursuit beyond the heights which the Prussians had been constrained to abandon.

Such was the battle of Ligny, in which the Prussians, as Blücher truly said, "lost the field, but not their honour." The French Emperor had struck a great blow – overpowered a stubborn and inveterate enemy, and opened the campaign with favourable auspices. The degree of advantage, however, which Napoleon might have derived from the Prussian retreat was greatly limited by the indifferent success of Ney.

About three o'clock in the afternoon the main attack commenced, but was repulsed. Ney attempted a general charge of heavy cavalry; but they were received with such a galling fire from the British infantry, joined to a battery of two guns, that it could not be sustained; the whole causeway was strewed with men and horses, and the fugitives, who escaped to the rear, announced the loss of an action which was far from being decided, considering that the British had few infantry and artillery, though reinforcements were coming fast forward. The battle of Quatre-bras terminated with the light. The British retained possession of the field, which they had maintained with so much obstinacy, because the Duke of Wellington conceived that Blücher would be able to make his ground good at Ligny, and was consequently desirous that the armies should retain the line of communication which they had occupied in the morning.

It was not till he found the English resolved to make a stand, and the Prussians determined to communicate with them, that Napoleon became aware of the plan arranged betwixt Wellington and Blücher, to concentrate the Prussian and English armies at Waterloo. This was the enigma on which his fate depended, and he failed to solve it.

CHAPTER LXXXIX

The gaining of the battle of Ligny had no marked results, still less had the indecisive action at Quatre-bras; but had these been followed by the retreat of the English army to Antwerp, and the capture of Brussels, they would then have attained the rank of great and decisive victories.

Napoleon pretended to look to still more triumphant results from such a victory, and to expect nothing less than the dissolution of the Alliance as the reward of a decided defeat of the English. Napoleon's belief that a single defeat of the Duke of Wellington would occasion a total change of government in England can only serve to show how very little he must have known of the English nation with which he had been fighting so long. It cannot, however, be denied, that any success gained by Napoleon in this first campaign, would have greatly added to his influence both in France and other countries, and might have endangered the possession of Flanders. The Duke of Wellington resolved, therefore, to protect Brussels, if possible, even by the risk of a general battle.

The Duke despatched intelligence of his position to Blücher, acquainting him with his resolution to give Napoleon the battle which he seemed to desire, providing the prince would afford him the support of two divisions of the Prussian army. The answer was worthy of the indefatigable and indomitable old man, who was never so much disconcerted by defeat as to prevent his being ready for combat on the succeeding day. He sent for reply, that he would move to the Duke of Wellington's support, not with two divisions, but with his whole army; and that he asked no time to prepare longer than was necessary to supply food and serve out cartridges to his soldiers.

It was three o'clock on the afternoon of the 17th when the British came on the field and took up their bivouac for the night in the order of battle in which they were to fight. It was much later before Napoleon reached the heights of Belle Alliance in person, and his army did not come up in full force till the morning of the 18th.

The plans of these two great generals were extremely simple. The object of the Duke of Wellington was to maintain his line of defence until the Prussians arrived to give him a decided superiority. They were expected about eleven or twelve o'clock; but the extreme badness of the roads detained them several hours later. Napoleon's scheme was equally plain and decided. He trusted, by his usual rapidity of attack, to break and destroy the British army before the Prussians should arrive; after which, he calculated to have an opportunity of destroying the Prussians by attacking them on their march through the broken ground.

The tempest which had raged with tropical violence all night, abated in the morning; but the weather continued gusty and stormy during the whole day. Betwixt eleven and twelve, on the memorable 18th June, this dreadful and decisive action commenced, with a cannonade on the part of the French, instantly followed by an attack, commanded by Jerome, on the advanced post of Hougomont. The troops of Nassau, which occupied the wood around the chateau, were driven out, but the utmost efforts of the assailants were unable to force the house, garden, and farm offices, which a party of the guards sustained with the most dauntless resolution. The French redoubled their efforts and precipitated themselves in numbers on the exterior hedge, which screens the garden-wall, not perhaps aware of the internal defence afforded by the latter. They fell in great numbers on this point by the fire of the defenders. The attack was at length repelled so far that the British again opened their communication with Hougomont, and that important garrison was reinforced.

Meantime, the fire of artillery having become general along the line, the force of the French attack was transferred to the British centre. It was made with the most desperate fury, and received with the most stubborn resolution. The assault was here made upon the farm-house of Saint Jean by four columns of infantry, and a large mass of cuirassiers, who took the advance. The four columns of French infantry forced their way forward beyond the farm of La Haye Sainte, and, dispersing a Belgian regiment, were in the act of establishing themselves in the centre of the British position, when they were attacked by the brigade of General Pack. Meanwhile, a brigade of British heavy cavalry wheeled round their own infantry and attacked the French charging columns in flank, at the moment when they were checked by the fire of the musketry. The results were decisive. The French columns were broken with great slaughter, and two eagles, with more than 2000 men, were made prisoners. The British cavalry, however, followed their success too far. They got involved amongst the French infantry and some hostile cavalry which were detached to support them, and were obliged to retire with considerable loss.

Shortly after, the scene of conflict again shifted to the right, where a general attack of French cavalry was made on the squares, chiefly towards the centre of the British. They came up with the most dauntless resolution, despite the continued fire of thirty pieces of artillery, placed in front of the line, and compelled the artillerymen by whom they were served, to retreat within the squares. The enemy had no means, however, to secure the guns, or even to spike them, and at every favourable moment the British artillerymen sallied from their place of refuge, again manned their pieces, and fired on the assailants. The British squares stood unmoved, and never gave fire until the cavalry were within ten yards, when men rolled one way, horses galloped another, and the cuirassiers were in every instance driven back.

The French have pretended that squares were broken, and colours taken; but this assertion, upon the united testimony of every British officer present, is a positive untruth. This was not, however, the fault of the cuirassiers, who displayed an almost frantic valour. They rallied again and again, and returned to the onset, till the British could recognise even the faces of individuals. At length they suffered so severely that they were compelled to abandon the attempt. In this unheard-of struggle, the greater part of the French heavy cavalry was absolutely destroyed.

During this long succession of the most furious attacks, the French had gained no success save occupying for a time the wood around Hougomont, from which they had been expelled, and the farm house of La Haye Sainte, which had been also recovered. The British, on the other hand, had suffered very severely but had not lost one inch of ground. 10,000 men were, however, killed and wounded.

But the French, besides losing about 15,000 men, together with a column of prisoners more than 2000 in number, began now to be disturbed by the operations of the Prussians on their right; and the secret of the Duke of Wellington was disclosing itself. It became now evident that the Prussians were to enter seriously into the battle, and with great force. Napoleon had still the means of opposing them, and of achieving a retreat, at the certainty, however, of being attacked upon the ensuing day by the combined armies. His celebrated Guard had not yet taken part in the conflict, and would now have been capable of affording him protection after a battle which he had fought at disadvantage, but without being defeated. But the circumstances by which he was surrounded must have pressed on his mind at once. It seemed as if all must be decided on that day, and on that field. Surrounded by these ill-omened circumstances, a desperate effort for victory, ere the Prussians could act effectually, might perhaps yet drive the English from their position.

About seven o'clock, Napoleon's Guard were formed in two columns and put under command of the dauntless Ney. Buonaparte told the soldiers, and, indeed, imposed the same fiction on their commander, that the Prussians whom they saw on the right were retreating. Perhaps he might himself believe that this was true. The Guard answered, for the last time, with shouts of *Vive l'Empereur*, and moved resolutely forward, having, for their support, four battalions of the Old Guard in reserve. The British were arranged in a line four men deep to meet the advancing columns, and poured upon them a storm of musketry which never ceased an instant. The soldiers fired independently, as it is called; each man loading and discharging as fast as he could.

At length the British moved forward, as if to close round the heads of the columns, and at the same time continued to pour their shot upon the enemy's flanks. The French gallantly attempted to deploy, for the purpose of returning the discharge. But in their effort to do so, under so dreadful a fire, they stopped, staggered, became disordered, were blended into one mass, and at length gave way, retiring, or rather flying, in the utmost confusion. This was the last effort of the enemy, and Napoleon gave orders for the retreat; to protect which, he had now no troops left, save the last four battalions of the Old Guard. These threw themselves into squares, and stood firm. But at this moment the Duke of Wellington commanded the whole British line to advance, so that whatever the bravery and skill of these gallant veterans, they also were thrown into disorder, and swept away in the general rout, in spite of the efforts of Ney, who, having had his horse killed, fought sword in hand, and on foot, in the front of the battle, till the very last.

Moving in oblique lines, the British and Prussian armies came into contact with each other on the heights so lately occupied by the French, and celebrated the victory with loud shouts of mutual congratulation. The French army was now in total and inextricable confusion and rout; and when the victorious generals met at the farm-house of La Belle Alliance, it was agreed that the Prussians, who were fresh in comparison, should follow up the chase.

During the whole action, Napoleon maintained the utmost serenity. He remained on the heights of La Belle Alliance, from which he had a full view of the field, which does not exceed a mile and a half in length. He expressed no solicitude on the fate of the battle for a long time, noticed the behaviour of particular regiments, and praised the English several times, always, however, talking of them as an assured prey. When forming his guard for the last fatal effort, he descended near them, half down the causeway from La Belle Alliance, to bestow upon them what proved his parting exhortation. He watched intently their progress with a spyglass, and refused to listen to one or two aides, who at that moment came to inform him of the appearance of the Prussians. At length, on seeing the attacking columns stagger and become confused, his countenance, said our informer, became pale as that of a corpse, and muttering to himself, "They are mingled together," he said, "All is lost for the present," and rode off the field; not stopping till he reached Charleroi, where he paused for a moment.

The loss on the British side during this dreadful battle was, as the Duke of Wellington truly termed it, immense. 100 officers slain, 500 wounded, many of them to death, 15,000 men killed and wounded, threw half Britain into mourning. It required all the glory and all the solid advantages of this immortal day, to reconcile the mind to the high price at which it was purchased. The commander-in-chief, compelled to be on every point of danger, was repeatedly in the greatest jeopardy. Only the Duke himself and one gentleman of his numerous staff escaped unwounded in horse and person. It would be difficult to form a guess at the extent of the French loss. Besides those who fell in the battle and flight, great numbers deserted. We do not believe, that of 75,000 men, the half were ever again collected under arms.

The laurels of Waterloo must be divided – the British won the battle, the Prussians achieved and rendered available the victory.

CHAPTER XC

That part of the French army which escaped from the field of Waterloo, fled in the most terrible disorder towards France. On the 19th of June the public ear of the capital had been stunned by the report of 100 pieces of cannon, which announced the victory at Ligny, and the public prints had contained the most gasconading accounts of that action; of the forcing the passage of the Sambre, the action at Charleroi, and the battle of Quatre-bras. The Imperialists were in the highest state of exultation, the Republicans doubtful, and the Royalists dejected. On the morning of the 21st, the third day after the action, it was first whispered, and then openly said, that Napoleon had returned alone from the army on the preceding night, and was now in the palace of Bourbon-Elysée. The fatal truth was not long in transpiring – he had lost a dreadful and decisive battle, and the army, which had left the capital so confident, so full of hope, pride, and determination, was totally destroyed.

Many reasons have been given for Napoleon's not remaining with his army, and endeavouring at least to bring it into a state of reorganisation; but the secret seems to be his apprehension of the Republicans and Constitutionalists in Paris. He must have remembered that Fouché, and others of that party, had advised him to end the distresses of France by his abdication, even before he placed himself at the head of his army. He was aware, that what they had ventured to suggest in his moment of strength, they would not hesitate to extort from him in the hour of his weakness, and that the Chamber of Representatives would endeavour to obtain peace for themselves by sacrificing him. "He is known," says an author friendly to his fame, "to have said, after the disasters of the Russian campaign, that he would confound the Parisians by his presence, and fall among them like a thunderbolt. But there are things which succeed only because they have never been done before, and for that reason ought never to be attempted again. His 5th flight from his army occasioned the entire abandonment of himself and his cause by all who might have forgiven him his misfortune, but required that he should be the first to arise from the blow."[iv]

The anticipations of Napoleon did not deceive him. It was plain that, whatever deference the Jacobins had for him in his hour of strength, they had no compassion for his period of weakness. They felt the opportunity favourable to get rid of him, and did not disguise their purpose. The two Chambers hastily assembled. All seemed to unite in one sentiment, that abdication was a measure absolutely necessary.

The gauntlet was now thrown down, and it was necessary that Napoleon should resist or yield; declare himself absolute, and dissolve the Chambers by violence; or abdicate. He dared neither venture on the desperate measures which might, for a short time, have preserved his power, nor could he bring himself to the dignified step of an apparently voluntary resignation. He clung to what could no longer avail him, like the distracted criminal, who, wanting resolution to meet his fate by a voluntary effort, must be pushed from the scaffold by the executioner.

On the morning of the 22nd June, only four days after the defeat at Waterloo, the Chamber of Representatives assembled at nine in the morning, and expressed the utmost impatience to receive the Act of Abdication. It was presented by Fouché, whose intrigues were thus far crowned with success, and was couched in the following terms:

Frenchmen! – In commencing war for maintaining the national independence, I relied on the union of all efforts of all wills, and the concurrence of all the national authorities. I had reason to hope for success, and I braved all the declarations of the powers against me.

Circumstances appear to me changed. I offer myself as a sacrifice to the hatred of the enemies of France. May they prove sincere in their declarations, and have really directed them only against my power! My political life is terminated, and I proclaim my son, under the title of Napoleon II, Emperor of the French.

The present ministers will provisionally form the council of the government. The interest which I take in my son induces me to invite the Chambers to form, without delay, the regency by a law.

Unite all for the public safety, in order to remain an independent nation.

NAPOLEON

The Republican party, having thus obtained a victory, proposed instantly several new models for settling the form of a constitution, in the room of that which, exactly three weeks before, they had sworn to in the Champ de Mai. This was judged somewhat premature; and they resolved for the present to content themselves with nominating a Provisional Government, vesting the executive powers of the state in five persons – two to be chosen from Buonaparte's House of Peers, and three from that of the Representatives.

Meanwhile, to preserve the decency due to the late Emperor, the Chamber named a committee to wait on him with an address of thanks, in which they carefully avoided all mention and recognition of his son. Napoleon, for the last time, received the committee in the imperial habit and surrounded by his state-officers and guards. He seemed pale and pensive, but firm and collected, and heard with a steady indifference the praises which they bestowed on his patriotic sacrifice. His answer recommended unanimity, and the speedy preparation of means of defence; but at the conclusion he reminded them, that his abdication was conditional, and comprehended the interests of his son. Lanjuinais, President of the Chamber, replied, with profound respect, that the Chamber had given him no directions respecting the subject. "I told you," said he, turning to Lucien, "they would not, could not do it. Tell the Assembly," he said, again addressing the President, "that I recommend my son to their protection. It is in his favour I have abdicated."

Thus the succession of Napoleon II came to be now the point of debate between the abdicated Emperor and the Legislative Bodies. It is certain the appointment could not have been rendered acceptable to the allies; and the influence which Buonaparte and his friends were likely to have in a regency, were strong arguments for all in France who had opposed him, uniting to set aside his family and dynasty. There seems to have been little to prevent Napoleon from still placing himself at the head of a small but formidable army. To remove him from this temptation, the Provisional Government required him to retire to the palace of Malmaison, near St. Germain, so long the favourite abode of the discarded Josephine. Napoleon had not been within its walls a single day, before, surrounded by Fouché's police, he found that he, who, not a month since, had disposed of the fate of myriads, was no longer the free master of his own actions. He was watched and controlled, though without the use of actual force, and now, for the first time, felt what it was to lose that free agency, of which his despotism had for so many years deprived so large a portion of mankind.

There was, however, a reason for his protracting his residence at Malmaison, more honourable than mere human reluctance to submit to inevitable calamity. The English and Prussian forces were now approaching Paris by rapid marches. When Paris was again to be girt round with hostile armies, honourable as well as political feelings might lead Napoleon to hope that the Representatives might be inclined to waive all personal animosity, and might permit him once more to assume the sword for protection of Paris. He offered to command the army as general in chief, on behalf of his son. He offered to take share in the defence, as an ordinary citizen. But the internal discord had gone too far. The popular party which then prevailed saw more danger in the success of Napoleon, than in the superiority of the allies. The latter they hoped to conciliate by treaty. They doubted, with good reason, the power of resisting them by force; and if such resistance was, or could be maintained by Napoleon, they feared his supremacy, in a military command, at least as much as the predominance of the allies. His services were therefore declined by them.

Like skilful anglers, the Provisional Government had been gradually drawing their nets around Napoleon, and it was now time to drag him upon the shallows. They proceeded to place him under a sort of arrest, by directing General Beker to watch over, and, if necessary, restrain his movements, that it should be impossible for him to make his escape. Orders were at the same time given for two frigates to transport him to the United States of America; and the surveillance of General Beker and the police was to continue until the late Emperor was on board the vessels. This order was qualified by directions that all possible care should be taken to ensure the safety of Napoleon's person. Napoleon submitted to his destiny with resignation and dignity.

CHAPTER XCI

Buonaparte arrived at Rochefort upon the 3rd July; so short had been the space between the bloody cast of the die at Waterloo, and his finding him-self an exile. Yet even this brief space of fifteen days had made his retreat difficult, if not impracticable. Means, indeed, were provided for his trans-portation. The two French frigates, the Saale and the Medusa, together with a corvette and a large brig, waited Buonaparte's presence and orders to sail for America from their station under the Isle d'Aix. But, as Napoleon himself said shortly afterwards, wherever there was water to swim a ship, there he was sure to find the British flag.

The news of Waterloo had been the signal to the Admiralty to cover the western coast of France with cruisers, in order to prevent the possi-bility of Napoleon's escaping. The commanders of these vessels had the strictest orders to suffer no vessel to pass unexamined. No less than thir-ty ships of different descriptions maintained this blockade. According to this arrangement, the British line-of-battle ship, the Bellerophon, cruised off Rochefort, with the occasional assistance of other small vessels. Captain Maitland, who commanded the Bellerophon, is a man of high character, of birth, of firmness of mind, and of the most indisputable honour. It is necessary to mention these circumstances because the national character of England herself is deeply concerned and identified with that of Captain Maitland, in the narrative which follows.

The resolution was taken by Napoleon to write to the British Prince Regent.

Rochefort, July 13, 1815
ROYAL HIGHNESS,
A victim to the factions which distract my country, and to the enmi-ty of the greatest powers of Europe, I have terminated my politi-cal career and I come, like Themistocles, to throw myself upon the hospitality of the British people. I put myself under the protection of their law; which I claim from your Royal Highness, as the most powerful, the most constant, and the most generous of my ene-mies.

NAPOLEON

Captain Maitland informed Count Las Cases, that he would despatch General Gourgaud to England, and himself prepare to receive Napoleon and his suite. On the 15th July, 1815, Napoleon finally left France. He was received on board the Bellerophon respectfully, but without any salute or distinguished honours. As Captain Maitland advanced to meet him on the quarterdeck, Napoleon pulled off his hat, and, addressing him in a firm tone of voice, said, "I come to place myself under the protection of your prince and laws." His manner was uncommonly pleasing, and he displayed much address in seizing upon opportunities of saying things flattering to the hearers whom he wished to conciliate.

As when formerly on board Captain Usher's vessel, Buonaparte showed great curiosity concerning the discipline of the ship, and expressed considerable surprise that the British vessels should so easily defeat the French ships, which were heavier, larger, and better manned than they. Captain Maitland accounted for this by the greater experience of the men and officers. The Ex-Emperor examined the marines also, and, pleased with their appearance, said to Bertrand, "How much might be done with 100,000 such men!" In the management of the vessel, he particularly admired the silence and good order of the crew while going through their manœuvres, in comparison to a French vessel, "where every one," he said, "talks and gives orders at once." He spoke, too, of the British army in an equal style of praise, and was joined by his officers in doing so. One of the French officers observing that the English cavalry were superb, Captain Maitland observed, that in England, they had a higher opinion of the infantry. "You are right," said the French gentleman; "there is none such in the world; there is no making an impression on them; you might as well attempt to charge through a wall; and their fire is tremendous." Bertrand reported to Captain Maitland that Napoleon had communicated to him his opinion of the Duke of Wellington in the following words "The Duke of Wellington, in the management of an army, is fully equal to myself with the advantage of possessing more prudence." This we conceive to be the genuine unbiased opinion of one great soldier concerning another. It is a pity that Napoleon could on other occasions express himself in a strain of depreciation, which could only lower him who used it, towards a rival.

During the passage, notwithstanding the painful uncertainty under which he laboured, Napoleon seemed always tranquil, and in good temper; at times, he even approached cheerfulness. He spoke with tenderness of his wife and family, complained of being separated from them, and had tears in his eyes when he showed their portraits to Captain Maitland. His health seemed perfectly good; but he was occasionally subject to somnolence, proceeding, perhaps, from the exhaustion of a constitution which had gone through such severe service. On 23rd July, they passed Ushant. Napoleon remained long on deck, and cast many a melancholy look to the coast of France, but made no observations. At daybreak on 24th, the Bellerophon was off Dartmouth.

The Bellerophon had hardly anchored when orders came from the admiral, Lord Keith, which were soon after seconded by others from the Admiralty, enjoining that no one, of whatever rank or station, should be permitted to come on board the Bellerophon, excepting the officers and men belonging to the ship. On the 26th, the vessel received orders to move round to Plymouth Sound. In the meantime, the newspapers which were brought on board tended to impress anxiety and consternation among the unhappy fugitives. The report was generally circulated by these publications that Buonaparte would not be permitted to land, but would be presently sent off to St. Helena, as the safest place for detaining him as a prisoner of war.

On the evening of the 30th of July, Major-General Sir Henry Bunbury, one of the Under Secretaries of State, arrived, bringing with him the final intentions of the British Government. Upon the 31st, Lord Keith and Sir Henry waited upon the Ex-Emperor, on board of the Bellerophon, to communicate to him the unpleasing tidings. The letter of Lord Melville (First Lord of the Admiralty) was read to the Ex-Emperor, announcing his future destination. It stated that "it would be inconsistent with the duty of the British ministers to their sovereign and his allies, to leave General Buonaparte the means or opportunity of again disturbing the peace of Europe – announced that the island of St. Helena was selected for his future residence, and selected as such, because its local situation would permit his enjoying more freedom than could be compatible with adequate security elsewhere – that, with the exception of Generals Savary and Lallemand, the General might select three officers, together with his surgeon, to attend him to St. Helena – that twelve domestics would also be allowed." The same document stated that "the persons who might attend upon him would be liable to a certain degree of restraint, and could not be permitted to leave the island without the sanction of the British Government." Lastly, it was announced that "Rear-Admiral Sir George Cockburn, appointed to the chief command of the Cape of Good Hope, would be presently ready to sail, for the purpose of conveying General Buonaparte to St. Helena, and therefore it was desirable that he should without delay make choice of the persons who were to form his suite."

The letter was read in French to Buonaparte by Sir Henry Bunbury. He listened without impatience, interruption, or emotion. When he was requested to state if he had any reply, he began, with great calmness of manner and mildness of countenance, to declare that he solemnly protested – that the British Ministry had no right to dispose of him in the way proposed – that he appealed to the British people and the laws – and asked what was the tribunal which he ought to appeal to. "I am come," he continued, "voluntarily to throw myself on the hospitality of your nation – I am not a prisoner of war, and if I was, have a right to be treated according to the law of nations. But I am come to this country a passenger on board one of your vessels, after a previous negotiation with the commander. If he had told me I was to be a prisoner, I would not have come. I asked him if he was willing to receive me on board and convey me to England. *Admiral* Maitland said he was, having received, or telling me he received, special orders of government concerning me. It was a snare, then, that had been spread for me; I came on board a British vessel as I would have entered one of their towns – a vessel, a village, it is the same thing. As for the island of St. Helena, it would be my sentence of death. I demand to be received as an English citizen. How many years entitle me to be domiciliated?"

Sir Henry answered that he believed four were necessary. "Well, then," continued Napoleon, "let the Prince Regent during that time place me under any superintendence he thinks proper – let me be placed in a country-house in the centre of the island, thirty leagues from every seaport – place a commissioned officer about me, to examine my correspondence and superintend my actions; or if the Prince Regent should require my word of honour, perhaps I might give it. I might then enjoy a certain degree of personal liberty, and I should have the freedom of literature. In St. Helena I could not live three months; to my habits and constitution it would be death. I am used to ride 20 miles a-day – what am I to do on that little rock at the end of the world? No! Botany Bay is better than St. Helena – I prefer death to St. Helena – And what good is my death to do you! I am no longer a sovereign. What danger could result from my living as a private person in the heart of England, and restricted in any way which the Government should think proper?"

He referred repeatedly to the manner of his coming on board the Bellerophon, insisting upon his being perfectly free in his choice, and that he had preferred confiding to the hospitality and generosity of the British nation. "Otherwise," he said, "why should I not have gone to my father-in-law, or to the Emperor Alexander, who is my personal friend? We have become enemies, because he wanted to annex Poland to his dominions, and my popularity among the Poles was in his way. But otherwise he was my friend, and he would not have treated me in this way. If your Government act thus, it will disgrace you in the eyes of Europe. Even your own people will blame it. Besides, you do not know the feeling that my death will create both in France and Italy. There is, at present, a high opinion of England in these countries. If you kill me, it will be lost, and the lives of many English will be sacrificed. What was there to force me to the step I took? The tri-coloured flag was still flying at Bordeaux, Nantes, and Rochefort. The army has not even yet submitted. Or, if I had chosen to remain in France, what was there to prevent me from remaining concealed for years amongst a people so much attached to me?"

He repeated again and again his determination not to go to St. Helena, and his desire to be suffered to remain in Great Britain. "No, no," repeated Buonaparte, with animation, "I will not go there – You would not go there, sir, were it your own case – nor, my Lord, would you." Lord Keith bowed and answered – "He had been already at St. Helena four times." Napoleon went on reiterating his protestations. "I *will not* go thither," he repeated; "I am not a Hercules," (with a smile,) "but you shall not conduct me to St. Helena. I prefer death in this place. You found me free, send me back again; replace me in the condition in which I was, or permit me to go to America."

After the admiral and Sir Henry Bunbury had left the cabin, Napoleon recalled Lord Keith, whom, in respect of his former attention to his lordship's relative, Captain Elphinstone, he might consider as more favourable to his person. Napoleon opened the conversation by asking Lord Keith's advice how to conduct himself. Lord Keith replied that he was an officer, and had discharged his duty, and left with him the heads of his instructions. If he considered it necessary to renew the discussion, Sir Henry Bunbury must be called in. Buonaparte said that was unnecessary. "Can you," said he, "after what is passed, detain me until I hear from London?" Lord Keith replied that must depend on the instructions brought by the other admiral, with which he was unacquainted. "Was there any tribunal," he asked, "to which he could apply?" Lord Keith answered that he was no civilian, but believed that there was none whatever. He added that he was satisfied there was every disposition on the part of the British Government to render his situation as comfortable as prudence would permit. "How so?" said Napoleon, lifting the paper from the table, and speaking with animation. Upon Lord Keith's observing that it was surely preferable to being confined to a smaller space in England, or being sent to France, or perhaps to Russia. "Russia!" exclaimed Buonaparte, "God preserve me from it!"

During this remarkable scene, Napoleon's manner was perfectly calm and collected, his voice equal and firm, his tones very pleasing. Once or twice only he spoke more rapidly, and in a harsher key. He used little gesticulation, and his attitudes were ungraceful; but the action of the head was dignified, and the countenance remarkably soft and placid, without any marks of severity. He seemed to have made up his mind, anticipating what was to be announced, and perfectly prepared to reply. In expressing his positive determination not to go to St. Helena, he left it to his hearers to infer whether he meant to prevent his removal by suicide, or to resist it by force.

CHAPTER XCII

Napoleon's spirit for some time seemed wound up to some desperate resolve, and though he gave no hint of suicide before Captain Maitland, otherwise than by expressing a dogged resolution not to go to St. Helena, yet to Las Cases he spoke in undisguised terms of a Roman death. The philosophic arguments of Las Cases determined Napoleon to survive and write his history. Had he consulted his military attendants, he would have received other counsels, and assistance to execute them if necessary. Lallemand, Montholon, and Gourgaud assured Captain Maitland that the Emperor would sooner kill himself than go to St. Helena, and that even were he to consent, they three were determined themselves to put him to death, rather than he should so far degrade himself. Captain Maitland, in reply, gave some hints indicative of the gallows, in case such a scheme were prosecuted.

It was now that Napoleon gave Captain Maitland the first intimation of his purpose to submit, by requesting that Mr. O'Meara, surgeon of the Bellerophon, might be permitted to attend him to St. Helena, instead of his own surgeon, whose health could not stand the voyage. This made it clear that no resistance was designed; and indeed, as soon as Napoleon observed that his threat had produced no effect, he submitted with his usual equanimity. About eleven o'clock on the morning of the 7th August, Lord Keith came in his barge to transfer Napoleon to the Northumberland. About one o'clock, when Buonaparte had announced that he was in full readiness, a captain's guard was turned out; Lord Keith's barge was prepared; and as Napoleon crossed the quarter deck, the soldiers presented arms under three ruffles of the drum, being the salute paid to a general officer. His step was firm and steady; his farewell to Captain Maitland polite and friendly.

Napoleon was received on board of the Northumberland with the same honours paid at leaving the Bellerophon. Sir George Cockburn, to whose charge the late Emperor was now committed, was in every respect a person highly qualified to discharge the task with delicacy towards Napoleon, yet with fidelity to the instructions he had received.

While on board the Northumberland, the late Emperor spent his mornings in reading or writing; his evenings in his exercise upon deck and at cards. The game was generally *vingt un*. But when the play became rather deep, he discouraged that amusement and substituted chess. Great tactician as he was, Napoleon did not play well at that military game and it was with difficulty that his antagonist, Montholon, could avoid the solecism of beating the Emperor. During this voyage, Napoleon's *jour de fête* occurred, which was also his birthday. It was a day for which the Pope had expressly canonised a St. Napoleon to be the Emperor's patron. And now, strange revolution, it was celebrated by him on board of an English man-of-war, which was conducting him to his place of imprisonment and, as it proved, his tomb. Yet, Napoleon seemed cheerful and contented during the whole day, and was even pleased with being fortunate at play, which he received as a good omen.

Upon the 15th October, 1815, the Northumberland reached St. Helena, which presents but an unpromising aspect. Its destined inhabitant surveyed it with his spy-glass. St. James' Town, an inconsiderable village, was before him, enchased in a valley amid arid and scarped rocks of immense height. Every platform, every opening, every gorge, bristled with cannon. Las Cases, who stood by him, could not perceive the slightest alteration of his countenance. The orders of Government had been that Napoleon should remain on board till a residence could be prepared suitable for the life he was to lead. But as this was likely to be a work of time, Sir George Cockburn readily undertook, on his own responsibility, to put his passengers on shore and provide in some way for the security of Napoleon until the necessary habitation should be fitted up. He was accordingly transferred upon the 16th October; and thus the Emperor of France, nay, well-nigh of Europe, sunk into the recluse of St. Helena.

CHAPTER XCIII

We are now to touch upon the arguments which seem to justify the Administration of England in the strict course which they adopted towards Napoleon, in restraining his person and abating the privileges of rank which he tenaciously claimed. A surrender ensured his life and gave him the hope of taking further advantages from the generosity of the British nation; for an unconditional surrender, as it secures nothing, so it excludes nothing. General Bertrand, when on board the Northumberland, said that Napoleon had been much influenced in taking the step by the Abbé Sièyes, who had strongly advised him to proceed at once to England, in preference to taking any other course, which proves that his resolution must of course have been formed long before he ever saw Captain Maitland. Even M. Las Cases, when closely examined, comes to the same result; for he admits that he never hoped that Napoleon would be considered as a free man, or receive passports for America; but only that he would be kept in custody under milder restrictions than were inflicted upon him. But as he made no stipulation concerning the nature of these restrictions, they must of course have been left to the option of the conquering party. The question, therefore, betwixt Napoleon and the British nation, was not one of *justice,* but of generosity and clemency, feelings which can only be wisely indulged with reference to the safety of those who act upon them.

Napoleon being thus a prisoner surrendered at discretion, became subjected to the common laws of war, which authorise belligerent powers to shut up prisoners of war in places of confinement, from which it is only usual to except such whose honour may be accounted as a sufficient guarantee for their good faith, or whose power of doing injury is so small that it might be accounted contemptible. But Buonaparte was neither situation. His power was great; the temptation to use it strong; and the confidence to be placed in his resolution or promise to resist such temptation, very slight indeed. His breach of the treaty of Fontainebleau altered entirely his relations with England and with Europe and placed him in the condition of one whose word could not be trusted and whose personal freedom was inconsistent with the liberties of Europe. The experiment of trusting to his parole had been tried and failed. The wise may be deceived once; only fools are twice cheated in the same manner.

In respect to Napoleon's personal treatment, Sir George Cockburn proceeded on his arrival to arrange this upon the system recommended:

In committing so important a trust to British officers, the Prince Regent is sensible that it is not necessary to impress upon them his anxious desire that no greater measure of severity with respect to confinement or restriction be imposed, than what is deemed necessary for the faithful discharge of that duty, which the admiral, as well as the governor of St. Helena must ever keep in mind – the perfect security of General Buonaparte's person. Whatever, consistent with this great object, can be allowed in the shape of indulgence, his royal highness is confident will be willingly shown to the general: and he relies on Sir George Cockburn's known zeal and energy of character, that he will not allow himself to be betrayed into any improvident relaxation of his duty.

The accommodation was by no means such as could be desired. There were only three houses of a public character, which were in any degree adapted for such a guest. Two residences were unfit for Napoleon, because they were within James Town, a situation which, for obvious reasons, was not advisable. The third was Plantation-house, a villa in the country, belonging to the governor, which was the best in the island. The British Administration had prohibited the selection of this house.

There was another residence in the country, occupied by the lieutenant-governor, called Longwood, which was chosen by Sir George Cockburn as the future residence of Napoleon. It lies detached from the generally inhabited places of the island, consequently none were likely to frequent its neighbourhood, unless those who came there on business. It was also distant from those points which were most accessible to boats. At Longwood, too, there was an extent of level ground, capable of being observed and secured by sentinels, presenting a space adapted for exercise, whether on horseback or in a carriage; and the situation, being high, was more cool than the confined valleys. The house itself was equal in accommodation (though that is not saying much) to any on the island, Plantation house excepted. It was approved of by Napoleon, who visited it personally, and expressed himself so much satisfied that it was difficult to prevail on him to leave the place.

On the 9th December, Longwood received Napoleon and part of his household; the Count and Countess of Montholon and their children; the Count Las Cases and his son. Upon the whole, the house at Longwood, when finished as well as it could be in the circumstances, was far inferior in accommodation to that which every Englishman would have desired that the distinguished prisoner should have enjoyed whilst in English custody.

A space of twelve miles in circumference was traced off, within which Napoleon might take exercise without being attended by anyone. A chain of sentinels surrounded this domain to prevent his passing, unless accompanied by a British officer. If he inclined to extend his excursions, he might go to any part of the island providing the officer was in attendance, and near enough to observe his motions. Such an orderly officer was always in readiness to attend him when required.

Chapter XCIV

The first loud subject of complaint was that the imperial title was not given to Napoleon and that he was only addressed and treated with the respect due to a general officer of the highest rank. On this subject Napoleon was particularly tenacious: he contended with great obstinacy, from the time he came to Portsmouth, on his right to be treated as a crowned head; nor was there a more fertile source of discord betwixt him and the gentlemen of his suite on one side, and the Governor of St. Helena on the other.

Napoleon, it cannot be denied, had been not only an Emperor, but perhaps the most powerful that has ever existed; and he had been acknowledged as such by all the continental sovereigns. But he had been compelled, in 1814, to lay aside and abdicate the empire of France, and to receive in change the title of Emperor of Elba. His breach of the treaty of Paris was in essence a renunciation of the empire of Elba; and the reassumption of that of France was so far from being admitted by the allies that he was declared an outlaw by the Congress at Vienna. Indeed, if this second occupation of the French throne were even to be admitted as in any respect re-establishing his forfeited claim, it must be remembered that he himself a second time abdicated, and formally renounced a second time the dignity he had in an unhappy hour reassumed. But if Napoleon had no just pretension to the Imperial title or honours after his second abdication, even from those who had before acknowledged him as Emperor of France, still less had he any right to a title which he had laid down, from a nation who had never acquiesced in his taking it up.

His purpose in tenaciously claiming the name of a sovereign was to establish his claim to the immunities belonging to that title. He had already experienced at Elba the use to be derived from erecting a barrier of etiquette betwixt his person and any inconvenient visitor. Once acknowledged as Emperor, it followed, of course, that he was to be treated as such in every particular; and thus it would have become impossible to enforce such regulations as were absolutely demanded for his safe custody. Who ever heard of an emperor restricted in his promenades, or subjected, in certain cases, to the surveillance of an officer? Those readers, therefore, who may be of opinion that it was necessary that Napoleon should be restrained of his liberty, must also allow that the British Government would have acted imprudently if they had gratuitously invested him with a character which they had hitherto refused him, and that at the very moment when their doing so was to add to the difficulties attending his safe custody.

Sir Hudson Lowe, at one time desirous to compromise this silly dispute, would have been contented to render Napoleon the title of Excellency, as due to a field-marshal, but neither did this meet with acceptation. Napoleon was determined either to be acknowledged as Emperor, or to retain his grievance in its full extent. No modifications could be devised by which it could be rendered palatable. Whether this pertinacity in claiming a title which was rendered ridiculous by his situation, was the result of some feelings which led him to doubt his own title to greatness, when his ears were no longer flattered by the language of humility; or whether the political considerations just alluded to, rendered him obstinate to refuse all epithets, except one which might found him in claims to indemnities and privileges, it is impossible for us to say. But the strife should certainly, for his own sake, have been abandoned, when the point remained at issue between the governor and him only, since even if the former had wished to comply with the prisoner's desires, his instructions forbade him to do so. To continue an unavailing struggle, was only to invite the mortification of defeat and repulse. Yet Napoleon and his followers retained so much sensibility on this subject that this unfortunate phrase of *General Buonaparte* occurring so often in their correspondence, seemed to render every attempt at conciliation a species of derogation and insult, and made such overtures resemble a coarse cloth tied over a raw wound, which it frets and injures more than it protects.

A subject, upon which we are called upon to express much more sympathy with Napoleon is the screen which was drawn betwixt him, and, it may be said, the living world, through which he was not permitted to penetrate by letter, even to his dearest friends and relatives, unless such had been previously read by the governor. It is no doubt true that this is an inconvenience to which prisoners of war are, in all cases, subjected; nor do we know any country in which their parole is held so sacred as to induce the government to dispense with the right of inspecting their letters. Yet the high place so lately occupied by the fallen monarch might, we think, have claimed for him some dispensation from a restriction so humiliating. If a third person, cold-blooded at best, perhaps to hold up to scorn the expressions of our grief or our affection, is permitted to have the review of the effusions of our heart towards a wife, a sister, a brother, or a bosom-friend, the correspondence loses half its value; and, forced as we are to keep it within the bounds of the most discreet caution, it becomes to us rather a new source of mortification, than the opening of a communion with, those absent persons, whose friendship and attachment we hold to be the dearest possession of our lives. We rather think that some exercise of this privilege might have been left to Napoleon, without any risk of endangering the safe custody of his person; because we are pretty well convinced that all efforts strictly to enforce this regulation must have proved, ineffectual, and that he and his followers would always acquire the means of transmitting private letters from the island without regard to the restriction.

Another especial subject of complaint pleaded upon, arose from a regulation which required that Buonaparte should be visible twice, or at least once, in the day, to the British orderly officer. If this regulation had been submitted to with equanimity, it would have given the strongest possible guarantee against the possibility of attempting an escape. It might easily have been arranged that the officer should have the opportunity to execute his duty with every possible respect to Napoleon's privacy and convenience, and the latter might himself have chosen the time and manner of exhibiting himself for an instant. In this case, and considering how many other precautions were taken to prevent escape, the chance of Napoleon's attempting to fly, even if permitted the unlimited range of St. Helena, was highly improbable, and the chance of his effecting his purpose next to an impossibility. But this security depended upon his submitting to see a British officer at a fixed hour; and, resolute in his plan of yielding nothing to circumstances, Napoleon resisted, in every possible manner, the necessity of complying. Indeed, Sir Hudson Lowe was on many occasions contented to wink at its being altogether neglected, when the orderly officer could not find the means of seeing Napoleon by stealth. This was not the way in which this important regulation ought to have been acted upon and enforced, and the governor did not reap a great harvest of gratitude from his conduct in dispensing with this act of super-intendence.

The situation was in every respect a painful one; nor is it possible to refuse our sympathy, not only to the prisoner, but to the person whose painful duty it became to be his superintendent. His duty of detaining Napoleon's person was to be done most strictly, and required a man of that extraordinary firmness of mind, who should never yield for one instant his judgment to his feelings, and should be able at once to detect and reply to all false arguments. But, then, there ought to have been com-bined with those rare qualities a calmness of temper almost equally rare, and a generosity of mind, which, confident in its own honour and integri-ty, could look with serenity and compassion upon the daily and hourly effects of the maddening causes, which tortured into a state of constant and unendurable irritability the extraordinary being subjected to their influence. Buonaparte, indeed, and the followers who reflected his pas-sions, were to be regarded on all occasions as men acting and speaking under the feverish and delirious influence of things long past, and alto-gether destitute of the power of cool or clear reasoning, on any grounds that exclusively referred to things present. The emperor could not forget his empire, the husband could not forget his wife, the father his child, the hero his triumphs, the legislator his power. It was scarce in nature that a brain agitated by such recollections should remain composed under a change so fearful. To have soothed him would have been a vain attempt; but the honour of England required that he should have no cause of irri-tation, beyond those which severely enough attached to his condition as a captive.

Sir George Cockburn was superseded by Sir Hudson Lowe, [whose] conduct has been censured, in several of the writings which have treated of Napoleon's confinement, with such extremity of bitterness as in some measure defeats its own end. On the other hand, it would require a strong defence on the part of Sir Hudson himself, to induce us to consider him as the very rare and highly exalted species of character, to whom this important charge ought to have been entrusted. Sir Hudson Lowe had risen to rank in the army while serving chiefly in the Mediterranean, in a foreign corps in the pay of England. In this situation he became master of French and Italian, circumstances which highly qualified him for the situation to which he was appointed. In the campaign of 1814, he had been attached to the army of the allies, and carried on a correspondence with the English Government, describing the events of the campaign, part of which was published, and intimates spirit and talent in the writer. Sir Hudson Lowe received from several of the allied sovereigns and generals the most honourable testimonies of his services. He had thus the opportunity and habit of mixing with persons of distinction in the discussion of affairs of importance; and his character as a gentleman and a man of honour was carefully inquired into, and highly vouched, ere his nomination was made out.

But there were other qualifications, and those not less important, his possession of which could only be known by putting him upon trial. The indispensable attribute, for example, of an imperturbable temper, was scarce to be ascertained, until his proceedings in the office entrusted to him should show whether he possessed or wanted it. The same must be said of that firmness and decision, which dictate to an official person the exact line of his duty – prevent all hesitation or wavering in the exercise of his purpose – render him, when it is discharged, boldly and firmly confident that he has done exactly that which he ought – and enable him fearlessly to resist all importunity which can be used to induce him to change his conduct.

Knowing nothing of Sir Hudson Lowe personally, and allowing him to possess the qualities of an honourable, and the accomplishments of a well-informed man, we are inclined, from a review of his conduct, divesting it so far as we can of the exaggerations of his personal enemies, to think there remain traces of a warm and irritable temper, which seems sometimes to have overborne his discretion, and induced him to forget that his prisoner was in a situation where he ought not, even when his conduct seemed most provoking, to be considered as an object of resentment, or as being subject, like other men, to retort and retaliation. Napoleon's situation precluded the possibility of his inflicting an insult, and therefore the temper of the person to whom such was offered, ought, if possible, to have remained cool and unruffled. It does not seem to us that this was uniformly the case. In like manner, Sir Hudson Lowe appears to have been agitated by an oppressive sense of the importance and the difficulties of his situation. This over-anxiety led to frequent changes of his regulations. All this uncertainty occasioned just subject of complaint to his prisoner.

It is probable that the warm temper of Sir Hudson Lowe was in some degree convenient to Napoleon, as it afforded him the means of reprisals upon the immediate instrument of his confinement. But Napoleon's interest in provoking the governor did not rest upon the mere gratification of spleen. His views went far deeper, and were connected with the prospect of obtaining his liberty, and with the mode by which he hoped to accomplish it. And this leads us to inquire upon what these hopes were rested, and to place before our readers evidence of the most indisputable credit, concerning the line of policy adopted in the councils of Longwood.

It must be premised that the military gentlemen, who, so much to the honour of their own fidelity, had attended on Buonaparte, to soften his calamity, were connected by no other link than their mutual respect for the same unhappy master. Being unattached to each other by any ties of friendship, or community of feelings, it is no wonder that these officers, given up to ennui, and feeling the acidity of temper which such a situation is sure to cause, should have had positive quarrels, not with the governor only, but with each other. In these circumstances, the conduct of General Gourgaud distinguished him. As he was in attendance upon the Ex-Emperor at the moment of his fall, he felt it his duty to accompany him to St. Helena. While upon that island, he took less share in Napoleon's complaints and quarrels with the governor than either Generals Bertrand and Montholon, or Count Las Cases, avoided all appearance of intrigue with the inhabitants, and was regarded by Sir Hudson Lowe as a brave and loyal soldier, who followed his emperor in adversity.

This officer had left in France a mother and sister, to whom he was tenderly devoted. General Gourgaud became desirous of revisiting his native country; and his resolution was the stronger that considerable jealousies and misunderstandings arose betwixt him and Count Bertrand. In these circumstances, he obtained permission from the governor to return to London. Before leaving St. Helena, he was very communicative both to Sir Hudson Lowe and Baron Sturmer, the Austrian commissioner, respecting the secret hopes and plans which were carrying on at Longwood. When he arrived in Britain in the spring 1818, he was no less frank with the Government; informing them of the various proposals for escape which had been laid before Napoleon; the facilities and difficulties which attended them, and the reasons why he preferred remaining on the island. At this period it was supposed that General Gourgaud was desirous of making his peace with the King of France; but whatever might be his private views, the minutes of the information which he afforded to Sir Hudson Lowe and Baron Sturmer at St. Helena, and afterwards at London to the Under Secretary at War, are still preserved in the Foreign Office. They agree entirely with each other, and their authenticity cannot be questioned. The communications are studiously made, with considerable reserve as to proper names, in order that no individual should be called in question for any thing; and in general they bear, as was to be expected, an air of the utmost simplicity and veracity.

It was not, according to General Gourgaud, for want of means of escape that Napoleon continued to remain at St. Helena. There was one plan for carrying him out in a trunk with dirty linen; and so general was the opinion of the extreme stupidity of the English sentinels that there was another by which it was proposed he should slip through the camp in disguise of a servant carrying a dish. When Baron Sturmer represented the impossibility of such wild plans being in agitation, Gourgaud answered, "There was no impossibility to those who had millions at their command. Yes, I repeat it," he continued, "he can escape from hence, and go to America whenever he has a mind." – "Why, then, should he remain here?" said Baron Sturmer. Gourgaud replied, "That all his followers had urged him to make the experiment of escape; but he preferred continuing on the island. He has a secret pride in the consequence attached to the custody of his person, and the interest generally taken in his fate. He has said repeatedly, 'I can no longer live as a private person. I would rather be a prisoner on this rock, than a free but undistinguished individual in the United States.'"

General Gourgaud said, therefore, that the event to which Napoleon trusted for liberty, was some change of politics in the court of Great Britain, which should bring into administration the opposition, and who, he rather too rashly perhaps conceived, would at once restore to him his liberty. General Gourgaud's communications further bear, what, indeed, can be collected from many other circumstances, that as Napoleon hoped to obtain his liberty from the impression to be made on the minds of the English nation, he was most anxious that the public mind should be carefully kept alive to it, by a succession of publications, modified according to the different temper and information of the various authors, but bearing all of them the stamp of having issued in whole or in part from the interior of Longwood. Accordingly, the various works of Warden, O'Meara, Santini, the letter of Montholon, and other publications upon St. Helena, appeared one after another, to keep the subject awake; which, although seemingly discharged by various hands, bear the strong peculiarity of being directed at identically the same mark, and of being arrows from the same quiver. Other papers, he said, would appear under the names of captains of merchantmen and the like, for Napoleon was possessed by a mania for scribbling, which had no interruption. It becomes the historian, therefore, to receive with caution the narratives of those who have thus taken a determinedly partial part in the controversy, and concocted their statements from the details afforded by the party principally concerned.

The evidence of O'Meara, contained in a *Voice from St. Helena,* is that of a disappointed man, bitterly incensed against Sir Hudson Lowe. He had no need to kindle the flame of his own resentment, at that of Buonaparte. But it may be granted that their vindictive feelings must have strengthened each other. The quarrel was the more irreconcilable, as it appears that Dr. O'Meara was originally in great habits of intimacy with Sir Hudson, and in the custom of repeating at Plantation-house the gossip which he had heard at Longwood. Some proofs of this were laid before the public, in the *Quarterly Review,* and Sir Hudson Lowe's correspondence with government contains various allusions to Dr. O'Meara's authority, down to the period when their mutual confidence was terminated by a violent quarrel. Count Las Cases is not, in point of impartiality, to be ranked much above Dr. O'Meara. He was originally a French emigrant, a worshipper by profession of royalty, and therefore only changed his idol, not his religion, when he substituted the idol Napoleon for the idol Bourbon. He embraces with passive obedience the interests of his chief, real or supposed, and can see nothing wrong which Napoleon is disposed to think right. He was also the personal enemy of Sir Hudson Lowe. We have no idea that he would falsify the truth; but we cannot but suspect the accuracy of his recollection, when we find he inserts many expressions and incidents in his Journal, long after the period at which it was originally written, and it is to be presumed from memory. Sir Hudson Lowe had the original manuscript for some time, and we have at present before us a printed copy, in which Sir Hudson has marked those additions which had been made since he saw it in its primitive state. It is remarkable that all, or almost all, the additions consist of passages highly injurious to Sir Hudson Lowe, which had no existence in the original manuscript. These additions must therefore have been made under the influence of recollection, sharpened by angry passions, since they did not at first seem important enough to be preserved. When memory is put on the rack by passion and prejudice, she will recollect strange things; and, like witnesses under the actual torture, sometimes avow what never took place.

Of Dr. Antommarchi it is not necessary to say much; he was a legatee of Buonaparte, and an annuitant of his widow, besides being anxious to preserve the countenance of his very wealthy family. He never speaks of Sir Hudson Lowe without rancour. Sir Hudson's first offence against him was inquiring for clandestine correspondence; his last was preventing the crowd at Napoleon's funeral from pulling to pieces the willow-trees by which the grave was sheltered, besides placing a guard over the place of sepulture. What truth is there, then, to be reposed in an author, who can thus misrepresent two circumstances – the one imposed on Sir Hudson Lowe by his instructions; the other being what respect to the deceased imperatively demanded?

The mass of evidence shows that to have remained upon good, or even on decent terms with the governor, would not have squared with the politics of one who desired to have grievances to complain of; and who, far from having the usual motives which may lead a captive and his keeper to a tolerable understanding, wished to provoke the governor, if possible, beyond the extent of human patience, even at the risk of subjecting himself to some new infliction, which might swell the list of wrongs which he was accumulating to lay before the public.

What we have stated above is exemplified by Napoleon's reception of Sir Hudson Lowe, against whom he appears to have adopted the most violent prejudices at the very first interview, and before the governor could have afforded him the slightest disrespect. We quote it, because it shows that the mind of the prisoner was made up to provoke and insult Sir Hudson, without waiting for any provocation on his part. The governor's first aggression (so represented,) was his requiring permission of General Buonaparte to call together his domestics, with a view to their taking the declaration required by the Government, binding themselves to abide by the rules laid down for the custody of Buonaparte. This permission was refused in very haughty terms. The servants, however, appeared, and took the necessary declaration. But the affront was not cancelled; "Sir Hudson Lowe had put his finger betwixt Napoleon and his valet-de-chambre." This was on the 27th April, 1816.

Upon the 30th, the governor again paid his respects at Longwood, and was received with one of those calculated bursts of furious passion with which Napoleon was wont to try the courage and shake the nerves of those over whom he desired to acquire influence. He spoke of protesting against the Convention of Paris, and demanded what right the sovereigns had to dispose of one, their equal always, and often their superior. He called upon the governor for death or liberty. Sir Hudson enlarged on the conveniences of the building which was to be sent from England, to supply the present want of accommodation. Buonaparte repelled the proposed consolation with fury. It was not a house that he wanted, it was an executioner and a line. These he would esteem a favour; all the rest was but irony and insult. Sir Hudson Lowe could in reply only hope that he had given no personal offence, and was reminded of his review of the domestics; which reproach he listened to in silence.

Every attempt at conciliation on the part of the governor seemed always to furnish new subjects of irritation. Sir Hudson sent a variety of clothes and other articles from England, which it might be supposed the exiles were in want of. The thanks returned were, that the governor treated them like paupers, and that the articles ought, in due respect, to have been left at the store, or governor's house, while a list was sent to the household. On [another] occasion, Sir Hudson resolved to be cautious. He had determined to give a ball; but he consulted Dr. O'Meara whether Napoleon would take it well to be invited. The doctor foresaw that the fatal address, General Buonaparte, would make shipwreck of the invitation. The governor proposed to avoid this stumbling-block, by asking Napoleon verbally and in person. But with no name which his civility could devise for the invitation, could it be rendered acceptable.

At length, on 18th August, a decisive quarrel took place. Sir Hudson Lowe was admitted to an audience. Dr. O'Meara has preserved the following account, as it was detailed by Napoleon to his suite, the day after it took place.

'That governor,' said Napoleon, 'came here yesterday to annoy me. He saw me walking in the garden, and in consequence, I could not refuse to see him. He wanted to enter into some details with me about reducing the expenses of the establishment. He had the audacity to tell me that things were as he had found them, and that he came up to justify himself; that he had come up two or three times before to do so, but that I was in a bath.' I replied, 'No, sir, I was not in a bath; but I ordered one on purpose not to see you. In endeavouring to justify yourself you make matters worse.' He said that I did not know him; that, if I knew him, I should change my opinion. 'Know you, sir!' I answered, 'how could I know you? People make themselves known by their actions – by commanding in battles. You have never commanded in battle. You have never commanded any but vagabond Corsican deserters, Piedmontese and Neapolitan brigands. I know the name of every English general who has distinguished himself; but I never heard of you, except as a *scrivano* [clerk] to Blücher, or as a commandant of brigands. You have never commanded, or been accustomed to men of honour.' He said that he had not sought for his present situation. I told him that such employments were not asked for; that they were given to people who had dishonoured themselves. He said, that he only did his duty, and that I ought not to blame him, as he only acted according to his orders. I replied, 'So does the hangman; he acts according to his orders. But when he puts a rope about my neck to finish me, is that a reason that I should like that hangman, because he acts according to his orders? Besides, I do not believe that any government could be so mean as to give such orders as you cause to be executed.' I told him, that if he pleased, he need not send up any thing to eat; that I would go over and dine at the table of the brave officers of the 53rd; that I was sure there was not one of them who would not be happy to give a plate at the table to an old soldier; that there was not a soldier in the regiment who had not more heart than he had; that in the Iniquitous bill of Parliament, they had decreed that I was to be treated as a prisoner; but that he treated me worse than a condemned criminal or a galley slave, as they were permitted to receive newspapers and printed books, of which he deprived me.' I said, 'You have power over my body, but none over my soul. That soul is as proud, fierce, and determined at the present moment, as when it commanded Europe.' I told him that he was a *sbirro Siciliano* (Sicilian thief-taker,) and not an Englishman; and desired him not to let me see him again until he came with orders to despatch me, when he would find all the doors thrown open to admit him.

It is not surprising that this extreme violence met with some return on Sir Hudson's part. He told Napoleon that his language was uncivil and ungentlemanlike, and that he would not remain to listen to it. Accordingly, he left Longwood without even the usual salutation. Upon these occasions, we think it is evident that Napoleon was the wilful and intentional aggressor, and that his conduct proceeded either from the stings of injured pride, or a calculated scheme, which made him prefer being on bad rather than good terms with Sir Hudson Lowe. They never afterwards met in friendship, or even on terms of decent civility.

CHAPTER XCV

Before entering upon such brief inquiry as our bounds permit, into the conduct of the new governor towards Napoleon, it may be necessary to show what were his, Sir Hudson Lowe's, instructions from the English Government on the subject of the custody of the Ex-Emperor:

Downing Street, 12th September, 1816.
You will observe, that the desire of his Majesty's Government is, to allow every indulgence to General Buonaparte, which may be compatible with the entire security of his person. That he should not by any means escape, or hold communication with any person whatsoever, excepting through your agency, must be your unremitted care; and those points being made sure, every resource and

amusement, which may serve to reconcile Buonaparte to his confinement, may be permitted.

A few weeks later, the Secretary of State wrote to Sir Hudson Lowe a letter to the same purpose with the former, 26th October, 1816:

> With respect to General Buonaparte himself, I deem it unnecessary to give you any further instructions. I am confident that your own disposition will prompt you to anticipate the wishes of his Royal Highness the Prince Regent, and make every allowance for the effect which so sudden a change of situation cannot fail to produce on a person of his irritable temper. You will, however, not permit your forbearance or generosity towards him to interfere with any regulations which may have been established for preventing his escape, or which you may hereafter consider necessary for the better security of his person.

The just and honourable principle avowed by Government is obvious. But it was an extraordinary and most delicate tax upon Sir Hudson, which enjoined him to keep fast prisoner an individual who, of all others, was likely to be most impatient of restraint, and, at the same time, to treat him with such delicacy as might disguise his situation from himself, if it could not reconcile him to it. If Sir Hudson failed, he may be allowed to plead that it was in a case in which few could have succeeded.

The first point of complaint, on the part of the family at Longwood, respected the allowance assigned by the British Government for their support, which they alleged to be insufficient. This was not a point on which Napoleon thought it proper to express his feelings in his own person. *His* attention was apparently fixed upon obtaining concessions in certain points of etiquette. The theme was not, however, left untouched, as those concerned were well aware that there was no subject of grievance which would come more home to the people of England. Montholon's letter was clamant on the subject; and Santini intimated that the Emperor must sometimes have gone with out a meal altogether, had he (Santini) not been successful with his gun. The true state of the case was this: The British Government had determined that Napoleon's table should be provided for at the rate of a general of the first rank, together with his military family. The expense of such an establishment was, by the regulations furnished to Sir Hudson Lowe, supposed to reach to £8000 a-year, with permission, however, to extend it as far as £12,000, should he think it necessary. The expense could not, in Hudson Lowe's opinion, be kept within £8000; and indeed it was instantly extended to £12,000. If, however, even £12,000 should, in the governor's opinion, be found, from dearth, high price of provisions, or otherwise, practically insufficient to meet the expense of a general's family, calculated on a liberal scale, Sir Hudson had liberty from Government to extend the purveyor's allowance without limitation. But if, on the other hand, the French should desire to add to their housekeeping any thing which the governor should think superfluous, in reference to the rank assigned to the principal person, they were themselves to be at the charge of such extraordinary expenditure.

It is apprehended that the British Government could not be expected to do more for Napoleon's liberal maintenance, than to give the governor an unlimited order to provide for it, upon the scale applicable to the rank of a general officer of the first rate. But yet the result, as the matter was managed, was not so honourable to Great Britain, as the intentions of the Government designed. Virtues as well as vices have their day of fashion in England; and at the conclusion of the peace, when the nation was cloyed with victory, men began, like epicures after a feast, to wrangle about the reckoning. Everyone felt the influence of the *Quart d'heure de Rabelais*. It ascended into the Houses of Parliament, and economy was the general theme of the day. There can be no doubt that a judicious restriction upon expenditure is the only permanent source of national wealth; but, like all other virtues, parsimony may be carried to an extreme, and there are situations in which it has all the meanness of avarice. The waste of a few pounds of meat, of 100 billets of wood, of a few bottles of wine, ought not to have been made the shadow of a question between Britain and Napoleon; and it would have been better to have winked at and given way to the prodigality of a family, which had no motives of economy, than to be called upon to discuss such petty domestic details in the great council of the nation.

But although such disputes arose, we think, from the governor mistaking the meaning of the British ministers, and descending, if he really did so, to details about the quality of salt or sugar to be used in the kitchen at Longwood, there is no reason to entertain the belief that the prisoners had any actual restriction to complain of, though it might not always happen that articles of the first quality could be procured at St. Helena so easily as at Paris. The East India Company sent out supplies to the purveyor, and they consisted of every luxury which could be imagined; so that delicacies very unusual in St. Helena could, during Napoleon's residence, be obtained. The wine was (generally speaking) excellent in quality, and of the first price;ᵛ and although there was rather too much said and thought about the quantity consumed, yet it was furnished in a quantity far beyond the limits of ordinary conviviality. Indeed, although the French officers, while hunting for grievances, made complaints of their treatment at table, yet when called on as men of honour to give their opinion, they did justice to the governor in this respect.

In a letter of General Bertrand to the governor, he expresses himself thus: "Be assured that we are well persuaded of the good intentions of the governor, to supply us with every thing necessary, and that as to provisions there will never be any complaints, or if there are, they will be made against the government, not against the governor, upon whom the matter does not depend." He adds, "that such were the sentiments of the Emperor. That indeed they had been under some difficulties when the plate was broken up, but that ever since then they had been well supplied, and had no complaint whatever to make." But we have also the opinion of the Ex-Emperor himself, transmitted by Dr. O'Meara, who was, as already noticed, in the habit of sending to the governor such scraps of information:

5th June, 1817

He (Buonaparte) observed that Santini's was a foolish production, exaggerated, full of coglionerie, and some lies: truths there were in it, but exaggerated. That there never had existed that actual want described by him; that there had been enough to eat supplied, but not enough to keep a proper table; that there had been enough of wine for them; that there certainly had been sometimes a deficiency of necessary articles, but that this might be accounted for by accidents; that he believed frequent purchases had been made, at the camp, of bread and other provisions, which might also have occasionally arisen from the same cause. He added he was convinced some Englishman had written it, and not Santini.

It was about the same time that Sir Hudson Lowe was desirous to keep the expense of the establishment within £12,000. A conference on this subject was held betwixt General Montholon, who took charge of the department of the household, and Major Gorrequer, belonging to Sir Hudson's staff. It appears that Sir Hudson had either misapprehended the instructions of the government, and deemed himself rigidly bound to limit the expenses of Longwood within £12,000; or else that he considered the surplus above £1000 per month, to consist of such articles as the French might, in a free interpretation of his instructions, be required to pay for themselves. General Montholon stated that the family could not be provided, even after many reductions, at a cheaper rate than £15,194 and that this was the *minimum of minimums*. He offered that the Emperor would draw for the sum wanted, providing he was permitted to send a sealed letter to the banking-house. This, Major Gorrequer said, could not be allowed. Count Montholon then declared that the Emperor had no other means left than to dispose of his property here.

This proposal was too rashly assented to by Sir Hudson, whose instructions empowered him to have prevented a circumstance so glaringly calculated to accredit all that had ever be said or written respecting the mean manner in which the late Emperor was treated. Napoleon had an opportunity, at the sacrifice of a parcel of old silver plate, to amuse his own moments of languor, by turning into ridicule the inconsistent qualities of the English nation – at one time sending him a house and furniture to the value of £60,000 or £70,000; at another, obliging him to sell his plate, and discharge his servants; and all for the sake of a few bottles of wine, or pounds of meat. Sir Hudson Lowe ought not to have exposed his country to such a charge; he ought to have paid the extra expense, without giving room to such scandal. But if the governor took too narrow a view of his duty upon this occasion, what are we to say of the poor conduct of Napoleon, who, while he had specie in his strong-box to have defrayed three times the alleged balance, yet preferred making the paltry sale alluded to, that he might appear before Europe *in forma pauperis*?

The communications of General Gourgaud put the governor in possession of the curious fact that the breaking up of the plate was a mere trick, resorted to on account of the impression it was calculated to produce; for that at the time they had at Longwood plenty of money. Sir Hudson Lowe conjectured that General Gourgaud alluded to the sale of some stock belonging to Las Cases, the value of which that devoted adherent had placed at Napoleon's disposal; but General Gourgaud replied, "No, no; before that transaction they had received 240,000 francs, chiefly in Spanish doubloons." He further said that it was Prince Eugene who lodged the money in the hands of the bankers.

CHAPTER XCVI

Napoleon's life, until his health began to give way, was of the most regular and monotonous character. Having become a very indifferent sleeper, perhaps from his custom of assigning, during the active part of his life, no precise time for repose, his hours of rising were uncertain. It followed from this, that during the day he occasionally fell asleep, for a few minutes, upon his couch or armchair. At times, his favourite valet-de-chambre, Marchand, read to him while in bed until he was composed to rest, the best remedy, perhaps, for that course of "thick-coming fancies," which must so oft have disturbed the repose of one in circumstances so singular and so melancholy.

So soon as Napoleon arose from bed, he either began to dictate to one of his generals, (Montholon or Gourgaud generally,) and placed upon record such passages of his remarkable life as he desired to preserve; or, if the weather and his inclination suited, he went out for an hour or two on horseback. He sometimes breakfasted in his own apartment, sometimes with his suite, generally about ten o'clock, and almost always *à la fourchette.*

The fore part of the day he usually devoted to reading, or dictating, and about two or three o'clock received such visitors as had permission to wait upon him. An airing in the carriage or on horseback generally succeeded to this species of levee, on which occasions he was attended by all his suite. On returning, he resumed the book, or caused his amanuensis take up the pen until dinner-time, which was about eight o'clock.

He preferred plain food, and eat plentifully, and with an apparent appetite. A very few glasses of claret, scarce amounting to an English pint in all, and chiefly drank during dinner, completed his meal. Sometimes he drank champagne; but his constitutional sobriety was such that a large glass of that more generous wine immediately brought a degree of colour to his cheek. No man appears to have been in a less degree than Napoleon, subject to the influence of those appetites which man has in common with the lower range of nature. He never took more than two meals a day, and concluded each with a small cup of coffee. After dinner, chess, cards, a volume of light literature, read aloud for the benefit of his suite or general conversation, in which the ladies occasionally joined, served to consume the evening till ten or eleven, about which time he retired to his apartment, and went immediately to bed.

We may add to this brief account of Napoleon's domestic habits, that he was very attentive to the duties of the toilet. He usually appeared in the morning in a white night-gown, with loose trousers and stockings joined in one, a chequered red Madras handkerchief round his head, and his shirt-collar open. When dressed, he wore a green uniform, very plainly made, and without ornament, similar to that which, by its simplicity, used to mark the sovereign among the splendid dresses of the Tuileries: white waistcoat, and white or nankeen breeches, with silk stockings, and shoes with gold buckles, a black stock, a triangular cocked hat, of the kind to be seen in all the caricatures, with a very small tri-coloured cockade. He usually wore, when in full dress, the riband and grand cross of the Legion of Honour.

The circumstance of the large portion of his time employed in dictation, makes us anxious to know with what he could have found means to occupy so many pages, and so many hours. The fragments upon military subjects are not voluminous enough to account for the leisure expended in this manner; and even when we add to them the number of pamphlets and works issuing from St. Helena, we shall still find room to suppose either that manuscripts remain which have not yet seen the light, or that Napoleon was a slow composer, and fastidious in the choice of his language. The last conjecture seems most probable, as the French are particularly scrupulous in the punctilios of composition, and Napoleon must have known that he would receive no mercy from the critics.

The works themselves, fragments as they are, are extremely interesting in a military point of view; and those in which the campaigns of Italy are described contain many most invaluable lessons on the art of war. Their political value is by no means considerable. Gourgaud seems to have formed a true estimation of them, when, in answer to Baron Sturmer's inquiries, whether Napoleon was writing his history, he expressed himself thus: "He writes disjointed fragments, which he will never finish. When asked why he will not put history in possession of the exact fact, he answers, it is better to leave something to be guessed at than to tell too much, it would also seem, that not considering his extraordinary destinies as entirely accomplished, he is unwilling to detail plans which have not been executed, and which he may one day resume with more success."

To these reasons for leaving blanks and imperfections, should be added the danger which a faithful and unreserved narrative must have entailed upon many of the actors in the scenes from which he was lifting the veil. It is no doubt true that Napoleon seems systematically to have painted his enemies, more especially such as had been once his adherents, in the most odious colours; but the same principle induced him to spare his friends, and to afford no handle against them for their past efforts in his favour, and no motive for taking from them the power of rendering him further service. These considerations operated as a check upon the pen of the historian; and it may be truly said, that no man who has written so much of his own life, and that consisting of such singular and important events, has told so little of himself which was not known before.

Napoleon's Memoirs, together with the labour apparently bestowed upon his pamphlets written against Sir Hudson Lowe, seem to have furnished the most important part of his occupation whilst at St. Helena, and probably also of his amusement. It was not to be expected that in sickness and calamity he could apply himself to study, even if his youth had furnished him with more stores to work upon. It must be remembered that his whole education had been received at the military school of Brienne, where indeed he displayed a strong taste for the sciences. But the studies of mathematics and algebra were so early carried on with a view to military purposes, that it may be questioned whether he retained any relish for prosecuting his scientific pursuits in the character of an inquirer into abstract truths. The practical results had been so long his motive, so long his object, that he ceased to enjoy the use of the theoretical means when there was no siege to be formed, no complicated manœuvres to be arranged, no great military purpose to be gained by the display of his skill – but when all was to begin and end with the discussion of a problem.

That Napoleon had a natural turn for *belles lettres* is unquestionable; but his leisure never permitted him to cultivate it, or to refine his taste or judgment. He read very extensively; but, like all young persons, with little discrimination, and more to amuse himself than for the purpose of instruction. Before he had arrived at that more advanced period when youths of such talent as his, and especially when gifted with such a powerful memory, usually think of arranging and classifying the information they have collected, the tumults of Corsica, and the siege of Toulon, carried him into those scenes of war which were his element during the rest of his life.

The want of information which we have noticed, he supplied, as most able men do, by the assistance derived from conversing with persons possessing knowledge, and capable of communicating it. No one was ever more dexterous than Napoleon at extracting the kind of information which each was best qualified to impart; and in many cases, while in the act of doing so, he contrived to conceal his own ignorance, even of that which he was anxiously wishing to know. But although in this manner he might acquire facts and results, it was impossible to make himself master, on such easy terms, of general principles, and the connection betwixt them and the conclusions which they lead to.

It was no less certain that though, in this manner, Napoleon could obtain insulated portions of information, and though the knowledge so acquired served his immediate purpose, these were not habits which could induce him to resume those lighter subjects of study so interesting and delightful in youth, but which an advanced age is unwilling to undertake, and slow to profit by. He had, therefore, never corrected his taste in the *belles lettres*, but retained his admiration for Ossian, and other books which had fascinated his early attention. The declamatory tone, redundancy of expression, and exaggerated character of the poetry ascribed to the Celtic bard, suit the taste of very young persons; but Napoleon continued to

retain his relish for them to the end of his life; and, in some of his proclamations, we can trace the hyperbolical and bombastic expressions which
pass upon us in youth for the sublime, but are rejected as taste and reason
become refined. There was indeed this apology for Napoleon's lingering
fondness for Ossian, that the Italian translation, by Cesarotti, is said to be
one of the most beautiful specimens of the Tuscan language. The work
was almost constantly beside him.

Historical, philosophical, or moral works seem more rarely to have
been resorted to. We have, indeed, been informed that the only books of
this description for which Napoleon showed a decided partiality, were
those of Machiavelli and Montesquieu, which he did not perhaps consider as fit themes of public recitation; Tacitus, who holds the mirror so
close to the features of sovereigns, he is said always to have held in aversion, and seldom to have mentioned without terms of censure or dislike.
Thus will the patient sometimes loathe the sight of the most wholesome
medicine. The French novels of the day were sometimes tried as a
resource; but the habits of order and decency which Napoleon observed,
rendered their levities and indelicacies unfitted for such society.

The drama occupied a considerable part of those readings with which
Napoleon used to while away the tedious hours of his imprisonment. This
was an indication that he still retained the national taste of France. He is
said to have read with taste and effect, which agrees with the traditions
that represent him as having been early attached to theatrical representations. It was in the discussions following these readings, which Las Cases
has preserved, that Buonaparte displayed his powers of conversation, and
expressed his peculiar habits and opinions. Corneille and Racine stood
much higher in his estimation than Voltaire. There seems a good reason
for this. They wrote their immortal works for the meridian of a court, and
at the command of the most monarchical of monarchs, Louis XIV. The
productions, therefore, contain nothing that can wound the ear of the
most sensitive sovereign. With Voltaire it is different. The strong and
searching spirit, which afterwards caused the French Revolution, was
abroad at this time, and though unaware of the extent to which it might
lead, the philosopher was not the less its proselyte. There were many passages, therefore, in his works, which could not but be instantly applied to
the convulsions of the period during which Napoleon had lived, to the

despotic character of his government, and to the plans of freedom which had sunk under the influence of his sword. On this account Voltaire, whose compositions recalled painful comparisons and recollections, was no favourite with Napoleon. The *Mahomet* of that author he particularly disliked, avowing, at the same time, his respect for the Oriental impostor, whom he accused the poet of traducing. Perhaps he secretly acknowledged a certain degree of resemblance between his own career and that of the youthful camel-driver, who, rising from a mean origin in his native tribe, became at once the conqueror and the legislator of so many nations.

The character of Caesar was another which Napoleon always strove to vindicate. The French general could not be indifferent to the Roman leader, who, like himself, having at first risen into notice by his victories, had, also like himself, ended the struggles between the patricians and plebeians of Rome, by reducing both parties equally under his own absolute dominion; who would have proclaimed himself their sovereign had he not been prevented by conspiracy; and who thought of nothing so much as extending an empire over the distant regions of Scythia and Parthia. The points of personal difference, indeed, were considerable; for neither did Napoleon indulge in the gross debauchery and sensuality imputed to Caesar, nor can we attribute to him the Roman's powers as an author, or the gentle and forgiving character which distinguished him as a man.

Yet, although Napoleon had something vindictive in his temper, which he sometimes indulged when Caesar would have scorned to do so, his intercourse with his familiar friends was of a character the most amiable. It is true, indeed, that he exacted from his followers the same marks of severe etiquette which distinguished the Court of the Tuileries; yet, in other respects, he permitted them to carry their freedom in disputing his sentiments almost beyond the bounds of ordinary decorum. He seemed to make a distinction between their duty towards him as subjects, and their privileges as friends. All remained uncovered and standing in his presence, and even the person who played at chess with him sometimes continued for hours without sitting down. But their verbal intercourse was that of free men, conversing with a superior, indeed, but not with a despot. Captain Maitland mentions a dispute betwixt Napoleon and General Bertrand. The latter had adopted a ridiculous idea that £30,000 a-year was spent in maintaining Blenheim. Napoleon's turn for calculation easily detected the improbability. Bertrand insisted upon his assertion, on which Buonaparte said with quickness, *"Bah! c'est impossible."* – "Oh!" said Bertrand, much offended, "if you are to reply in that manner, there is an end of all argument;" and for some time would not converse with him. Buonaparte, so far from taking umbrage, did all he could to soothe him and restore him to good-humour. But although Napoleon tolerated freedoms of this kind to a considerable extent, he still kept in his own hands the royal privilege of starting the topic of conversation, and conducting it as he should think proper; so that, in some respects, it seemed that, having lost all the substantial enjoyment of power, he had become more attached than ever to the observance of its monotonous, wearisome, unprofitable ceremonial.

We return to Napoleon's habits of amusement. Music was not one of the number. Though born an Italian, and possessing something of a musical ear, so far as was necessary to hum a song, it was probably entirely without cultivation. He appears to have had none of the fanaticism for music which characterises the Italians; and it is well known that he put a stop to the cruel methods which had been used in that country to complete their concerts. Neither was Napoleon, as we have heard Denon reluctantly admit, a judge or an admirer of painting. He had some pretence to understand sculpture, and there was one painting in the Museum before which he used to pause, terming it his own; nor would he permit it to be ransomed for a very large sum by its proprietor the Duke of Modena. But he valued it, not on account of its merits, though a masterpiece, but because he had himself been the means of securing it at a great sacrifice. The other paintings in that immense collection he seldom paid much attention to. He also shocked admirers of painting by the contempt he showed for the durability of the art. Being informed that a first-rate picture would not last above 500 or 600 years, he exclaimed, "Bah! a fine immortality!" Yet by using Denon's advice, and that of other sçavans, Napoleon sustained a high reputation as an encourager of the arts. His medals have been particularly and deservedly admired.

In respect of personal exercise at St. Helena, he walked occasionally, and, while strong, did not shun steep, rough, and dangerous paths. But although there is some game on the island, he did not avail himself of the pleasure of shooting. It does not indeed appear that he was ever much attached to field sports, although, when Emperor, he replaced the hunting establishment upon a scale still more magnificent than formerly. It is supposed he partook of this princely pastime rather out of a love of magnificent display than any real attachment to the sport.

The society of St. Helena receives a great temporary increase at the seasons when vessels touch there on their way to India, or on their return to Europe. Of course, every officer and every passenger on such occasions was desirous to see Napoleon; and there might sometimes occur individuals among them whom he too might have pleasure in receiving. Of these interviews, some who enjoyed them have published an account; and the memoranda of others we have seen in manuscript. All agree in extolling the extreme good grace, propriety, and appearance of benevolence with which Napoleon clothed himself whilst holding these levees; and which scarce left the spectators permission to believe that, when surprised by a fit of passion, or when choosing to assume one, he could appear the rude, abrupt, and savage despot. His questions were uniformly introduced with great tact, so as to put the person interrogated at his ease, by leading to some subject with which he was acquainted, while, at the same time, they induced him to produce any stock of new or curious information which he possessed.

The Journal of Captain Basil Hall of the Royal Navy affords a pleasing example of what we have been endeavouring to express, and displays at the same time the powerful extent of Buonaparte's memory. He recognised the name of Captain Hall instantly, from having seen his father, Sir James Hall, Bart., when he was at Brienne. Buonaparte explained the cause of his recollecting a private individual, after the intervention of such momentous events. "It is not," he said, "surprising. Your father was the first Englishman that I ever saw; and I have recollected him all my life on that account." He was afterwards minute in his inquiries respecting the Royal Society of Edinburgh, of which Sir James Hall was long President. He then came to the very interesting subject of the newly-discovered island of Loo-Choo.[24]

"Having settled where the island lay, he cross-questioned me about the inhabitants with a closeness – I may call it a severity of investigation – which far exceeds every thing I have met with in any other instance. His questions were not by any means put at random but each one had some definite reference to that which preceded it, or was about to follow. I felt in a short time so completely exposed to his view, that it would have been impossible to have concealed or qualified the smallest particular. Such, indeed, was the rapidity of his apprehension of the subjects which interested him, and the astonishing ease with which he arranged and generalised the few points of information I gave him, that he sometimes outstripped my narrative, saw the conclusion I was coming to before I spoke it, and fairly robbed me of my story."

Several circumstances, however, respecting the Loo-Choo people, surprised even him a good deal; and I had the satisfaction of seeing him more than once completely perplexed, and unable to account for the phenomena which I related. Nothing struck him so much as their having no arms. *'Point d'armes!'* he exclaimed, *'c'est a dire point de cannons – ils ont des fusils?'* Not even muskets, I replied. *'Eh bien donc – des lances, ou, au moins des arcs et des flèches?'* I told him they had neither one nor other. *'Ni poignards?'* cried he, with increasing vehemence. 'No, none.' *'Mais!'* said Buonaparte, clenching his fist, and raising his voice to a loud pitch, *'Mais! sans armes, comment se bat-on?'*

I could only reply, that as far as we had been able to discover, they had never had any wars, but remained in a state of internal and external peace. 'No wars!' cried he, with a scornful and incredulous expression, as if the existence of any people under the sun without wars was a monstrous anomaly.

In like manner, but without being so much moved, he seemed to discredit the account I gave him of their having no money, and of their setting no value upon our silver or gold coins. After hearing these facts, he mused for some time, muttering to himself in a low tone, 'Not know the use of money – are careless about gold and silver.' Then, looking up, he asked sharply, 'How then did you contrive to pay these strangest of all people for the bullocks and other good things which they seem to have sent on board in such quantities?' When I informed him that we could not prevail upon the people of Loo-Choo to receive payment of any kind, he expressed great surprise at their liberality, and made me repeat to him twice the list of things with which we were supplied by these hospitable islanders.

The low state of the priesthood in Loo-Choo was a subject which he dwelt on without coming to any satisfactory explanation. Captain Hall illustrated the ignorance of the people of Loo-Choo with respect to all the world, save Japan and China, by saying they knew nothing of Europe at all – knew nothing of France and England – and never had even heard of his Majesty; at which last proof of their absolute seclusion from the world, Napoleon laughed heartily. During the whole interview, Napoleon waited with the utmost patience until his questions were replied to, inquired with earnestness into every subject of interest, and made naturally a most favourable impression on his visitor.

'Buonaparte,' says the acute traveller, 'struck me as differing considerably from the pictures and busts I had seen of him. His face and figure looked much broader and more square, larger indeed, in every way, than any representation I had met with. His corpulency, at this time universally reported to be excessive, was by no means remarkable. His flesh looked, on the contrary, firm and muscular. There was not the least trace of colour in his cheeks; in fact, his skin was more like marble than ordinary flesh. Not the smallest trace of a wrinkle was discernible on his brow, nor an approach to a furrow on any part of his countenance. His health and spirits, judging from appearances, were excellent; though at this period it was generally believed in England that he was fast sinking under a complication of diseases, and that his spirits were entirely gone. His manner of speaking was rather slow than otherwise, and perfectly distinct: he waited with great patience and kindness for my answers to his questions, and a reference to Count Bertrand was necessary only once during the whole conversation. The brilliant and sometimes dazzling expression of his eye could not be overlooked. It was not, however, a permanent lustre, for it was only remarkable when he was excited by some point of particular interest. It is impossible to imagine an expression of more entire mildness. I may almost call it of benignity and kindliness, than that which played over his features during the whole interview. If, therefore, he were at this time out of health and in low spirits, his power of self-command must have been even more extraordinary than is generally supposed for his whole deportment, his conversation, and the expression of his countenance, indicated a frame in perfect health, and a mind at ease.'

The date of this meeting was 13th August, 1817.

CHAPTER XCVII

Reports had been long current concerning the decline of Buonaparte's health, even before the battle of Waterloo; and many were disposed to impute his failure in that campaign, to the decrease of his own habits of activity. There seems no room for such a conclusion. The rapid manner in which he concentrated his army upon Charleroi ought to have silenced such a report forever. He was subject occasionally to slight fits of sleepiness, such as are incident to most men, especially after the age of forty, who sleep ill, rise early, and work hard.

When he landed at St. Helena, so far did he seem from showing any appearance of declining health, that one of the British grenadiers, who saw him, exclaimed, with his national oath, "They told us he was growing old; he has forty good campaigns in his belly yet, d—n him!" Yet at this time, viz. July, 1817, Napoleon was alleging the decline of his health as a reason for obtaining more indulgence, while, on the other hand, he refused to take the exercise judged necessary to preserve his constitution, unless a relaxation of superintendence should be granted. It is probable, however, that he felt, even at that period, the symptoms of that malady which consumed his life. It is now well known to have been the cruel complaint of which his father died, a cancer in the stomach, of which he had repeatedly expressed his apprehensions. The progress of this disease, however, is slow and insidious, if indeed it had actually commenced so early as 1817.

Gourgaud, at a much later period, avowed himself a complete disbeliever in his illness. He allowed, indeed, that he was in low spirits to such an extent as to talk of destroying himself and his attached followers, by shutting himself and them up in a small apartment with burning charcoal – an easy death, which Berthollet the chemist had, it seems, recommended. Nevertheless, "on the subject of General Buonaparte's health, General Gourgaud stated, that the English were much imposed upon; for that he was not, as far as bodily health was concerned, in any degree materially altered, and that the representations upon this subject had little, if any, truth in them. Dr. O'Meara was certainly the dupe of that influence which General Buonaparte always exercises over those with whom he has frequent intercourse, and though he (General Gourgaud) individually had only reason *de se louer de Mr. O'Meara,* yet his intimate knowledge of General Buonaparte enabled him confidently to assert, that his state of health was not at all worse than it had been for some time previous to his arrival at St. Helena."

Yet, as before hinted, notwithstanding the disbelief of friends and foes, it seems probable that the dreadful disease of which Napoleon died was already seizing upon the vitals, though its character was not decisively announced. Dr. Arnott, surgeon to the 20th regiment, who attended on Napoleon's death-bed, has made the following observations upon this important subject:

> We are given to understand that this affection of the stomach cannot be produced without a considerable predisposition of the parts to disease. I will not venture an opinion: but it is somewhat remarkable that he often said that his father died of scirrhus of the pylorus; that the body was examined after death, and the fact ascertained. His faithful followers, Count and Countess Bertrand, and Count Montholon, have repeatedly declared the same to me.
>
> If, then, it should be admitted that a previous disposition of the parts to this disease did exist, might not the depressing passions of the mind act as an exciting cause? It is more than probable that Napoleon Buonaparte's mental sufferings in St. Helena were very poignant. By a man of such unbounded ambition, and who once aimed at universal dominion, captivity must have been severely felt.
>
> The climate of St. Helena I consider healthy. The air is pure and temperate, and Europeans enjoy their health, and retain the vigour of their constitution, as in their native country.

Dr. Arnott proceeds to state that, notwithstanding this, dysentery, and other acute diseases of the abdominal viscera prevailed among the troops. This he imputes to the carelessness and intemperance of the English soldiers, and the fatigue of the working parties; as the officers, who had little night duty, retained their health and strength as in Europe.

I can therefore safely assert, that anyone of temperate habits, who is not exposed to much bodily exertion, night air, and atmospherical changes may have as much immunity from disease in St. Helena as in Europe; and I may therefore further assert, that the disease of which Napoleon Buonaparte died was not the effect of climate.

In support of Dr. Arnott's statement, it may be observed, that of Napoleon's numerous family of nearly fifty persons, English servants included, only one died during all their five years' residence on the island; and that person (Cipriani, the major-domo) had contracted the illness which carried him off, being a species of consumption, before he left Europe.

Dr. Arnott, to whose opinion we are induced to give great weight, both from the excellence of his character and his having the best opportunities of information, states that the scirrhus, or cancer of the stomach, is an obscure disease; the symptoms which announce it being common to, and characteristic of, other diseases in the same region; yet he early conceived that some morbid alteration of the structure of the stomach had taken place, especially after he learned that his patient's father had died of scirrhus of the pylorus. He believed, as already hinted, that the disease was in its incipient state even so far back as the end of the year 1817, when the patient was affected with pain in the stomach, nausea, and vomiting, especially after taking food; which symptoms never left him from that period, but increased till the day of his death.

From this period, therefore, Napoleon was in a situation which, considering his great actions, and the height of his former fortunes, deserved the compassion of his most bitter enemies, and the sympathy of all who were disposed to take a moral lesson from the most extraordinary vicissitude of human affairs which history has ever presented. Nor can we doubt that such reflections might have eventually led to much relaxation in the severity with which the prisoner was watched, and, it may be, at length, to his entire emancipation. But to attain this end, it would have been necessary that Napoleon's conduct should have been of a very different character. He ought to have permitted the visits of some medical person, whose report might be held as completely impartial. This could not be the case with Dr. O'Meara, engaged as he was in the prisoner's intimate and even secret service; and Napoleon's positive rejection of all other assistance seemed to countenance the belief, however unjust, that he was either feigning indisposition, or making use of some slight symptoms of it to obtain a relaxation of the governor's vigilance. Nor was it to be supposed that Dr. Antommarchi's evidence, being that of an individual entirely dependent on Napoleon, could be considered as more authentic, till corroborated by some indifferent, and, at the same time, competent medical authority.

About the 25th of September, 1817, Napoleon's health seems to have been seriously affected. He complained much of nausea, his legs swelled, and there were other unfavourable symptoms, which induced his physician to tell him that he was of a temperament which required much activity; and that without exercise he must soon lose his health. He immediately declared that while exposed to the challenge of sentinels, he never would take exercise, however necessary. Dr. O'Meara proposed calling in the assistance of Dr. Baxter, a medical gentleman of eminence on Sir Hudson's staff. "He could but say the same as you do," said Napoleon, "and recommend my riding abroad; nevertheless, as long as the present system continues, I will never stir out." At another time he expressed the same resolution, and his determination to take no medicines. Dr. O'Meara replied that, if the disease should not be encountered by remedies in due time, it would terminate fatally. His answer was remarkable: "I will have at least the consolation that my death will be an eternal dishonour to the English nation, who sent me to this climate to die under the hands of ****." The physician again represented, that, by neglecting to take medicine, he would accelerate his own death. "That which is written is written," said Napoleon, looking up. "Our days are reckoned."

This deplorable course seems to have been adopted partly to spite Sir Hudson Lowe, partly in the reckless feelings of despondency inspired by his situation, and in some degree, perhaps, was the effect of the disease itself, which must necessarily have disinclined him to motion. When the governor sent to offer him some extension of his riding ground, and Dr. O'Meara wished him to profit by the permission, he replied, that he should be insulted by the challenge of the sentinels, and that he did not choose to submit to the caprice of the governor.

The removal of Dr. O'Meara from Napoleon's person, which was considered by him as a great injury, was the next important incident in the monotony of his life. Sir Hudson again offered the assistance of Dr. Baxter, but this was construed into an additional offence. It was even treated with suspicion. The governor tried, it was said, to palm his own private physician upon the Emperor, doubtless that he might hold his life more effectually in his power. Dr. Stokoe, surgeon on board the Conqueror, was next called in to visit at Longwood. But differences arose betwixt him and the governor, and after a few visits his attendance on Napoleon was discharged.

After this, the prisoner expressed his determination, whatever might be the extremity of his case, not to permit the visits of an English physician; and a commission was sent to Italy to obtain a medical man of reputation. At the same time, Napoleon signified a desire to have the company of a Catholic priest. The proposition for this purpose came through his uncle, Cardinal Fesch, and readily received the assent of the British ministry. Napoleon had declared his resolution to die in the faith of his fathers. He was neither an infidel, he said, nor a philosopher. If we doubt whether a person who had conducted himself towards the Pope in the way which history records of Napoleon, and who had at one time been excommunicated, (if, indeed, the ban was yet removed,) could be sincere in his general professions of Catholicism we must at least acquit the Exile of the charge of deliberate atheism. On various occasions, he expressed, with deep feelings of devotion, his conviction of the existence of the Deity, the great truth upon which the whole system of religion rests; and this at a time when the detestable doctrines of atheism and materialism were generally current in France.

The vessel which arrived at St. Helena on the 18th September, 1819, with these physicians for the mind, brought with them Dr. F. Antommarchi, anatomic pro-sector (that is, assistant to a professor of anatomy) to the Hospital of St. Marie Neuve at Florence, attached to the University of Pisa. Dr. Antommarchi seems to have been acceptable to Napoleon, and the rather that he was a native of Corsica. His lost hopes aggravating the progress of the cruel disease, which had its source in the stomach, it now affected the whole frame, and undermined the strength of the constitution. The symptoms of disorganisation in the digestive powers became more and more apparent, and his reluctance to take any medicine, as if from an instinctive persuasion that the power of physic was in vain, continued as obstinate as ever. On one of the many disputes which he maintained on this subject, he answered Antommarchi's reasoning thus: "Doctor, no physicking. We are, as I already told you, a machine made to live. We are organised for that purpose, and such is our nature. Do not counteract the living principle. Let it alone – leave it the liberty of defending itself – it will do better than your drugs. Our body is a watch that is intended to go for a given time. The watchmaker cannot open it; and must, on handling it, grope his way blindfolded and at random. For once that he assists and relieves it by dint of tormenting it with his crooked instruments, he injures it ten times, and at last destroys it." This was on the 14th of October, 1820.

As the Ex-Emperor's health grew weaker, it cannot be thought extraordinary that his mind became more and more depressed. In lack of other means of amusing himself, he had been somewhat interested in the construction of a pond and fountain, which was stocked with small fishes. A mixture of copperas in the mastick employed in cementing the basin had affected the water. The creatures which had been in a good measure the object of Napoleon's attention, began to sicken and to die. He was deeply affected by the circumstance, and, in language strongly resembling the beautiful verses of Moore, expressed his sense of the fatality which seemed to attach itself to him. "Every thing I love – every thing that belongs to me," he exclaimed, "is immediately struck. Heaven and mankind unite to afflict me." At other times he lamented his decay of energy. The bed was now a place of luxury, which he would not exchange for all the thrones in the universe. The eyes, which formerly were so vigilant, could now scarcely be opened. He recollected that he used to dictate to four or five secretaries at once. "But then," he said, "I was Napoleon – now I am no longer any thing – my strength, my faculties, forsake me – I no longer live, I only exist." Often he remained silent for many hours, suffering, as may be supposed, much pain, and immersed in profound melancholy.

About the 22nd January, 1821, Napoleon appeared to resume some energy, and to make some attempt to conquer his disease by exercise. He mounted his horse, and galloped, for the last time, five or six miles around the limits of Longwood, but nature was overcome by the effort. He complained that his strength was sinking under him rapidly. Towards the end of March the disease assumed a character still more formidable, and Dr. Antommarchi became desirous of obtaining a consultation with some English medical men. The Emperor's aversion to their assistance had been increased by a well-meant offer of the governor, announcing that a physician of eminence had arrived, whom he placed at General Buonaparte's devotion. This proposal, like every other advance on the part of Sir Hudson, had been received as a meditated injury; "He wants to deceive Europe by false bulletins" said Napoleon; "I will not see anyone who is in communication with him." To refuse seeing every physician but his own was certainly an option which ought to have been left in Napoleon's choice. But in thus obstinately declining to see an impartial medical man, whose report must have been conclusive respecting his state of health, Napoleon unquestionably strengthened the belief that his case was not so desperate as it proved to be.

At length the Ex-Emperor consented that Dr. Antommarchi should consult with Dr. Arnott. But the united opinion of the medical gentlemen could not overcome the aversion of Napoleon to medicine, or shake the belief which he reposed in the gloomy doctrines of fatalism. "Quod scriptum scriptum," he replied in the language of a Moslem; "All that is to happen is written down. Our hour is marked, and it is not in our power to claim a moment longer of life than Fate has predestined for us."

Dr. Antommarchi finally prevailed in obtaining admittance for Dr. Arnott into the apartment and presence of the patient, who complained chiefly of his stomach, of the disposition to vomit, and deficiency of the digestive powers. He saw him for the first time on 2nd April, 1821, and continued his visits regularly. Napoleon expressed his opinion that his liver was affected. Dr. Arnott's observations led him to think that, though the action of the liver might be imperfect, the seat of the disease was to be looked for elsewhere. And here it is to be remarked that Napoleon, when Dr. Antommarchi expressed doubts on the state of his stomach, had repelled them with sharpness, though his own private belief was that he was afflicted with the disease of his father. Thus, with a capricious inconsistency, natural enough to a sick bed, he communicated to some of his retinue his sense of what disease afflicted him, though, afraid perhaps of some course of medicine being proposed, he did not desire that his surgeon should know his suspicions. From the 15th to the 24th of April, Napoleon was engaged from time to time in making his testamentary bequests.

As the strength of the patient gradually sunk, the symptoms of his disease became less equivocal, until, on the 27th April, the ejection of a dark-coloured fluid gave further insight into the nature of the malady. Dr. Antommarchi persevered in attributing it to climate, which was flattering the wish of the patient, who desired to lay his death upon his confinement; while Dr. Arnott expressed his belief that the disease was the same which cut off his father in the pure air of Montpellier. Upon the 28th of April, Napoleon gave instructions to Antommarchi, that after his death his body should be opened, but that no English medical man should touch him, unless in the case of assistance being absolutely necessary, in which case he gave Antommarchi leave to call in that of Dr. Arnott. He directed that his heart should be conveyed to Parma, to Maria Louisa; and requested anxiously that his stomach should be particularly examined, and the report transmitted to his son. "The vomitings," he said, "which succeed one another without interruption, lead me to suppose that the stomach is, of all my organs, the most diseased; and I am inclined to believe that it is attacked with the same disorder which killed my father – I mean a scirrhus in the pylorus." On the 2nd May, the patient returned to the same interesting subject, reminded Antommarchi of his anxiety that the stomach should be carefully examined. "The physicians of Montpellier had announced that the scirrhus in the pylorus would be hereditary in my family. Their report is, I believe, in the hands of Louis. Ask for it, and compare it with your own observations, that I may save my son from the sufferings I now experience."

During the 3rd May, it was seen that the life of Napoleon was drawing evidently to a close; and his followers, and particularly his physician, became desirous to call in more medical assistance; that of Dr. Shortt, physician to the forces, and of Dr. Mitchell, surgeon of the flagship. Dr. Shortt, however, thought it proper to assert the dignity belonging to his profession, and refused (being under the same roof with the patient,) to give an opinion on a case of so much importance, and attended with so much obscurity, unless he were permitted to examine him. The officers of

Napoleon's household excused themselves by professing that the Emperor's strict commands had been laid on them that no English physician, Dr. Arnott excepted, should approach his dying bed. They said that even when he was speechless they would be unable to brook his eye, should he turn it upon them in reproof for their disobedience.

About two o'clock of the same day, the priest Vignali administered the sacrament of extreme unction. Some days before, Napoleon had explained to him the manner in which he desired his body should be laid out in state, in an apartment lighted by torches, or what Catholics call *une chambre ardente*. "I am neither," he said, "a philosopher nor a physician. I believe in God, and am of the religion of my father. It is not every body who can be an atheist. I was born a Catholic, and will fulfil all the duties of the Catholic Church, and receive the assistance which it administers." He then turned to Dr. Antommarchi, whom he seems to have suspected of heterodoxy. "How can you carry it so far?" he said. "Can you not believe in God, whose existence every thing proclaims, and in whom the greatest minds have believed?"

A dreadful tempest arose on the 4th May, which preceded the day that was to close the mortal existence of this extraordinary man. A willow, which had been the Exile's favourite, and under which he had often enjoyed the fresh breeze, was torn up by the hurricane; and almost all the trees about Longwood shared the same fate. The 5th of May came amid wind and rain. Napoleon's passing spirit was deliriously engaged in a strife more terrible than that of the elements around. The words *"tête d'armée,"* the last which escaped his lips, intimated that his thoughts were watching the current of a heady fight. About eleven minutes before six in the evening, Napoleon, after a struggle which indicated the original strength of his constitution, breathed his last.

The officers of Napoleon's household were disposed to have the body anatomised in secret. But Sir Hudson Lowe had too deep a sense of responsibility to permit this to take place. He declared that even if he were reduced to make use of force, he would insure the presence of English physicians at the dissection. Generals Bertrand and Montholon, with Marchand, the valet-de-chambre, were present at the operation, which took place on the 6th of May. It was also witnessed by Sir Thomas Reade, and some British staff-officers. Drs. Thomas Shortt, Archibald Arnott,

Charles Mitchell, Matthew Livingstone, and Francis Burton, all of them medical men, were also present. The cause of death was sufficiently evident. A large ulcer occupied almost the whole of the stomach. It was only the strong adhesion of the diseased parts of that organ to the concave surface of the lobe of the liver, which, being over the ulcer, had prolonged the patient's life by preventing the escape of the contents of the stomach into the cavity of the abdomen. All the other parts of the viscera were found in a tolerably healthy state. The report was signed by the British medical gentlemen present. Dr. Antommarchi was about to add his attestation, when, according to information which we consider as correct, General Bertrand interdicted his doing so, because the report was drawn up as relating to the body of General Buonaparte. Dr. Antommarchi's own account does not, we believe, greatly differ from that of the British professional persons, though he has drawn conclusions from it which are apparently inconsistent with the patient's own conviction, and the ghastly evidence of the anatomical operation. He continued to insist that his late patron had not died of the cancer which we have described, but of a *chronic gastro hepatitis,* a disease he stated to be endemic in the island of St. Helena; although we do not observe it asserted or proved that the hospital of the island at any time produced a single case like that of the deceased.

The gentlemen of Napoleon's suite were desirous that his heart should be preserved and given to their custody but Sir Hudson Lowe did not feel himself at liberty to permit this. He agreed, however, that the heart should be placed in a silver vase, filled with spirits, and interred along with the body; so that, in case his instructions from home should so permit, it might be afterwards disinhumed and sent to Europe. The place of interment became the next subject of discussion. On this subject Napoleon had been inconsistent. His testamentary disposition expressed a wish that his remains should be deposited on the banks of the Seine; a request which he could not for an instant suppose would be complied with, and which appears to have been made solely for the sake of producing effect.

A grave for the Emperor of France, within the limits of the rocky island to which his last years were limited, was the alternative; and sensible that this was likely to be the case, he had himself indicated the spot where he wished to lie. It was a small secluded recess, called Slane's or

Haines' Valley, where a fountain arose, at which his Chinese domestics used to fill the silver pitchers which they carried to Longwood for Napoleon. The spot had more of verdure and shade than any in the neighbourhood; and the illustrious Exile was often accustomed to repose under the beautiful weeping willows which overhung the spring.

The body, after lying in state in his small bedroom, during which time it was visited by every person of condition in the island, was, on the 8th May, carried to the place of interment. The pall which covered the coffin was the military cloak which Napoleon had worn at the battle of Marengo. The members of his late household attended as mourners, and were followed by the governor, the admiral, and all the civil and military authorities of the island. All the troops were under arms upon the solemn occasion. As the road did not permit a near approach of the hearse, a party of British grenadiers had the honour to bear the coffin to the grave. The prayers were recited by Abbé Vignali. Minute guns were fired from the admiral's ship. The coffin was then let down into the grave, under a discharge of three successive volleys of artillery from fifteen pieces of cannon. A large stone was then lowered down on the grave, and covered the moderate space now sufficient for the man for whom Europe was once too little.

CONCLUSION

Napoleon was not imposing at first glance, his stature being only five feet six inches. His person, thin in youth, and somewhat corpulent in age, was rather delicate than robust in appearance, but cast in the mould most capable of enduring privation and fatigue. He rode ungracefully, without the command of his horse which distinguishes a perfect cavalier. But he was fearless, sat firm in his seat, rode with rapidity, and was capable of enduring the exercise for a longer time than most men. We have already mentioned his indifference to the quality of his food, and his power of enduring abstinence. A morsel of food and a flask of wine hung at his saddle-bow, used, in his earlier campaigns, to support him for days. In his latter wars, he more frequently used a carriage; not, as has been surmised, from any particular illness, but from feeling in a frame so constantly in exercise the premature effects of age.

The countenance of Napoleon is familiar to almost everyone. The dark-brown hair bore little marks of the attentions of the toilet. The shape of the countenance approached more than is usual to a square. His eyes were grey and full of expression, the pupils rather large, and the eye-brows not very strongly marked. The brow and upper part of the countenance was rather of a stern character. His nose and mouth were beautifully formed. The upper lip was very short. The teeth were indifferent, but were little shown in speaking. His smile possessed uncommon sweetness, and is stated to have been irresistible. The complexion was a clear olive, otherwise in general colourless. The prevailing character of his countenance was grave, even to melancholy, but without any signs of severity or violence. After death, the placidity and dignity of expression which continued to occupy the features rendered them eminently beautiful, and the admiration of all who looked on them.

His personal and private character was decidedly amiable, excepting in one particular. His temper, when he received, or thought he received, provocation, especially of a personal character, was warm and vindictive.

He was, however, placable in the case even of his enemies, providing that they submitted to his mercy; but he had not that species of generosity which respects the sincerity of a manly and fair opponent. On the other hand, no one was a more liberal rewarder of the attachment of his friends. He was an excellent husband, a kind relation, and, unless when state policy intervened, a most affectionate brother. General Gourgaud, whose communications were not in every case to Napoleon's advantage, states him to have been the best of masters, labouring to assist all his domestics, giving them the highest credit for such talents as they actually possessed, and imputing; in some instances, good qualities to such as had them not.

There was gentleness, and even softness, in his character. He was affected when he rode over the fields of battle, which his ambition had strewed with the dead and the dying, and seemed not only desirous to relieve the victims – issuing for that purpose directions – but showed himself subject to the influence of that more acute and imaginative species of sympathy, which is termed sensibility. As he passed over a field of battle in Italy, with some of his generals, he saw a houseless dog lying on the body of his slain master. The creature came towards them, then returned to the dead body, moaned over it pitifully, and seemed to ask their assistance. "Whether it were the feeling of the moment," continued Napoleon, "the scene, the hour, or the circumstance itself, I was never so deeply affected by any thing which I have seen upon a field of battle. That man, I thought, has perhaps had a house, friends, comrades, and here he lies deserted by everyone but his dog. How mysterious are the impressions to which we are subject? I was in the habit, without emotion, of ordering battles which must decide the fate of a campaign, and could look with a dry eye on the execution of manœuvres which must be attended with much loss; and here I was moved – nay, painfully affected – by the cries and the grief of a dog. It is certain that at that moment I should have been more accessible to a suppliant enemy, and could better understand the conduct of Achilles in restoring the body of Hector to the tears of Priam." The anecdote at once shows that Napoleon possessed a heart amenable to humane feelings, and that they were usually in total subjection to the stern precepts of military stoicism. It was his common and expressive phrase, that the heart of a politician should be in his head; but his feelings sometimes surprised him in a gentler mood.

A calculator by nature and by habit, Napoleon was fond of order, and a friend to that moral conduct in which order is best exemplified. The libels of the day have made some scandalous averments to the contrary, but without adequate foundation. Napoleon respected himself too much, and understood the value of public opinion too well, to have plunged into general or vague debauchery. Considering his natural disposition, then, it may be assumed that if Napoleon had continued in the vale of private life, and no strong temptation of passion or revenge had crossed his path, he must have been generally regarded as one whose friendship was every way desirable, and whose enmity it was not safe to incur.

But the opportunity afforded by the times and the elasticity of his own great talents raised him with unexampled celerity to a sphere of great power, and at least equal temptation. Ere we consider the use which he made of his ascendency, let us briefly review the causes by which it was accomplished. The consequences of the Revolution, however fatal to private families, were the means of filling the camps of the nation with armies of a description which Europe had never seen before, and it is to be hoped, will never witness again. There was neither safety, honour, nor subsistence, in any other profession than the military; and accordingly it became the refuge of the best and bravest of the youth of France, until the army ceased to consist, as in most nations, of the miserable and disorderly, but was levied in the bosom of the state, and composed of the flower of France. With such men, the generals of the republic achieved many and great victories, but without being able to ensure corresponding advantages. This may have been in a great measure occasioned by the dependence in which these leaders were held by the various administrators of the republic – a dependence accounted for by the necessity of having recourse to those in power at Paris, for the means of paying and supporting their armies. From the time that Napoleon passed the Alps, he inverted this state of things; and made the newly conquered countries not only maintain the army, but even contribute to support the government. Thus war, which had hitherto been a burden to the republic, became a source of public revenue; while the youthful general was enabled to assert the freedom at which he speedily aimed, and correspond with the Directory upon a footing approaching to equality. His talents as a soldier and situation as a victorious general soon raised him from equality to pre-eminence.

In strategy, he applied upon a gigantic scale the principles upon which Frederick of Prussia had acted, and gained a capital or a kingdom, when Frederick would have won a town or a province. His system was, of course, that of assembling the greatest possible force upon the vulnerable point of the enemy's position, paralysing, perhaps, two parts of their army, while he cut the third to pieces, and then following up by destroying the remainder in detail. For this purpose, he taught generals to divide their armies upon the march, with a view to celerity of movement and facility of supply, and to unite them at the moment of contest, where an attack would be most feebly resisted, because least expected. For this, also, he first threw aside all species of baggage which could possibly be dispensed with – supplied the want by the contributions exacted from the country, or collected by a regular system of marauding – discontinued the use of tents, and trusted to bivouacking, where hamlets could not be found, and there was no time to erect huts. His system was ruinous in point of lives, for even the military hospitals were often dispensed with; but although Moreau termed Napoleon a conqueror at the rate of 10,000 men a-day, the sacrifice for a length of time uniformly attained the object for which it was designed. The enemy who had remained in their extensive cantonments, distracted by the reports of various columns moving in different directions, were surprised and defeated by the united force of the French, which had formed a junction where and when it was least expected. It was not till they had acquired the art of withdrawing from his attack so soon as made, that the allies learned to defeat the efforts of his movable columns.

Napoleon was not less original as a tactician than as a strategist. His manœuvres on the field of battle had the promptness and decision of the thunderbolt. In the actual shock of conflict, his object was to amuse the enemy upon many points, while he oppressed one by an unexpected force of numbers. The breaking through the line, the turning of a flank, which had been his object from the commencement, lay usually disguised under a great number of previous demonstrations, and was not attempted until both the moral and physical force of the enemy was impaired by the length of the combat. It was at this period that he brought up his guards, who had been held in readiness for hours, and now, springing forward like wolf-dogs from the leash, had the glorious task, in which they rarely failed, of deciding the long-sustained contest. It may be added that he preferred employing the order of the column to the line; perhaps on account of the faith which he might rest in the extreme valour of the officers by whom the column was headed.

The interest which Napoleon preserved in the French soldier's affection by a frequent distribution of prizes and distinctions, joined to his possession of absolute and independent command, rendered it no difficult matter for him to secure their support in the revolution of the eighteenth Brumaire, and in placing him at the head of affairs. Most part of the nation were heartily tired of the continually unsettled state of the government, and the people in general desired a settled form of government, which, if less free, should be more stable in duration, and better calculated to assure to individuals the protection of property and of personal freedom. A successful general, of a character more timid, or conscience more tender, might have attempted the restoration of the Bourbons. But Napoleon foresaw the difficulties which would occur by an attempt to reconcile the recall of the emigrants to the assurance of the national sales and aptly concluded that the parties which tore France to pieces would be most readily amalgamated under the authority of one, who was in a great measure a stranger to them all.

Arrived at the possession of supreme power, a height that dazzles and confounds so many, Napoleon seemed only to occupy the station for which he was born, to which his peculiar powers adapted him, and his brilliant career of success gave him, under all circumstances, an irresistible claim. He continued, therefore, with a calm mind and enlightened wisdom, to consider the means of rendering his power stable, of destroying the republican impulse, and establishing a monarchy, of which he destined himself to be the monarch. To most men, the attempt to revive, in favour of a military adventurer, a form of government which had been rejected by what seemed the voice of the nation, would have appeared an act of desperation. The partisans of the Republic were able statesmen and men of superior talent, accustomed also to rule the fierce democracy and organise intrigues; and it was hardly to be supposed that such men would, were it but for shame's sake, have seen their ten years' labour at once swept away by the sword of a young though successful general. But Napoleon knew himself and them; and felt the confidence that those who had been associates in the power acquired by former revolutions, must be now content to sink into the instruments of his advancement, and the subordinate agents of his authority, contented with such a share of spoils as that with which the lion rewards the jackal.

To the kingdom at large, upon every new stride towards power, he showed the certificate of superior efficacy, guaranteed by the most signal success; and he assumed the empire of France under the proud title, *Detur dignissimo*. Neither did his actions up to this point encourage anyone to challenge the defects of his title. In practice, his government was brilliant abroad, and, with few exceptions, liberal and moderate at home. The abominable murder of the Duke d'Enghien showed the vindictive spirit of a savage; but, in general, the actions of Napoleon, at the commencement of his career, were highly laudable. The battle of Marengo, with its consequences – the softening of civil discord, the reconciliation with the Church of Rome, the recall of the great body of the emigrants, and the revivification of National Jurisprudence – were all events calculated to flatter the imagination, and even gain the affections, of the people.

But, with a dexterity peculiar to himself, Napoleon proceeded, while abolishing the Republic, to press into his service those very democratic principles which had given rise to the Revolution. His sagacity had not failed to observe that the popular objections to the ancient government were founded less upon any objection to royal authority, than a dislike, amounting to detestation, of the privileges which it allotted to the nobles and the clergy. When, therefore, Napoleon constructed his new form of monarchical government, he wisely considered that he was not, like hereditary monarchs, tied down to any particular rules arising out of ancient usage, but was at liberty to model it according to his own pleasure. He had been raised also so easily to the throne, by the general acknowledgment of his merits, that he had not needed the assistance of a party of his own; consequently, being unfettered by the necessity of gratifying old partisans, or acquiring new ones, his conduct was in a very unusual degree free and unlimited.

Having, therefore, attained the summit of human power, he proceeded, advisedly and deliberately, to lay the foundation of his throne on that democratic principle which had opened his own career, and which was the throwing open to merit, though without further title, the road to success in every department of the state. This was the secret key of Napoleon's policy; and he was so well aided in the use of it by acute perception of character, as well as by good nature and good feeling (both of which, in his cooler moments, he possessed,) that he never, through all his vicissitudes, lost an opportunity of conciliating and pleasing the multitude by evincing a well-timed attention to distinguish and reward talent. Unhappily, his love of merit, and disposition to reward it, were not founded exclusively upon attention to public welfare, far less on a purely benevolent desire to reward what was praiseworthy; but upon a principle of selfish policy, to which must be ascribed a great part of his success, no small portion of his misfortunes, and almost all his political crimes.

"His conduct," said his brother,[25] "is entirely regulated by his policy, and his policy is altogether founded upon egotism." No man, perhaps, ever possessed so intense a proportion of that selfish principle which is so common to humanity. It was planted by nature in his heart, and nourished by the half monastic, half military education, which so early separated him from social ties; it was encouraged by the consciousness of possessing talents which rendered him no mate for ordinary men; and became a confirmed habit, by the desolate condition in which he stood at his first outset in life, without friend, protector, or patron. The praise, the promotion he received, were given to his genius, not to his person; and he who was conscious of having forced his own way, had little to bind him in gratitude or kindness to those who only made room for him because they durst not oppose him. His ambition was a modification of selfishness, sublime indeed in its effects and consequences, but yet, when strictly analysed, leaving little but egotism in the crucible. Our readers are not, however, to suppose, that the selfishness of Napoleon was of that ordinary and odious character which makes men miserly, oppressive, and fraudulent; or which, under milder features, limits their exertions to such enterprises as may contribute to their own profit, and closes the heart against feelings of patriotism, or of social benevolence. Napoleon's egotism and love of self was of a far nobler and more elevated kind, though founded on similar motives – just as the wings of the eagle, who soars into the regions of the sun, move on the same principles with those which cannot bear the dunghill fowl over the pales of the poultry-yard.

To explain our meaning, we may add that Napoleon loved France, for

France was his own. He studied to confer benefits upon her, for the profit redounded to her emperor. He represented, as he boasted, the People as well as the Sovereign of France; he engrossed in his own person her immunities, her greatness, her glory, and was bound to conduct himself so as to exalt at the same time the emperor and the empire.

When we conceive the powerful mind of Napoleon, animated by an unbounded vivacity of imagination and an unconquerable tenacity of purpose, moving forward, without deviation or repose, to the accomplishment of its purpose, which was nothing less than to acquire the dominion of the whole world, we cannot be surprised at the immense height to which he raised himself. But the egotism which governed his actions, subject always to the exercise of his excellent sense, and the cultivation of his interest in the public opinion, did him in the end much more evil than good; as it instigated his most desperate enterprises, and was the source of his most inexcusable actions.

Moderate politicians will agree that after the imperial system was substituted for the republican, the chief magistrate ought to have assumed and exerted a considerable strength of authority in order to maintain that re-establishment of civil order, that protection of the existing state of things, which was necessary to terminate the wild and changeful recurrence of perpetual revolutions. Had Napoleon stopped here, his conduct would have been unblameable, unless by the more devoted followers of the House of Bourbon. But his principles of egotism would not be satisfied until he had totally destroyed every vestige of those free institutions which had been acquired by the perils, the blood, the tears of the Revolution, and reduced France, save for the influence of public opinion, to the condition of Constantinople, or of Algiers. The nation lost, under his successive encroachments, what liberty the ancient government had left them and all those rights which had been acquired by the Revolution. Political franchises, individual interests, the property of municipalities, the progress of education, of science, of mind and sentiment, all were usurped by the government. France was one immense army, under the absolute authority of a military commander, subject to no control nor responsibility. In that nation, so lately agitated by the nightly assembly of thousands of political clubs, no class of citizens under any supposable circumstances had the right of uniting in the expression of their opinions.

Neither in the manners nor in the laws did there remain any popular means of resisting the abuses of the administration. France resembled the political carcass of Constantinople, without the insubordination of the Pachas, the underhand resistance of the Ulemas, and the frequent and clamorous mutinies of the Janizaries.

Whilst Napoleon destroyed successively every barrier of public liberty – while he built new state prisons and established a high police, which filled France with spies and jailors – while he took the press into his own hand – his policy at once, and his egotism, led him to undertake those immense public works which were sure to be set down as monuments of the Emperor's splendour. The name given to him by the working classes, of the General Undertaker, was by no means ill bestowed; but in what an incalculably greater degree do such works succeed, when raised by the skill and industry of those who propose to improve their capital by the adventure, than when double the expense is employed at the arbitrary will of a despotic sovereign! Yet it had been well if bridges, roads, harbours, and public works had been the only compensation which Napoleon offered to the people of France for the liberties he took from them. But he poured out to them, to drown all painful and degrading recollections, the intoxicating and fatal draught of military glory and universal domination. To lay the whole universe prostrate at the foot of France, while France, the nation of Camps, should herself have no higher rank than the first of her own Emperor's slaves, was the gigantic project at which he laboured with such tenacious assiduity. It was the Sisyphæan stone which he rolled so high up the hill, that at length he was crushed under its precipitate recoil.

Napoleon's career of constant and uninterrupted success under the most disadvantageous circumstances, together with his implied belief in his Destiny, conspired, with the extravagant sense of his own importance, to impress him with an idea that he was not "in the roll of common men," and induced him to venture on the most desperate undertakings, as if animated less by the result of reason than by an internal assurance of success. After great miscarriages, he is said sometimes to have shown a corresponding depression; and thence he resigned four times the charge of his army when he found his situation embarrassing, as if conceiving he was deserted for the moment by his guardian genius. There were similar alternations, too, according to General Gourgaud's account, in his conversation. At times, he would speak like a deity, at others, in the style of a very ordinary person.

To the egotism of Napoleon we may also trace the general train of deception which marked his public policy, and, when speaking upon subjects in which his own character was implicated, his private conversation. In his public capacity, he had so completely prostituted the liberty of the press, that France could know nothing whatever but through Napoleon's own bulletins. The battle of Trafalgar was not hinted at till several months after it had been fought, and then it was totally misrepresented; and so deep and dark was the mantle which covered the events in which the people were most interested, that, on the very evening when the battle of Montmartre was fought, the *Moniteur* was occupied in a commentary on *nosographie*, and a criticism on a drama on the subject of the chaste Susannah. Hiding the truth is only one step to the invention of falsehood, and, as a periodical publisher of news, Napoleon became so eminent for both, that, to "lie like a bulletin," became an adopted expression, and the more disgraceful to Napoleon, that he is well known to have written those official documents in most instances himself.

Even this deceptive system, this plan of alternately keeping the nation in ignorance, or abusing it by falsehood, intimated a sense of respect for public opinion. Men love darkness, because their deeds are evil. Napoleon dared not have submitted to the public an undisguised statement of his perfidious attacks upon Spain, than which a more gross breach of good faith and treaties could scarce have been conceived. Nor is it more likely that, could the public have had the power of forming a previous judgment upon the probable event of the Russian campaign, that rash enterprise would ever have had an existence. In silencing the voice of the wise and good, the able and patriotic, and communicating only with such counsellors as were the echoes of his own inclinations, Napoleon, like Lear,

> Kill'd his physician, and the fee bestow'd
> Upon the foul disease.

This was the more injurious, as Napoleon's knowledge of the politics, interests, and character of foreign courts was, excepting in the case of Italy, exceedingly imperfect. The peace of Amiens might have remained uninterrupted and the essential good understanding betwixt France and Sweden need never have been broken if Napoleon could, or would, have understood the constitution of England, which permits every man to print or publish what he may choose; or if he could have been convinced that the institutions of Sweden did not permit their government to place their fleets and armies at the disposal of a foreign power.

Self-love, so sensitive as that of Napoleon, shunned especially the touch of ridicule. The gibes of the English papers, the caricatures of the London print-shops, were the petty stings which instigated, in a great measure, the breach of the peace of Amiens. The laughter-loving Frenchmen were interdicted the use of satire. During the time of the consulate, Napoleon was informed that a comic opera, something on the plan of the English farce of *High Life Below Stairs,* had been brought forward on the stage, and that, in this audacious performance, three valets mimicked the manners, and even the dress of the three Consuls, especially his own. He ordered that the actors should be exposed at the Grève, in the dresses they had dared to assume, which should be there stripped from their backs by the executioner; and he commanded that the author should be sent to St. Domingo, and placed at the disposal of the commander-in-chief. The sentence was not executed, for the offence had not existed to the extent alleged; but the intention shows Napoleon's ideas of the liberty of the stage.

But no light, which reason or information could supply, was able to guide the intensity of a selfish ambition, which made Napoleon desire that the whole administration of the whole world should not only remotely, but even directly and immediately, depend on his own pleasure. When he distributed kingdoms to his brothers, it was under the express understanding that they were to follow in every thing the course of politics which he should dictate; and after all, he seemed only to create independent states for the purpose of resuming them. In his wild and insatiable extravagance of administering in person the government of every realm he conquered, he brought his powerful mind to the level of that of the spoiled child, who will not be satisfied without holding in its own hand whatever has caught its eye. The system, grounded on ambition so inordinate, carried with it in its excess the principles of its own ruin. The runner who will never stop for repose must at last fall down with fatigue. Had

Napoleon succeeded both in Spain and Russia, he would not have rested, until he had found elsewhere the disasters of Baylen and of Moscow.

The consequences of the unjustifiable aggressions of the French Emperor were an unlimited extent of slaughter, fire and human misery, all arising from the ambition of one man, who, never giving the least sign of having repented, seemed, on the contrary, to justify and take pride in the ravage he had occasioned. This ambition, equally insatiable and incurable, justified Europe in securing his person, as if it had been that of a lunatic, whose misguided rage was not directed against an individual, but against the civilised world.; which had a natural right to be guaranteed against repetition of the frantic exploits of a being who seemed capable of employing in execution of his purpose more than human strength.

The same egotism, the same spirit of self-deception, which marked Napoleon during his long and awful career of success, followed him into adversity. He framed apologies for the use of his little company of followers, as he had formerly manufactured bulletins for the Great Nation. Those to whom these excuses were addressed, being too much devoted to him, and too generous to dispute, received whatever he said as truths delivered by a prophet, and set down doubtless to the score of inspiration what could by no effort be reconciled to truth. The horrid evils which afflicted Europe during the years of his success were represented to others, and perhaps to his own mind, as consequences which the Emperor neither wished nor contemplated, but which were necessarily and unalterably attached to the execution of the great plans which the Man of Destiny had been called upon earth to perform.

Some crimes he committed of a different character, which seem to have sprung, not like the general evils of war, from the execution of great and calculated plans, but must have had their source in a temper naturally passionate and vindictive. The Duke d'Enghien's murder was at the head of this list; a gratuitous act of treachery and cruelty, which, being undeniable, led Napoleon to be believed capable of other crimes of a secret and bloody character – of the murder of Pichegru – and of other actions of similar atrocity. We pause before charging him with any of those which have not been distinctly proved. For while it is certain that he had a love of personal vengeance – proper, it is said to his country – it is equally evident, that, vehement by temperament, he was lenient and calm by policy; and that, if he had indulged the former disposition, the security with which he might have done so, together with the ready agency of his fatal police, would have made his rage resemble that of one of the Roman emperors. He was made sensible, too late, of the general odium drawn upon him by the murder of the Duke d'Enghien, and does not seem to have been disposed to incur further risks of popular hatred in prosecution of his individual resentment. The records of his police, however, and the persecutions experienced by those whom Napoleon considered his personal enemies, show that, by starts at least, nature resumed her bent, and that he upon whom there was no restraint, save his respect for public opinion, gave way occasionally to the temptation of avenging his private injuries. He remarked it as a weakness in the character of his favourite Caesar that he suffered his enemies to remain in possession of the power to injure him; and Antommarchi, the reporter of the observation, admitted, that when he looked on the person before him, he could not but acknowledge that he was unlikely to fall into such an error.

When Napoleon laid aside reserve, and spoke what were probably his true sentiments, he endeavoured to justify those acts which transgressed the rules of justice and morality, by political necessity and reasons of state; or, in other words, by the pressure of his own interest. This, however, was a plea, the full benefit of which he reserved to vindicate his own actions, never permitting it to be used by any other sovereign. It is no less remarkable that Napoleon, though himself a soldier, and a distinguished one, could never allow a tribute of candid praise to the troops and generals by whom he was successively opposed. In mentioning his victories, he frequently bestows commendation upon the valour and conduct of the vanquished. This was an additional and more delicate mode of praising himself and his own troops by whom these enemies were overthrown. But he never allows any merit to those by whom he was defeated in turn. He professes never to have seen the Prussian troops behave well save at Jena, or the Russians save at Austerlitz. Those armies of the same nations, which he both saw and felt in the campaigns of 1812 and 1813, and before whom he made such disastrous retreats as those of Moscow and Leipzig, were, according to his expressions, mere *canaille*. In the same manner, when he details an action in which he triumphed, he is sure to boast, like the old Grecian (very justly perhaps,) that in this Fortune had no share; while his defeats are exclusively attributed to the rage of the elements, the combination of some most extraordinary and unexpected circumstances, the failure of some of his lieutenants, or, finally, the obstinacy of the general opposed, who, by mere dint of stupidity, blundered into success through circumstances which should have ensured his ruin.

In a word, from one end of Napoleon's works to the other, he has scarcely allowed himself to be guilty of a single fault or a single folly, excepting of that kind, which, arising from an over confidence and generosity, men secretly claim as merits, while they affect to give them up as matters of censure.

But the most extraordinary instance of Napoleon's deceptive system, and of his determination, at all events, to place himself under the most favourable light to the beholders, is his attempt to represent himself as the friend and protector of liberal and free principles. He had destroyed every vestige of liberty in France – he had persecuted as ideologists all who cherished its memory – he had boasted himself the restorer of monarchical government. The war between the Constitutionalists and him, covered, after the return from Elba, by a hollow truce, had been renewed, and the Liberalists had expelled him from the capital. He had left in his Testament the appellation of *traitor* with La Fayette, one of their earliest and most sincere chiefs – yet, notwithstanding all this constant opposition to the party which professes most to be guided by them, he has ventured to represent himself as a friend of liberal ideas! He has done so, and he has been believed.

There is but one explanation of this. The friends of revolution are upon principle the enemies of ancient and established governments – Napoleon became the opponent of the established powers from circumstances; not because he disputed the character of their government, but because they would not admit him into their circle; and though there was not, and could not be, any real connection betwixt his system and that of the Liberalists, yet both had the same opponents, and each loved in the other the enemy of their enemies. It was the business of Napoleon in his latter days to procure the sympathy and good opinion of any or every class of politicians; while, on the contrary, it could not be indifferent to those to whom he made advances, to number among their disciples, even in the twelfth hour, the name of Napoleon. It resembled what sometimes happens in the Catholic Church when a wealthy and powerful sinner on his deathbed receives the absolution of the Church on easy terms, and dies after a life spent in licentious courses, wrapped up in the mantle, and girded with the cord, of some order of unusual strictness. Napoleon, living a despot and a conqueror, has had his memory consecrated and held up to admiration by men who term themselves emphatically the friends of freedom.

The faults of Buonaparte, we conclude as we commenced, were rather those of the sovereign and politician, than of the individual. Wisely is it written, that "if we say we have no sin we deceive ourselves, and the truth is not in us." It was the inordinate force of ambition which made him the scourge of Europe; it was his efforts to disguise that selfish principle that made him combine fraud with force, and establish a regular system for deceiving those whom he could not subdue. Had his natural disposition been coldly cruel, like that of Octavius, or had he given way to the warmth of his temper, his private history, as well as that of his campaigns, must have been written in letters of blood. If, instead of asserting that he never committed a crime, he had limited his self-eulogy to asserting that, in attaining and wielding supreme power, he had resisted the temptation to commit many, he could not have been contradicted. And this is no small praise.

His system of government was false in the extreme. It comprehended the slavery of France, and aimed at the subjugation of the world. But to the former he did much to requite them for the jewel of which he robbed them. He gave them a regular government, schools, institutions, courts of justice, and a code of laws. In Italy, his rule was equally splendid and beneficial. The good effects which arose to other countries from his reign and character, begin also to be felt, though unquestionably they are not of the kind which he intended to produce. His invasions, tending to reconcile the discords which existed between the governors and governed, by teaching them to unite together against a common enemy, have gone far to loosen the feudal yoke, to enlighten the mind both of prince and people, and have led to many admirable results, which will not be the less durably advantageous that they have arisen, and are arising slowly, without contest.

In closing the 'Life of Napoleon Buonaparte', we are called upon to observe that he was a man tried in the two extremities, of the most exalted power and the most ineffable calamity, and if he occasionally appeared presumptuous when supported by the armed force of half a world, or unreasonably querulous when imprisoned within the narrow limits of St. Helena, it is scarce within the capacity of those whose steps have never led them beyond the middle path of life, to estimate either the strength of the temptations to which he yielded, or the force of mind which he opposed to those which he was able to resist.

ℰNDNOTES

1. Scott mixes up the two younger sisters. Marie-Paulette, or Pauline, was born on 10 October 1780, Marie-Annonciade, later Caroline, was born on 25 March 1782.

2. He was appointed in 1771.

3. Pius signed the Concordat on 15 August 1801, Napoleon signed it on 8 September; it was ratified on 10 September.

4. The place was formally awarded in December 1778. Napoleon took it up in May 1779.

i. *Walter Scott*: The following is a copy of de Keralio's report: "M. de Buonaparte, (Napoleon,) born 15th August, 1769, height four feet, ten inches, ten lines, has finished his 4th course; of good constitution, excellent health, of submissive character, upright, grateful, and regular in conduct; has always been distinguished for application to the mathematics. He is tolerably well acquainted with history and geography; he is deficient in the ornamental branches, and in Latin, in which he has only completed his 4th course. He will make an excellent sailor: he deserves to pass to the military school at Paris."

5. This occurred in 1791. Napoleon did not win the prize.

6. Probably written in 1791.

7. Napoleon's actual first taste of combat was a failed descent on Sardinia in February 1793.

8. He was appointed brigade-general in December 1793.

9. 5th October 1795.

10. Marie-Joseph-Rose de Tascher de La Pagerie is the current orthography.

11. She was born on 23 June 1763 and was therefore six years older than Napoleon.

12 Piacenza.

13. Scott occasionally uses this ancient measure; the *toise de l'académie* equals 1.949 metres.

14. It began on the 21st.

15. The last attempt was made on 10th May, the siege was lifted on the 20th.

ii. *Walter Scott*:

French Republic – Sovereignty of the People-Liberty-Equality.

Buonaparte, First Consul of the Republic, to his Majesty the King of Great Britain and Ireland

Paris, 5th Nivôse. 8th year of the Republic,

(25th Dec. 1799)

"Called by the wishes of the French nation to occupy the first magistracy of the Republic, I think it proper, on entering into office, to make a direct communication of it to your Majesty. The war, which for eight years has ravaged the four quarters of the world, must it be eternal? Are there no means of corning to an understanding? How can the two most enlightened nations of Europe, powerful and strong beyond what their safety and independence require, sacrifice to ideas of vain greatness the benefits of commerce, internal prosperity, and the happiness of families? How is it that they do not feel that peace is the first necessity as well as the first glory? These sentiments cannot be foreign to the heart of your Majesty, who reign over a free nation, and with the sole view of rendering it happy. Your Majesty will only see, in this overture, my sincere desire to contribute efficaciously, for the second time, to a general pacification, by a proceeding prompt, entirely confidential. and disengaged from those forms which, necessary perhaps to disguise the dependence of weak States, prove only in the case of the strong the mutual desire of deceiving each other. France and England, by the abuse of their strength, may still, for a long time, for the misfortune of all nations, retard the period of their being exhausted. But I will venture to say, the fate of all civilised nations is attached to the termination of a war which involves the whole world.

BUONAPARTE

16. Scott's narrative may mislead. The *Lycées* were established before the National University.

17. 27th October 1807.

18. Soult.

19. Scott gets his chronology off by one day. The French actually began crossing on the evening of 4th July.

iii. *Walter Scott*: The Abbé de Pradt represents Vandamme at Warsaw, as beating with his own hand a priest, the secretary of a Polish bishop, for not having furnished him with a supply of Tokay, although the poor man had to plead in excuse that King Jerome had the day before carried off all that was in the cellar. A saying was ascribed to Buonaparte, "that if he had had two Vandammes in his service, he must have made the one hang the other.".

20. 11th February.

21. The island rich in mines of inexhaustible iron.
22. *La* violette.
23. *Une.*
iv. *Walter Scott:* Hobhouse Letters from Paris, written during the Last Reign of Napoleon.

v. *Walter Scott:* The claret, for example, was that of Carbonel, at L.6 per dozen without duty. Each domestic of superior rank was allowed a bottle of this wine, which is as choice, as dear certainly, as could be brought to the table of sovereigns. The labourers and soldiers had each, daily, a bottle of Tenerife wine of excellent quality.

24. The Ryukyu Islands.
25. Lucien.

On Walter Scott

W.E.K. Anderson ed., *The Journal of Sir Walter Scott* (Oxford, 1972)

H.J.C. Grierson et al. eds., *The Letters of Sir Walter Scott* (12 vols., London, 1932-79)

J. Buchan, *Sir Walter Scott* (London, 1932)

E. Johnson, *Sir Walter Scott, The Great Unknown* (2 vols., London 1970)

G.J. Lockhart, *The Life of Sir Walter Scott bart., 1771-1832* (repr., London, 1896)

J. Sutherland, *The Life of Walter Scott. A Critical Biography* (1995)

A.N. Wilson, *The Laird of Abbotsford: A View of Sir Walter Scott* (Oxford, 1980)

Criticism of *The Life of Napoleon Buonaparte*

L. Bonaparte, *Réponse à sir Walter Scott sur son histoire de Napoléon* (Paris, 1829)

G. Gourgaud, *Réfutation de la vie de Napoléon par sir Walter Scott, par le general G**** (Paris, 1827)

J.O. Hayden, *Walter Scott: The Critical Heritage* (repr. 1995)

J. S. Mill, 'Review of *The Life of Napoleon Buonaparte*', *Westminster Review*, ix (April 1828), 251-313

The Athenaeum, xiv (11 March 1828)

Scott as an historian

J.A. Anderson, *Sir Walter Scott and History* (Edinburgh, 1981)

J.H. Alexander, D. Hewitt (eds.), *Scott and his Influence* (Aberdeen, 1983)

D. Brown, *Walter Scott and the Historical Imagination* (London, 1979)

J.P. Farrell, *Revolution as Tragedy. The Dilemma of the Moderate from Scott to Arnold* (Ithaca, 1980)

H. Ben-Israel, *English Historians on the French Revolution* (Cambridge, 1968)

G. Lukács, *The Historical Novel* (London, 1962)

G.M. Young, 'Scott the Historian' in *Sir Walter Scott Lectures 1940-1948*
(Edinburgh, 1950)

On Napoleon

Napoleon's has generated more studies than almost any other individual in history. There follows a brief list of some of the classics, as well as the better recent ones:

L. Bergeron, *France under Napoleon* (Princeton, 1981)

M. Broers, *Europe under Napoleon, 1799-1815* (London, 1996)

D.G. Chandler, *Napoleon* (London, 2001)

O. Connelly, *Blundering to Glory: Napoleon's Military Campaigns* (Revised ed.,
Wilmington, 1999)

E.F. Heckscher, *The Continental System: An Economic Interpretation* (Oxford, 1922)

P. Geyl, *Napoleon: For and Against* (London, 1949)

G.J. Ellis, *The Napoleonic Empire* (London, 1991)

G.J. Ellis, *Napoleon* (London, 1997)

F. McLynn, *Napoleon: A Biography* (London, 1997)

A. Thiers, *Histoire du Consulat et de l'Empire* (1845-62)

J. Tulard, *Napoleon: The Myth of the Saviour* (1984)

S.J. Woolf, *Napoleon's Integration of Europe* (1991)